Allied Coastal Forces

Allied
Coastal
Forces
of World War II

Volume II:
Vosper MTBs and US Elcos

John Lambert
Al Ross

Conway Maritime Press

Frontispiece: Felixstowe – March 1943. A feast of Vospers at HMS *Beehive. Row 1 – 234 with 1st foredeck 20mm Oerlikon, with 223 and 241 (21st Flotilla); Row 2 – 32, 34, 72, 69 and 70 (4th Flotilla); Row 3 – Three British Power Boat MGBs, including 74 (8th MGB Flotilla); Row 4 – Five 70ft British Power Boat MGBs, including 67 (6th MGB Flotilla).*
Imperial War Museum

First published in 1993. Reprinted 2002 by
Conway Maritime Press
64 Brewery Road
London
N7 9NT
www.conwaymaritime.com

A member of **Chrysalis** Books plc

9 8 7 6 5 4 3 2

A CIP catalogue record for this book is available from the British Library.

ISBN 0 85177 602 7

Printed and bound by The Bath Press, Bath

Contents

Foreword and acknowledgements

A great many people, both in the UK and overseas, have assisted with this second volume of Allied Coastal Forces of World War II, and without their help this volume would not be as comprehensive as it is.

I would particularly thank Leslie G Brown BSc Eng AMIEE Chief Weapons Systems Designer of Vosper Thornycroft (UK) Ltd, Woolston, Southampton, who over many years has provided copies of original Vosper drawings. Every one of my requests or queries has been answered by Les and in some cases copies of full size drawings or part sheets have been sent by return. My task has been simply to redraw Vosper wartime efforts. Vosper photographic cover has been provided from my visit of July 1986, when I obtained all the negative numbers from their lists. Without these records taken at the time I would have been lost. The photographs have the added bonus of being working views taken at the period when Britain was at war and the Vosper yard(s) was virtually in the front line with little defence against bombing raids.

Much background information has been provided by my contacts in the Coastal Forces Veterans' Association and letters from retired workers from the company. Geoffrey Hudson, the CFVA historian, again has filled in many gaps. The mass of engineering drawings have been provided by the loan of Packard manuals both from Al Ross and Bill Hollick. Mr CS Woolridge provided information on Vosper's only 'long' boat. Dave Fricker and Philip Simons did the honours with 'the survivors'.

Finally, my thanks to Sheila who read through masses of material, squared up my spelling, checked through the drawings for obvious errors and put up with my moods over the time I have taken.

Most of the drawings are available on large sheets – in some cases several sheets; ships from Traplet Publications Ltd, Traplet House, Severn Drive, Upton upon Severn, Worcestershire WR8 0SL; weapons from David MacGregor Plans, 99, Lonsdale Road, London SW13 9DA; or from Al Ross or myself. I know that several first-class models have been produced from our previous efforts.

The ships and weapons are the meat of this study and we are pleased to be able to record the wartime efforts of draughtsmen and designers.

John Lambert

Many people provided invaluable assistance in the preparation of the Elco section of this volume, among them: AD Baker III, Tom Peltin, Bob Sattler, Tim Howard, Wayne Traxel, Dave Shadell, Mark Wertheimer, Geoff Hudson, Tom Walkowiak, Dr WAB Douglas and Donald Graves of the Canadian Directorate of History, Capt Robert Kelly, Cdr Albert Ross, Chuck Haberlein, Mike West, Dr Norman Friedman, Erminio Bagnasco, Capt S Sanvold of the Royal Norwegian Navy Museum, Tom DelRossi, 'Tubby' Tong, Bill Last, Dr Jan Spek, Les Brown, and many PT and Coastal Forces veterans who shared their experiences during the Second World War. To these the authors express their sincere gratitude.

Special thanks go to Alyce Newberry and the staff of the PT Boat Museum/PT Boats Inc, a veterans' group dedicated to the preservation of the history of the PT boat. To this end, the organisation has preserved two boats, PT 617 (80ft Elco) and PT 796 (78ft Higgins) at Fall River, Massachusetts and maintains a large collection of historical material and memorabilia at its Memphis office. Readers interested in more information on the organisation should contact: PT Boats Inc, PO Box 38070, Memphis, TN 38183–0070, United States of America, (Telephone (901) 755–8440).

Another organisation of interest is the American Patrol Boat Museum, which is restoring patrol and air/sea rescue craft from the Second World War through to Vietnam. Of particular relevance to this volume, the APBM has acquired the ex-*PT 695*, one of the Annapolis-built Vospers, and is considering acquiring a second Vosper. Further information is available from: APBM, PO Box 641, Rio Vista, CA 94571, United States of America.

Al Ross

Request for information

As part of the research process for these volumes on Coastal Forces craft, Al Ross is developing a comprehensive database (using dBase III+) on all of the US-built boats and will eventually expand it to include Royal Navy and Royal Canadian Navy boats. A sample of the information contained on the current database can be found at the end of this section.

While the existing database is quite comprehensive, there are still major gaps, particularly in the following areas:

- Modifications to armament
- Camouflage schemes
- Squadron assignments for boats serving in navies other than the US Navy
- Pennant numbers for boats transferred to the Soviet Navy
- Current status of surviving boats

Consequently, he welcomes correspondence with any and all readers who can fill in the gaps or who are themselves looking for information on a particular boat or group of boats.

Key for PT Database

Field	Data contained in field
PT	USN boat number
PREFIX	Boat number prefix (*PT*, *PTC*, etc)
BLDR	Builder
TYPE	Type of boat; eg, 77ft Elco
SERIES	Series of which the individual boat is a member; eg, *PT 20–44*
HULLNO	Builder's hull number
NICK	Boat's nickname, if any; eg, 'Sad Sack' (*PT 369*)
LAID	Date keel laid
LAUNCH	Date launched
COMP	Date completed
INSERVICE	Date placed in service with USN
HISTORY	Capsule history, including squadron assignments, transfers, and eventual fate
CAUSE	Cause of loss
TRANSFER	Navy to which transferred
TDATE	Date of transfer
NEWNO	Boat number other than original
RON	Squadron(s) to which assigned
FLEET	Area of operations
CAMOBUILT	Camouflage applied at the factory
CAMOFLEET	Camouflage applied after entering service
ARMBUILT	Armament as designed
ARMMODS	Changes to armament in service
RADAR	Type of radar, IFF carried
EXIST	Information on boat if still surviving
LENGTH	Length
BEAM	Beam
DRAFT	Mean draft
DISP	Displacement
SPEED	Rated speed in knots
RADIUS	Radius of action
POWER	Power plant
PROPS	Size and number of propellers
SHP	Rated horsepower
SMOKE	MK of smoke canister
FUEL	Fuel capacity
WATER	Potable water capacity
OIL	Lube oil capacity
RADIO	MK of radio gear carried
NOTES	Information not addressed by other fields

Abbreviations

ASR	Air/Sea Rescue
BU	Broken up
BuShips	Bureau of Ships
CT	Controlled target
CTL	Constructive total loss
DY	Dockyard
FF	Free French
Fl	Flotilla
HB	Houseboat
HO	Handed over
KM	Kreigsmarine
PO	Paid off
RAF	Royal Air Force
RAN	Royal Australian Navy
RCN	Royal Canadian Navy
RIN	Royal Indian Navy
RN	Royal Navy
R Neth N	Royal Netherlands Navy
SC	Surface craft
TL	Total loss
TS	Training ship
USN	United States Navy
WD	War Department (RASC)

Vosper Ltd

It is significant, in view of the later developments of the firm of Vosper, that the company began as engineers. Herbert Edward Vosper himself was an engineer with a very considerable talent for innovation. The first recorded instance of this is his 1870 patent (No 2657) when he was 19 or 20, for a direct-acting steam engine – the device being a lost motion linkage to the slide valve. He also designed a simplified boiler feed pump, using a rotating piston to distribute the steam, which Vosper & Co continued to manufacture up to the mid-1920s.

H E Vosper, at an early age, must have allied business ability and resources to his technical knowledge and inventiveness, for in 1871, when he was 21, he was setting up workshops on the Camber, the small commercial dock on the east side of the entrance to Portsmouth Harbour, which were to form the base for the work of Vosper & Co until the late 1930s.

The early years were employed largely in refitting and repairing coasting vessels, but Vosper quickly built up its own range of steam reciprocating engines, compound (ie, two cylinders) and triple-expansion. These were fitted to a variety of craft – yachts, tugs, tenders, and launches for the War Office and Admiralty. Many orders were for export, particularly in South American river boats.

In those days before specialisation, the works were remarkably self-contained, with ferrous and non-ferrous foundries, machine and fitting shops, forge, boiler shop, and woodworking shops for refit work.

Vosper was a pioneer of the internal combustion engine, developing in parallel vaporising paraffin engines and crude oil engines – semi-diesels. The latter were compression ignition engines but, as was normal at that period, when cold they did not compress the air charge enough to raise its temperature to a value which would cause the injected fuel to ignite. They therefore had an iron mass at the cylinder head which was preheated by a blowlamp; part of this mass projected into the cylinder to provide a local hot spot to help ignite the fuel. The Vosper oil engine also had fresh water injection for piston cooling, so that alongside the fuel injection pump was a water injection pump.

Both types of engine were manufactured in ranges of powers, the semi-diesels from 5 to 320bhp, and the paraffin engines 7 to 100 bhp until about 1916. They showed considerable originality in design and when Vosper sold his vaporiser patent rights to Thornycroft, this design was embodied in the range of Thornycroft

A view of Vosper's Portsmouth yard in late 1939. These units are probably MTBs 20, 21 and 23 before handing over to Romania.
Vosper Thornycroft (UK) Ltd

paraffin engines which were widely used in the 1920s and '30s.

In those early days, mechanical design resulted from discussion on the shop floor, aided at the most by chalk sketches, and engines were built and run, modified and refined into successful products, with facilities which today would seem very primitive. However, in the process skills were developed which were to be an important foundation for later advances.

Although Vosper & Co Ltd (as it was then called) was still describing itself as 'engineers and boiler makers' well into the twentieth century, the building of small ships and launches began in the 1880s and ranged from dinghies and lifeboats to yachts and tugs of 70–80ft long and mainly powered by their own steam and oil engines.

What did make Vosper & Co an unusual company, particularly as it was quite small, was its wide range of skills and capacities. Apart from designing, developing and building its own range of different engine types, boilers, made pumps, and manufactured patent anchors were also built. On the shipbuilding side they tackled steel hulls – both solid, workmanlike tugs and lightly plated launches for tropical waters, where the destructive shipworm would have attacked wood; robust wooden barges on grown oak frames, and light-timbered cedar launches; many workboats for the Admiralty and ship's boats, whalers, dinghies and tenders, requiring between them most forms of the shipwright's craft in wood or metal.

The First World War saw a rapid expansion of these activities, with the addition of shell manufacture. After the war the company shared in the country's problems of retrenchment, reverting largely to refit work. The company was kept intact, although at the end of the 1920s the total workforce was reduced to about sixty. However the basic facilities remained and the shipyard ways could accommodate vessels of up to 200 tons, with berths afloat for larger ships, the boatbuilding shop for wooden craft, and the engineering facilities.

The two essential elements for achieving higher speeds on water – engines providing enough power for their weight and hulls which would plane – were first brought together in the early years of the twentieth century. Much work was done, notably by Sir John I Thornycroft in reciprocating engines, and Sir Charles Parsons with the steam turbine, to develop plants of high power/weight ratio and fit them in easily driven hulls of narrow beam and rounded sections. For example, the torpedo boat HMS *Lightning*, designed and built by Thornycroft in 1876 with a waterline length of 81ft, achieved a speed of 18½ knots with a two-cylinder compound steam engine of just 390ihp. She was a pioneer in the field of naval torpedo-carrying small craft, the forerunner of the destroyer. Sir Charles Parsons produced *Turbinia*, which achieved 35 knots at the Fleet Review of 1897, and there was nothing there to catch her.

The idea of planing craft, designed to lift – or in the terms of the patent Office's definition 'reduce their draught' – is attributed to the Rev C M Ramus, who was granted a patent in 1872. His design was for a stepped hydroplane of roughly flat bottom form. Thornycroft patented in 1877 another stepped hydroplane form, with injection of air under pressure at the step.

The ground for development after the turn of the century was motor boat racing, the major annual events being held in Monaco.

Launch of the 70ft MTB 22.
Vosper Thornycroft (UK) Ltd

With the development of petrol engines and refinement of round-bilge hull forms, boats such as *Ursula*, designed by S E Saunders, were by 1910 achieving speeds of over 35 knots. Hydroplanes began to make an impact on racing in 1908, and for a while were attaining much the same speeds as the then conventional round hull, but with smaller powers and hence lower fuel consumption.

The type of hull which we know today as a hard-chine planing form began to emerge in 1908–9. Among the more successful pioneers in the field were W H Fauber, who patented a multi-step chine form in 1909. Thornycroft was developing what he called his 'skimmers', notably the *Miranda* series, and S E Saunders was applying the Fauber ideas. Meanwhile, H E Vosper won a gold medal in 1904 at the reliability trials held in Southampton with his paraffin-engined launch – speed was not his objective.

Naval authorities were seeking to apply the speeds attainable in petrol engined craft to torpedo boats. A French boat with a central forward-firing torpedo reached 20 knots on trials in 1907, whilst a 110ft torpedo boat, built by Yarrow, with four 180hp Napier engines, reached 30 knots in 1908. The direct application of the benefits of planing hard-chine stepped hull forms as developed in racing came with the coastal motor boats (CMBs) which Thornycroft designed and built at the outset of the First World War. These in turn stemmed from the successful racing hydroplane *Miranda IV*, built in 1910, which attained 35 knots. Two classes of torpedo-carrying CMBs were built, of 40ft and 55ft, and later some 70 footers as minelayers. Their speeds were in the range of 30–40 knots. A variety of engines were used, mainly of US origin, but others, were specially developed by Thornycroft. These vessels proved the possibility of the type, proving that planing craft could be designed to carry a useful weapon load, be it torpedo or mine, with a practical measure of sea-keeping ability and service reliability.

H E Vosper had continued to head the firm until he retired in 1919; he died in 1943.

It was at the end of the decade of retrenchment which followed the First World War that development began to surge forward again. The rapid advances in aero engines made it possible for the Thornycroft-designed and built *Miss England III* to gain the world water speed record for Lord Wakefield in 1932 at 119.81mph (104 knots), with two Rolls-Royce engines developing about 4720bhp. It was a time to look again at the practical application of what was being learnt in racing and record-breaking craft, and for design to catch up with the possibilities opened up by innovation and development.

This was the time when the firm of Vosper began to concentrate on fast craft. One of the leading designers of hydroplanes and related types, Fred Cooper (who had designed *Miss England II*, Sir Henry Segrave's record-breaker of 1930 with a speed of 110mph), joined the company in 1930 and was responsible for a number of craft, and in July 1931 Commander Peter Du Cane joined Vosper. He established the policy of concentrating on fast craft and his enthusiasm for speed on the water was largely responsible for Vosper's development. In particular his prewar ideas and drive gave new pace to the development of MTBs and their improvement during the years of hostilities. When Commander Du Cane joined Vosper it was a private company with Portsmouth coal merchants Fraser & White having a majority interest. Among his first projects was responsibility for liaison with Commander Glen Kidston, for whom Vosper was building the picket boat *Advance*. Commander Kidston was negotiating for the purchase of control of Vosper & Co but was killed in a flying accident in 1931, and the controlling interest was bought in 1932 by Du Cane and the Earl of Hardwicke.

Peter Du Cane was born in Northumberland in 1901, and in his early years spent much time in the coal mines and quarries owned by neighbouring cousins. He was educated at the Royal Naval Colleges of Osborne, Dartmouth, Keyham and Greenwich, and visited HMS *St Vincent* during 1917 where he took an interest in stoking the boilers and learning the intricacies of efficient firing. Later as a midshipman he joined HMS *Revenge* in 1919, followed by HMS *St Vincent* and HMS *Whitby* in which he took a particular delight in the steam picket boats. He later said that the highlights of his service were '. . . about three years running steam picket boats, taking charge of the gunnery transmitting station whilst still a midshipman in wartime and qualifying in engineering at Keyham and Greenwich'. In 1928 he resigned his commission as, being qualified as an engineer, he was unable to re-enter the executive officer stream. He joined the Auxiliary Air Force in 1929 after flying tuition in a Renault Avro and gained his flying licence from the Air Ministry in September 1928. He went on to gain his 'B' licence to fly for hire or reward, and a certificate of the Fédération Aéronautique Internationale, having obtained his wings in a DH9A, a former First World War light bomber with a V12 Liberty engine. He joined 601 Squadron of the Auxiliary Air Force in 1933.

Advance was the first of the new generation of fast craft for Vosper, and she was followed by the fast cruiser *Silver Star* in 1931–32. Two hydroplanes, stepped racing boats, were built for Horace E Dodge, and shipped to the United States. The second, *Delphin*, was completed in 1933. These craft were to Fred Cooper designs, but it was at about this time that he left the company and Du Cane took charge of all aspects of the work, recognising that a reputation for first class workmanship and design were vital to the future of the company. Sir Malcolm Campbell had *Bluebird II* designed and built by Vosper, and secured the water speed record at 141.7mph.

Soon Vosper, under the helm of its new manager, was among the leading builders of fast motor boats, powered by their own marine conversion of the Ford V8, which the Admiralty acknowledged in 1938 when the firm was entrusted with the design and construction of the Royal Barge. A fast 40ft boat with three Vosper-Ford engines, she was completed in 1939.

Another area of engineering development at that time was the V-drive gearbox, which was used by Vosper as a means of installing the engines of small, fast launches right aft, in small machinery spaces. This arrangement also made it easier to locate the fuel tanks amidships, where the consumption of fuel has the least tendency to alter the boat's trim, which is critical in many high speed hull designs. Many centre engines in Vosper's wartime MTBs utilised this idea.

In the late 1930s came the change of emphasis from single orders, carried out as special designs to individual owners' requirements, towards the development of a range of standard Vosper basic designs, which could be adapted to various purposes. This began with jolly boats. These were small planing boats, predominantly with the four-cylinder Ford engine, which could either be open or have folding or removable rigid shelters for helmsman and passengers. The prototype was a 16ft boat which the company used for trials, demonstrations and general odd jobs. Others of 13ft, 15ft and 18ft were also built, but the original 16-footer was the most successful, becoming the basis for the 'skimming dishes' carried by many Royal Navy ships throughout the war. Speeds of up to 27 knots were achieved by these boats, depending upon load. Clinker built, about 130 of the 16-footers were built during the late 1930s. About 30 such craft of other sizes were also completed.

Shortly after the jolly boats came a 25ft design with a single Vosper-Ford V8 engine, used both as a captain's boat and as a general fleet workhorse in the Royal Navy. Nearly one hundred of these were built during 1935–39, and in their turn they were followed by 35ft picket boats and barges with twin V8 engines. The range extended to 45ft picket boats, with four V8 engines, which were carried by battleships to replace old steam pinnaces. In the later 1930s, Vosper designed and built a number of 40ft seaplane tenders for the Air Ministry, followed by more than seventy 45ft seaplane refuelling barges, the construction of which continued well into the war years.

These changes in the character and scope of the company's activities called for an expansion of facilities. Firstly the premises on the Camber were modernised, and later a second shipyard, Flathouse Yard, on the north side of Portsmouth Dockyard, was purchased. Meanwhile, in 1936, the firm was incorporated as Vosper Ltd, and became a public company, with a Stock Exchange quotation. Control remained with the directors.

The Admiralty purchase of 60ft motor torpedo boats designed and built by Vosper's rival, the British Power Boat Co of Hythe in 1936 encouraged Du Cane to furious efforts to obtain a similar order. Failure culminated in a decision, involving considerable initiative and financial risk, to build a private venture boat to incorporate new ideas on hull lines and more powerful engines. Job 1763 was designed, reviewed, modified and built, completing in the summer of 1937. She underwent many trials of both ideas and weapons systems and is covered in depth elsewhere in this Volume. She was purchased by the Admiralty to become MTB 102, and formed the basis of the later Vosper short MTB designs.

If Hubert Scott-Paine started Admiralty departments thinking about MTBs as a weapons system, to Vosper and Du Cane must go the credit of putting them along the right lines. The development work undertaken by Job 1763 proved the concept that torpedoes could be mounted in a new way and fired forward towards the target, and twin 21in torpedo tubes became the standard armament for 'short' boats.

With some foresight, Vosper started its Portchester Yard in 1939 and built overhaul shops at Blackbrook, near Farnham, in 1940 – the works on Broad Street were bombed in 1941.

After careful study Du Cane chose the Italian Isotta-Fraschini petrol engine of 1150bhp for his private venture (PV) boat. It was of proven design and in production. He attempted to persuade the British Government to produce it under licence, but to no avail, and Vosper was committed to using a few of the engines purchased to fulfil export orders for 60ft and 70ft MTBs (many of which were subsequently requisitioned for the Royal Navy before delivery). The entry of Italy into the war on the Axis side, however, prevented substantial numbers of the engines being used in later units.

When the Italian engines became unobtainable, the only alternative was to purchase engines elsewhere and eventually the US-manufactured Packard engine was supplied under Lend-Lease and this development is related in the equipment section. In the meantime the lower powered supercharged Hall-Scott Defender of 900hp (see Volume I) was fitted to several Vosper craft with added problems of changed layout, weight, positioning and pipework, and loss in performance.

Fortunately the Packard 4M–2500 was in production and all further Vosper MTBs were powered by these engines. Of course Vosper was not the only company engaged on the development of craft of the MTB type in the 1930s, and probably their main rival was the British Power Boat Co (to be a subject in Volume III). As demand for units for the flotillas of light coastal forces grew, many of the country's best known ship, yacht and boat-building concerns were drawn in, some developing their own designs, while others built to the plans of the Admiralty or other builders.

There was, however, still some controversy over whether or not hulls for MTBs were better designed with a hard-chine form, such as MTB 102, or with a step as in the earlier CMBs and related hydroplanes. The Admiralty therefore ordered such a stepped MTB (MTB 103) from Vosper, to be powered by two of the up-

rated 1500bhp Isotta-Fraschini engines in a V-drive arrangement. There was some delay in her completion due to the interrupted supply of Italian engines, and with a redesigned engine room eventually she was fitted with the 1350bhp Packard engines from the United States. She was completed as a target boat.

A number of MTBs were built at the Flathouse shipyard, but in 1938 these premises were compulsorily purchased by the Admiralty as a northwards extension of the Royal Dockard. Vosper retained the use of some trials facilities there, while acquiring the site on the border of Portchester and Portsmouth near Portchester Castle on the northern extremity of Portsmouth Harbour. This became the company headquarters until amalgamation with Thornycroft after the War. The sale price of Flathouse fell short of the sum required for the new shipyard at Portchester and a rights issue was made early in 1939.

The new site was marshland enclosed by an embankment, which had been built during the Napoleonic wars by French prisoners of war. Vosper filled this area with chalk, and drove piles as foundations for a new boatbuilding shed and offices, together with an enclosed non-tidal fitting-out basin under cover. These upper reaches of Portsmouth Harbour are mudflats at low tide, and the access channel to the new yard was, and remained, usable only at certain stages of the tide. Later an extension gave a much larger non-tidal basin in the open. The Portchester yard came into use in 1940, by which time German air raids were causing much damage in the Portsmouth area.

Vosper's achievements in MTB production during the Second World War were firstly in the number of craft constructed to their designs – 127 in the United Kingdom and 64 in the United States for the Royal Navy, 100 in the United States for the USSR and a number for other Allied navies, making a total of over 300. The second was that, despite increasing requirements involving additional equipment and armament with the resulting increased displacement, their performance did not substantially fall off. This is best illustrated by a comparison between their 1938 and 1943 programme boats. The former had a displacement of 35.8 tons, a length overall of 71ft, with a maximum speed of 42 knots. The latter had a displacement of 44.4 tons, a length overall of 73ft, a percentage increase in military load of 60 per cent over the 1938 units, and a speed of 40.5 knots. The main engine power increased by 9 per cent but against this various refinements, including increase of generator output, prevented a substantial improvement in the overall machinery power/weight ratio. The following year performance fell, as might be expected, to 36 knots at 48.8 tons displacement due to further increases in military load, in particular the addition of the 6-pounder Mark VII gun mounting forward.

The drawings shown in this volume give an indication of the effort, particularly in design, which went into the building of these craft, compared with the Fairmile system of construction as shown in the drawings of Volume I. All have been redrawn from Vosper originals.

At the beginning there was no operational experience to guide the formulation of requirements and as operational experience became available, it was often difficult to accept the demand for alternative, improved and invariably heavier equipment, particularly in view of the state of production. The builders, and for that matter the design sections of the Admiralty, were regarded as obstructionists if they did not immediately accept revised requirements which frequently upset all ideas of displacement, centre of gravity, trim, propellers, and consequently speed.

Nevertheless, to quote W G Holt, 'It is in the function of design to be servant of the operational requirements as far as possible and as far as good reason will allow', and in this respect Du Cane's team made every effort to meet the Royal Navy's requirements whatever

*MTB 33, destroyed by bombing on
26 September 1940.*
Vosper Thornycroft (UK) Ltd

the difficulty. The problems confronting the designer seldom presented themselves singly, whether they were fundamental characteristics of the craft or requirements of the user, such as the interrelated problems of propellers, supercharged engines and silencing. When the war began very little information regarding high speed cavitating propellers was available. The difficulties of insufficient immersion, rake of propeller shaft, and the proximity of hull, shaft brackets, rudders and other propellers soon presented themselves, as did the questions of boss size and blade thickness, to give adequate strength yet not affect efficiency, and accurate manufacture. In 1942 the new cavitation tunnel at the Admiralty Experimental Works began to produce results, one of the first and most startling of which was that the two-bladed propellers gave the units for which they were designed nearly four knots additional speed, albeit at the expense of some vibration. The method of strength calculation was revised and the propeller manufacturers were persuaded to accept closer tolerances. Thus propellers became more efficient and at the same time designers were able to design them accurately for maximum boat speed conditions. Whilst satisfying these conditions, even for short periods, the highly supercharged engines provided from the United States now showed symptoms of serious detonation at lower speeds with a consequent reduction in their already limited working life. Carefully constructed curves of engine and boat performance on the axes rpm and bhp revealed that the former curve was steeply inclined while the latter humped over the range of speed when the boat changed its attitude relative to the water, that is from full displacement to the planing condition. This hump touched or crossed the permissible maximum power line, engine trouble resulted, and this in turn involved a reduction in propeller size to suit the transitional condition and consequently a loss of top speed. These considerations forced the Admiralty and the builders to undertake a great deal of experimentation with reduction gears, two-speed gears and variable-pitch propellers – all involving new propeller designs.

Up to the end of the 1942 programme it was the practice to fit a V8 cruising engine, driving through gearing and a centrifugal clutch, to each wing shaft, for silent approach, but the speeds attained, around eight knots, were considered by the Naval Staff (and COs) to be inadequate. Accordingly, in early 1943 much experimentation was carried out by Vosper with underwater exhausts, beneath the engineroom (not through the transom, as in the British Power Boat craft, which involved heavy lengths of water-cooled piping). It will be appreciated that it was not possible to provide exhaust orifices, which remained under water at all speeds and conditions, in the sides of a hard chine boat, and that it was difficult enough to find spaces, in the honeycombed bilges of the engineroom, which were in a suitable proximity to the engine and did not result in unacceptable convolutions of the exhaust piping. Moreover, the position selected could not upset the function of the cooling water scoops, the rudders and above all, the propellers, and had to be such that the underwater pressure, which varied with the engine speed, did not adversely affect the performance of the engines by increasing the back pressure. Cases were recorded of considerable loss of propeller efficiency and of the complete loss of rudder effect due to entrained exhaust gases. Nevertheless, ideas of running boats on cushions of exhaust gas and of feeding controlled quantities of the gas to the rudders and propellers for greater quietness and efficiency were urgently considered but, alas, the difficulties associated with the experimentation were insurmountable. As a result, the main engines of later units were not arranged with underwater exhausts, as intended, but were provided with silencers.

The dumbflow silencer, shaped like a dustbin, was remarkably small, relatively easy to accommodate into the exhaust system, one per engine, and effective; at low power the hot exhaust gases were diverted through the tank under continuous water spray, while at high powers the exhaust passed straight through.

To meet the ever growing demand for boats of increased armament and speed, and to overcome the resultant loss of speed of the Fairmile Ds to about 30 knots as their payload increased, the company proposed and built their only one-off 'long' design MTB 510, 100ft 6in length overall. With improved Packard engines and revised engineroom ideas she was never operational, but paved the way for postwar engineering gearbox developments. Fortunately a complete set of her drawings is available to show her development.

During the early postwar years, the Admiralty took advantage of the vast reservoir of design and manufacturing facilities then available and, having in mind the explosive fuel required for and the inadequate power of the wartime engines, directed attention to diesel and gas turbine development. Vosper was in the forefront of these new fields and exported a number of new postwar designs and gas turbine developments.

Early in 1966 Vosper Ltd, assisted by the strength and financial expertise of the David Brown Corporation, agreed terms with its earlier rival, John I Thornycroft & Co Ltd, Southampton, for a merger of the two companies. This at once made available to Vosper the facilities for building larger ships, and experience in warship design and construction, to which they in turn brought a fresh approach to the problems encountered in marketing vessels for overseas navies in particular, based on their earlier success with smaller craft. The two companies were complementary in many respects, as well as being geographically close neighbours. Thornycroft also had a substantial ship repair organisation in Southampton, as well as a thriving boatbuilding subsidiary in Singapore. Both are very active, and enjoy long-term order books.

Vosper 70ft MTB (Short Type) – comparison of military loads

	1938	1939	1940	1942	1943	1944
Admiralty numbers	20–23	31–40	73–98	347–362	380–395	523–537
Petrol (lb)	11,100	14,120	18,818	19,055	18,870	18,870
Lubricating oil (lb)	435	610	1090	796	1525	1100
Fresh water (lb)	500	930	450	500	450	450
Crew and effects (lb)	2160	2400	1800	1800	2160	2880
Miscellaneous equipment constituting additions (lb)	360	713	703	809	1384	1572
Armament, ammunition and armour protection (lb)	12,860	14,805	15,147	16,294	18,362	19,000
W/T and radar or A/S (lb)	540	927	836	1064	1800	3632
Total weight (lb)	27,955	34,505	38,844	40,318	44,551	47,504
Percentage increase in military or useful load compared with 1938 MTBs		23.2	38.5	44.0	59.2	69.5
Total displacement on trials (tons)	35.79	39.70	46.90	44.73	44.39	48.80
Percentage of total displacement made up by military load	34.9	38.8	36.9	40.3	44.7	43.4

Note: These data were produced by Vosper at the conclusion of hostilities and proved beyond doubt their aim in improving MTB performance.

The Ferry Dock at Dover. MTBs, MASBs and Royal Air Force HS launches 123 and 122. Vosper units identified include MTBs 44 and 231.
Imperial War Museum

Construction list

Vessel	Vosper hull	Keel laid	Launched	Delivered	Fate

Ordered 6.10.37

Bloodhound	VP (1909)			1937	Wrecked at Bincleaves 31.1.43

Ordered by Sweden 1938

| T 3 | VP (1983) | | | 28.12.39 | Gas turbine experimental vessel 1952–59. Sunk as target 1963 |
| T 4 | VP (1984) | | | 28.12.39 | Gas turbine experimental vessel 1952–59. Sunk as target 1963 |

1 purchased from builder 30.10.37 (Vosper PV boat)

| 102 | VP (1763) | | 5.37 | 25. 5.38 | To WD 1.43 and RASC 21.1.43 and renamed *Vimy*; returned Admiralty 14.3.45; for disposal 2.5.45. Sold J van der Ould 1948. Still in use as Sea Scouts TS |

Ordered by Norway 1938

| No 5 | VP (2018) | 1. 7.39 | | 18. 5.40 | Requisitioned by RN. Lost following accidental explosion 1.7.41 |
| No 6 | VP (2020) | 14. 8.39 | | 21. 5.40 | Abandoned 26.9.40 |

Ordered 8.9.38

28	Th			10. 7.40	Lost by fire 7.3.41
29	C&N (2023)	1. 9.39		2. 6.40	Lost following collision during action with E-boats in North Sea 6.10.42
30	C&N (2024)	1. 9.39		11. 7.40	Mined, sunk, North Sea, 18.12.42

No	Builder (hull no)	Laid down	Launched	Completed	Fate

6 ordered 15.8.38 (4 from Vosper, 2 from Thornycroft, Hampton)

20	VP (1943)			12.39	To Romania 1939, renamed *Viforul*. Sunk by debris from exploding steamer *Ungvar* which ran on to minefield off Ilyichevka 9.11.41
21	VP (1942)			12.39	To Romania 1939, renamed *Viscolul*. Captured by USSR 9.44 and renamed TKA 955. Returned Romania 22.9.45. BU after 1947
22	VP (1944)	17.10.38	3. 4.39	9. 6.39	Sold 1945. Became HB *Gemini XXII*
23	VP (1945)			12.39	To Romania 1939, renamed *Vijelia*. Sunk by debris from exploding steamer *Ungvar* which ran on to minefield off Ilyichevka 9.11.41

1 ordered 10.12.38 (stepped hull Vosper design)

| 103 | VP (1980) | 29. 8.39 | 1940 | 6.41 | Completed as CT 05 6.41. Stricken 1947 |

26 ordered 27.9.39 (10 from Vosper)

31	VP (2037)	16.11.39	7. 6.40	5. 7.40	CT 22 1943. For disposal 1.46
32	VP (2038)	22.11.39	22. 6.40	24. 7.40	CT 24 1943. For disposal 10.45
33	VP (2039)	4.12.39			Bombed on stocks 26.9.40. TL
34	VP (2040)	18. 1.40	5. 8.40	13. 8.40	CT 23 1943. For disposal 9.45
35	VP (2041)	18. 4.40	9. 1.41	2. 4.41	For disposal 11.43
36	VP (2042)	29. 2.40	12.40	10. 3.41	For disposal 11.44
37	VP (2043)	28. 2.40			Bombed on stocks 10–11.1.41. TL
38	VP (2044)	13. 5.40		26. 5.41	To Bexleyheath Sea Scouts 10.44. Sold
39	VP (2045)	6. 5.40			Bombed on stocks 10–11.1.41. TL
40	VP (2046)	17. 6.40			Bombed on stocks 10–11.1.41. TL

10 ordered 26.2.40 (all from Vosper)

57	VP (2069)	14.11.40	16. 5.41	23.10.41	For disposal, Mediterranean, 10.44
58	VP (2070)	11.12.40	27. 5.41	8.12.41	For disposal, Mediterranean, 10.44
59	VP (2071)	26. 1.41	30. 7.41	18.12.41	For disposal, Mediterranean, 4.44
60	VP (2072)	19. 2.41	20. 8.41	23.12.41	For disposal, Mediterranean, 9.44
61	VP (2073)	9. 4.41	27. 8.41	9. 1.42	Wrecked off Kelibia, Tunisia, following action damage 9.5.43

Key to builders

Be	Berthon Boat Co, Lymington
C&N	Camper & Nicholson, Gosport and Northam
H&W	Harland & Wolff, Belfast
Mc	H McLean, Renfrew
McG	McGruer, Clyder
MG	Morgan Giles, Teignmouth
Th	Thornycroft, Hampton
VP	Vosper, Portsmouth and Portchester
VW	Vosper, Wivenhoe

These data are based on material in *Warships Supplement* No 65 (Summer 1981) by JJ Colledge, the 'Pink Lists', 'Red Lists' and 'Particulars of War-vessels' in the Naval Library (MOD (Navy)) and Naval Historical Branch records, and correspondence with Geoff Hudson, the Coastal Forces Veterans' Association historian.

Vessel	Vosper hull	Keel laid	Launched	Delivered	Fate
62	VP (2075)	30. 5.41	25.11.41	18. 2.42	In collision with MTB 64, sunk, off Benghazi 2.4.43
64	VP (2076)	31. 5.41		23. 2.42	In collision with MTB 63, sunk, off Benghazi 2.4.43
65	VP (2077)	4. 9.41		16. 3.42	For disposal, Malta, 9.45
66	VP (2078)	9. 9.41		18. 4.42	For disposal 11.44–7.45

6 requisitioned 4.40–5.40 (2 Finnish, 2 Greek, 2 Norwegian; 4 being built by Vosper)

69	VP (1993)			2. 6.40	Under construction as T4 (Greek). Requisitioned by RN 1940. CT 18 1943; for disposal 4.46
70	VP (1992)			4. 6.40	Under construction as T 3 (Greek). Requisitioned. CT 19 1943; for disposal 9.45. Became HB *Chrysalis*
71	VP (2019)	28. 7.39		5. 6.40	Under construction as No 7 (Norwegian). Requisitioned. To WD 6.43; sold 1945. For restoration 1993
72	VP (2021)	1. 1.40		5. 7.40	Under construction as No 8 (Norwegian). Requisitioned. To WD 7.43; sold 1946

26 ordered 14.5.40 plus replacement for MTB 75 (27 Vosper designs plus 1)

73	VP (2081)	5. 9.40	12. 9.41	3.10.41	Bombed, sunk, by German aircraft off Maddalena, Sardinia, 24.11.43
74	VP (2082)	12. 3.41	3. 9.41	12.12.41	Sunk by shore batteries gunfire off St Nazaire 28.3.42
75(I)	VP (2083)	27. 3.41	24.11.41	3. 1.42	Bombed on stocks 11.1.41
75(II)	VP (2083)	27. 3.41	24.11.41	3. 1.42	For disposal, Mediterranean, 10.44
76	VP (2084)	28. 3.41		14. 3.42	For disposal, Mediterranean, 4.44
77	VP (2085)	5. 4.41	29. 9.41	28. 5.42	Sunk by German aircraft off Vibo Valencia, SW Italy, 8.9.43
78	VW (2086)	8. 9.41	14. 4.42	18. 5.42	For disposal, Mediterranean, 7.45
79	VW (2087)	17. 9.41	2. 7.42	5. 8.42	For disposal 4.44
80	VP (2088)	14.10.41		18. 1.43	For disposal 12.45
81	VP (2089)	20. 3.42	24. 8.42	14. 1.43	For disposal, Mediterranean, 8.45
82	VP (2090)	8. 9.41		26. 6.42	For disposal, Mediterranean, 5.45
83	VP (2091)	17. 9.41		22. 5.42	For disposal 3.48
84	VP (2092)	14.10.41		13. 7.42	Scuttled Mediterranean 3.46
85	VP (2093)	29.11.41		6. 8.42	Scuttled Mediterranean 3.46
86	MG (2094)			18. 5.42	Scuttled Mediterranean 3.46
87	H&W (2095)		2. 5.42	12. 6.42	Mined in North Sea 31.10.42
88	H&W (2096)	20.10.41	20. 5.42	22. 6.42	For disposal 12.44–7.45
89	H&W (2097)	20.11.41	6. 7.42	5. 8.42	Scuttled Mediterranean 3.46
90	H&W (2098)		13. 8.42	4. 9.42	To FF 11.42. Returned RN 1946; sold 15.3.48
91	H&W (2099)	15. 1.42	10. 9.42	12.10.42	To FF 11.42. Returned RN 1946; sold 21.9.48
92	H&W (2100)	29. 1.42	28.11.42	1. 1.43	To FF 12.42. Returned RN 1946; sold 11.2.48
93	Be (2101)			10. 9.42	Sunk following collision with MTB 729 off Harwich 18.8.44
94	Be (2102)			24.12.42	To FF 12.42. Returned RN 5.46; sold 29.1.48
95	MG (2103)	11.41		17. 7.42	For disposal 10.44
96	MG (2104)	15. 2.42		28.10.42	To FF 11.42. Returned RN 5.46; sold 27.1.48
97	VP (2105)			4. 9.42	For disposal 7.45
98	VP (2106)	16. 1.42	5. 5.42	24.10.42	To FF 10.42. Returned RN 5.46; sold 4.3.48; become HB *Grayling*

1 ordered 14.11.40 (experimental 45ft)

108	VP (2079)				Bombed on stocks 10–11.1.41. TL

(Note Admiralty numbers 100–200 are experimental designs)

HMS Hornet, *Gosport 1944, Q 163 (a Fairmile 'B' Type) and MTBs 205 and 210. The majority carry a 20mm gun forward. The others are of the 202–212 batch).*
Imperial War Museum

Vessel	Vosper hull	Keel laid	Launched	Delivered	Fate
4 ordered 7.12.40 (ordered by Greece)					
218	VP (2057)	9. 5.40	10. 2.41	9. 6.41	Building as T3. Taken over by RN. Mined, sunk, during action with German SC, Dover Strait, 18.8.42
219	VP (2058)	4. 5.40	19. 2.41	3. 7.41	Building as T4. Taken over by RN. To Staines Sea Scouts 1945. Sold by 1948. Became HB
220	VP (2059)	1. 7.40	4. 3.41	30. 7.41	Building as T5. Taken over by RN. Sunk by E-boat gunfire off Ambleteuse, NE France, 13.5.42
221	VP (2060)	9. 7.40	2. 4.41	30. 9.41	Building as T6. Taken over by RN. For disposal 11.45
20 ordered 22.2.41					
222	Mc (2115)	22. 5.41	19. 1.42	15. 2.42	To R Neth N 4.42, renamed *Sperwer*. Mined, sunk, North Sea, 10.11.43
223	Mc (2116)	9. 6.41		9. 4.42	For disposal 3.45
224	Mc (2117)	10. 7.41	9. 4.42	12. 5.42	For disposal 1.45; became HB *Freedom*. BU 1991
225	Mc (2118)	5. 8.41	14. 5.42	12. 6.42	For disposal 2.45
226	Mc (2119)	15. 8.41	27. 7.42	28. 8.42	For disposal 7.45
227	Mc (2120)	22. 8.41	19. 9.42	10.11.42	To FF 12.42. Returned RN 1945. Sold 16.1.48
228	Mc (2121)	21. 4.42		22. 5.43	For disposal 1.47
229	McG (2122)	24. 5.41	3. 2.42	19. 2.42	To R Neth N 7.43, renamed *Geir*. Returned RN 1946. For disposal 1946
230	McG (2123)	21. 9.41	15. 4.42	5. 5.42	Rammed, sunk, by MTB 222 during action in North Sea 9.11.43
231	McG (2124)	30.12.41	7. 7.42	31. 7.42	To R Neth N 8.43, renamed *Stormvogel*. Returned RN and BU 1946
232	Be (2157)	15. 4.41	24. 9.41	2. 4.42	For disposal 12.44
233	Be (2158)			12. 1.42	For disposal 6.45
234	Be (2159)	16. 5.41	21.10.41	12. 4.42	For disposal 1.45

Vessel	Vosper hull	Keel laid	Launched	Delivered	Fate
235	Be (2160)	3. 7.41	11.11.41	16. 6.42	To R Neth N, renamed *Sperwer* (II) 6.42. Returned RN and BU 1946
236	C&N (2161)	28. 5.41	8. 3.42	15. 4.42	To R Neth N renamed *Havik* 8.43. Returned RN and BU 1946
237	C&N (2162)			18. 6.42	Sunk by German SC gunfire off Barfleur 7.8.42
238	C&N (2163)			18. 9.42	For disposal 12.44
239	C&N (2164)	24. 3.42	15. 9.42	5.12.42	To FF 12.42. Returned RN 1945. Sold 5.1.48. Became HB *Sarie Marais*
240	MG (2165)			11. 2.42	To R Neth N 6.42, renamed *Buizerd*. Returned RN and BU 1946
241	MG (2166)			30. 3.42	Sunk by German SC gunfire off Ijmuiden 31.3.44

4 ordered 2.12.40 (MTB 33, 37, 39, 40 replacements)

Vessel	Vosper hull	Keel laid	Launched	Delivered	Fate
242	VP (2156)	20. 2.42	17. 8.42	23.10.42	Lost in tow for Malta 7.45
243	VP (2153)	20. 3.42	13. 7.42	18.11.42	Sunk as target, Mediterranean, 22.8.44
244	VP (2154)	17. 4.42	8. 9.42	12.12.42	For disposal 12.44
245	VP (2155)	25. 1.42	14. 7.42	29.12.42	Sold 4.46. Became HB *Meridian*

16 ordered 17.4.42

Vessel	Vosper hull	Keel laid	Launched	Delivered	Fate
347	VP (2187)	15. 5.42		18. 3.43	Sunk by German SC gunfire off Ijmuiden 1.10.44
348	VP (2188)	29. 9.42		1. 5.43	For disposal 10.45
349	VP (2189)	8.10.42		3. 6.43	For disposal 10.45
350	H&W (2190)	16. 9.42		8. 5.43	For disposal 10.45
351	VW (2191)	29. 6.42		21. 4.43	For disposal 10.45
352	VW (2192)	18. 7.42		31. 5.43	Sunk following collision, North Sea, 26.3.44
353	VW (2193)	10. 8.42		23. 6.43	CT 38 3.45. For disposal 7.46
354	VW (2194)	19. 9.42		7. 9.43	CT 39 3.45. For disposal 1.47
355	H&W (2195)	16. 9.42	19. 5.43	10. 6.43	For disposal 10.45
356	H&W (2196)		7. 6.43	21. 6.43	Scuttled following damage in action with German SC off Netherlands 16.10.43
357	H&W (2197)		1. 7.43	9. 8.43	Foundered following gunfire damage in action with German SC, North Sea, 23.12.43
358	H&W (2198)	21.11.42	28. 7.43	17. 8.43	CT 34 3.45. For disposal 7.46
359	H&W (2199)	7.12.42	21. 8.43	16. 9.43	CT 35 1.45. For disposal 4.46
360	MG (2200)	2. 6.42	4. 6.43	19. 6.43	Sunk by German SC gunfire off Ijmuiden 1.10.44
361	MG (2201)	2. 6.42		8. 9.43	CT 36 1944. For disposal 1947
362	MG (2202)	2. 6.42		19. 1.44	CT 37 3.45. For disposal 7.46

16 ordered 22.7.42 under Lend-Lease

MTBs 363–378 See under Licence-built Vospers

1 ordered 9.11.42 (experimental 73ft)

Vessel	Vosper hull	Keel laid	Launched	Delivered	Fate
379	VP (2225)	18. 1.43		22. 1.44	Sold 17.9.47

16 ordered 10.3.43 (all 73ft new Vosper design)

Vessel	Vosper hull	Keel laid	Launched	Delivered	Fate
380	VP (2239)			12. 5.44	For disposal 6.46
381	VP (2240)			5. 6.44	For disposal 1.48
382	VP (2241)			3. 7.44	Sold 1947
383	VP (2242)			21. 7.44	For disposal 6.46
384	VP (2243)			5. 9.44	For disposal 10.46
385	VP (2244)			5.10.44	For disposal 10.45
386	VP (2245)			7.11.44	MTB 1001 1949. Sold 21.6.49. Became HB *Brincadeira*
387	VP (2246)			21.11.44	Sold 25.10.45
388	VP (2247)			9. 1.45	For disposal 9.45
389	VP (2248)			1. 2.45	Sold 4.6.48
390	VW (2249)		29. 5.44	4. 8.44	For disposal 10.45
391	VW (2250)			15. 7.44	For disposal 9.47
392	VW (2251)	25.10.43		11.11.44	MTB 1002 1949. Hulk 1956–12.57
393	VW (2252)			22.12.44	Sold 28.1.48

Coastal Forces HMS Beehive *at Felixstowe with mainly Vosper MTBs – Nos 72, 34, 32, 69 and 70 of the 4th Flotilla, and MGB 74 (8th MGB Flotilla). The front line is the 21st Flotilla, including Nos 234, 223 and 241.*
Imperial War Museum

Vessel	Vosper hull	Keel laid	Launched	Delivered	Fate
394	VW (2253)	14.12.43		2. 6.45	Sold 1948
395	VW (2254)	6. 4.44		21. 4.45	Sold 4.8.48

16 ordered 15.3.43 under Lend-Lease
MTBs 396–411. See under Licence-built Vospers

Ordered 2.4.42

510 (MGB)	VP (2186)	25. 7.42	14. 8.43	12.43	For disposal 9.47

20 ordered 2.12.43 as MGBs and completed as MTBs (16 Vosper designs)

523	VP (2285)	4. 4.44	13. 2.45	5. 7.45	To Denmark 1949, MTB 1023. Lost by explosion at Aarhus 17.5.53
524	VP (2286)	27. 4.44	15. 3.45	1.12.46	To Denmark 1949, MTB 1024. For disposal 9.54
525	VP (2287)	19. 8.44	11. 5.45	31.10.45	To Denmark 1949, MTB 1025. For disposal 9.54
526	VP(2288)	14. 9.44	30. 3.45	2. 1.46	To Denmark 1949, MTB 1026. Hulk 11. 56–10.58
527	VP (2289)			28. 2.46	To Denmark 1949, MTB 1027, FC 26 1952. Sold 24.1.58
528	VP (2290)			16. 4.46	Sold 1.3.48
529	VP (2291)	27.11.44		23. 5.46	To Denmark 1949, MTB 1029. For disposal 6.53
530	VP (2292)	2.12.44	17. 1.46	9. 8.46	To Denmark 1949, MTB 1030. Lost following collision with 1032 (see below) 28.3.52
531	VP (2293)			23. 9.47	CT 44 12.45. Sold 3.10.58
532	VW (2294)			13. 2.46	To Denmark 1949, MTB 1032. FC 27 1952. Sold 4.57
533	VW (2295)			5.12.45	To Denmark 1949, MTB 1033. FC 42 1952. Sold 21.10.58. Became HB *Latona*; BU 1989
534	VP (2296)	15. 5.45			Cancelled 20.10.45
535	VP (2297)	1. 7.45			Cancelled 1945; hull sold
536	VP (2298)				Cancelled 6.45
537	VP (2299)				CT 45 12.45. Sold 3.10.58
538	VP (2300)	11. 9.45	1. 9.47	27. 8.48	MTB 1601 7.49. Sold 20.8.57

Elco – a short history

The roots of Elco can be traced to the Electric Launch & Navigation Company, which was created in 1892 ostensibly to bid on the building of fifty electric launches for the 1893 World's Fair in Chicago. The company was successful in acquiring the contract and built fifty-five 36ft launches, establishing itself as a quality boat-building firm. In 1895 the original company was dissolved and emerged as the Electric Launch Company. Four years later, Elco was purchased by Isaac Rice, owner of the Electro Dynamic Company, and merged with the Holland Torpedo Boat Company. A final merger with the Electric Storage Battery Company consolidated all four companies into the Electric Boat Company, the forerunner of the current General Dynamics.

Henry Sutphen, an employee of the original corporation, became Elco's general manager in 1902 and was joined in 1906 by young Irwin Chase, a naval architect. Chase would be the chief designer for Elco until 1923, when he became plant manager, his position as chief designer being filled by Glenville Tremaine. Ultimately, these three men would develop Elco into a premier supplier of fine yachts and naval small craft.

Elco's first government contracts came in 1906, when the company was selected to design and build six lifeboats for the Life Saving Service. After that, government contracts waned and the company concentrated on fine yachts until the outbreak of the First World War. The Royal Navy, hard-pressed to control increasingly effective U-boat operations, became interested in acquiring anti-submarine motor launches. On 9 April 1915, the Admiralty awarded Elco a contract for fifty 75ft motor launches (ML1–50), the first twenty-five of which were to be delivered by the end of November. Then, on 8 June, an order was placed for a further 500, enlarged to 80ft, to be delivered by 16 November 1916. Four-

hundred and eighty-eight days later, all 550 motor launches had been delivered, a feat that established Elco as a premier supplier of naval craft. By the end of the First World War, Elco built a further 152 80-footers for the Royal Navy, French, and Italians.

Between the wars, Elco returned to yacht construction and began to concentrate on standardised construction techniques. These efforts would pay off during the Second World War, culminating in the superb 80ft PT. With the exception of twelve boats (PT 372–383) assembled by Harbor Boat Company from kits supplied by Elco, a total of 385 PTs would be constructed at the Bayonne plant, twenty-two 70ft, forty-nine 77ft, and three hundred and fifteen 80ft boats. Contracts for a further thirty-two 80ft boats (PT 761–790) were cancelled at the end of the war.

Unfortunately, the end of the Second World War brought about the collapse of Elco. There were a number of factors contributing to the demise of the company:

- the plant had been doubled in size in 1939 to handle the expected PT contracts;
- the expected postwar boom in yachting had not materialised; and
- Electric Boat viewed Elco as a liability, despite the company's profitability during the war.

On 31 December 1949 the company closed its doors for ever.

Towards the end of the Second World War, Elco produced a colour film on the development and construction of the 80ft boats. It contains a lot of good footage of all aspects of construction and initial trials. For anyone interested in how the Elcos were built, this is an excellent reference. This film, as well as others on the PTs, is available on video tape from the PT Boat Museum, PO Box 38070, Memphis, TN 38183–070, United States of America.

PT20 on trials. See page 117.
USN

Vosper's private venture (MTB 102) and *Bloodhound*

The 1935–36 Naval Estimates were presented to Parliament on 1 March 1935. There was a Supplementary Estimate in December to cover seven destroyers of a new type (the large Tribal class). This represented the first stage in covering the 'naval deficiencies', as reported by the Defence Requirements Committee, the Estimates being £60,050,000 (including Supplementary), whilst the actual cost was £64,887,613. Six motor torpedo boats were ordered, to a new design by British Power Boat Co (MTBs 1–6), the first since the end of the Great War. But there was no Admiralty order for Vosper.

The 1936–37 Estimates were presented on 16 March 1936. With the acceleration of shipbuilding abroad and the imminent end of treaty restrictions it was recognised that British shipbuilding would have to be stepped up, and shipyards modernised. Consequently three Supplementary Estimates were presented and approved during the year: one on 28 April for £10,300,000, one on 7 July for £1,100,000 and one in the autumn for a smaller sum, to start a cruiser and a flotilla of destroyers. Four additional MTBs were ordered. Three from British Power Boat Co (MTBs 7, 8 and 9), with an experimental steel hydrofoil design from White at Cowes. (MTB 101). But there were still no Admiralty orders for Vosper.

The company had not been idle, however. From 1931, Vosper had been developing a range of standard basic designs, beginning with jolly boats. These were small hard chine, fast, semi-planing boats, the 16ft prototype and later other production versions of 13ft, 15ft and 18ft. In 1934 Peter Du Cane took over the responsibility for design for the company with an increasing design staff.

In 1935 a 25ft motor boat was placed in production, being used by the Royal Navy as a captain's boat and for general duties. This was followed by a larger, 35ft version, to be employed as picket boats or aboard capital ships. At the same time the Vosper workforce gained experience in standardisation and improved their craft.

With orders for the Admiralty's new motor torpedo boats going to their rivals, Vosper considered the possibility of developing a larger, faster and more powerful vessel, which would be more seaworthy and faster than those of their competitors. The company approached the Admiralty on a number of occasions, with a request to design and construct such a prototype, but without success. A few were impressed with the idea, however, and it was indicated that if a contract were placed, it would be for a boat with a speed in excess of 40 knots and capable of carrying two 21in torpedoes, as well as being armed with a small calibre anti-aircraft gun in a

MTB 102 off Southsea, March 1939.
Courtesy Geoffrey Hudson

revolving turret. In addition this 1936 'ghost' specification included the ability to operate in the open sea, for example the
English Channel and the North Sea, in moderate sea condition –
Beaufort scale 5 (Fresh Breeze). Additionally, the boat's cruising
speed and range should be such that a crossing could be made
during the hours of darkness from, for example, Dover to the
French coast, or Felixstowe to the Hook of Holland, allowing for an
engagement with opposing forces during the night before return to
base.

After a great deal of consideration the directors decided to design
and build at the company's own expense a private venture boat
which, provided she met the suggested performance envelope in all
respects, would be submitted for Admiralty official trials in the
hope that this would result in her eventual purchase for the Royal
Navy and pave the way for more orders.

Starting with no preconceived ideas and a blank sheet of paper,
the designers soon realised that the vessel would have to be a complete rethink, and larger than the 60ft British Power Boat MTBs
then under construction. For the required performance, it was
necessary to select suitable engines. Whilst Du Cane could design
the hull form, its performance and ride characteristics, especially at
maximum and cruising speeds, would depend on, and have to be
matched to, the weight and output of the power units. At the same
time the weight and position of the torpedo and gun armament
would have to be considered.

It was known that Scott-Paine had developed a marine version of
the Napier Lion for his 60ft MTBs, but as this only developed
500bhp it was considered that something more powerful was required. Vosper had to look abroad, and the choice was limited. It
narrowed down to a power plant built by the Isotta-Fraschini company of Milan, Italy. This petrol engine was in limited production
and the only one currently available, but it had been developed
specifically for marine high-speed craft. The original development

*Vosper's PV boat in 1937. It has no upper deck
torpedo tubes, but is fitted with bow door and
launch rails aft.*
Courtesy Geoffrey Hudson

contract had been provided by the Russians, who at that time required engines for MTBs they were building. There had also followed further development through its use in the Italian Navy's
MAS boats (MTBs) since 1929.

The Asso 1000 engine was produced in a number of models –
ASM 180 to ASM 183, with output ranging between 1000 and
1150bhp at 1800 to 2000rpm. The type fitted to Vosper's PV (MTB
102) was rated at 1050bhp. Whilst no output figures for these engines have been traced, the ASM 183 model fitted in the Thornycroft 1938 class boats (MTBs 24, 25 and 28 – to be dealt with in
Volume III), completed 2½ years later, produced the following
figures on trials:

1150bhp at 1850rpm maximum emergency rating
950bhp at 1660rpm maximum continuous rating

In MTB 102, 1500rpm gave her a normal cruising speed of 31
knots.

A great deal of design work was undertaken with Job 1763 and
plans have been redrawn from a set of her originals which formed
the basis for all Vosper's following wartime design and their subsequent development. According to the plans, all three engines are
shown with direct drive to their respective propellers. In the event,
the centre engine was reversed and sited further aft, to drive its
shaft through a 'V' drive arrangement. There was no reduction gear
fitted.

Two Vosper V8 75bhp auxiliary engines, each driving a single
0.5kW generator, were fitted. They could be coupled into the outer

propeller shafts and used for manoeuvring or silent approach. The maximum speed on auxiliary engines was about 9 knots.

Originally 630 gallons of 87 octane petrol aft in three tanks of 210 gallons each was carried. This was later increased to 990 gallons in tanks of 330 gallons each. At normal fuel load at a maximum speed of 35 knots she was capable of 240 nautical miles. With a full fuel load at a cruising speed of 17½ knots the range was increased to 340 nautical miles. Using just her two auxiliary engines at 9 knots gave her a range of some 1100 nautical miles. The fuel consumption was critical. At maximum speed the three engines consumed some 230 gallons per hour and at maximum continuous speed this was reduced to about 180 gallons per hour.

The design of Vosper's new PV boat was completed in 1936. The lines plan is dated 31 August, the construction plan 16 September and the G/A, 1 October 1936. She was laid down later that year, being launched in May 1937, and later that month carried out the first works trials. On further trials, her maximum speeds of 47.8 knots in light condition and 43.7 knots in loaded condition were achieved. One of the results of these early trials was to reveal the need to increase the strength of the boat's hull, which required that the number of frames was doubled, increasing hull strength and rigidity but adding to her displacement.

Even so, the shape of things to come was apparent. Vosper's PV was the guideline to future development. A much improved seagoing MTB compared with Scott-Paine orders for the Admiralty – 22 tons in service trim with three Napier Lions giving a maximum speed of 33 knots and a top continuous speed of about 29 knots. Their armament was two 18in Mark VIII torpedoes and two clusters of four .303in machine guns on slip ring mounts. Originally they had been classified as coastal motor boats (CMBs), but this was changed in 1936 when they were reclassified as motor torpedo boats. (They will be dealt with in Volume III.)

On the basis of their new design's performance, Vosper considered that she should be submitted to the Admiralty, who then arranged official trials. Part of this evaluation included rough-weather trials, which took place in the English Channel, south of the Isle of Wight, on a day when there was a southwesterly gale, officially recorded as Force 7. This trial took place in competition with one of the 60ft British Power Boat MTBs and accompanied by a destroyer, which had been supplied by the Commander-in-Chief Portsmouth to provide assistance in case of accident. Du Cane himself drove the Vosper boat from inside the closed wheelhouse, instead of from the more normal upper steering position, but spray caused problems as the so-called clear-view screens could not cope with the prevailing sea conditions.

Following those trials and after some discussion, the Admiralty decided to acquire the boat and according to the 1938 *Navy Estimates* she was purchased for £22,529. Peter Du Cane refers to Vosper selling the boat for about £16,500, while records at the Naval Historical Branch give a figure of £50,000. These variations could well have been due to the various additions and alterations carried out between the date of purchase and her commissioning in May 1938 as MTB 102.

After purchase there followed a short period of fitting out for Royal Navy service, which the company completed by December 1937, after which she was based at HMS *Vernon* for some four months for further evaluation, before being accepted into service. She was crewed by Royal Navy personnel under Lt Harry Glyn, but was still the responsibility of her builders and flew the Red Ensign.

Torpedo trials

By late 1936, experience gained at HMS *Vernon* with the torpedo launching arrangements in MTB–1, the first 60ft design, revealed a

number of limitations, and the 8in Mark VIII torpedo with its warhead of 320lb of TNT was considered too small. The torpedo launching system was little improved from the CMBs of the Great War, therefore Du Cane considered alternative methods of torpedo launching, eventually deciding upon a means of bow discharge.

The original intention was to recess into the foredeck, immediately above the crew mess deck, a single torpedo tube arranged on a declivity firing through the stem of the boat. (See Vosper redrawn Drawing No 7685). To meet the requirements for two torpedoes, a second torpedo was to be carried on deck aft as a reload. Reloading would be through the door at the rear of the torpedo tube, which extended aft of the small wheelhouse. Of interest was the helmsman's seat, astride the tube, when the boat was being steered from the open bridge. When the boat first appeared on works trials, although the foredeck was 'bulged' upwards to accommodate the tube, neither the tube or the bow door, which was to cover the exit port in the stem, had been fitted.

Concern about the inability to fire more than one torpedo at a time, plus the delay and difficulty of reloading the tube, in action, at night or in rough weather, led to the arrangements for the reload centre torpedo being redesigned. Despite specific problems in current MTBs, principally caused by the torpedo stowage and launching arrangements, there was still support from within the Admiralty for the stern discharge method, which was proved to work and gave steady and straight running. This led to Vosper fitting a frame discharge launching gear on the deck aft, which enabled the second torpedo to be launched astern, tail first, in a similar manner to the system employed in the First World War.

Up to September 1937 not one torpedo had been fired from the boat. At *Vernon* they carried out trials with the existing bow discharge tube, which was soon found to be unsatisfactory, leading to a decision to abandon the bow and stern launching methods. In their place a new system of torpedo discharge was evolved which officers at *Vernon* had considered for some time and was thought likely to give better results. The Whitehead department at *Vernon*

MTB 22, followed by 102, flying the Royal Standard at the Reserve Fleet Review, Weymouth, August 1939.
Courtesy Geoffrey Hudson

had developed a lightweight slack-fit 21in tube, with cordite firing, for use as an upper deck fitting. In the early spring of 1938, still prior to commissioning, 102 was returned to Vosper's Camber yard for modifications, including the fitting of the upper deck tube. It was fitted starboard abreast the wheelhouse, with the forward end projected outboard, slightly beyond the beam of the boat, on a small sponson which was supported by two brackets extending upwards from the boat's side. This was required in order that the torpedo cleared the deck edge when discharged, resulting in the tube being inclined outboard by 7½ degrees. This *Vernon*-type tube gave the impression of being inverted when compared with the more usual views of later tubes (see drawing). Within a few weeks the *Vernon* tube was replaced by another with the normal overhang. The Vosper drawing (not shown) for this light construction (LC) tube was dated May 1938. Torpedo firing trials continued with this second tube after MTB 102 was commissioned. During this trials period she retained the bow door in her stem, covering the exit port for the original torpedo tube recessed into the hull forward. As a counterweight to the deck tube on the starboard, she carried a canvas-wrapped torpedo secured to chocks on the port side. In addition, during these discharge trials, a further torpedo was carried on the deck aft, as a reload. This avoided the need to keep returning to harbour for additional reload torpedoes.

As a result of the experience gained from trials with her single upper deck tube, it was decided that trim would be improved and

Bow view of MTB 102.
Courtesy D J Marshall

there would be less risk of damage to the torpedo tube end whilst coming alongside if further modifications were carried out. In early summer 1938 she returned to Vosper for the fitting of the second, port tube. Other alterations included locating the tubes further inboard and moving them about 8 feet nearer the bow, plus the provision of deck edge scallops. With this revised tube position, scallops about 10ft long were added to ensure that the torpedoes had sufficient clearance over the deck edge when launched. The opportunity was used for the removal of her internal bow tube and the bow door in her stem.

When she emerged from the yard in August she had dummy tubes on the upper deck, presumably while waiting for the completion of production versions of the 21in LC Mark I tube. The new tubes were fitted shortly after, following trials with the 20mm Oerlikon gun, and the arrangements were retained for her service with the Royal Navy although some minor changes were made. These included fitting 18in tubes for a short time around August–September 1939 and, later in 1939, adjusting the position and angle (to 6½ degrees) of her 21in tubes when initial trials with the prototype twin 0.5in Mark V power-operated gun mounting were carried out.

After the initial deck trials in 102 had proved the satisfactory operation of this method of torpedo discharge, it was adopted for all subsequent production boats, the first being ordered on 15 August 1938. They were six 70ft boats (MTBs 20–23 from Vosper and MTBs 24 and 25 from Thornycroft), these being the initial line of 'short' MTBs, which served in the Royal Navy throughout the war and into the early 1950s.

During the remainder of 1938 and for much of 1939, 102 conducted exhaustive torpedo running trials, developing techniques such as boat firing speeds, shallow water firing, horizontal rudder control settings and testing equipment such as the Duplex pistol. Thus it was the prolonged torpedo running by her from HMS *Vernon* which provided the foundation on which was based the whole of the torpedo equipment of British MTBs.

Gun trials

The 1936 'ghost' staff requirement had included an anti-aircraft gun in a revolving turret, but as designed and completed Job 1763 had no gun armament. Soon after completion, the small bipod mast, originally stepped over the forward edge of frame 12, was moved forward 2ft 4in, to the forward edge of frame 13. This resulted in the deck layout allowing the fitting of two gun mountings. These positions were sided and immediately inboard of the extensions running aft from the wheelhouse. Two sided positions, rather than a single one on the centreline, were determined by the need to keep the deck area on the centreline clear in order to reload the designed-in bow tube.

Geoff Hudson, the Coastal Forces Veterans' Association historian, has stated that there are references to her having two quadruple 0.303in Bren machine-gun mountings fitted. However, at that time it may have been intended to fit experimental quadruple mountings aboard for trial, prior to the spring of 1938. (During 1937 and 1938, the 60ft British Power Boat MTBs were fitted with two quadruple 0.303in Lewis guns, but by 1939 the new 70ft Vosper and Thornycroft 1938 class boats received two quadruple 0.303in Vickers K guns. Both are described in Volume I.)

A number of sources mention the fitting of a 20mm Oerlikon gun, but in single, two singles, a twin, and even two twin mountings. However, photographic evidence establishes that MTB 102 did have a single 20mm gun fitted. Geoff Hudson mentions a Vosper drawing dated December 1937 for a 'mounting for an automatic gun'. This showed a 'dustbin', of 33in diameter and 37in high, to be fitted port and starboard, midway between frames 12

*MTB 102 in early 1940, sporting polished
ventilators and the crew wearing smart
submarine sweaters.*
Courtesy Geoffrey Hudson

and 13, inboard of the side extensions running aft from the wheel-house. Apparently the drawing did not include the gun, but there is little doubt that it was the Oerlikon. Photographs of 102 taken in January and February 1938 show her fitted with a single 'dustbin' on the port side position only, as described above. A 20mm Oerlikon gun can be seen. The gun was later removed but the 'dustbin' remained.

Other independent sources state that Peter Du Cane and Lord Mountbatten organised the trials to have the gun accepted by the Royal Navy. A later Vosper drawing dated July 1938 showed a larger improved dustbin 44in in diameter and again 37in high, to be mounted 2¼in to port of the centreline and over frame 12, with a slip ring fitted to the top of the dustbin. The larger mounting does not appear to have been fitted until 1939.

In mid-1939 an experimental smoke apparatus was fitted right aft. Prior to this, in the autumn of 1938, 102 was damaged due to side planking tearing away from her gunwale, when the boat was being driven at speed in the Needles Channel. This gave a very clear indication of hull stresses caused when hard chine boats are driven at speed into head seas. The increased weight in the form of torpedo tubes and gun turret had added to these stresses, so steps were taken to strengthen the structure. This included the fitting of a plank about 12in deep and 1in thick over the sheer plank. This extended from frame 17 to the stern.

In August 1939, when 102 attended the Reserve Fleet Review in Weymouth Bay, she still retained the large dustbin type turret, but the actual gun(s) and CSA gear had been removed. Before the end of that year another prototype gun mounting was fitted for trials. This was later to become the twin 0.05in Mark V (power-operated) mounting, hydraulically operated from a pump running off one of the boat's engines, and she carried out the initial sea trials with this weapon in early 1940. This turret went into production that year and the first production mounting was fitted in one of the new Vosper 70ft boats in July 1940. The original mounting was re-turned to 102 for permanent installation after modification.

In addition to the above, yet another weapons system was carried for a short period. In May 1940 while her prototype twin 0.5in turret was being modified, 102 was devoid of guns. On 26 May prior to sailing from Portsmouth to Dover en route to take part in the evacuation of the British Expeditionary Force from Dunkirk, she was fitted with a small gun turret mounting four Vickers K 0.303in machine guns on a slip ring, apparently 'borrowed' from

HMS *Vernon* and fitted by the base staff at HMS *Hornet*.

On her safe return, and following the permanent fitting of her twin Mark V mounting, the only other change to her gun fit was the addition of light 0.303in machine guns in 1941. These were mounted forward on stanchions. These shoulder shooting (SS) guns were to become a standard fit in 'short' MTBs of that period. They were either 0.303in stripped Lewis or 0.303in Savage Lewis from the USA. From 1942 these were gradually replaced by the twin 0.303in Vickers GO guns, mounted on short stanchions or 'saddle' mountings on the torpedo tubes (see Volume 1).

To summarise, MTB 102 spent the early part of the war in trials and training based at *Vernon*, and at *Hornet* across the water at Gosport. She made eight round trips in the Dunkirk evacuation and, for a time, flying the flag of the Naval Force Commander, Rear-Admiral Wake-Walker, her distinguished evacuees included General Alexander and Captain William Tennant, the SNO Dunkirk. From then her war service was not so distinguished and by late 1942 she was regarded as surplus to requirements, being transferred to the Army for target towing.

MTB 102 was taken over by the Royal Army Service Corps on 21 January 1943, and named *Vimy*, being based at the Gunwharf, Portsmouth. She was returned to the Royal Navy at Poole on 14 March 1945, put up for disposal on 25 October and sold into private ownership in 1948. She survived as a motor cruiser until 1973 when she was sold to the Blofield and Brundall Sea Scouts. Since then she has been re-engined, and updated for a part in the film *The Eagle has Landed* and is now (1993) owned by the Norwich Area Scout Council '102' Trust, taking scouts to sea, and making appearances at Navy days, reunions and other events.

Vospers PV Boat has been given special attention because of her place in the history and development of wartime units, but she was not the only Vosper design to undertake torpedo development. In addition to the above, a 68ft mobile torpedo discharge vessel, MTDV *Bloodhound*, was ordered on 6 October 1937 under Contract No CP BR 8A/28281/37. She has been redrawn from the 'as fitted' Drawings Nos 8195 and 8196, dated 19 September 1938. Unfortunately it was not possible to acquire a photograph, but as can be seen she is a motor launch 68ft overall with a beam of 19ft on a displacement of 35 tons. She has a small wheelhouse situated well forward, a simple mast and a single trainable 21in torpedo tube mounted amidships. This tube is described more fully in the chapter covering torpedo tubes. She was of limited range, only 700 gallons of fuel being carried, and was powered by a pair of French Lorraine 'Orion' petrol engines of 1600bhp to give a maximum speed of 25 knots, but as she was only used for torpedo testing locally there was not a requirement for more. She was fitted with small but adequate mess facilities for a small crew on daily routines to the ranges and back. Unfortunately *Bloodhound* was wrecked on 31 January 1943 at Bincleaves and became a total loss.

A second *Bloodhound* (motor craft) was ordered by the Indian Government on 22 June 1941 from Thornycroft, Singapore, and was lost in January 1942 at the capture of the area by Japanese forces.

MTB 102 data (as built)

Displacement 32 tons, loaded 31.16 tons, light 18.59 tons
Later armament fitting increased her weight with a consequent reduction of performance — 33 tons, maximum speed 41 knots, maximum continuous 35 knots

Dimensions 68ft 0in overall, 69ft 6in including trailing rudders, 14ft 9in beam, 3ft 2in draught

Armament two 21in Mark VIII*E torpedoes (bow tube + reload)

Complement two officers, eight ratings

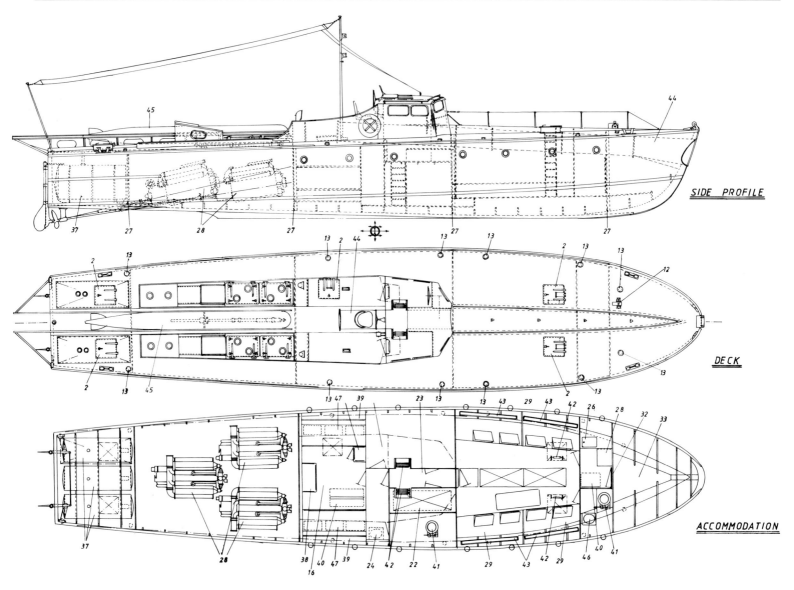

SIDE PROFILE

DECK

ACCOMMODATION

**Private venture boat Job 1763,
later MTB 102: side profile, deck and accommodation.**

1	Plush hatch	16	Officers' cabin
2	Hatch	17	Step
3	Fuel filling cap	18	Table
4	Engine hatches	19	Sideboard
5	Emergency hatch to officers' cabin	20	Officers' WC
6	Sliding hatch over	21	Wireless cabin
7	Alternative steering position	22	Fresh water tank under (75gal)
8	Fresh water filling cap	23	Passage
9	Control position	24	Folding washbasin
10	Forecastle hatch	25	Dresser
11	Chain pipe	26	Sink
12	Windlass	27	WT bulkhead
13	Mushroom ventilator	28	Three Isotta-Fraschini Asso 1000 petrol engines
14	Chain locker	29	Seat lockers
15	Pullman berth settee	30	Crews toilet

31	Hatch to chain locker	47	Settee
32	WT door	48	Cot
33	Forepeak	49	Centre main engine
34	Store	50	Fuel tank (210gal) (original)
35	Fixed window	51	Fuel tank compartment
36	Window (to open)	52	Wheelhouse
37	Fuel tank (130gal)	53	Lobby
38	Chest of drawers	54	Auxiliary and astern engine
39	Shelf	55	Bilge pump
40	Folding table	56	Stove
41	WC	57	Dynamo
42	Ladder	58	Turtle deck
43	Folding cot	59	Air compressor
44	21in torpedo tube	60	Forecastle mess
45	Reload torpedo		
46	Washbasin		

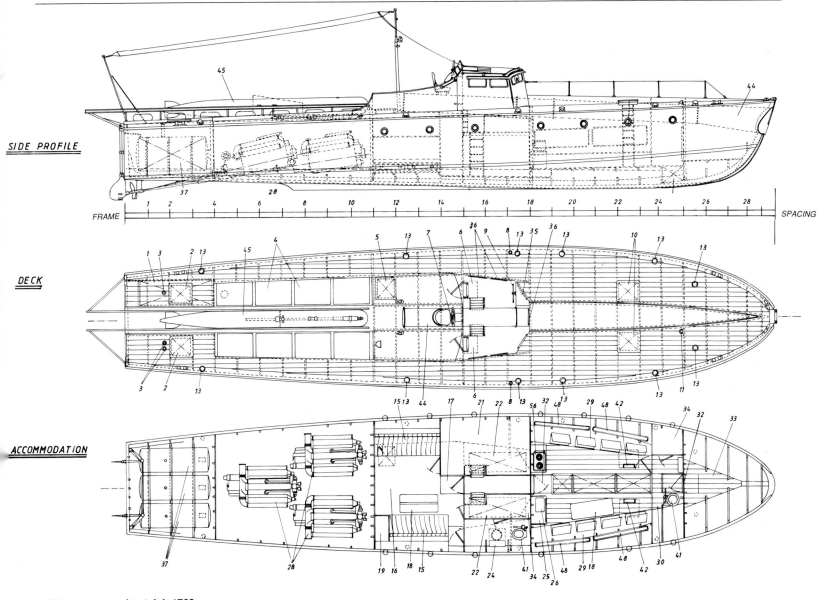

SIDE PROFILE

FRAME

SPACING

DECK

ACCOMMODATION

**Private venture boat Job 1763,
side profile, deck and accommodation.**

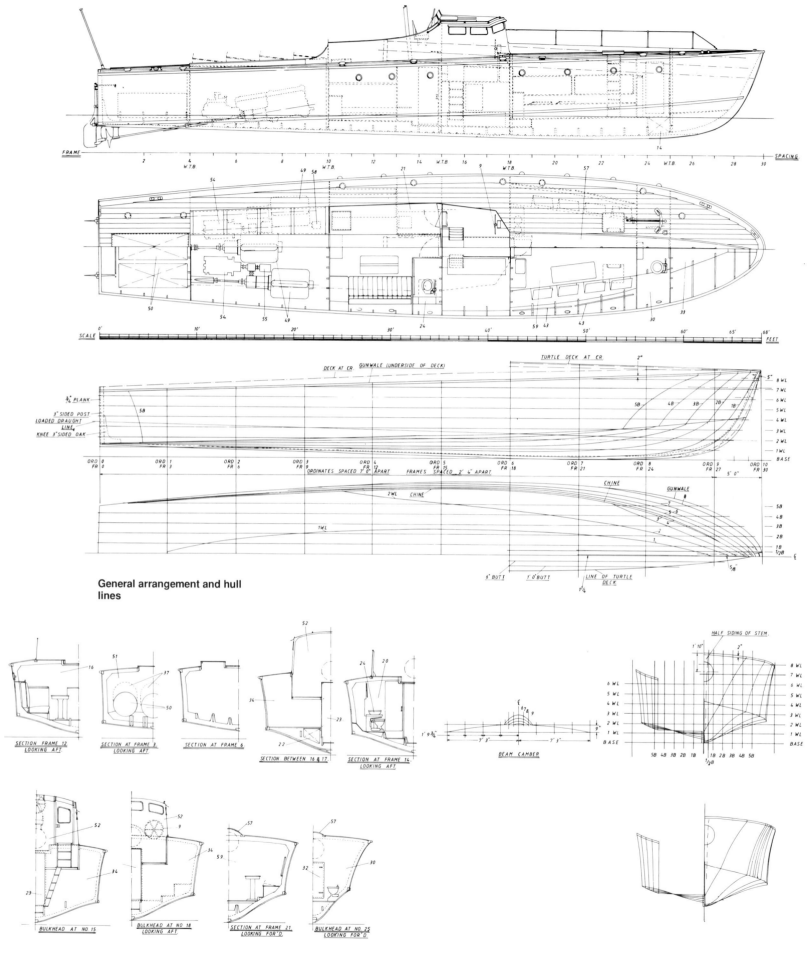

General arrangement and hull lines

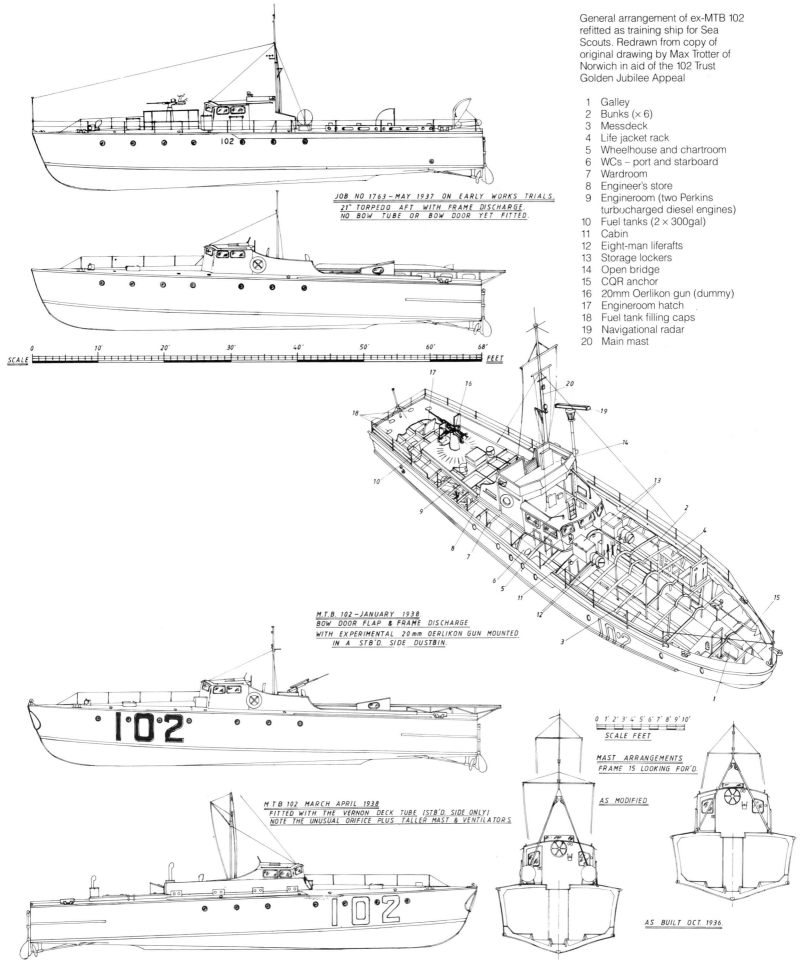

General arrangement of ex-MTB 102
refitted as training ship for Sea
Scouts. Redrawn from copy of
original drawing by Max Trotter of
Norwich in aid of the 102 Trust
Golden Jubilee Appeal

1 Galley
2 Bunks (× 6)
3 Messdeck
4 Life jacket rack
5 Wheelhouse and chartroom
6 WCs – port and starboard
7 Wardroom
8 Engineer's store
9 Engineroom (two Perkins
   turbocharged diesel engines)
10 Fuel tanks (2 × 300gal)
11 Cabin
12 Eight-man liferafts
13 Storage lockers
14 Open bridge
15 CQR anchor
16 20mm Oerlikon gun (dummy)
17 Engineroom hatch
18 Fuel tank filling caps
19 Navigational radar
20 Main mast

JOB NO 1763 – MAY 1937 ON EARLY WORKS TRIALS.
21" TORPEDO AFT WITH FRAME DISCHARGE.
NO BOW TUBE OR BOW DOOR YET FITTED.

SCALE 0 10' 20' 30' 40' 50' 60' 68' FEET

M.T.B. 102 – JANUARY 1938.
BOW DOOR FLAP & FRAME DISCHARGE
WITH EXPERIMENTAL 20mm OERLIKON GUN MOUNTED
IN A STB'D. SIDE DUSTBIN.

M.T.B. 102 MARCH APRIL 1938
FITTED WITH THE VERNON DECK TUBE [STB'D. SIDE ONLY]
NOTE THE UNUSUAL ORIFICE PLUS TALLER MAST & VENTILATORS

0 1' 2' 3' 4' 5' 6' 7' 8' 9' 10'
SCALE FEET

MAST ARRANGEMENTS
FRAME 15 LOOKING FOR'D.

AS MODIFIED

AS BUILT OCT. 1936.

29

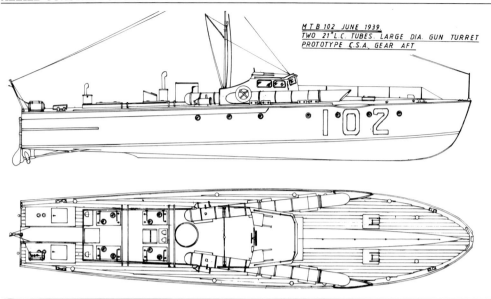

M.T.B.102 JUNE 1939
TWO 21" L.C. TUBES. LARGE DIA. GUN TURRET
PROTOTYPE C.S.A. GEAR AFT

MTB development vessel
Bloodhound detail

1	Fuel tank (350gal)	35	WT manhole
2	Wireless battery stowage	36	Passage
3	Pyrene junior fire extinguisher	37	Ladder
4	Aluminium chequer plate flooring	38	WC
		39	Tip-up seat
5	Lorraine Orion petrol engine	40	Mess rack
6	Fire extinguisher cylinder	41	Windlass
7	Hydraulic steering gear	42	Sink
8	CAV Bosch exhaust fan	43	Folding table
9	Vortex bilge pump	44	Masthead lights
10	Engineroom companion	45	Chest of drawers
11	Stuart lighting set	46	Wardrobe
12	Paraffin radiator	47	Cooker
13	21in Mark IX torpedo	48	2in pillar
14	6in mushroom ventilator	49	Seat
15	3in mushroom ventilator	50	Oil cooler
16	Forepeak	51	Water cooler
17	Chain locker	52	Fresh water tank
18	Crew's WC	53	Navigation lights
19	Officers' WC (port)	54	Fuel tank
20	Wireless cabin on centreline	55	Switchboard
21	Freshwater tank (25gal)	56	Lubricating oil tank
22	Galley (starboard)	57	Air bottles
23	Officers' cabin (port)	58	Bilge pump
24	Crew space	59	Wheelhouse
25	Air trunking	60	Store
26	Engineroom	61	Buoyant cushion
27	Tank room	62	Table
28	Afterpeak	63	Rungs
29	CQR anchor	64	Cupboard
30	18in searchlight	65	Engineroom telegraph
31	Sliding hatch	66	Magnetic compass
32	Hatch	67	Steering wheel
33	6in cowl ventilator	68	Fold-up washbasin
34	Flush hatch		

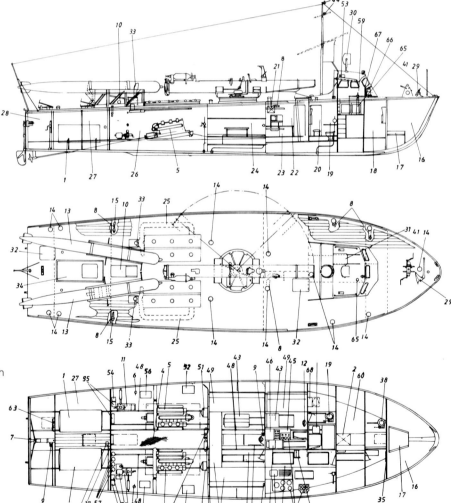

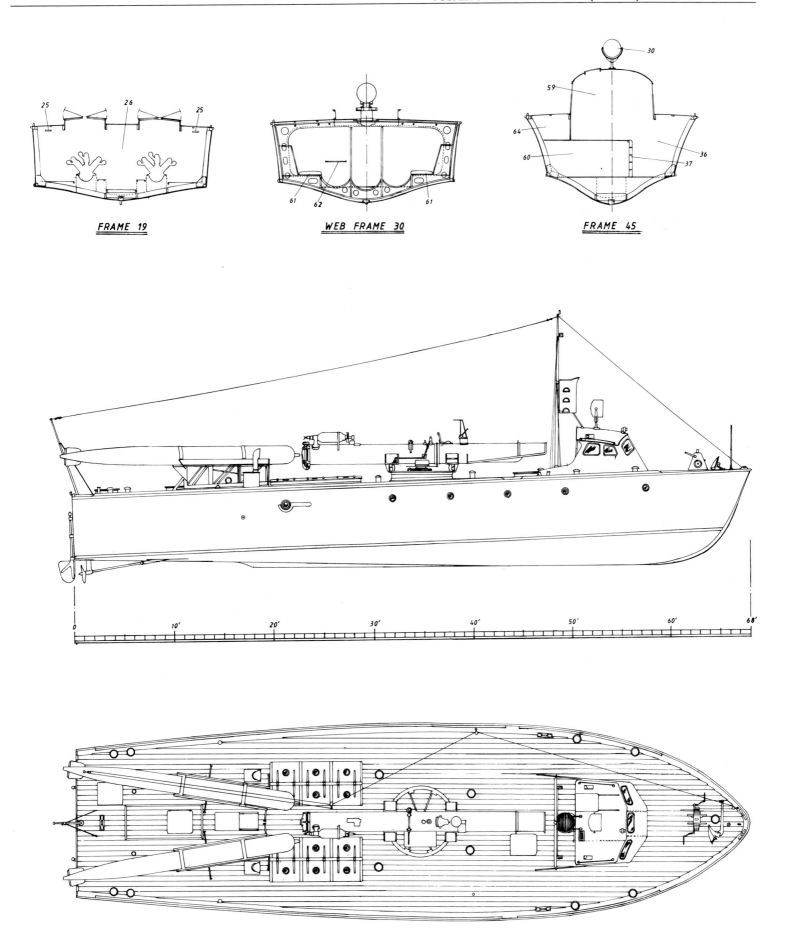

FRAME 19   WEB FRAME 30   FRAME 45

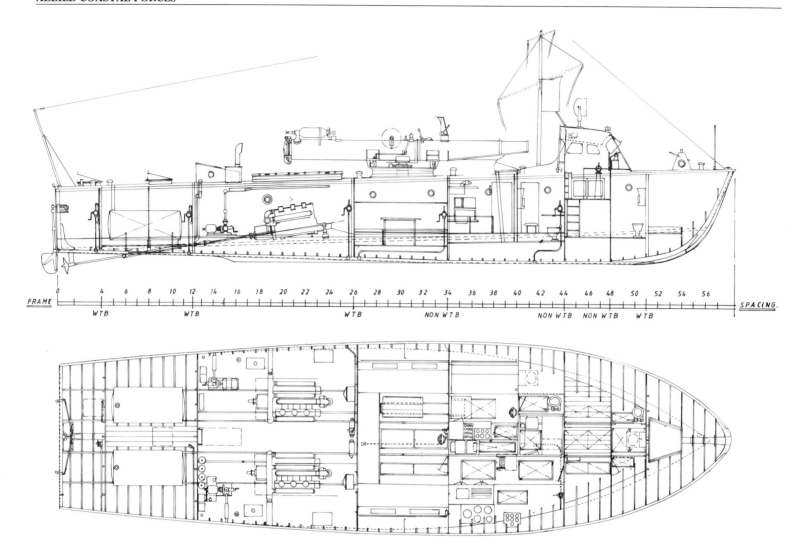

FRAME 0 4 6 8 10 12 14 16 18 20 22 24 26 28 30 32 34 36 38 40 42 44 46 48 50 52 54 56 SPACING.

WTB   WTB   WTB   NON WTB   NON WTB NON WTB WTB

Bloodhound

Vosper MTB designs 1938–39

The year 1938 was a very busy period for Vosper, with capacity orders, both for home and export. A small number of new staff were taken on and the yard was very busy indeed.

The economic problems of the world were still predominant. The 1938–39 Naval Estimates were presented to Parliament on the last day of February 1938. Two destroyer flotillas were included in the original Draft Estimates but drastic financial restrictions caused the deletion of one flotilla, a battleship, an aircraft carrier and four submarines. The Cabinet then cut one flotilla of destroyers, leaving none at all, a situation which nearly caused the First Sea Lord to resign. The financial limit was later increased by three 'Supplementary Estimates' (the first in May for £2,410,000) plus a sum from 'Appropriations in Aid' under the 1937 Defence Loans Act. The initial estimates and other figures were:

1938–39 Estimates	£93,707,000
1938–39 Supplementaries	£ 2,410,000
1938–39 Expenditure	£96,396,000
Appropriations in Aid	£30,000,000

Seemingly the purchase of Vosper's PV boat had indeed turned heads and the company was given its first Admiralty order on 15 August 1938 – four motor torpedo boats – MTBs 20, 21, 22 and 23. Thornycroft gained the other half of the total order, for MTBs 24, 25, 26 and 27. It was later decided that three of the Vosper boats would be sold to Romania on their completion. MTB 22 was used as a prototype, being completed in June 1939, and the three Romanian boats completed in December. As a result of this sale three more were ordered as replacements on 8 September 1938, to the same basic design. However Vosper did not have further capacity so they (MTBs 28, 29 and 30) were sub-contracted to other builders, one to Thornycroft at Hampton, the other two to Camper & Nicholson at Gosport. Another Vosper design, the experimental MTB 103, was ordered on 10 December and she is described separately.

The gathering war clouds in Europe had caused other nations to consider rearming, and motor torpedo boats were seen as a relatively inexpensive method of providing protection in a short time. As had happened in the late 1880s with the birth of the destroyer, British boatyards had full order books for building torpedo boats of their own design for many foreign navies and when the Admiralty placed MTB contracts in 1938 and 1939, some forty boats were under construction for France, Romania, Greece, Siam, the Netherlands, Sweden, Finland, Norway, the Philippines and Ireland. Vosper had a share in these export orders, which provided full employment for their workforce and added to their building skills and expertise, and included the laying down of the first line for series production.

In a brief examination of the company's first Admiralty order, MTBs 20, 21, 22 and 23, the subjects have not been drawn in the usual detail, but concentrating on the general arrangement and sections. It is obvious that the design office put in a great deal of work as Drawing 8264 shows the preliminary layout of the contract, and the later drawing 8632 shows the 'as fitted' layout of the completed boats. In the same period the Vosper design office was undertaking alternative 70ft designs. Drawing 8663 (undated) shows a projected G/A with a differing hull line and changed engineroom layout. The two 21in tubes are further aft and no torpedo troughs are built into the hull, although in general the basic layout and armament of two gun tubs is the same. Detailed drawings of

the bridge and wheelhouse layout for the first Admiralty order (Drawing 8226) is included in the chapter on bridge development. These designs provided both the design staff and the builders with a sound basis for what was to come. The Italian engines proved sound and many teething troubles were overcome.

Order dates for the foreign units are lacking, but 1939 saw Vosper's yard further committed to building and expansion. The 1939–40 Estimates were presented to Parliament on 28 February 1939. Expenditure levels rose quickly and the difference was met by extra receipts and a Vote of Credit from Parliament for securing the 'Defence of the Realm' and there was also a sum of money from 'Appropriations in Aid' under the 1937 Defence Loans Act. The 1939–40 figures were:

1939–40 Estimates	£63,399,000
1939–40 Expenditure	£99,429,000
Appropriations in Aid	£80,000,000

These included orders for two battleships (not built), one carrier (*Indefatigable*), two cruisers, a fast minelayer, sixteen fleet destroyers, twenty escort destroyers, two sloops, fifty-six Flower class corvettes, twenty fleet minesweepers, a gunboat (later cancelled) the first Fairmile motor launch (ML 1000), and six MTBs (31–36) ordered 27 September 1939.

The 1939 War Programme details are apparently still classified, and little is known of the particulars apart from Parliament's approval of an initial £20,000,000 Supplementary Vote and the implementation of a vast shipbuilding programme involving a further six light cruisers, twenty-four fleet destroyers, thirty-six escort destroyers, twenty-six submarines, sixty Flowers, twenty-two minesweepers, twenty minesweeping escorts from Australia, thirty-nine MTBs (37–56 and 57–68), twenty-two motor A/S boats. In addition there were to be built 183 motor launches, as well as many other lesser types.

Vosper received orders both from the Admiralty and from abroad. Two 60ft MTBs were ordered by Sweden in 1938, Jobs 1983–84 as T 3 and T 4, which were handed over on 28 December 1939. They displaced 25 tons with a hull length of 60ft and a beam of 15ft 3in. They were armed with two 18in Swedish tubes (see section on torpedo tubes), twin 8mm guns in a type KSP M/36 mounting, and two single 6.5mm guns type KGM/21. They were powered by two Isotta-Fraschini petrol engines giving a maximum speed of 42.5 knots and 41 knots maximum continuous sea speed. The complement was between six and eight. The 'as fitted' general arrangement has been redrawn from Vosper Drawing 8839. The gun armament lacks detail and was, it is assumed, fitted on arrival in Sweden.

Four similar 60ft units were ordered by Norway. These were builder's Jobs 2018–21 for which the 'as fitted' layout from Drawing 9216 has been redrawn. All six 60ft units have common hull lines (Drawing 8282). They displaced 25 tons on the 60ft hulls. The two Isotta-Fraschini engines of 2300bhp gave a sea speed of 35 knots. They were armed with 18in tubes as shown and four depth charges, and had a complement of ten. The shorter 60ft units look quite dumpy in comparison with the more usual 70ft boats. Whilst both the Swedish and Norwegian units have been drawn in detail, additional views have been added for the two later-requisitioned Norwegian units, which were refitted with Admiralty 18in tubes and the new twin 0.5in power-operated Mark V turret, which was just coming into production.

There is a slight difference in the dates for 'handed over' and completed between the records held by Vosper and by the World Ship Society, thus:

Job No	Vosper (handed over)	WSS (completed)	
2019 MTB 71 (RN)	5.6.40	2.7.40	(ex-Norwegian No 7)
2021 MTB 72 (RN)	5.7.40	6.7.40	(ex-Norwegian No 8)

The two units delivered to Norway were lost in war service, MTB 71 was transferred to the War Office in June 1943, sold in 1945, and eventually became the houseboat *Wild Chorus*; MTB 72 was transferred to the War Office in July 1943 and was sold in 1946.

Two 70ft units were ordered for Greece as T 3 and T 4, and although full G/As have not been drawn, Vosper have provided excellent photographs of them, as completed with shiny bright-work. Drawing 9183 'as fitted' hull sections and wheelhouse G/As for these two units, which became the Royal Navy MTBs 69 and 70, have been redrawn. They were very similar to the 70ft Admiralty designs, carried two 21in torpedo tubes and had standard light gun tubs for .303in guns.

Six units building for foreign navies were requisitioned between April and May 1940, and apart from the four previously mentioned units built by Vosper there were two CMB types building for Finland in the Thornycroft yard at Hampton. These became Royal Navy MTBs 67 and 68 and were lost in the Mediterranean in 1941 (MTB 67 in Suda Bay on 23 May, and MTB 68 following a collision off the Libyan coast).

Under the 1939 Programme and the later 1939 War Programme, Vosper received the bulk of the MTB orders and, looking to the future, undertook the development of a new yard at Portchester. It was also building the former French MTB 40K which had been requisitioned in September 1939 whilst on the stocks, and the experimental design MTBs 104 and 105 which were requisitioned on 9 January 1940.

The G/A layout for MTBs 31–40 (Admiralty Contract CP/BB/45405/39) has been redrawn from Drawing 9239. These vessels were fitted with three Isotta-Fraschini petrol engines with a total 3450bhp giving a speed of 40 knots. They were of 35–38 tons displacement, armed with two 21in torpedo tubes and a single twin 0.5in PO Mark V mounting. The majority of Isotta-engined units were reduced to controlled target duties in 1943, when problems with spares for their main engines proved a problem and individual units were cannibalised to provide spares for others. The supply of Italian engines dried up with MTB 34 and alternatives had to be sought.

The only engine available was the American built Hall-Scott supercharged petrol engine of 900hp (see Volume I), and engine-room redesign was undertaken to accommodate these heavier and less powerful units.

The vessels displaced 39.75 tons and were constructed of double diagonal mahogany throughout. The maximum speed was some 25–28 knots – nowhere near the required 40 knots envisaged – but no trials figures are known to exist. They were built at Vosper Portsmouth and the new yard at Portchester. The drawing number is omitted but it is 94— with the bullet-proof bridge and wheelhouse layout (Drawing 9462) is shown in the relevant chapter.

The detailed G/A 'as fitted' AD Contract CPBR 8b/45405/39 and the later contract for follow up Greek orders CPBR 8b/63971/39 (MTBs 218–221) has been redrawn.

By now construction was improved and laid out along the lines of series production. Many more women were employed as can be seen from the photographs taken at the launch of new units. The standard of equipment gradually improved. Gone was the light inverted 'Y' mast of the early 1938 designs, and there was a gradual reduction of the dangerous upper deck fuel tanks with their highly explosive contents of high octane petrol. A great deal of design improvement was undertaken by Vosper's design office.

Later developments are shown in the G/A drawings of MTBs 57–66 which follow similar lines to 31–40 but have improvements in power with the introduction of the US-built Packard as a number were re-engined after completion with Hall-Scott engines. These ten units were built under Contract 8B/20689/40. Other improvements included the addition of Type 286 RDF (see Volume 1) fitted during 1941. Fuel capacity was increased to a total of 2725 gallons (1025 centre tank and 850 gallons each wing tank).

The vessels were re-engined during 1942 with three Packards each of 1200hp (as drawn), and 4050hp gave a 37.5 knot maximum speed and 33 knots at 3600hp. Additional equipment became standard, CSA (see Volume I) was fitted and the small dinghy carried by the earlier boats was removed and replaced by Carley floats. The complement was increased to twelve, two officers and ten ratings. The armament became standardised with two 21in tubes and twin power-operated 0.5in Vickers machine guns. Two twin 0.303in Vickers gas operated machine guns were carried (not shown – but detailed in Volume I) for close-range defence. It was now usual to carry a box of grenades for close-in fighting.

MTBs 49–56 were all withdrawn from naval service on 2 December 1942 with cracked frames, and after local repair and strengthening were passed over to the War Office for use by the Royal Army Service Corps.

As 1939 came to an end and the future seemed dark indeed, Vosper had successfully ironed out many production problems, a new yard at Portchester was under consideration and the company was steadily producing standard boats.

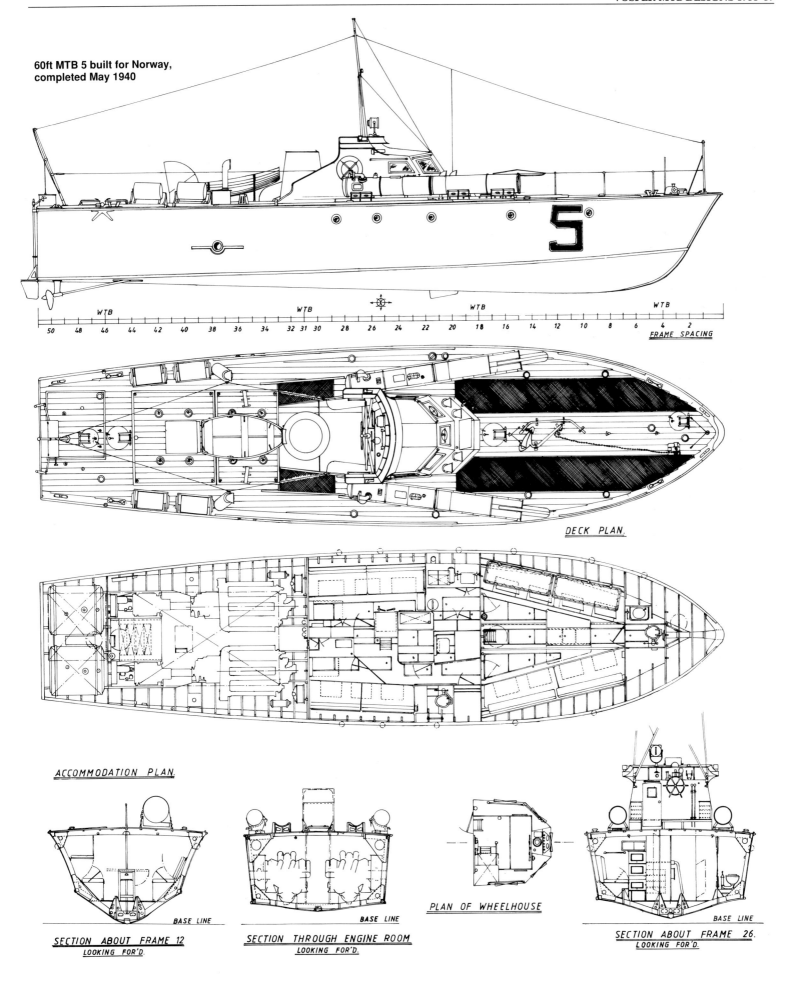

60ft MTB 5 built for Norway, completed May 1940

WTB WTB WTB WTB

50 48 46 44 42 40 38 36 34 32 31 30 28 26 24 22 20 18 16 14 12 10 8 6 4 2

FRAME SPACING

DECK PLAN.

ACCOMMODATION PLAN.

PLAN OF WHEELHOUSE

BASE LINE   BASE LINE   BASE LINE

SECTION ABOUT FRAME 12
LOOKING FOR'D.

SECTION THROUGH ENGINE ROOM
LOOKING FOR'D.

SECTION ABOUT FRAME 26.
LOOKING FOR'D.

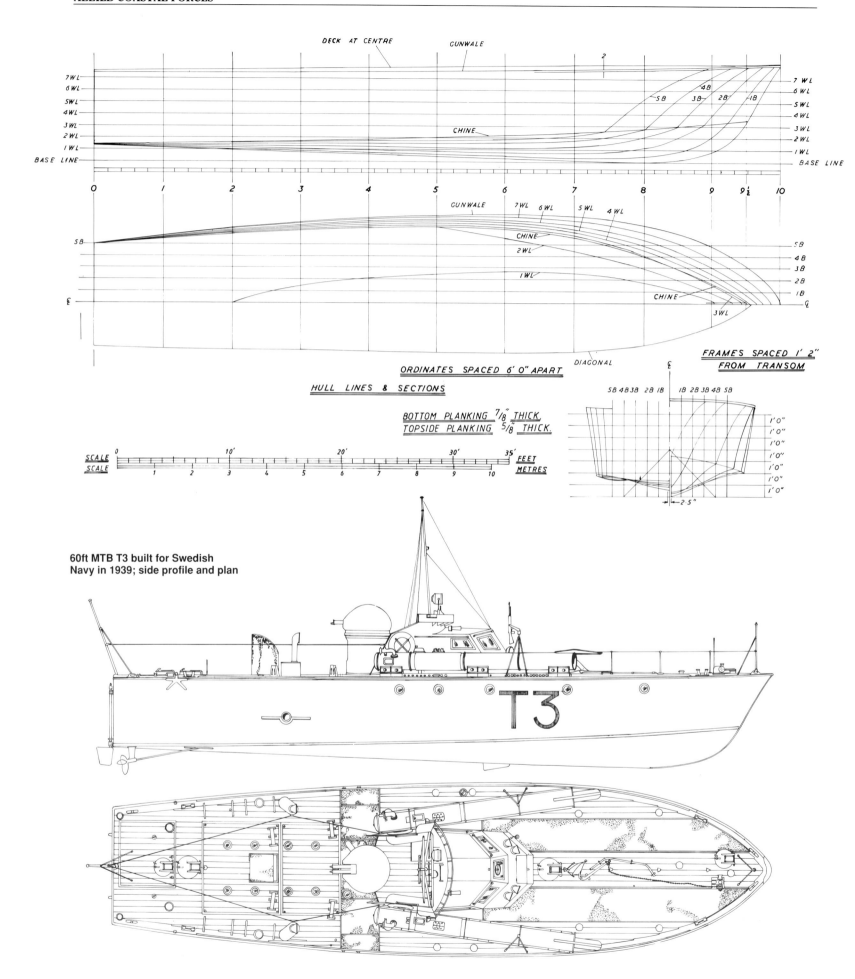

DECK AT CENTRE   GUNWALE

2

7 WL
6 WL
5 WL
4 WL
3 WL
2 WL
1 WL
BASE LINE

4B
5B   3B   2B   1B

7 WL
6 WL
5 WL
4 WL
3 WL
2 WL
1 WL
BASE LINE

CHINE

0   1   2   3   4   5   6   7   8   9   9½   10

GUNWALE   7 WL 6 WL   5 WL   4 WL

CHINE
2 WL

5B
4B
3B
2B
1B

1 WL

CHINE

3 WL

SB

₵

₵

DIAGONAL

ORDINATES SPACED 6' 0" APART

FRAMES SPACED 1' 2"
FROM TRANSOM

HULL LINES & SECTIONS

SB 4B 3B 2B 1B   1B 2B 3B 4B 5B

BOTTOM PLANKING 7/8" THICK.
TOPSIDE PLANKING 5/8" THICK.

1' 0"
1' 0"
1' 0"
1' 0"
1' 0"
1' 0"
1' 0"

SCALE   0   10'   20'   30'   35' FEET
SCALE   1   2   3   4   5   6   7   8   9   10 METRES

2.5"

**60ft MTB T3 built for Swedish
Navy in 1939; side profile and plan**

T3

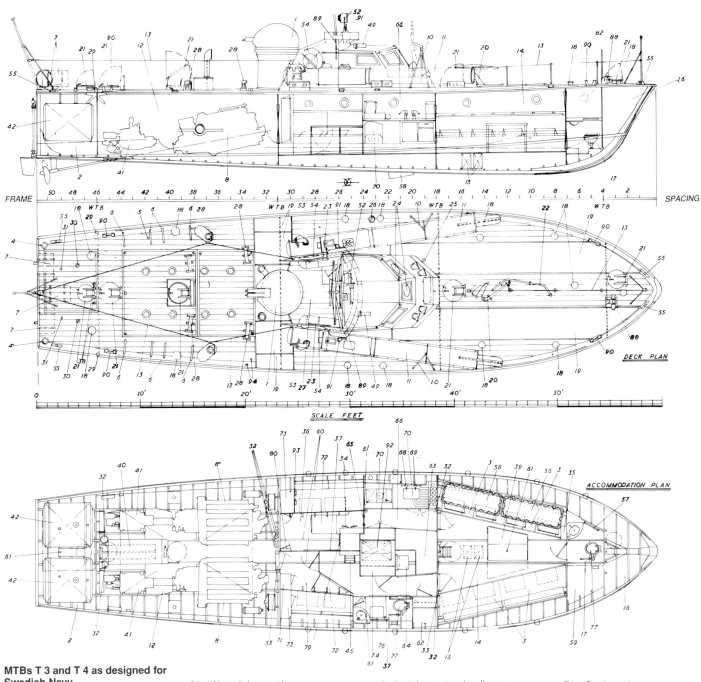

FRAME 50 48 46 44 42 40 38 36 34 32 30 28 26 24 22 20 18 16 14 12 10 8 6 4 2 SPACING

DECK PLAN

0 10' 20' 30' 40' 50'

SCALE FEET

ACCOMMODATION PLAN

MTBs T 3 and T 4 as designed for Swedish Navy

1 Mounting for twin 8mm guns
2 Fuel tank compartment
3 Cushioned seats with lockers under
4 Deck plate for access to steering sheave
5 Filling pipe for heating fresh water tank
6 Chocks for depth charge chutes
7 Smoke fluid containers – if fitted
8 Isotta-Fraschini petrol engine
9 Fire extinguisher – remote control
10 6.5mm machine gun mounting
11 18in torpedo tube
12 Engineroom
13 Lifeline
14 Forecastle
15 Two food bins
16 Forepeak
17 Crew's WC
18 Mushroom ventilator
19 Rubber deck covering
20 CQR anchor

21 Watertight scuttle
22 Emergency tiller
23 Handrail
24 Clear view screens
25 Fresh water filling cap
26 Vent from heating boiler
27 Raised steering platform
28 Torpedo loading chocks
29 Lifting lug
30 Fuel tank filling cap port and starboard
31 Fuel tank sounding cap port and starboard
32 Fire extinguisher
33 Watertight door
34 Voice pipe
35 First aid box
36 Commander's cabin
37 Sliding door
38 Air pipe
39 Table with hinged flaps
40 Batteries under
41 Vosper V8 engine
42 Petrol tank
43 Torpedo release levers
44 Door to wheelhouse

45 Ladder up to wheelhouse
46 Canvas screen
47 Sponge rubber covering
48 Fresh water tank sounding pipe
49 Klaxon
50 Windscreen
51 Wind deflector
52 Searchlight
53 Seat
54 Life buoy
55 Fairlead
56 Canvas cot
57 Storm rail
58 Centre fin
59 Shelf
60 Girder
61 Pillar
62 Store
63 W/T office
64 Hinged seat
65 Serving hatch
66 Galley
67 Sink
68 Fresh water pump
69 Salt water pump
70 Boiler – under

71 Cupboard
72 Table
73 Wardrobe
74 Magazine
75 Notice board
76 Passage
77 WC
78 Officers' WC
79 Officers' cabin
80 Key board
81 Locker
82 Life line stanchion
83 Flag locker
84 Drawers
85 Chart table
86 Standard compass
87 Dashboard
88 Windlass
89 Steering wheel
90 Bollard
91 Navigation light
92 Fresh water tanks
93 Clock
94 Filling and air pipes to fresh water tank for priming pump

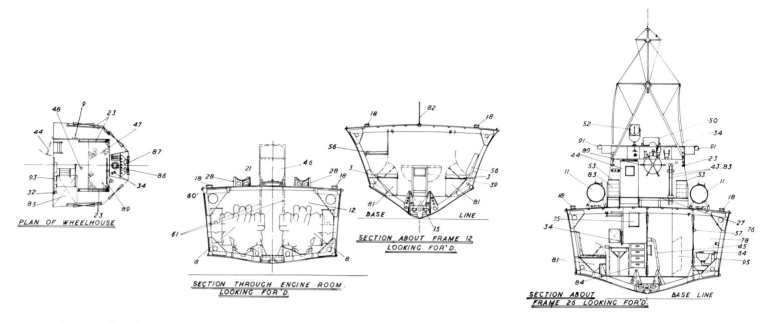

Wheelhouse and sections

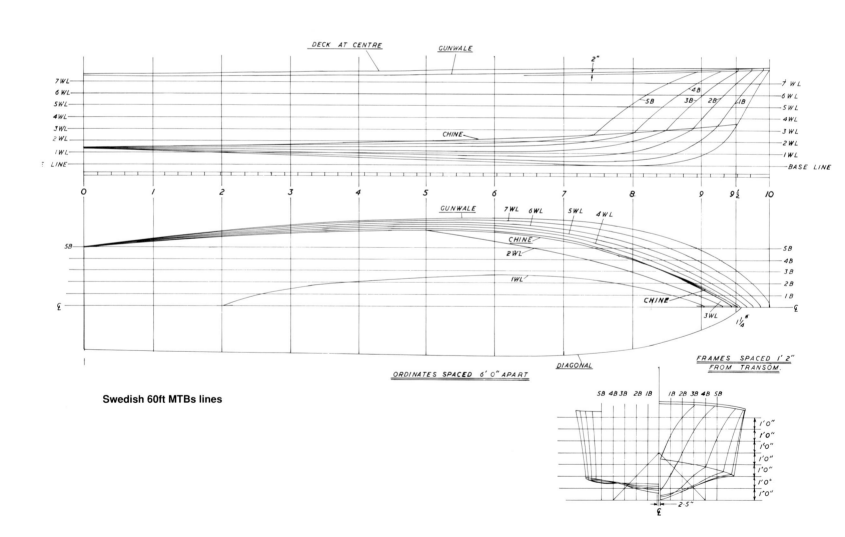

Swedish 60ft MTBs lines

The Vosper 45ft MTB design

The Vosper design for a 45ft MTB is redrawn from their Drawing 8572 (Admiralty Reference CP 8b/24437/39) and was the result of an invitation to tender dated 16 May 1939, from the Director of Navy Contracts, Admiralty (Branch 8b) 2–6 Bainbridge Street, London WC1. Similar invitations to tender were sent to – British Power Boat Co Ltd, Hythe, Southampton; J S White & Co Ltd, Cowes; J I Thornycroft & Co Ltd, London; James Taylor (Chertsey) Ltd, Chertsey, Surrey; Wm Denny & Bros Ltd, Dumbarton; and Fred Cooper, Pennington, Hampshire.

The proposals had arisen from a meeting held by the Director of Naval Estimates on 15 March 1939, when discussions had taken place on the characteristics of a 'Cruiser-carried MTB' with a view to taking action as a result of earlier meetings which had taken place during 1938. Then the position was summarised as determining the line which experiment in fast motor boat design should take. The position as seen then was that existing MTBs met the requirement of the 'offensive-defensive' type, and that the obvious development was to provide a MTB designed to attack enemy ports and for rapid emergency production. The sphere of possible operations outlined a demand of endurance ranging from 460 to 1080 miles. The director of production considered towing to be undesirable and a minimum speed on passage of 20 knots a necessity. An 'offensive' MTB was seen to be either (1) a small MTB which could be hoisted into (a) a cruiser (about 8 tons) or (b) a special MTB carrier (20 tons), or (2) a large MTB with greatly increased endurance and better accommodation.

The Director of Naval Construction was not optimistic over the design and construction of a satisfactory MTB carrier of moderate size and considered that the choice lay between the small 8-ton MTB and the large option. The estimated characteristics of each were:

	Small type	Large type
Displacement	8 tons	75 tons
Length	40–45ft	90ft
Cost	£17,000	£70,000
Armament	2 × 18in torpedoes	Uncertain
Speed	50 knots	
HP	at least 1000bhp	
Endurance	100 miles at 2/3 power	Endurance would be the most difficult to provide.

Their relative advantages and disadvantages were considered to be:

	Small type	Large type
Advantages	Small silhouette Cheaper and easier to produce in numbers	Larger armament Independent of transport
		May be developed for anti-MTB work or work with the fleet
Disadvantages	Small armament Require transport	Larger silhouette Less handy Cost

The earlier discussions in 1938 suggested that there was a practical limit to the size of MTBs of about 100ft and it also seemed doubtful whether a large MTB could be given the necessary speed and en-

A Greek 70ft MTB on trials in 1939.
Vosper Thornycroft (UK) Ltd

*The 70ft MTB T3, built for Greece and later
taken over by the RN as MTB 69.*
Vosper Thornycroft (UK) Ltd

durance with existing engines to carry out the longer operations contemplated, and still less to work with the fleet. In view of this doubt, the probable cost and the disadvantages of the large MTB in an attack on a harbour, it was considered that an experiment with a 90ft MTB was hardly justifiable, at any rate until experience had been gained with the 70ft 1938 (Vosper) MTBs and possibly with the British Power Boat 70ft boat then under consideration. Summarising, it seemed the small MTB was more viable for experiment if the required endurance could be imparted either by hoisting in or towing, and it was conceived that it may be of value for a specific offensive operation if hostilities broke out.

The following 'secret' report was duly dispatched to the companies which had been asked to tender:

Gentlemen,
I have to request that you will submit a tender for the design, construction, completion in all respects and delivery at your own risk and expense, free from defect at HM Dockyard, Portsmouth, of one Small Type Motor Torpedo Boat of 40 to 45ft in length, suitable for carrying aboard ship and to meet the requirements as set out hereunder.

The tender is subject to the attached General Conditions of Contract and Schemes of Payment by Instalments of the price of Hull, Machinery and Electrical Work. The prices quoted will be taken to cover all the requirements of the letter, and, so far as is practicable, separate prices should not be quoted for any items other than as shown on the tender form. The company tender is to be made out on the enclosed Tender form and lodged at the Admiralty in a sealed cover, addressed by means of the label provided, not later than 12 noon on Thursday, 8th June 1939.

Then followed the principal requirements to be met:

1) Length to be from 40 to 45 feet.
2) The displacement fully loaded and complete in every respect not to exceed 8 tons. The lifting weight you are prepared to guarantee is to be stated.
3) The speed when fully loaded (ie all petrol, lubricating oil, armament, stores, full equipment and crew, but excluding slings), is to be not less than 50 knots. The speed you are prepared to guarantee with the boat in this condition with the engines at full throttle is to be

*Upper deck aft view of a Greek 70ft MTB,
which later became the Royal Navy's MTB 69
or 70, June 1940. Note the twin gun tubs,
lifting eyes and polished ventilators.*
Vosper Thornycroft (UK) Ltd

stated. This speed will be taken as the mean of four runs over an approved measured mile during the ¼ hour trial at full throttle. In addition, the speed you are prepared to guarantee for continuous running. In this case, the trials are to be of two hours duration during which six consecutive runs are to be made over an approved measured mile.

4) The boats are to have a layout generally as shown on the accompanying print DNC 28/A/769. Construction is to be suitable for sea-going qualities similar to those of 45 foot fast motor picket boats. The boats are to be capable of being lifted by crane.

5) The fuel carried should be sufficient for obtaining an endurance of 100 nautical miles at 2/3 full power.

6) The armament is to consist of two 18 inch torpedoes in upper deck tubes to be supplied free of charge by the Admiralty. The weight of the torpedoes and tubes is to be taken as 2 tons.

7) The crew is to consist of four men.

8) All fittings, spare gear, stores etc, necessary for equipping the boat in all respects ready for service are to be provided by the boatbuilder, except items for which supply will be arranged by the Admiralty, viz compass, anchor and cable and navigating lanterns; the weight of these fittings being taken as 150lbs. All necessary stowages are to be provided for the general equipment. Sling fittings for lifting by crane are to be provided and secured in the boat by the boatbuilder. Slings are also to be provided and tested to Admiralty standard by the boatbuilder.

9) Delivery is required by the earliest possible date.

Other stipulations followed. The electrical installation was to be fitted as in fast motor boats of similar size, and modified as required to suit the new design. Quotations for the electrical equipment on

The launch of a Norwegian 60ft boat in the summer of 1939.
Vosper Thornycroft (UK) Ltd

Former MTB 21, 20 or 23, which was sold to Romania, in immaculate condition.
Vosper Thornycroft (UK) Ltd

those lines was to be 'obtained from approved firms and submitted with your tender'.

> Alternative proposals which may be put forward with the object of saving weight will be considered. All fittings should, however, be sufficiently robust to ensure reliability and the required degree of watertightness under service conditions. Full details of such proposals with the cost of the same should be submitted with your tender.

The following were to be supplied in duplicate with the tender:

(a) A general arrangement drawing in profile, plan and section. The estimated lifting weight with full equipment to be stated.

(b) A general arrangement drawing of the machinery

MTB 30 in July 1940, slowly moving astern, with empty depth charge racks and long-range tanks aft.
Vosper Thornycroft (UK) Ltd

MTB 30 in summer 1940. She carries a single 0.303in Lewis gun forward, two 21in torpedo tubes and a twin 0.5in Vickers Mark V power mounting aft. She was mined on 18 December 1942 in the North Sea.
Imperial War Museum

installation.

(c) A detailed hull specification.
(d) A detailed machinery specification.
(e) A detailed electrical specification.
(f) A list of equipment.

Your tender price should cover the supply and performance of the following items which will be required if an order is placed with you:

(a) Two in number additional copies of the General Arrangement Drawings and specifications, Hull, Machinery and Electrical, as submitted with your tender are to be forwarded to the Admiralty immediately after the order is placed for transmission

to Inspecting Officers.

(b) A drawing showing details of the slings for lifting by crane, sling plates and fastenings proposed is to be submitted for approval before work is taken in hand. Prints of the General Arrangement of the slings as approved are to be supplied by you through the Warship Production Superintendent to the Dockyard or Overseers concerned for information and guidance.

(c) A sheer draft 'as built' on tracing cloth to be forwarded as soon as possible after completion.

(d) A General Arrangement drawing on tracing cloth with permanent black lines in profile, plan and three sections 'as built', to be forwarded as soon as possible after completion.

(e) A list of hull fixtures on Form D6C and of Principal dimensions, etc, on Form D463 to be prepared in quadruplicate. The forms will be supplied to you by the Overseer. A rigging warrant is to be prepared in quadruplicate and a list of the equipment supplied with the boat in duplicate. Each of these lists will be verified by the Overseer and is to be forwarded to the Admiralty through the Warship Production Superintendent. The lists are to be prepared and forwarded as soon as possible after the completion of the boat.

(f) Form D127b to be prepared in quadruplicate in the usual manner.

(g) Sea trials in accordance with paragraph 6(3) and the Statement of Machinery Requirements. Ballast is to be used if required to make up the full load displacement.

(i) The boat is to be weighed in the presence of, and to the satisfaction of the Overseer immediately before the inclining experiment.

(ii) An inclining experiment will be carried out on the boat, with full equipment and fuel and four men, by an Admiralty Officer. The boatbuilder is to supply ballast, pendulum and labour, and afford any assistance required, including weighing the ballast in the presence

The newly commissioned MTB 32 in summer 1940. Note the upper deck fuel tanks, a recently fitted twin 0.5in mounting and stump ensign staff.
Vosper Thornycroft (UK) Ltd

MTB 32 – another pass of the camera on the same day.

of the Overseer. A tracing is to be forwarded showing the disposition of the ballast and the items on board. Hydrostatic curves are to be supplied on tracing cloth.

The boat to be built under Admiralty supervision and the standard of workmanship, care of the boat whilst building, quality of materials used, etc, are to be those usual in Admiralty work of this type.

The boat to be completed by the boatbuilder ready for service.

The torsional characteristics of the machinery installation are to be investigated, and the result, together with the calculations involved and proposals for the elimination of undesirable effects of torsional oscillation at all engine speeds are to be submitted to the

MTB 48 in 1940, a Vosper design built by J S White, Cowes.
Imperial war Museum

The newly completed MTB 36 in March 1941. Gone are the days of polished ventilators.
Vosper Thornycroft (UK) Ltd

Admiralty for approval. The stresses arising in any part of the machinery installation on account of torsional oscillations are not to exceed approved limits.

The measured course over which it is proposed to run the official full power trials, should the order be placed with you, is to be named on the tender form.

The delivery date given must be that on which the Admiralty can absolutely rely. In completing the Tender Form the date given for delivery should be based on the assumption that Admiralty orders already placed with you are completed according to contract, but should not take into account the effect on delivery which would arise if orders for fast boats of any other type than that referred to herein were placed with you at the same time as an order for the boat to which this enquiry relates.

All drawings are to be signed and all drawings forwarded to the Admiralty in illustration of the tender will be retained unless their return is specially requested.

It is desired that all work in connection with the supply of the engines and installation in the boat should be placed in the hands of the Machinery Sub-Contractor. Any proposed departures from this should be indicated in your tender, together with full particulars as to the division of work between yourselves and the Machinery Sub-Contractors.

Tenders should be self-contained so far as is practicable, in particular if it is desired to make reference back to conditions, drawings, submissions or the like which applied to or were submitted in connection with previous orders; such reference must be accompanied by a full statement of the conditions and copies of the drawings, submissions, etc, to which it applies.

Please acknowledge receipt of this letter and state whether it is your intention to deliver a tender by the date named in paragraph 5 of this letter. Should you be unable to tender on this occasion, please return all the enclosed documents to this Office as soon as possible with a statement to that effect.

I am, Gentlemen,
Your Obedient Servant

(and signed by the Director of Navy Contracts)

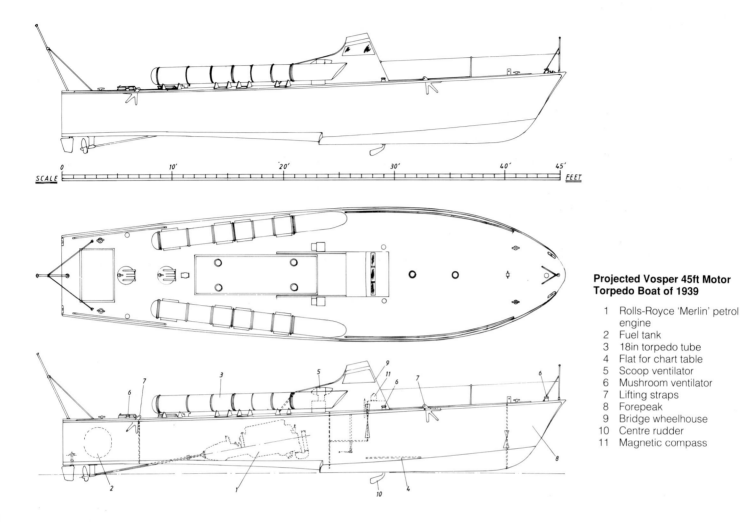

Projected Vosper 45ft Motor Torpedo Boat of 1939

1   Rolls-Royce 'Merlin' petrol engine
2   Fuel tank
3   18in torpedo tube
4   Flat for chart table
5   Scoop ventilator
6   Mushroom ventilator
7   Lifting straps
8   Forepeak
9   Bridge wheelhouse
10 Centre rudder
11 Magnetic compass

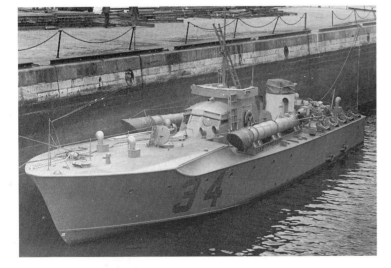

A lonely looking MTB 34 alongside the wall whilst on builder's trials.
Vosper Thornycroft (UK) Ltd

This is an Admiralty Tender document described in full, as of May 1939.

The original 'MTB small type' general layout as supplied with the tender, and Vosper's reply GA drawing, have been redrawn. It is similar to the offered GA, but has a stepped hull, similar to the later MTB 103 (CT 05 as completed). Power was to be provided by a single Rolls-Royce Merlin engine. The hull was to be divided into four watertight sections, with a flat for a chart table. The bridge is more like a shelter and the fuel tank was carried aft. It did not have a mess deck or galley, and the crew would not have lived on board.

The Vosper design was never completed – the experimental 45ft MTB 108 ordered on 14 November 1940 was bombed and destroyed by enemy action on 10 January 1941 whilst under construction. (Other sources show her as having two Packard engines.)

A GA drawing of two of Thornycroft's 45ft designs will be redrawn for Volume III. Both are stepped hull designs. The first, MTB 104, was very similar to the designs of First World War coastal motor boats, and carried two 18in torpedoes. The later, MTB 105, had a modified but similar hull, but only a single trainable 18in torpedo, similar to that carried by Vosper's *Bloodhound*, but these vessels were both requisitioned.

One other listed design is MTB 109, which is shown as 43ft long, with a weight of 9 tons. This was ordered on 28 February 1942 from William Denny, but never completed and was disposed of incomplete in December 1945. There is a mention of a 45ft MTB by British Power Boat, but again I have no details of her layout.

Vosper designs 1940

Under the 1940 Naval programme the hundreds of vessels ordered included eighty-nine MTBs, of which ten were ordered from Vosper on 26 February 1940. These were Nos 57–66. Six other units (Nos 67–72), were requisitioned whilst completing and a further twenty-six were ordered on 14 May (Nos 73–99; there was also a replacement for MTB 75 bombed on the stocks whilst under construction). A further twelve were ordered on 20 May (201–212) from J S White at Cowes (from Vosper drawings). Five improved Coastal Motor Boat types were ordered from Thornycroft on 7 June; four were ordered on 7 December (218–221, ex-Greek orders) and the last four (242–245) were replacements for MTBs 33, 37, 39 and 40. The majority of these were to Vosper design.

The first ten units were built under contract No 8B/20689/40, MTBs 57–66 are shown after being re-engined, but they generally had similar lines to the earlier MTBs 31–40. They were completed with the heavy Hall-Scott engines and subsequently re-engined with the US-built Packards. Other improvements included the addition of Type 286 RDF (see Volume I) which was fitted during

MTB 73 ready for trials under the red ensign, in October 1941.
Vosper Thornycroft (UK) Ltd

1941. Fuel capacity was increased to a total of 2725 gallons (1025 gallons centre tank and 850 gallons each wing tank).

Re-engined during 1942 with three Packard units of 1200hp (as drawn), 4050hp gave a 37.5 knot maximum speed at 2400rpm and 33 knots were produced at 3600hp/2200rpm. Additional equipment included CSA (chemical smoke apparatus – see Volume I), and the small clinker built dinghies carried by the earlier boats were deleted and replaced by Carley floats. The complement had increased to twelve – two officers and ten ratings. The armament was standardised – two 21in tubes and the twin power operated 0.5in Vickers machine gun turret. Two twin 0.303in Vickers gas-operated machine guns were carried for close range defence. It was now usual to carry a box of Mills grenades for close-in fighting.

The further 26 units ordered on 14 May 1940 (73–98) and the replacement for MTB 75 and repeat orders for MTBs 222–245 (ordered 22 February 1941) were built under Contract Nos CP BR8b/45096/40, CP BR8E/17205/41 and CP BR8E/21272/41. These groups had undergone considerable redesign.

The 'as fitted' Drawings 9859 and 9860 for these have been redrawn. These vessels incorporate several design changes and additions from the earlier boats. They were the first series to be equipped with Packard engines supplied under Lend-Lease. The hull was still hard chine double skin, diagonal mahogany

The launch of MTB 78 at Wivenhoe on 14 April 1942. She completed on 18 May. Note the number of female workers looking on. The only uniform visible is that of the petty officer on the upper deck.
Vosper Thornycroft (UK) Ltd

throughout, with two rudders right aft on the transom as usual, but a third centreline rudder was added to decrease the turning circle, as shown. Displacement had increased to 47 tons when new and dry, which increased to about 55 tons with added armament and equipment and the soakage of the hull timbers.

They had three Packard engines each of 1250hp. The two wing engines drove direct through thrust blocks to the outboard shafts. The centre shaft was driven by V-drive, reversing the power back aft. The two Ford V8 auxiliary engines could be clutched to the

wing shafts for silent running at 6.5 knots. By 1943 the main engines were modified with Dumbflow silencers and weight was reduced by removing one auxiliary engine.

When completed from late 1941 to the summer of 1942 maximum speed was reduced by an increase in displacement and the
craft were not as fast as the early, lighter Isotta-engined boats, but
overall they were more potent units, with a longer range. This
group had a maximum speed of 38.94 knots at 2400rpm and 35.9
knots at 2200rpm continuous. Additional fuel tankage was built in
aft (1078gal) with 1605gal in the main tanks amidships. The
2683gal of 100 octane petrol gave a range of about 400 miles at 20
knots.

The two steering positions, bridge and wheelhouse, were retained as in the earlier boats, and the wheelhouse was armoured.
This was a big improvement on the earlier days when a small
armoured plate was swung down from the deckhead. Type 286
radar was fitted soon after completion, but it was little used and was

*MTB 73, completed and ready for acceptance
trials in October 1941. Note the Type 286
radar at the masthead.*
Vosper Thornycroft (UK) Ltd

not reliable.

By 1942 the complement comprised two officers, with frequently a third along for the ride, or under training, two petty officers and nine ratings. This was increased as weapons and equipment were added.

The armament as built was little changed from before – two 21in tubes, the standard twin 0.5in Vickers machine gun PO and two twin 0.303in Vickers gas-operated machine guns mounted on the torpedo tubes. Four depth charges were usually standard (see Volume I for details of depth charges).

By late in the war, most of this series were modified by changing the 0.5in turret for the more potent twin 20mm Oerlikon Mark IX mounting, and a single 20mm Oerlikon mounted forward of the bridge. By June 1944 many were fitted for minelaying (see Drawing 9627) off the French, Belgian and Netherlands coasts.

The vessels built as 1940 follow-on orders continued along similar lines, and others included 218–221, ordered on 7 December 1940 by Greece, but requisitioned upon the fall of that country. These were powered by the supercharged Hall-Scott engines. A further four vessels, ordered on 2 December 1940, became 242–245 and were the same as 73 onwards. These replaced 33, 37, 39 and 40.

MTB 80 under the white ensign in early 1943, and now haing Type 291 'U' and Type 240 or 241 IFF and a single 0.303in Vickers GO gun forward.
Imperial War Museum

MTB 97 on builder's trials in September 1942. Note the Type 286 radar and IFF right forward.
Vosper Thornycroft (UK) Ltd

MTB 218 on builder's trials in June 1941. She had no radar and was powered by supercharged Hall-Scott petrol engines.
Vosper Thornycroft (UK) Ltd

70ft MTBs 35, 36, 38 and 218–221

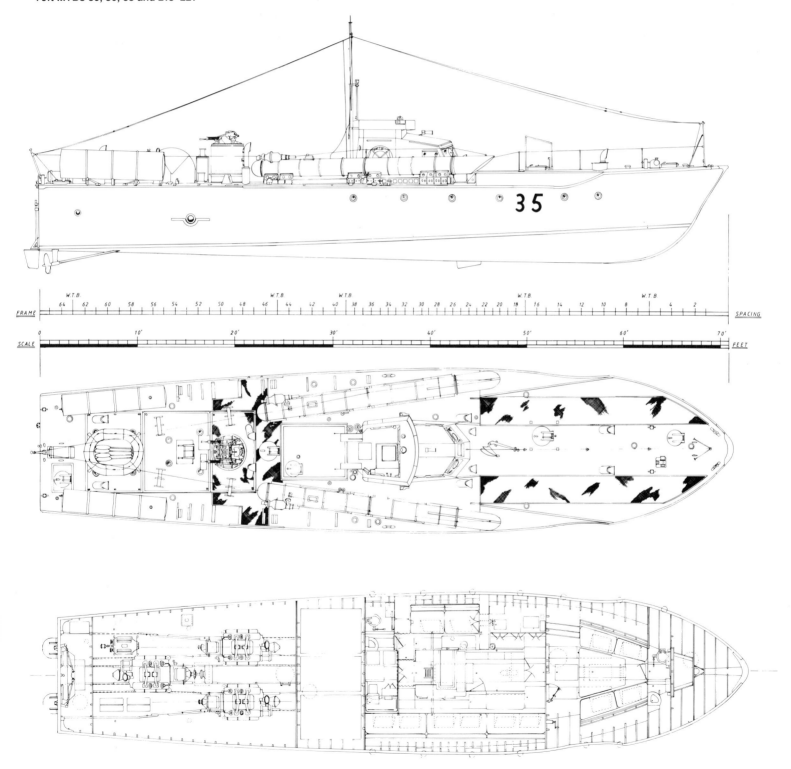

MTBs 35, 36, 38 and 218–221 detail

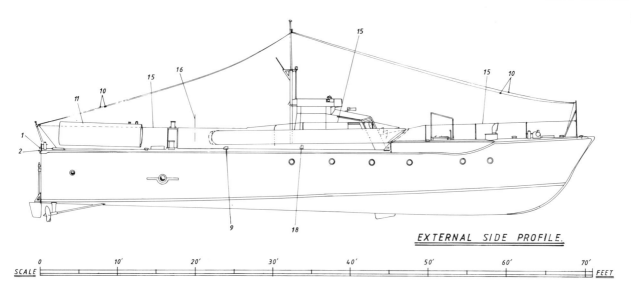

EXTERNAL SIDE PROFILE.

SCALE | 0 10' 20' 30' 40' 50' 60' 70' | FEET

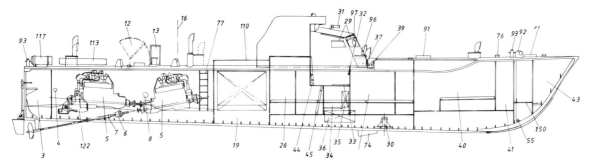

INTERNAL SIDE PROFILE

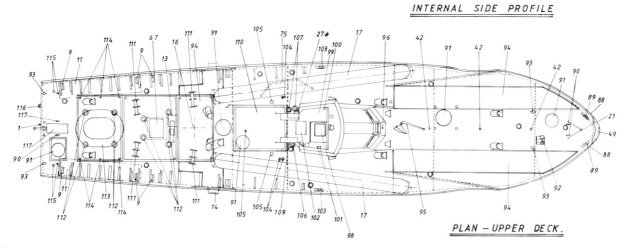

PLAN – UPPER DECK.

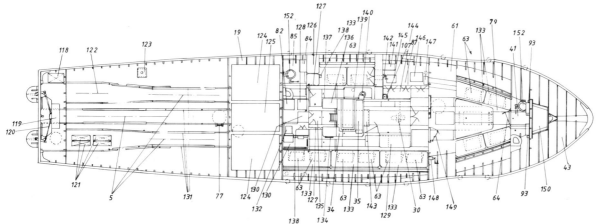

PLAN – LOWER DECK.

1   Overtaking light
2   Stern light
3   After peak
4   Centre engine exhaust
    (starboard side only)
5   Supercharged Hall-Scott
    Defender petrol engine
6   Thrust block
7   Stern tube
8   Wing engine exhausts port and
    starboard
9   Portable tripping chocks for
    mines
10 Insulators
11 Auxiliary deck fuel tank
    (350gal) port and starboard
12 Folding plywood screen
13 Ready use ammunition box
14 Side ladder eyeplates
15 Lifeline
16 Twin 0.5in power-operated
    Mark V mounting
17 21in torpedo tubes (note – two
    types)
18 Fixed tripping chocks for mine
    port and starboard
19 Fuel tank space
20 Lightning conductor
21 Jack stay
22 Masthead light
23 Aerial feeders to W/T office po
    and starboard
24 Telescopic mast
25 Cleats for mast and signal
    halyards
26 W/T office
27 Ensign
28 Handrail
29 Wood battens for blinds
30 Asdic
31 Horn
32 Telescope clip
33 2in rubber matting
34 Magazine
35 Fresh water tank (45gal)
36 Fresh water tank (50gal)
37 Air pipe to fresh water tank
38 A/S room
39 Raised deck bracket
40 Forecastle
41 Crew's WC
42 Lifeline stanchion sockets
43 Forepeak
44 Ladder – up to bridge
45 Ladder – down to lobby
46 Fresh water tank filling cap
47 Engineroom telegraph
48 Magnetic compass
49 Stem deck pad
50 Dashboard
51 Engine throttles
52 Torpedo firing levers
53 Sponge rubber mat
54 Voice pipe
55 Cable clench
56 Crew's scuttle
57 Canvas canopy – over
58 Scuttle stanchion
59 Lifeline stanchion
60 Shelf
61 Shelves
62 Berth
63 Locker
64 Door to crew's WC
65 2in pillar
66 Folding table

67 Engineroom scuttle
68 Torpedo sight bracket
69 Wood cleat
70 Bow light
71 Life buoy port and starboard
72 Flag locker
73 Armoured door to wheelhouse
74 Forward rudder
75 Auxiliary tiller
76 Mushroom ventilator
77 Engineroom escape ladder
78 Fixed mine trip
79 Crew space
80 Book cupboard
81 Door into lobby
82 Radio receiver
83 Generator
84 Toilet rack
85 Officers' WC
86 Mirror
87 Cupboard
88 Brass sheathing – port and starboard
89 Enclosed fairleads – port and starboard
90 Aerial cleats
91 W/T scuttle
92 Windlass
93 Samson posts – port and starboard
94 Rubber deck covering
95 CQR plough anchor
96 Lifeline eyebolt
97 Kent clear view screen
98 Steering stool
99 Raised platform
100 Lockheed fluid header tank
101 Voice pipes to wardroom, W/T office and wheelhouse
102 Portable flooring
103 Warping bollard – port and starboard
104 Air pipes to fuel tanks
105 Fuel tank sounding pipe
106 Mast socket
107 Fire extinguishers
108 Emergency tiller stowage
109 Insulated gland to W/T office
110 Raised tank space hatch
111 Portable torpedo loading chocks – port and starboard
112 Glass deck light
113 DNC Carley life float
114 Deck eyeplates for auxiliary fuel tanks
115 Filling cap and air pipes
116 Auxiliary tiller bearing
117 Chemical smoke-producing apparatus (CSA)
118 Reserve lubricating oil tank
119 A/S battery
120 Lockheed hydraulic steering gear
121 Kathanode batteries
122 Vosper V8 engine
123 Lubricating oil storage tank
124 Fuel tank (681gal)
125 Fuel tank (642gal)
126 Wardrobe
127 Curtain
128 Radio transmitter
129 Table
30 Hinged flap of table
31 Engine girders
32 Hinged seat
33 Hinged back berth
34 Notice board
35 Lobby
36 Drawers
37 Wardroom

138 Clock
139 Keyboard
140 Hinged table lamp
141 Plate rack
142 Fresh water pump
143 Platform over tank
144 Galley
145 Sink
146 Oven
147 Hot water tank
148 Hand-operated bilge pump
149 Watertight door
150 Wooden platform
151 Canopy over engineroom scuttle
152 WC

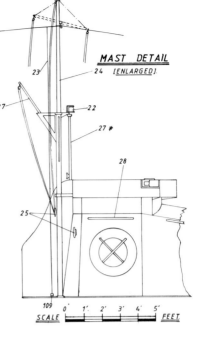

MAST DETAIL [ENLARGED]

SCALE FEET

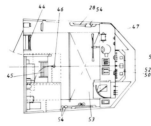

PLAN OF WHEELHOUSE

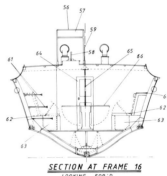

SECTION AT FRAME 16
LOOKING FOR'D.

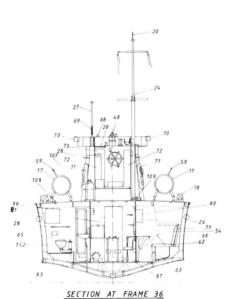

SECTION AT FRAME 36
LOOKING FOR'D.

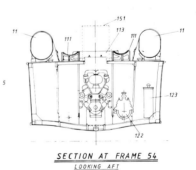

SECTION AT FRAME 54
LOOKING AFT

MTB 206 recovering a practice torpedo during her workup at HMS *Bee, Weymouth, in 1942. She was built to Vosper's design by J S White, Cowes.*
Courtesy Geoffrey Hudson

General arrangement, plan and lines of MTB 218, one of the later units

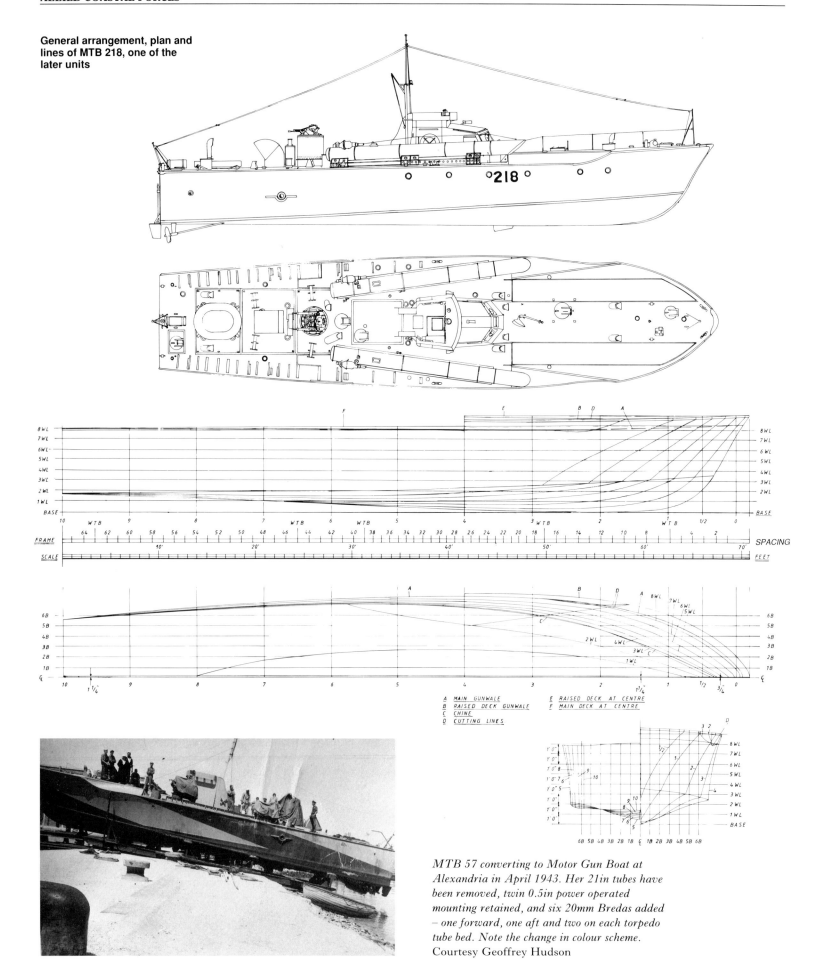

A MAIN GUNWALE
B RAISED DECK GUNWALE
C CHINE
D CUTTING LINES

E RAISED DECK AT CENTRE
F MAIN DECK AT CENTRE

MTB 57 converting to Motor Gun Boat at Alexandria in April 1943. Her 21in tubes have been removed, twin 0.5in power operated mounting retained, and six 20mm Bredas added – one forward, one aft and two on each torpedo tube bed. Note the change in colour scheme.
Courtesy Geoffrey Hudson

Fittings and instruments

1 Buzzer
2 Plug switch – engineroom orders telegraph
3 Walker electric log
4 Engineroom orders telegraph
5 Engineroom reply and change switch
6 Chart table light
7 Loudspeakers – Admiralty pattern M317
8 Switch roof light (wheelhouse)
9 Engineroom order push
10 Telephone handset
11 Fire extinguisher remote control
12 Junction box – electric wiring
13 Kent clear view screen
14 Bullet-proof sliding shutter
15 Lockheed valves (steering gear)
16 Telescope clips
17 Fire extinguisher
18 Binocular stowage box
19 Torpedo director mounting
20 Drip trough
21 Voice pipe
22 Voice pipe to wheelhouse and W/T office
23 Voice pipe to wheelhouse and wardroom
24 Voice pipe to wheelhouse steering position
25 Spy hole
26 Handrails
27 Chart stowage
28 Fresh water sounding pipe
29 Drain to bilges
30 Recorder
31 Amplifier
32 Aldis lamp socket
33 Flag locker
34 Bookshelves and pencil rack
35 Access trap
36 Canvas blind
37 Lockheed fluid header tank
38 Locker seat
39 Sliding door
40 Hatch stowage for signal cone and ball
41 Horn
42 Limit stops for B/P shutter bolts
43 Stowage for recognition pistol and cartridges
44 Sponge rubber mat
45 Roof light
46 Life line eyebolt
47 Plugs for mast, anchor, NUC and recognition lights
48 Semaphore flag locker
49 Mast
50 Mast socket

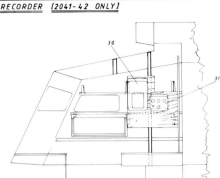
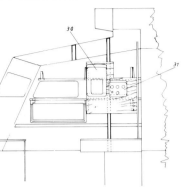

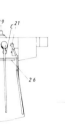

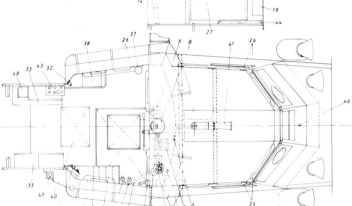
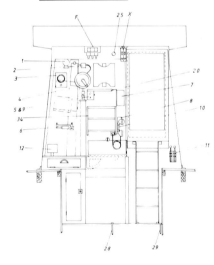
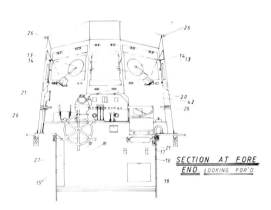
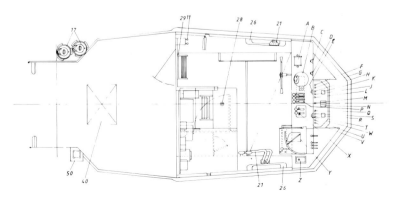

STARBOARD SIDE OF WHEELHOUSE SHOWING ARRGT OF ECHO SOUNDING AMPLIFIER & RECORDER [2041-42 ONLY]

SECTION LOOKING TO PORT.

SECTION LOOKING FOR'D. ON AFT BULKHEAD.

SECTION LOOKING AFT ON AFT BULKHEAD.

PLAN VIEW

SECTION AT FORE END. LOOKING FOR'D

Deck plan and interior
Dashboard instruments

A Engineroom telegraph
B Magnetic compass
C Telegraph illumination socket
D Compass illumination socket
E Navigation lights dimmer
F Alarm push
G Port wiper
H Anchor light
J Shaded stern light
K Trip clock
L Navigation lights switch
M Helm motor warning light
N Revolution counters
P Engine throttles
Q Instrument panel light
R Helm indicator
S Compass illumination switch
T Helm indicator switch
U Starboard wiper
V Siren
W Instrument light dimmer
X Torpedo firing levers
Y A/S recorder
Z A/S signalling key

**MTB 74 as modified for St Nazaire
Raid**

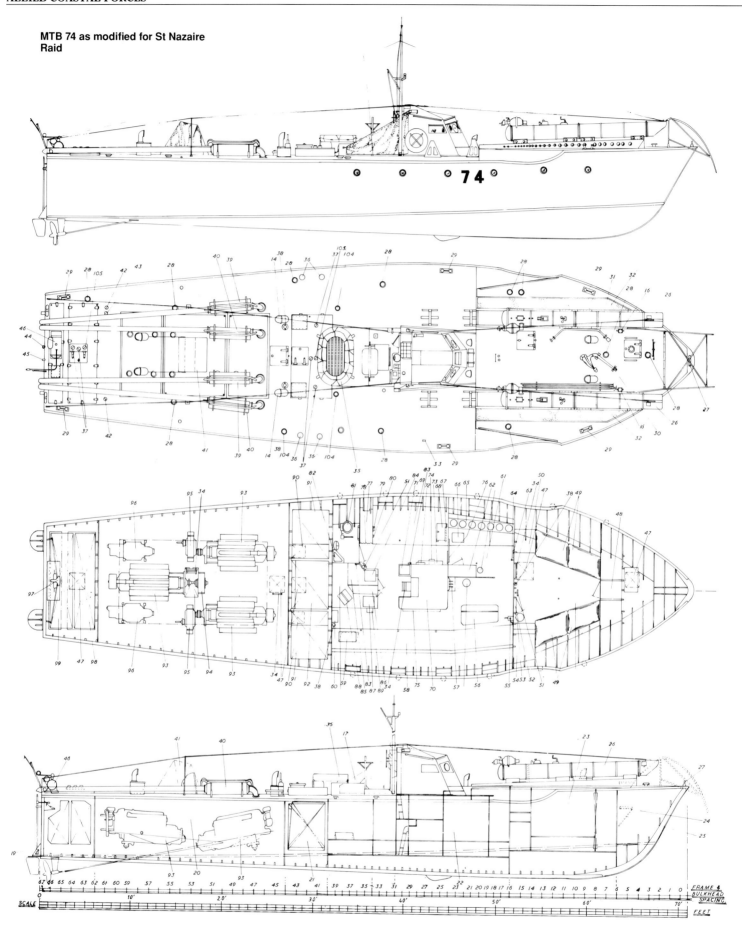

1 Aerial socket
2 Folding seat
3 Life belt
4 Blackout curtains
5 Sorbo mat
6 Ship's wheel
7 Quick release mast band
8 Torpedo sight socket
9 Torpedo firing levers
10 Main engine throttles
11 Standard compass
12 Recognition board
13 Klaxon horn
14 Cowl vent port and starboard
15 Impulse charge box
16 Towing bollard
17 Canvas dodger
18 Bottle screw slip
19 Aft tank compartment (1073 gal)
20 Engineroom
21 Midship tank compartment (1605gal)
22 Accommodation
23 Forecastle
24 Forepeak
25 Look-out platform
26 18in torpedo tube
27 Fairlead
28 Mushroom vent
29 Bollard port and starboard
30 CQR anchor
31 Emergency tiller stowed
32 Non-slip rubber port and starboard
33 Keel fin plate
34 Ladder
35 Carley life float – no boat carried
36 Plate covers port and starboard
37 Petrol filling caps
38 Fire extinguisher
39 Port bank silencer
40 Starboard bank silencer
41 Hatch canopy
42 Lubricating oil filling port and starboard
43 Distilled water filling
44 Stern light
45 Shaded stern light
46 Chemical smoke-producing apparatus (CSA)
47 WT hatch (over)
48 Store
49 Float on air cushions
50 Oilskin stowage
51 Electric fan

52 WT door
53 Aladdin heater
54 Blanket stowage
55 Hand bilge pump
56 Hinged table
57 Rifle rack
58 Seat
59 Locker
60 W/T cupboard
61 Galley
62 Food cupboard
63 Mirror
64 Draw-off cock
65 Thermos rack
66 Sink
67 Wine glass rack
68 Wine locker
69 Chart table
70 Magazine
71 Drawers
72 Key case
73 Chart rack
74 Revolver cabinet
75 Sliding door
76 Serving hatch
77 Wardrobe
78 Curtain
79 Barometer
80 Clock
81 WC
82 Washbasin
83 Voice pipe
84 Hinged seat
85 W/T office
86 Hinged flap
87 W/T receiver
88 W/T transmitter
89 Loudspeaker
90 Flush scuttle (over)
91 Fuel tank (514gal)
92 Fuel tank (577gal)
93 Packard main engine
94 Return drive
95 Reduction gear
96 Vosper V8
97 Steering gear
98 Fuel tank (573gal)
99 Fuel tank (500gal)
100 Masthead light
101 Starboard navigation light
102 Port navigation light
103 Torpedo loading chock
104 Mushroom vent with fan
105 Tank vent
106 Kent clear view screen
107 Permanently rigged lifelines

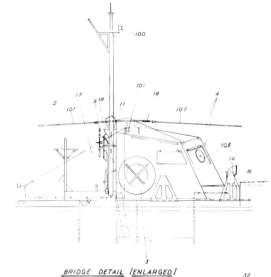

BRIDGE DETAIL [ENLARGED]

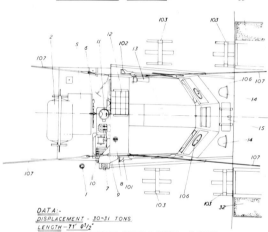

DATA:-
DISPLACEMENT – 30~31 TONS
LENGTH – 71' 0½"
MACHINERY – 3 PACKARD ENGINES. 3600bhp = 39 KNOTS
FUEL – 2678 GALLONS
ARMAMENT – TWO 18" TORPEDO TUBES & .303" M.G's
COMPLEMENT – 2 OFFICERS 8 MEN

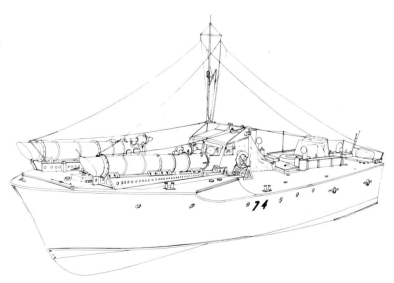

MTB 74

A one-off modification by the company, MTB 74, was ordered by the Admiralty under contract CP BR8b/45096/40 as a special unit, being converted from one of the series of twenty-six 70ft boats ordered on 14 May 1940. She replaced the original 75 which was bombed on the stocks in the air raid of 11 January 1941. Job 2082 was laid down 12 March 1941, launched on 3 September and completed for trials on 17 December.

Why was conversion undertaken and for what reason? The aim, originally, was to provide a means of firing a torpedo or ground mine over a net defence system such as those found protecting major warships. With two 18in torpedo tubes mounted forward on the forecastle deck, the extra height provided the clearance required to fire the tubes from close range above the net and its buoyancy floats.

The idea was suggested by her commanding officer Sub Lieutenant R C M V Wynn (more generally known as 'Micky'). The plan was set up for an attack on the German heavy cruiser *Scharnhorst*, when she was lying at Brest. The project was considered, thought feasible, and the boat was adapted for the purpose. The two 18in torpedoes, which came to be known as 'Wynn's weapons', containing 1800lb of explosive were designed to detonate by delayed-

A bow view of MTB 74 fitting out for the St Nazaire raid. Note her uncluttered upper deck and sided colour scheme.
Vosper Thornycroft (UK) Ltd

action fuses after lying for an interval on the sea bed. After a slow, quiet approach up to the nets surrounding the moored target, the two torpedoes would be fired so as to jump over the nets and hit the vessels. They would then sink to the bottom and after a predetermined period would explode directly beneath the hull, breaking the ship's back with the 'water hammer' effect, the same theory used later with great effect on the Möhne, Sorpe and Eder dams.

What practical changes were undertaken to achieve this aim? Vosper's 'as fitted' Drawing 9886 has been redrawn to show these, and two excellent photographs show her fitting out in the Vosper yard. Attention is particularly drawn to the two tubes right forward, and to the fact that the bridge has been cut away; the wheel and helmsman only have the protection of a canvas screen. Further aft the upper deck is devoid of depth charge chutes and the more usual upper deck fittings, guard rails, etc although she retains CSA. The impression is of a very low silhouette aided by multicolour camouflage paintwork. (The colour scheme is not known.) As can be seen in the starboard bow view, the upper deck is very uncluttered.

In referring to the drawings it is noted that there are a number of further additions. Right forward is a pipe gantry suspended over the bow. The emergency tiller bar is stowed adjacent to the CQR anchor, with boathooks secured in a stowage to starboard. At the break of the forecastle are the four torpedo loading chocks. The bridge detail has been enlarged to show its simplicity. To starboard is the quick release mast band to reduce the outline further. The life lines are permanently rigged from the bridge roof, which allows her outline to be further disguised if canvas is hung from it. To aid in pin-point navigation, there is a recognition board or navigation table to port of the helmsman. A folding seat for the commander was fitted directly behind the helmsman and the wheel, with its 'Sorbo' mat to give some protection from underwater shock.

There are four main engine exhaust pipes running aft from the forward end of the engineroom, along the upper deck to the transom. They are not shown in the photographs, but there is evidence of her being so equipped (David Mason, *Raid on St Nazaire* p41) and these are Vosper's 'as fitted' drawings.

After the raid on the target, a high speed retreat was to be made at full power, giving some 40 knots, aided by her lightened condition. But in February 1942, after the celebrated dash through the Dover Strait by the intended target (the heavy cruisers *Scharnhorst* and *Gneisenau*), Wynn and his converted boat found themselves out of a job.

The boat was therefore introduced into the team of light forces for the raid on St Nazaire in France, with the object of firing the torpedoes at the southern caisson if the converted 'Town' Class destroyer HMS *Campbeltown*, with her cargo of explosives charges, failed to ram successfully. The plan had been devised earlier and on 26 February 1942 Commander R E D Ryder was summoned to a meeting in London chaired by the new Director of Combined Operations, Lord Louis Mountbatten. He was informed that he would command the operation's naval forces, and was introduced to his army opposite number, Lieutenant-Colonel AC Newman.

The St Nazaire Raid during the night of 27/28 March 1942 proved to be a masterpiece of combined operations planning. Its main purpose was to destroy the massive gates of the graving dock which had been constructed in 1935 for the building of the French liner *Normandie* and was now the only dock outside Germany capable of accommodating the modern German pocket battleship *Tir-*

pitz. The presence of such a warship this far south would have posed a grave threat to Atlantic convoys. The aim was to smash the lock gates by using the obsolete destroyer as a ram, and destroy them by explosive charges loaded in the forward part of the destroyer and timed to go off after the raiding party had departed.

Sixteen Fairmile B motor launches, four of them with 21in torpedo tubes, led by the Fairmile C MGB 314 aided by MTB 74 took part in 'Operation Chariot', which left Falmouth at 1400 on Thursday 26 March, escorted by two 'Hunt' class destroyers which were towing the MGB and MTB owing to their restricted range. (They carried upper deck long-range fuel tanks).

Towards midnight the convoy was in the reaches of the Loire estuary, and the drone of the diversionary RAF bomber raid could be heard. At 0122 'Chariot's' luck started to run out. Two searchlights settled on *Campbeltown*, which had been converted to resemble a German destroyer. Signals were exchanged, but eventually the defending forces, unable to identify the ships in midriver, opened fire. The German naval ensign was struck and the white ensign run up in its place. Steaming at 8 knots the force fought its way on. At 0134 *Campbeltown* smashed into the caisson, tearing back 40 feet of her bows.

There was a tremendous firefight. Some of the commandos were landed but others could not be, owing to the weight of the firepower. Within the initial phase of the river battle five Fairmile Bs had been destroyed or were sinking. Meanwhile the MGB waited at the old entrance while Ryder went ashore to ascertain how effectively *Campbeltown* had been placed. By the time he returned, he

MTB 74 fitting out, with two 18in tubes right forward and modified bridge. The upper deck engine exhausts are yet to be fitted. Note, too, the camouflage scheme.
Vosper Thornycroft (UK) Ltd

found that almost half the old destroyer's crew had boarded the gunboat and MTB 74 was alongside. Satisfied with *Campbeltown's* position, Ryder ordered Wynn to fire his delayed action torpedoes at the old entrance lock gates. At a mere 20 yards range this operation was not without considerable risk, and had the delayed action mechanisms failed, both the MTB and the MGB would have been severely damaged.

With the major objectives accomplished, and encouraged by the sound of the commandos' subsidiary demolitions, those in command felt justified in removing the wounded and starting to withdraw. Taking some of the destroyer's crew from the gunboat, the MTB was ordered to make for home. Sadly, while steaming down the river Wynn stopped to pick up two men from a raft, and the MTB received a direct hit, knocking him insensible across the bridge. By the time he regained consciousness the boat had been abandoned. With the assistance of Chief Motor Mechanic Lovegrove, Wynn reached a raft and survived to be taken prisoner. In all thirty-three men were lost from the MTB. Of the 611 men who sailed in the force, 169 were killed. Five Victoria Crosses were awarded for the raid, all posthumously.

MTB 103

The coastal motor boat of the First World War had a stepped hull and was very successful within the limits imposed by engine power, range and armament, and perhaps it is significant that in the 1939–45 war the stepped hull was not employed to any great extent. It was, however, always used in the case of flying boats, as it allowed air under the hull to break the surface tension and enable the air-craft to lift off.

'sit on its step', increase to flying speed and to become airborne.

There are a number of variations to the stepped hull form, the best known consisting of what is termed as the single step, which is in reality a boat running on two steps, one formed by the step built on amidships and the other formed by the aft part of the bottom near the transom.

It must be appreciated that at fairly slow speeds and before true planing conditions have been attained, the aft side of the step will cause additional drag; in other words, the stepped hull form is more inefficient than any other type at low speeds, and whilst this is a disadvantage in a boat required for military purposes, where the maximum range at low speeds is a highly desirable quality, how does it perform in the case of a high speed MTB?

Vosper had expressed an interest in this theory, and the single prototype MTB 103, Vosper No 1980, was ordered by the Admiralty on 10 December 1938, with Vosper carrying out the design work. She was to be 70ft long, and powered by two, rather than the usual three, Isotta-Fraschini petrol engines of improved design giving slightly more power. She was laid down on 28 August 1939.

Design and construction went ahead, but GA drawings of her as designed with torpedo tubes have not been seen. There was a considerable delay as the more powerful engines were never delivered due to Italy's entry into the war. With no comparable engine available until the introduction of the Packard engine from the United States, the boat was put on 'hold'. However, with the arrival of this standard engine under Lend-Lease, design went ahead and re-

design of the engineroom was undertaken to accept the revised power plant. It will be noted the engines are situated right aft with the weight just ahead of the after planing step, and the shafts driven by V drives. The remainder of the design follows generally the standard MTB layout.

The original contract was agreed in 1938, but Vosper Drawing 10841 (Contract 8E/73697/42), which has been redrawn for this book, shows the design as 70ft motor boat CT 05 – a change from the original design envelope. The later drawing 11812 shows her 'as fitted' as a target-towing boat, used to tow high-speed targets. It is of interest to note that the earlier drawing shows a single 20mm Oerlikon on a hand-raised mounting, and the later with other detail changes shows her with the Mark VII 20mm mounting. The hull lines showing the single stepped hull are redrawn from the Vosper Drawing 8548 with a sketch of the petrol powered towing winch. A feint copy of Drawing 9424 for her revised engineroom layout as redesigned for Packard engines, dated 7 December 1940, was not suitable for redrawing. Drawing 9879, her hull construction plan, still as Admiralty No 103, is shown in the chapter covering Vosper construction.

CT 05 was completed in June 1941 but no record of her performance or war service has been found, though she is said to have been very fast. She was some 34 tons displacement, with a defensive armament of a single 20mm Oerlikon and two twin 0.303in Vickers gas-operated machine guns, and two Packard power units giving 2400bhp. Her maximum speed is not recorded.

The side launching of MTB 103 (later CT 05).
This was the only Vosper stepped hull design,
with two engines, but reputed to be very fast.
Vosper Thornycroft (UK) Ltd

70ft target towing boat CT 05

1 After peak
2 Engineroom
3 Fuel tank space
4 Accommodation
5 Forecastle
6 Forepeak
7 Engineroom hatch
8 Tank hatch
9 18in scuttle
10 22in scuttle
11 Fairlead
12 Bollards
13 Samson post
14 Wood cleat
15 8in cowl vent
16 10ft dinghy
17 6in cowl vent
18 Dinghy davit
19 Side ladder
20 Electric horn
21 Officers' WC
22 Wardroom
23 W/T office
24 Towing winch (canvas covered)
25 Chemical smoke-producing
   apparatus (CSA)
26 Awning stanchions
27 Canvas awning
28 Deck lights
29 Oerlikon gun safety rail
30 CQR plough anchor
31 Liferaft
32 Loud hailer
33 Wooden sparred gun platform
34 Twin 0.303in Vickers guns
35 Ready use ammunition locker
36 Kent clear view screen
37 Bridge platform
38 Mushroom vent
39 Position of mast
40 20mm Oerlikon on Mark VII
   mounting
41 20mm ready use lockers
42 Packard petrol engines
43 Main fuel tanks
44 Galley
45 Crew's WC
46 Sink
47 Three shelves
48 Settee berths
49 Two lockers under
50 Serving hatch
51 Bilge pump
52 Oilskin locker
53 Hinged table
54 Hinged seat
55 Drawers
56 Cupboard
57 Hinged Perspex windscreen
58 Compass mounting
59 Signal lamp
60 Telescopic mast
61 Life belt
62 Canopy frame
63 Boat hook stowage
64 Auxiliary rudder
65 Masthead lamp
66 Magazine
67 Refrigerator
68 Electric stove
69 Searchlight
70 Ladder to upper deck
71 Generator
72 Heater
73 Washbasin
74 Two shelves
75 Three lockers under

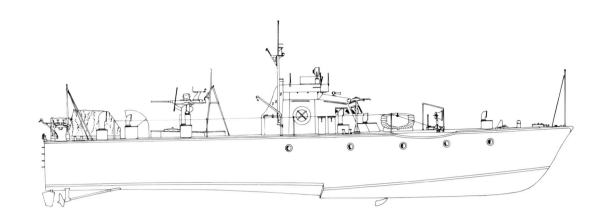

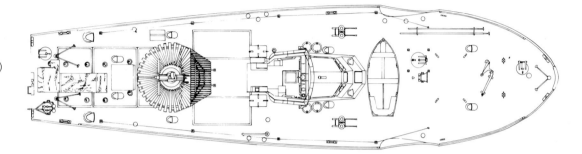

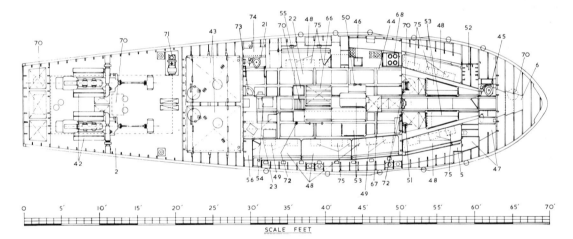

SCALE FEET

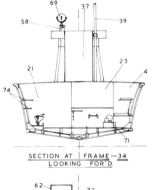

SECTION AT FRAME —34
LOOKING FOR'D.

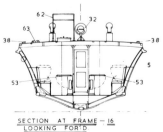

SECTION AT FRAME —16
LOOKING FOR'D

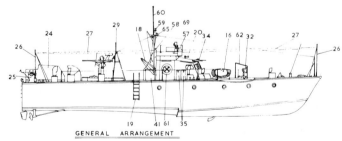

GENERAL ARRANGEMENT

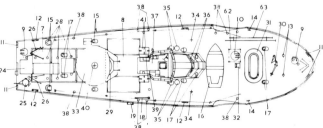

Vosper designs 1941

I do not have the cost figures for the 1941 Programme, but orders for the fleet continued to be placed in vast numbers. Although ordered during 1941, many of the larger units were not completed by the end of hostilities, were delayed in completion and their design modernised postwar.

Motor torpedo boats to Vosper designs continued to play a major part in the ongoing building programme, and twenty (MTBs 222–241) were ordered on 22 February 1941. These were a follow-on of the previous series, but built under contract at other British yards with Vosper supervising their construction. Vosper was building four units to replace those destroyed in the bombing of the Vosper yard (33, 37, 39 and 40). Twelve more to Vosper's designs were ordered from Samuel White at Cowes on 26 April (MTBs 246–257).

By now Lend-Lease had been passed by Congress and, with the United States now in the war, the British Government had sent purchasing commissions over to arrange the construction of Vosper-design craft under the terms of the agreement.

Fifty-eight units were ordered for the Royal Navy and these were numbered 258–326. The first, 258, was the original 70ft British Power Boat design sent to the United States and formed the basis of many US designs but in fact became MASB S 09 of the Royal Canadian Navy. Numbers 259–268 were US-built Elco designs with Hall-Scott engines. Numbers 269–274 were US Navy PT 5–8, 3 and 4 respectively, which were made available to the Royal Navy but never entered operational service. PT 6 was the second boat of this series, the first having been sold earlier to the Royal Navy to become MGB 68. PT 7 and 8 were of aluminium construction and the latter was eventually retained by the US Navy as their YP 110. PT 3 and 4 were 25-ton boats with a length of 59ft; PT 5 and 6 were of 34 tons with a length of 81ft, as were PT 7 and 8.

Numbers 275–306 were built in US boatyards to Vosper design and were repeats of the British-built boats, from drawings sent over by Vosper. They displaced 37 tons, were 72ft 6½in in length overall, of 19ft 3in beam and drew 2ft forward and 6ft 3in aft. The twin 0.5in Mark V power-operated gun turrets were manufactured in Canada. They were equipped with supercharged Packards of

MTB 226 alongside at Hvar, Yugoslavia, in 1944.
Courtesy Geoffrey Hudson

The US-built MTB 298 in the Adriatic, 22 December 1943.
Courtesy Geoffrey Hudson

4050bhp giving a maximum speed of some 39½ knots and 35 knots at 2200rpm. The standard 21in torpedo tubes were retained and the complement had increased to thirteen.

Numbers 307–326 were Elco types described in the US Navy section. Five CMB types ordered on 12 June 1940 from Thornycroft, Hampton, for the Philippines Government were requisitioned on their completion in November to become 327–331. A further three experimental boats (344–346) were purchased from Thornycroft on their completion late in the year.

The Vosper designs mentioned above were repeat orders and were detailed in the previous chapter in the MTB 73–98 and repeat 222–245 series, but Al Ross's detailed drawing of MTB 234 built by Berthon Boat Co of Lymington is shown as an example. MTB 234 was one of the twenty units ordered on 22 February 1941, and was one of four of that group (232–235) built under Vosper supervision, and completed on 14 May 1942. She is drawn later in her service, probably late 1943, as she would not have mounted the 20mm Oerlikon on completion. She has Type 286 radar and Type 240 or 241 IFF (identification friend or foe, described in Volume I). Only two depth charges are carried, and also reproduced is a sketch of her camouflage pattern by Al Ross.

As can be imagined with these additional 1941 orders, shipyards were still fully stretched by expanding order books and the armaments industry increasing its production, but were unable to keep up with the orders. Fortunately the Royal Navy and the Allied navies in exile were being compensated by the steady supply of Lend-Lease units provided by the United States. These were firstly the US designed craft provided during 1941, and then the increasing number of Vosper designs which arrived during 1942 as orders were completed, with many being shipped out to the Mediterranean and Indian theatres of war.

United States-built Vospers of the Royal Indian Navy under refit in 1944 (numbers unknown).
Courtesy Geoffrey Hudson

MTB 306, a US-built Vosper of the Royal Indian Navy, in 1944.
Courtesy Geoffrey Hudson

MTB 57 side elevation

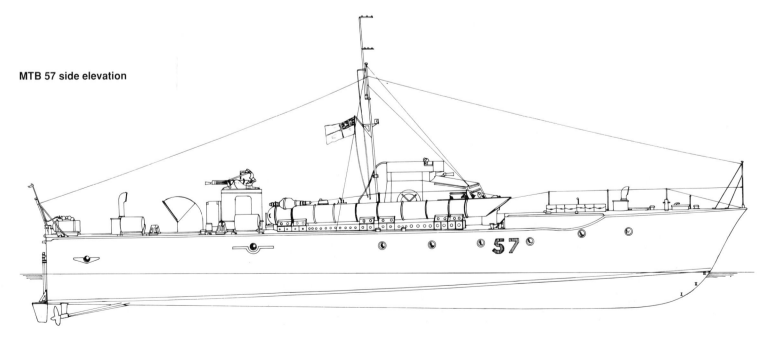

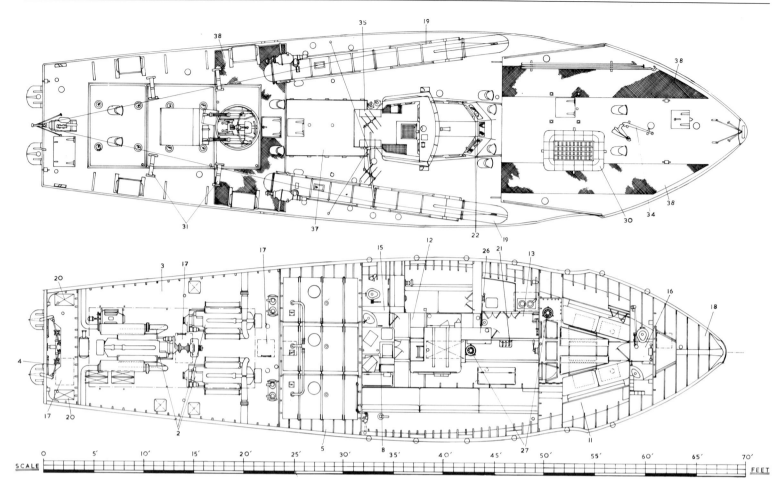

Vosper 70ft MTBs 57–66, plan, sections, wheelhouse and frames

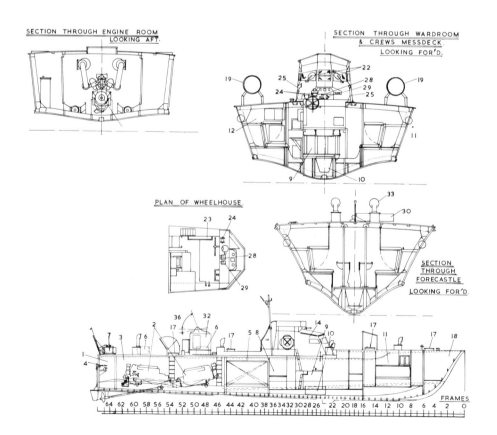

SECTION THROUGH ENGINE ROOM
LOOKING AFT.

SECTION THROUGH WARDROOM
& CREWS MESSDECK.
LOOKING FOR'D.

PLAN OF WHEELHOUSE

SECTION
THROUGH
FORECASTLE
LOOKING FOR'D.

FRAMES

 1 Aft peak
 2 Packard petrol engine
 3 Engineroom
 4 Lockheed hydraulic steering gear
 5 Fuel tank space
 6 Depth charge
 7 Chemical smoke apparatus
 8 Radio cabin
 9 Magazine
10 Fresh water tank
11 Crew's messdeck
12 Wardroom
13 Galley
14 Wheelhouse
15 Officers' WC
16 Crew's WC
17 WT hatch
18 Forepeak
19 21in torpedo tube
20 Lubricating oil storage tank
21 Rifle rack
22 Kent clear view screen
23 Chart rack
24 Engineroom telegraph
25 Voice pipe
26 Food cupboard
27 Oil heater
28 Engine throttles
29 Torpedo firing gear
30 Life raft
31 Torpedo loading chocks
32 Twin 0.5in machine guns in Mark
   V mounting
33 Ventilators
34 CQR anchor
35 Flag locker
36 Ready use ammunition locker
37 Fuel tank hatch
38 Pyramid rubber deck cover

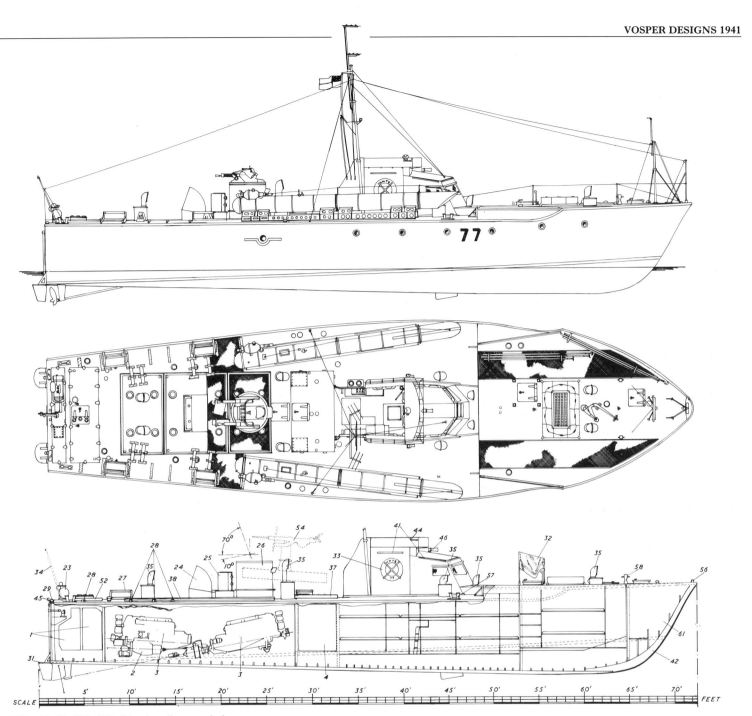

MTBs 73–98, 222–245 side elevations and plan

 1 Aft fuel tanks (1078gal)
 2 Ford V8 auxiliary engine
 3 Packard engine
 4 Main fuel tanks (1605gal)
 5 Small arms and 5in magazine
 6 Officers' WC
 7 W/T office
 8 Wardroom
 9 Galley
10 Sink
11 Hinged table
12 Settee berth
13 Rifle rack
14 Chart stowage
15 Forecastle
16 Crew's WC
17 Chain locker
18 Bosun's locker
19 Fresh water tank (48gal)
20 Open bridge
21 Standard compass
22 Type 286 radar aerials

23 Chemical smoke apparatus
24 Companion to engineroom
25 Ready use ammunition locker
26 Twin 0.5in Mark V mounting
27 Depth charge chute
28 Mine stowage (influence type)
29 Fairleads
30 Torpedo firing levers
31 Cavitation plate
32 Canvas cover over frame
33 Life buoy
34 Aerial spreader
35 6in ventilator
36 Foam fire extinguisher
37 Fuel tank hatch
38 Engine hatch
39 Pyramid rubber deck cover
40 CQR anchor
41 Handrail
42 Stem
43 Forward messdeck
44 Navigation light

45 Overtaking light
46 Electric horn
47 Flag locker
48 Mediterranean ladder
49 Engine throttles
50 Food cupboard
51 21in torpedo tube
52 Aft fuel hatch
53 Accommodation
54 Twin 20mm Oerlikon on Mark IX
   mounting
55 Bookcase
56 Bullring
57 Bollard
58 Towing bitt
59 Steering wheel
60 Chequer plates
61 Forepeak
62 Pillars

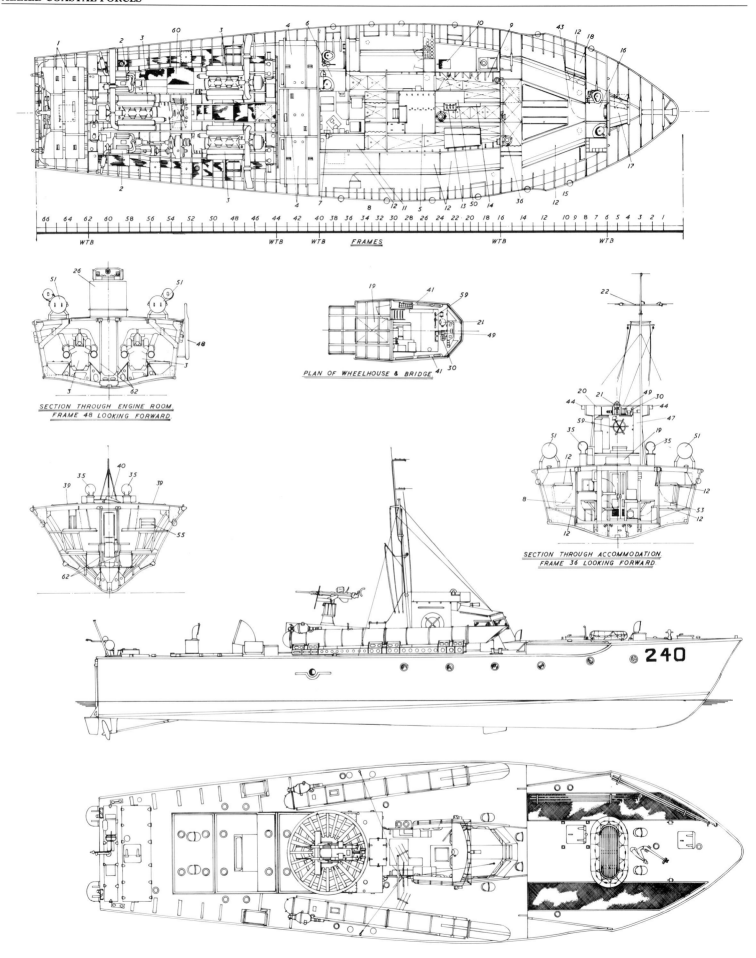

SECTION THROUGH ENGINE ROOM.
FRAME 48 LOOKING FORWARD.

PLAN OF WHEELHOUSE & BRIDGE

SECTION THROUGH ACCOMMODATION.
FRAME 36 LOOKING FORWARD.

WTB   WTB   WTB   *FRAMES*   WTB   WTB

240

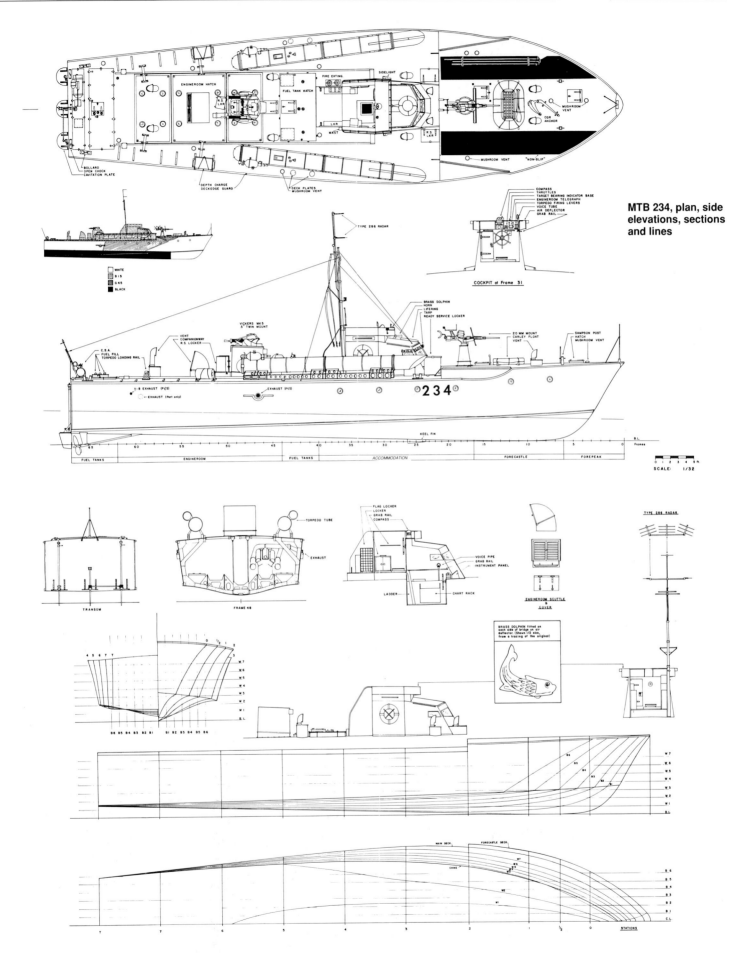

MTB 234, plan, side
elevations, sections
and lines

Vosper designs 1942

The 1942 naval building programme continued and even increased on the warship construction of the previous year. Eighteen aircraft carriers (some never to be completed) and two 6in cruisers headed a substantial new building list.

What of motor torpedo boats? By this period in the war material was becoming scarce, and hard woods such as mahogany had to be imported at great cost in valuable shipping space when the U-boat offensive was at its height. Sixteen units (347–362) were ordered from Vosper on 17 April. These were to be a modified 70ft layout utilising the same hull, but with some internal rearrangement. A general arrangement plan of MTB 347 from Drawing 10307, Contract CP35093/42, is shown. This group displaced 44.75 tons on the standard 70ft hull with a draught of 2ft 9in forward and 5ft 6in aft. The three supercharged packard engines of 4050bhp gave a maximum speed of 39.5 knots at 2400rpm. The standard armament of two 21in tubes and the twin 0.5in Mark V turret was retained, later to be replaced in some units by a single 20mm Oerlikon. The complement had increased to twelve. In an effort to reduce displacement, depth charges were reduced to two, now sited amidships. The photograph below shows MTB 347 just prior to her launch. Changes to note from the earlier units are the less cluttered layout, a single 12in cowl ventilator situated amidships above the after part of the engineroom and new type of CSA amidships aft. The two 0.5in machine guns and radar and IFF aerials have yet to be mounted. The fittings on the upper deck have been reduced and simplified to cut displacement. Automatic control was provided by a teleflex conduit cover from the bridge for release of the two depth charges. The emergency tiller is stowed below the port torpedo tube. An innovation is that the vessel is only steered from the open bridge position and the wheelhouse is now known as the 'chartroom'. The additional fuel tanks fitted right aft in the previous series are omitted and fuel capacity has reverted to that of the 1940 units, presumably in an effort to reduce displacement, redistribute hull loadings and increase performance without overloading the main engines.

Internal arrangements are redrawn from the same source and in the engineroom Dumbflow silencers are now standard and only one generator is fitted. The IFF was fitted on the bridge, and 286 with its trainable aerial and the pully system can be seen on the starboard side of the bridge.

Sixteen units (363–378) were ordered on 22 July 1942 under Lend-Lease, all being built to Vosper design by Annapolis Yacht Yard, and the first eight (363–370) were shipped to the USSR in February 1944. One further order was received by Vosper late in the year, and this required a new, larger and completely revised updated redesign to suit the role of combined MTB/MGB on the short hull. A single 73ft experimental boat (MTB 379) was ordered on 9 November 1942. This single unit was the prototype of the 1943 Vosper designs – an attempt to get a 'quart into a pint pot'.

MTB 347 on the stocks almost complete. One of sixteen ordered on 17 April 1942, she was to be sunk in action off the Netherlands coast on 1 October 1944.
Vosper Thornycroft (UK) Ltd

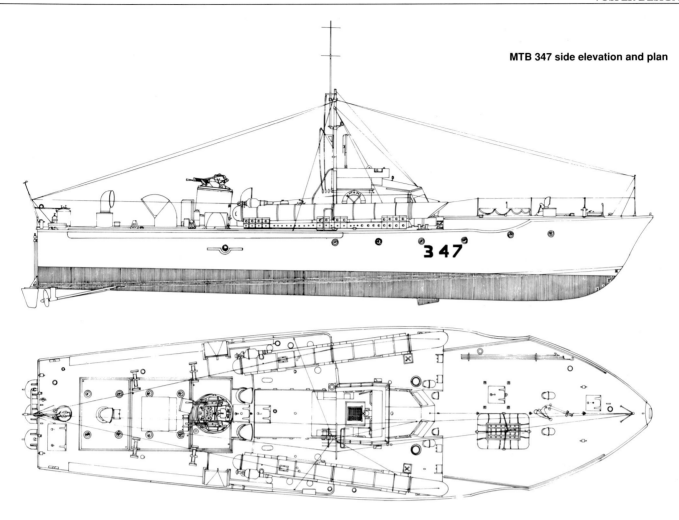

MTB 347 side elevation and plan

MTB 355 on sea trials in June 1943. This boat was fitted with Type 291 radar, Type 242 interrogator and Type 253 transponder. A new type of CSA is aft, but the vessel is still awaiting 20mm Oerlikon guns for the mountings.
Vosper Thornycroft (UK) Ltd

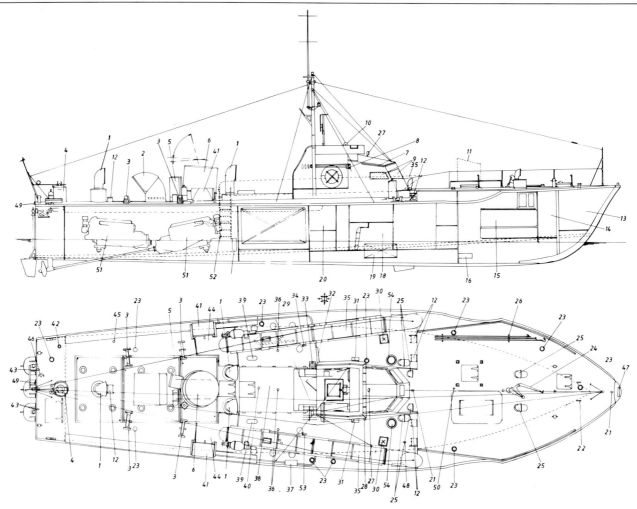

MTBs 347–362 – external detail

1 12in cowl vent
2 Folding screen
3 Torpedo loading chock
4 Chemical smoke-producing apparatus (CSA)
5 Ready use ammunition locker
6 Power operated Mark V mounting
7 Handrail
8 Radar aerial turning gear
9 Windows permanently blacked out

10 Magnetic compass
11 Canvas canopy
12 Hand grenade box
13 Forepeak
14 Crew's WC
15 Forecastle
16 Canister
17 Crew space
18 Magazine
19 Fresh water tank (50gal)
20 Radio cabin
21 Alignment plate
22 Aerial inlet
23 Mushroom vent
24 CQR anchor
25 6in cowl vent

26 Boat hook stowage
27 Navigation horn
28 Fresh water ear vent
29 Tank hatch lifting eye
30 Mounting for Vickers 0.303in GO gun
31 Port and starboard side lights
32 Teleflex conduit cover
33 Foam fire extinguisher
34 Port – fuel tank air pipe
35 21in torpedo tube
36 Sounding pipe
37 Hydrophone pad
38 Raised tank hatch
39 Tank access hole
40 Filling pipe

41 Depth charge
42 Distilled water filling
43 Torpedo outhaul bracket
44 Phendglaze covering
45 Reserve lubricating oil filling pipe
46 Slave bypass control
47 Rolling fairlead
48 Docking tally
49 Stern light
50 Plug for shore lighting
51 Packard main engine
52 Side ladder
53 Starboard fuel tank air pipe
54 0.303in ready use ammunition bucket

MTB 356 out of the water and being washed down. Her mast is unshipped. She had a short life, being completed on 1 July 1943 and lost on 16 October the same year: scuttled with action damage off the Netherlands coast.
Imperial War Museum

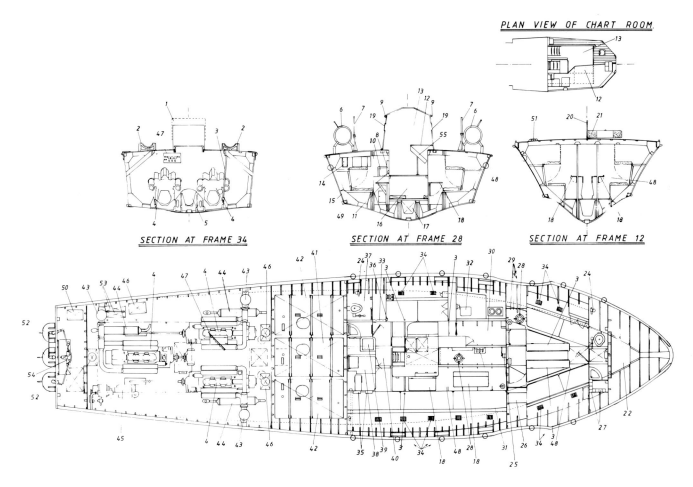

PLAN VIEW OF CHART ROOM.

SECTION AT FRAME 34

SECTION AT FRAME 28

SECTION AT FRAME 12

General arrangement MTBs 347–362

1 Folding screen
2 Torpedo loading chocks (port and starboard)
3 2in diameter pillar
4 Packard marine engine
5 Vosper V-drive
6 21in torpedo tube
7 Vickers 0.303in gun pedestal
8 Keyboard
9 Handrail
10 Serving hatch
11 Table
12 Chart table

13 Chartroom
14 Revolver rack
15 Wardroom
16 Magazine
17 Fresh water tank (50gal)
18 Folding table
19 Windows permanently blacked out
20 Lifeline stanchion
21 Carley raft
22 Forepeak
23 Crew's WC
24 CAV exhaust fan
25 Bilge pump
26 Shelves for blanket stowage
27 Toilet boxes

28 Heater
29 Oilskin hooks
30 Galley
31 Rifle rack
32 Sink
33 Curtain
34 Vent spills
35 Junction boxes
36 Clock
37 Officers' WC
38 Radio cabin
39 Transmitter
40 Lobby
41 Fuel tank (1026gal)

42 Fuel tank (850gal)
43 Dumbflow silencer
44 Cooler
45 Generator
46 Lubricating oil tank
47 Control panel
48 Crew's quarters
49 Voice pipe
50 Distilled water tank
51 Boathook stowage
52 Cavitation plate
53 Battery
54 Lockheed steering gear
55 Chart stowage

MTB 378, US built and one of sixteen units ordered on 22 July 1942. She completed on 15 December 1943 and transferred to the Royal Navy. She has a single 20mm forward with a twin 20mm aft, and two whip aerials.
Imperial War Museum

MTB 510

This unit was a one-off prototype and Vosper's only 'long' design of the war. A very complete set of her drawings revealed the many facets of her design. Little information has been disclosed about her, but copies were available of the original notes made by her chief mechanic before he joined her.

She was an experimental unit for trials of the Synchro-Self-Shift (SSS) two-speed gearbox designed to improve the performance of the 'long' boats, such as the Fairmile D. These had a top speed of about 30–31 knots with a good combined armament. MTB 510 had the added bonus of two propeller shafts (less weight and drag) and four high performance engines, two on each shaft, which with two engines shut down, would much improve range and maximum speed with all four in use.

She was ordered from Vosper on 2 April 1942, laid down on 25 July, launched on 14 August 1943 and handed over for trials the following December. Built at Portchester in great secrecy, she was never operational but was engaged on engine, gearbox and propeller trials until the end of hostilities, to be sold off for disposal in September 1947.

Job No 2186 as she was then, was certainly the most sophisticated design in coastal forces at that time. She was designed to cruise long distances and still have a good turn of speed, 36½ knots being attained during her trials. Being an engineering test bed, she carried three specially-trained mechanics, and prior to joining the ship when its engines and gearboxes were being fitted in the early spring of 1943, they had been to the David Brown works at Huddersfield to see the first gearbox assembled after manufacture, and to Hydraulic Couplings, Isleworth, who had designed the gearboxes and hydraulic couplings, for trials testing on their test bed.

The following is from the original notes:

> This boat is a prototype built for experiments with the SSS two-speed reduction gear. She is a hard chine boat with the usual square stern and is designed for high

The only Vosper 'long' design was MTB 510. No forward gun was mounted, but otherwise she was fully equipped. Note the spray strip fitted to reduce bow spray and standard Home Waters paint scheme.
Vosper Thornycroft (UK) Ltd

speeds. 75 tons. The respected measurements of the boat are,

Overall length	100ft 6in
Beam	19ft 0in
Draught forward	– –
Draught aft	5ft 6in

She is a twin screw ship and is propelled by four Packard W14 engines of 1500bhp each, making a total 6000bhp. One or two engines may be used on each propeller as required.

Her armament consists at the present stage of construction of – two 18in torpedo tubes, one Vickers 2-pounder power-operated turret fitted forward of the bridge, two Vickers 0.5in power-operated turrets fitted one either side of the bridge and a twin Oerlikon turret power-operated situated amidships aft of the radio-cabin.

There is also a Holman projector situated astern. Two depth charge racks are fitted. All the lighting in the ship is 220 volt and Oldham emergency lamps are fitted, these are fitted with relays and automatically light when the main lighting sets fail.

20 crew. 36½ knots.

Description of engine room
The chief things in the engine room are the main engines, these run into the SSS gear boxes, through hydraulic oil couplings, the main drive being taken out of the gearbox's [sic] under the after engines through 'Michelin' type plumber blocks and so on to the logs.

The auxiliary engines for charging and generating are of the Mawdsley type having an output of 220 volts, 57 amps, 12½ kilowatts. There are two of these generating sets and they are situated in the forward wings of the engine room. The control panel for the 220 volt lighting is situated on the forward bulkhead amidships and is very accessible.

There is a gangway running through the centre of the

MTB 510 with a 6pdr power operated gun forward, but with much reduced radar and communication array (see drawings).
Vosper Thornycroft (UK) Ltd

engine room and on either side of the gangway halfway up are the two control positions port and starboard. The operator faces aft and the control panels and instruments are all placed in a convenient position facing him. Fire extinguishers, of the methol bromide type situated, on the forward bulkhead. This is dual controlled and can be operated from the bridge as well as the engine room.

Petrol cocks from the forward tanks are situated in the gangway below the bilge boards near the forward bulkhead. Petrol cocks from the after tanks are situated on the after bulkhead near the bilge boards in the centre gangway.

The reserve oil tank is in the port wing and a rotary pump is installed to transfer oil. The reserve fresh water tank is fitted in the starboard wing and four semi-rotary pumps are used, one to each main engine to deliver fresh water.

There is also an oil tank fitted under the centre gangway for use with the oil couplings. Oil filters are of the 'Volks' type, and the thermostats are of the bi-metallic type and all are adjustable. Petrol priming pumps are of the plunger type instead of the usual diaphragm type.

Packard W14 main engines
The main propelling machinery of the boat consists of four Packard W14 engines of 1500bhp each. These engines are modified types of Packard 4M, the only difference being that the blower speed of the W14 is higher than the 4M.

The W14 is a 4 cycle, liquid cooled supercharged, 12 cylinder 60° V-type unit. It has a bore of 6⅜in and a stroke of 6½in. The standard compression ratio is 6.4 to

1 and has a total piston capacity of 2490 cubic inches.

The engine is rated at 1500bhp at 2400rpm.

Cooling

The engine is fresh water cooled except for the exhaust manifolds, these being salt water cooled. The fresh water is cooled in a 'Serk' type cooler by sea water, the cooler also provides for the cooling of the lubricating oil. The sea water is picked up by scoops when under way but a pump is provided for use when the boat is stationary and all the temperatures are thermostatically controlled by the use of bi-metallic thermostat. Each engine is provided with its own cooling equipment, but I will illustrate it as simply as possible (see engine room layout drawing).

Carburettor

The engines are equipped with a 'Holley' model 168f F modified carburettor of the single throat downdraught type, installed on the inlet side of the supercharger. A diaphragm mechanism is used instead of the conventional float chamber, float and needle. This design allows perfect operation in any position on the engine. Control of the main throat as air passage is accomplished by means of a variable venturi which also functions as a throttle. This takes the place of the usual butterfly throttle and fixed venturi.

Boost readings	100 octane fuel	36° ignition advance
RPM	MAX CON	MAX PERM
800	−2.5	−1.5
1000	−2	−0.75
1200	−1.25	0
1400	−0.5	+1
1600	+0.75	+3.25
1820	+2	+3.25
1840	+2.15	+3.37
1860	+2.45	+3.5
1880	+2.6	+3.75
1900	+2.75	+3.87
1920	+2.9	+4.0
1940	+3.05	+4.13
1960	+3.2	+4.25
1980	+3.35	+4.38
2000	+3.5	+4.5
2020	-	+4.63
2040	-	+4.75
2060	-	+5.0
2080	-	+5.13
2100	-	+5.25
2140	-	+5.37
2160	-	+5.5
2180	-	+5.63
2200	-	+5.75
2400	-	+7.25
2500	-	+8.0

Ignition

The ignition system comprises of a single high tension, double spark magneto, two separate gear driven distributors and a 24 volt booster coil to assist starting. The magneto is a Bendix Scintilla. It is of the rotating magnet type and provides two simultaneous sparks for

every 90° of magneto shaft rotation. Spark control is manually controlled (baked to the throttle lever) and has a range of 20 magneto 30 crankshaft degrees.

Booster coil

A booster coil is provided for starting purposes, it is of the battery operated, vibrating type. The coil supplies a series of sparks which are distributed by a separate electrode on the inlet distributor finger. This finger is retarded 30° and prevents 'kicking' when starting.

Cooling

The main engines are cooled by distilled water except for the exhaust manifolds these being cooled by seawater. The distilled water is cooled by sea water in a 'Serk' heat exchanger. This heat exchanger also cools the lubricating oil. The sea water is picked up by scoops (3in diameter) when under way but when the boat is stationary a gear type pump situated on the forward end of the engine circulates sufficient water through the cooler to keep the temperature down, the capacity of the sea water pump being 28 gallons per minute. The circulating pump for distilled water is of the centrifugal type and delivers 250 gallons per minute and is driven at 1½ crankshaft speed.

Fuel tanks etc

The total fuel capacity of MTB 510 is 5400 gallons. It is carried in ten tanks, six forward and four aft. The forward tanks are made of copper and they are covered by 'Linatex'. The after tanks being made of aluminium and are also covered with 'Linatex'.

The capacities of the respective tanks is as follows:

Port For'd 500	Centre For'd 900	Starb'd For'd 500
Port Aft 500	Centre Aft 900	Starb'd Aft 500
Port Wing 400	Port Centre 400	Starb'd Wing 400
		Starb'd Centre 400

Care must be taken when fuelling that the tanks are not filled more than 90% of their total capacity as injury is caused to the tank if they are filled right up. The fuel is delivered to distribution boxes as shown in the diagram where all tanks may be turned on or off as required. All the respective cocks are clearly labelled. Any engines may be run on any tank by shutting off all the cocks except those for the engine or engines required and the cock from the tanks that the fuel is wanted from.

Purolators

Purolator filters are employed and there is one on each engine of the 'self cleaning' type, the priming lines and auxiliary engines having the smaller type of filter. Non return valves are fitted on the main petrol lines in between the filter and the 'Pesco' pump. This also simplifies the priming as the fuel cannot run back, the priming pumps are of the plunger type.

For fuel transfers, a portable semi-rotary pump is supplied, fitted on a pedestal the pump has two very long hoses and by putting the hose in the tank desired to empty or fill the other hose may be run ashore or to another tank and vice-versa.

SSS Gearbox's [sic]

The most important feature of MTB 510 is the installation of the SSS gear boxes. (SSS standing for Synchro Self Shift).

There are two of these gear box's [sic] installed port and starboard, they are each driven by two Packard W14 engines driving through hydraulic oil couplings (details to follow) and each gear box drives one propeller. The main features of the gear boxes are:

1) They are reducing gears.
2) They allow opposite rotation of propellors [sic] although the propelling engines are of equal rotation.
3) They have a two speed ratio, the high ratio being 2.828 – 1rpm and the low ratio being 4.218 – 1rpm. The ratio doesn't work out exactly, this is done deliberately so that the teeth do not mesh in the same place, only in many revolutions, thus allowing equal wear on all the gear teeth.

The two ratios allow the use of two engines in high gears and the use of one engine by using low gear.

The gear boxes are completely self contained with

MTB 510, looking aft. Her twin 20mm Mark V power mounting is covered, but she still retains a Holman Projector right aft. Her depth charge racks are now much reduced compared with her original design specification.
Vosper Thornycroft (UK) Ltd

each being equipped with its own lubrication and cooling system. The boxes are made of fabricated steel with struts in the appropriate positions to take all the stress and strain. The bearings are of the 'Hoffman' roller and ball type. There is also a thrust bearing fitted, this being of the 'Timken' taper roller type. There is one set of phosphor bronze bearings fitted inside the main gear wheels of which there are two and allow the gears to run at different speeds on the main shaft.

This concludes the handwritten notes provided.

The first sheet of four drawings shows her as projected in January 1943 and is redrawn from Vosper Drawing 9894 dated 14 January 1943. She is armed with a Holman right forward, two

2-pounder Mark XVI power-operated mountings, one forward and one aft, and two twin 0.5in power-operated turrets and a twin 20mm Oerlikon Mark V mounting on a bandstand amidships. She has two 21in torpedo tubes, and is shown as having eighteen smoke floats stowed right aft. Her simple mast is devoid of any aerials, but it is assumed that this is as she was projected, and only gives her general layout.

Sheet two, redrawn from Drawing 9854, shows her hull lines, which are quite different to those of the Fairmile D, which was much fuller back aft. Here there are only two shafts, as opposed to four of the earlier design.

The ordinates are spaced 10ft, the waterlines 1ft and the buttocks 2ft apart. The hull planking is typical Vosper two skin. The bottom had an inner ½in mahogany on 45 degrees diagonal, the outer skin ¾in mahogany laid fore and aft, with oiled calico between the skins. The topside was of ½in mahogany, the inner skin on 30 degrees diagonal sloped aft from the chine, the outer skin was on 45 degrees diagonal sloped forward from the chine, again with oiled calico between. The camber of the deck is 8in in 23ft of beam. The frame spacing is 1ft 2in from frames 0–21, 10in from 21–37, and reverts back to 1ft 2in from frames 37–96. The next drawing on that sheet is of the rigging arrangement, redrawn from Drawing 10767 (30 August 1943). Here the armament has been reduced to only a single 2-pounder mounted forward and no torpedo tubes are shown. The mast is detailed as collapsible, falling back on to the charthouse roof, where it can be secured.

Sheet 3 shows a number of details. Firstly detail of a mock up of the bridge and charthouse redrawn from Drawing 10018 (24 August 1942). Here the whole of the upper deck structure is planned out, with a generous W/T office and chartroom behind the lobby and open bridge. The drawing is self-explanatory and also shows the adjacent armament layout.

Next is the detail of the DNC life float and life buoy stowage, redrawn from Drawing 11132 (16 September 1943). Here the larger Carley floats are stowed on each side of the chartroom. The easy release fastening of the securing gripes is also shown.

The final drawing details the bridge arrangement, redrawn from Drawing 10927 (12 May 1943), and much improved from the earlier arrangement shown. This was the production drawing and is noted: 'All fittings with the exception of the depth charge firing levers did not have holes drilled in the bullet proof plating for securing bolts etc'. Half-inch plywood panels were arranged for mounting fittings panels secured to light section grounds which were secured to stiffeners. This produces a small cramped bridge control area, but with every control close at hand.

Sheet 4 shows a number of fine details of the 18in torpedo tubes and bed arrangements, and fills in the missing mast detail, as well as depth charge loading and stowage details. The 18in torpedo tube seats and loading chocks are redrawn from Drawing 11025 (15 July 1943). Note that the tube seat webs were adjusted or raised to suit the deck mushroom vents when they were in the fully open position.

The missing detail of the mast and fittings is redrawn from Drawing 10767 (25 August 1943), with a modification shown, dated 19 September 1944, where fighting lights were fitted to the yard arm and the ASM aerial moved forward to give 12in clearance from the inner fighting lights. Besides radar and radio aerials, the hailing apparatus and horn are all mast fittings, which is still able to be dropped. All the stays, lift and shrouds to be ⅜in circular G/T construction copper wire cord, and gunmetal thimbles were to be used throughout. A simplified layout showing the mast and fittings dimensions is also provided.

The final items on this sheet are the depth charge arrangements redrawn from Drawing 10549 (9 March 1943), which shows the

positioning for two standard depth charges and item 10, a rack of small Mark XII depth charges is shown (see Volume I, p163 for Royal Navy depth charge details).

The final sheet adds more detail. First is a diagrammatic layout of the engineroom, redrawn from the chief mechanic's notebook, which gives a simplified plan view of her machinery layout. In the opposite corner are more views of the hull construction and depth charge arrangements redrawn from Drawing 10549/1 (7 March 1943). This shows the hull about the depth charge loading davit and depth charge chutes.

The final drawings show two general arrangements of MTB 510 redrawn from Vosper photographs. The first shows her as completed in January 1944. A new item is the spray strake under the forward chine. She only carries two depth charges. The armament has been reduced from the original proposal. She now has two 18in torpedo tubes, a 2-pounder Mark XVI mounting on the forecastle, two twin 0.5in Mark V mountings each side of the bridge, a twin 20mm Oerlikon Mark V mounting aft, and the Holman has been relocated aft, near the CSA.

The final general arrangement shows her in April 1945. Her 2-pounder gun has been replaced by the much more potent 6-pounder 7cwt QF Mark IIA gun on Mark VII mounting with autoloader. The other bonus is that the Holman has been removed, as has much of her radar and communications gear.

Little has been previously published about MTB 510 and she is rarely mentioned in other publications on this subject, probably because she was never operational, like the Fairmile F, but as a result of her trials of the SSS gearbox a great deal of new ground was covered which, with further development, led to the gearboxes used in frigates with their combined gas turbine engines.

MTB 510 as projected January 1943

1	Holman projector Mark IIA	26	Settee berth with hinged back
2	2-pounder Mark VIII gun on Mark XVI (power) mounting	27	Galley
		28	Sink
3	0.5in Vickers machine gun on twin Mark V (power) mounting	29	Stove
		30	Hinged table
4	Twin 20mm Oerlikon on Mark V (power) mounting	31	Petty officers' cabin
		32	Echo-sounder receiver unit (under)
5	Chemical smoke floats Mark III	33	Settee berth
6	Chlorine sulphonic acid (CSA) chemical smoke-producing apparatus	34	Lockers
		35	Crew's WC
		36	Forepeak
7	Open bridge	37	Magazine – 8 boxes H33, 2 Oerlikon loading frames, 12 boxes ASA/N43, 2 boxes H29, 1 box Holman grenades
8	W/T office and chartroom	
9	21in torpedo tubes LC Mark II	
10	Wind deflector	
11	2-pounder ready use lockers	
12	20mm Oerlikon ready use lockers	38	Engineroom
		39	Packard marine petrol engine model 4M-2500 type W8 (four off)
13	Engineroom ventilators	
14	A/S davit	
15	Side ladder sockets port and starboard	40	Windlass
		41	10ft dinghy
16	0.5in ammunition ready use locker	42	Forward messdeck
		43	Fuel tank (900gal)
17	Torpedo impulse charge ready use locker	44	Fuel tank (500gal)
		45	Fuel tank (400gal)
18	Holman illuminant ready use locker	46	Twin rudders
		47	Standard compass
19	2-pounder ammunition tank	
20	Aft fuel tanks (1600gal)	
21	Forward fuel tanks (3400gal)	
22	Petty officers' WC	
23	Officers' WC	
24	Wardroom	
25	Wardrobe	

**Side elevations and plans as
projected 1943**

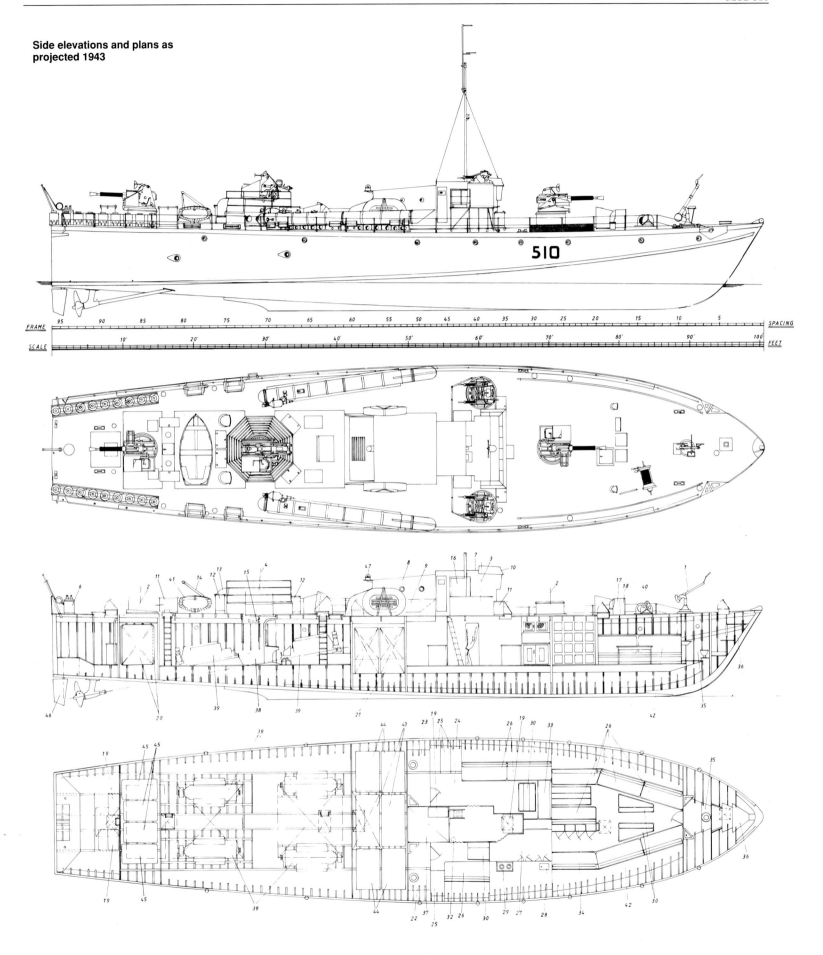

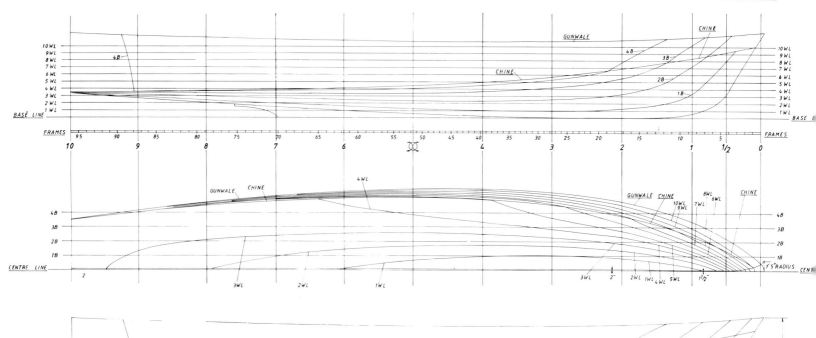

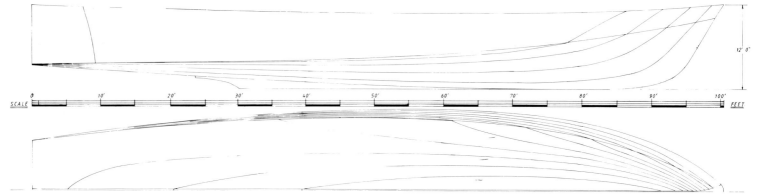

MTB 510 lines

A view of the engineroom of MTB 510. The SSS gearboxes are seen between the four Packard W14 engines on two shafts.
Vosper Thornycroft (UK) Ltd

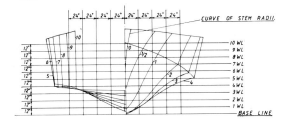

HULL LINES REDRAWN FROM DRG. NO. 9854
CONTRACT NO. C.P. 8E/33925/42.

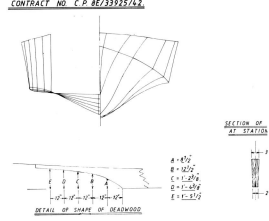

SECTION OF
AT STATION

A = 8¹⁄₂
B = 12¹⁄₂"
C = 1'-2³⁄₈"
D = 1'-4³⁄₈"
E = 1'-5¹⁄₂"

DETAIL OF SHAPE OF DEADWOOD

Upper deck detail: mock-up of bridge and charthouse

1 Perspex top
2 Rail round platform
3 2-pounder gun turret
4 0.5in machine gun turret
5 Platform
6 Handrails
7 Standard compass
8 Deck at centreline
9 9in coaming above deck
10 5ft × 1ft 8in clear opening
11 Ready use ammunition locker
12 W/T office and chartroom
13 A/S recorder
14 Lobby
15 5ft × 1ft 6in sliding doors port and starboard
16 Flag lockers
17 Revolutions order telegraph
18 Bow light box
19 Teleflex depth charge levers port and starboard
20 21¾in × 21¾in scuttle
21 Door
22 Lamp
23 Switch
24 Writing pad
25 Books
26 Mast tabernacle
27 Engineroom orders telegraph
28 Semaphore flag stowage
29 Recognition pistol and cartridge stowage
30 Voice pipe
31 Ladder
32 Bridge
33 Aldis lamp cupboard
34 Gun telephone

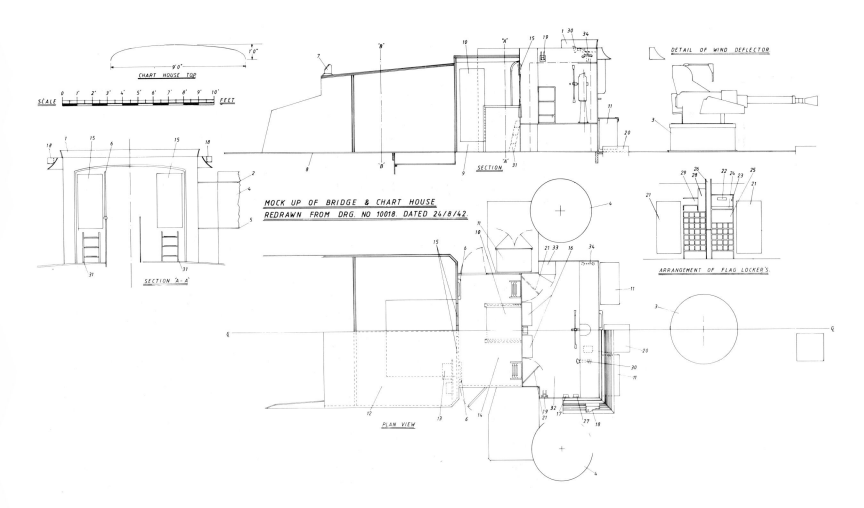

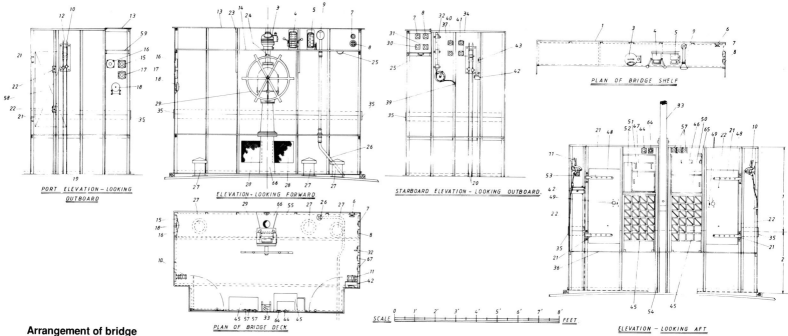

Arrangement of bridge

1 Bullet-proof bridge plating
2 Plywood bridge plating
3 Pattern 1151A steering compass
4 Engineroom telegraph
5 Revolutions order telegraph
6 Engineroom signal push
7 W/T bell
8 Engineroom horn
9 Megaphone type mouthpiece to voice pipe
10 Teleflex firing levers for port depth charges
11 Teleflex firing levers for starboard depth charge
12 ¾in multiply panel for depth charge firing levers
13 Instrument covers
14 Bridge shelf
15 Armament horn
16 Plug and socket for Aldis lamp
17 Engineroom reply horn

18 Bell from W/T office
19 Teleflex conduit to port depth charges
20 Teleflex conduit to starboard depth charges
21 Door hinge
22 Door fastener
23 Plywood bracket
24 Compass magnet box below shelf
25 Recognition light switch
26 Voice pipe
27 Ventilators
28 Ventilator grid in bridge front
29 Mark VI steering pedestal and steering wheel
30 Alarm buzzer
31 Gun communication buzzer
32 MRC type engineroom orders telegraph

33 Mast carrying hailing apparatus, recognition, NUC, masthead lights and RDF
34 Dimmer for engineroom telegraph, orders telegraph and revolutions orders telegraphs
35 Buttstrap
36 Bridge deck
37 Steering compass dimmer
38 Recognition light switch
39 Conduit to engineroom orders telegraph
40 Navigation light dimmer
41 Stern and shaded stern light dimmer
42 Mark X telephone
43 Telephone plug box
44 Klaxon push control
45 Signal flag locker
46 Light

47 Recognition pistol rack
48 Bullet-proof plate door
49 Door handle and lock
50 Bookshelf
51 Aldis lamp
52 Semaphore flag stowage
53 Telephone plug box Admiralty Pattern 9874 and 9875
54 Mast tabernacle
55 Helm indicator
56 Bulkhead under bridge deck
57 Plugs for recognition NUC and masthead lights
58 Door in open position
59 Bridge shelf
60 Bracket ¾in multiply
61 1¾in × ¾in mahogany stiffener
62 Canada rock elm handrail
63 1¼in Birmabright angle stiffener
64 Klaxon socket
65 Switch
66 Pedestal support
67 Dimmer switches

As completed January 1944

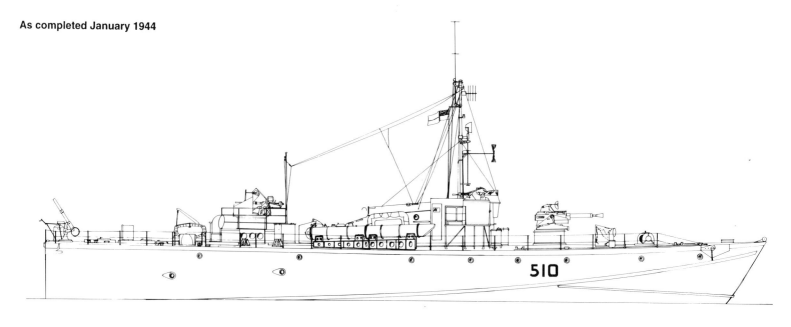

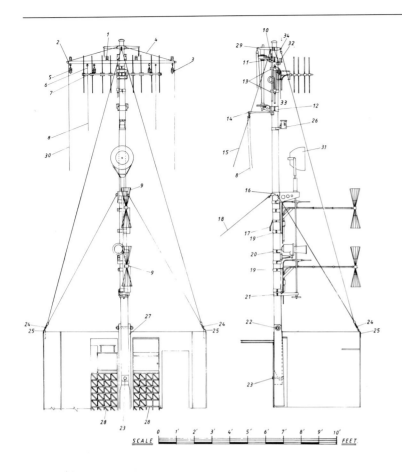

Mast arrangement 1943

1 Brackets for fighting light secured to yard with 2 – 1in No 10 brass right hand screws
2 1⅛in diameter eyes spliced in lifts and shrouds. Shroud slipped on ferrule before lift
3 Insulator to take TCS aerial
4 Yard lifts taken through eye and round seized
5 Insulator to take receiver (second channel aerial)
6 ⅛in gm shackles with 1¼in gm blocks Admiralty pattern 5006
7 Insulators plug and socket to take transmitting aerials (TW12)
8 No 4 plaited signal halliards with 2½in brass Inglefield flag swivels Admiralty pattern 100 and 101
9 ASH aerials 2in off centreline of mast to clear hailing apparatus control rod
10 Junction box securing clip and bracket
11 RDF pedestal upper securing band
12 RDF pedestal lower securing band
13 Transformer and matching unit securing band
14 Ensign spur with ⅛in gunmetal shackle and 1¼in gunmetal block, Admiralty Pattern 5001
15 Top backstay secured to spur with ³⁄₁₆in diameter gunmetal shackle
16 Hailing apparatus top bracket and bearing
17 Guides for RDF training wires
18 Lower backstay secured to bracket with ³⁄₁₆in diameter gunmetal shackle
19 ASH securing bands and bracket
20 Klaxon horn bracket
21 Hailing apparatus lower bracket and bearing
22 1in diameter × 11½in manganese bronze stud
23 ½in diameter × 8¼in manganese bronze stud
24 Fore stays secured to eyeplate with gunmetal thimbles and ⅜in circ Hambro lashing
25 Brass eyeplate
26 Masthead lamp
27 Ply tabernacle
28 Flag lockers
29 Twin spur
30 Signal yard shrouds
31 Hailing apparatus Admiralty pattern W2041
32 Fighting lights Admiralty pattern 3933. Two red glasses for port lanterns, two green glasses for starboard lanterns
33 ASM bracket
34 Top forestays secured to spur with ³⁄₁₆in diameter gunmetal bow shackle

In April 1945

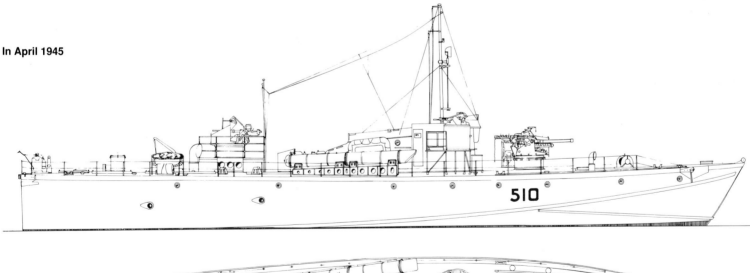

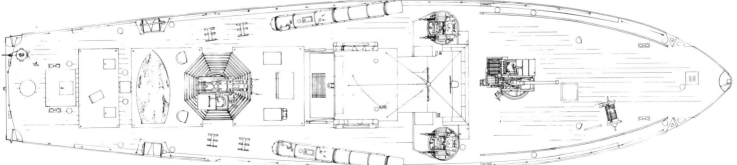

Vosper designs 1943–45

By late 1943 the Allies were beginning to gain the upper hand. War production was increasing and throughout the year warships joined the fleet in increasing numbers, replacing previous losses and increasing potential power. At last convoys were protected by more than a hotchpotch of different types of escort vessels, perhaps an old fleet destroyer, a couple of corvettes and coal-fired trawlers. At last there were sufficient units to form hunting groups, to search for the U-boat.

Training methods had been modified and the three armed services had improved their co-operation. New equipment and improved armament was coming off the production line, together with new radar, better radio communications, TBS (Talk Between Ships), new weapons systems and more lethal explosives. All three

services were becoming more and more reliant on new technology and although each item had its weight penalty and many required additional electrical power and extra crew, a great number of new combat aids were being fitted to warships.

The standard 70ft MTB had slowly developed as the result of operational experience and technical innovations. Now it was de-

MTB 380 in the Vosper yard at Portsmouth in May 1944, fitted with four 18in tubes and a twin 20mm forward. This was a complete redesign and update.
Vosper Thornycroft (UK) Ltd

MTB 380 on trials under the red ensign in
May 1944.
Vosper Thornycroft (UK) Ltd

cided that the motor torpedo boat should combine its tasks with that of motor gun boat and be more offensively armed. To this end, contract CP 8E/85759/42 was awarded to Vosper on 9 November 1942 and a complete redesign and update of the 70ft unit was undertaken. The prototype experimental boat, MTB 379, was laid down on 18 January 1943 and completed on 22 January 1944. She was a flush deck design, carrying the Vosper lines, but somewhat similar to US Navy types. Built at Portchester she had a completely new type of bridge, and this is shown in detail in the relevant chapter. The mast was mounted to port with a formidable array of radar and IFF aids. The main access below deck was a companion way to port alongside the bridge, although there was a watertight hatch on the forecastle, forward of the twin 20mm Oerlikon Mark IX mounting bandstand, with its four adjacent ready use ammunition lockers. The main offensive punch came from the mounting of four 18in torpedo tubes. On the prototype the after pair of tubes was set at 15 degrees to the centreline.

It was obvious that the new design was impressive as a further sixteen production units (MTBs 380–395), known collectively as the Vosper Type I 73ft, were ordered off the drawing board on 10 March 1943 under Contract CP 8E/63688/43/V1012. The only change from the prototype was that the after tubes were set at 15½ degrees. It is fair to say that a great deal of 'meat' had been added to the boat with only a slight increase size. The prototype was built at Portchester, as were the first 10 production boats, and the last six were built by Vosper at Wivenhoe in Essex.

The hull lines have been redrawn from Drawing 11245 (25 November 1943) which, although referring to the later or Type II 73ft, was common to both types. It will be noted that no torpedo troughs are built into the flush hull, with only a slight sponson or extension built out in the gunwale below the orifice of the after tube. The class design was overseen by Peter du Cane who had obtained a great deal of feedback from operational officers as to what was required or could be improved upon.

Unfortunately displacement had increased to some 46.7 tons, but

the three supercharged Packard engines each producing 1400bhp would provide additional power. The centre engine was geared and the two outer engines direct drive. Dumbflow silencers were now standard and only a single improved capacity generator was provided; 39.9 knots could be reached at the maximum 2400rpm with speed reduced to 34 knots at 2000rpm continuous. Fuel capacity in three tanks was 2500 gallons at 95 per cent full (698 gallons in each wing tank and 1114 gallons in the centre tank). These tanks were of the self sealing type. The endurance was some 470 miles at 20 knots. The crew comprised two officers and eleven ratings, although additional members under training were slotted in on operations. All the Vosper Type I and Type II 73ft served in home waters.

Their construction was slightly modified to save some building time. Although the hull construction followed the former lines of double skin mahogany, the upper deck was bonded sheets of plywood. The three underslung rudders were not carried on the transom as with previous designs, and cavitation plates were not fitted.

As previously mentioned the armament fit was greatly increased with twin 20mm Oerlikons in the manually-operated Mark IX mounting forward, twin 0.303in Vickers gas-operated light machine guns on pedestal mounts on the after 18in tubes and two single 2in rocket flare projectors on the forward tubes.

Below-deck equipment had improved too. The galley was now all-electric, with electric radiators in the messdeck, and an upper deck connection for shore supply power. The wheelhouse was armoured and had an emergency steering wheel aft. Communication was now state of the art with three radar sets, radio, inter-ship radio, telephones between departments rather than voice tubes,

plus the usual hydrophone position for when lying stopped, and chemical smoke-producing apparatus port side aft. The new units were completed from early summer 1944.

Sixteen more Vosper 70ft designs (396–411) were ordered on 15 March 1943 to be built under Lend-Lease and a further five units (419–423), originally intended for the USSR, were transferred to the Royal Navy in April. Elsewhere the request to combine the duties of MGB with that of MTB had been undertaken, with British Power Boat Co updating their 71ft 6in design, and the numbering of MGBs caused some confusion upon their numbering as MTBs (to be listed in Volume III).

Further orders for MTBs followed – six units (424–429) were ordered on 29 June 1943 from J Samuel White at Cowes to their own design and powered by the US Sterling Admiral petrol engine. These were Polish manned upon completion in 1944 and were S 5– S 10. Three were ordered on 7 April 1942 as MGBs 120–122 to become MTBs 439–441 in September 1943 on their completion by British Power Boat Co Ltd. A further eight were ordered as MGBs 123–130 from the same source to be reclassified as MTBs 442–449. The change in requirements continued, with a further sixty 71ft 6in British Power Boat vessels ordered during the year all to be completed as MTBs with two 18in tubes authorised.

Eight interchangeable MTB/MGB Camper & Nicholson long (117ft overall) types were ordered on 21 January 1943 as MGBs to be renumbered MTBs 511–518 on their completion (these are to be listed in Volume III).

The final orders for short boats completed (or intended for completion) during the war, were shared by British Power Boat Co and Vosper with 20 units ordered on 2 December 1943 as MGBs but completed as MTBs; 519–522 were BPB Co 71ft 6in units with the remainder (523–537) being 73ft (Type II) boats. Based on the earlier hull, but with an updated gun armament, they came under Admiralty contract CP 8E/112282/43. MTB 523 has been redrawn from Vosper drawings 11722 and 12222, in which there are a number of subtle changes. The mast with its loud hailer was carried amidships on the bridge, and a much improved Type 268U radar was introduced from 1945. New designs of watertight ventilators were introduced forward on the forecastle. Improved bridge instruments were fitted with some changes to design (see relevant chapter). Below deck two 40 gallon pool petrol tanks were fitted aft.

MTB 385, a 1943 Class (Type I), on trials in October 1944.
Vosper Thornycroft (UK) Ltd

A bow view of MTB 523, a 1944 Type II on trials in 1945. A 6pdr gun is forward. She has only two 18in tubes, and is fitted with British Type 268 radar at the masthead.

There is a radar office amidships with a W/T office to starboard.

The major difference between the Type I and Type II design was in the armament fit. The forward twin 20mm Oerlikon was replaced by the more potent QF 6-pounder Mark IIA gun on the power-operated Mark VII mounting (to be shown in Volume III). The twin 20mm Oerlikon guns have been moved aft above the fuel tank hatch and are now carried in the more sophisticated twin Mark XII mounting. Only the two after 18in torpedo tubes have been retained as there was a shortage of large targets, and the design would have been overloaded by two sets.

Displacement had increased again to some 49 tons, with the same three Packard engines providing about 40 knots at 2500rpm and 38 knots at 2000rpm continuous. Endurance had increased to 480 miles at 20 knots. The crew remained as two officers and eleven ratings. The first Type II did not complete before hostilities in Europe ended. MTB 523 was laid down on 4 April 1944, launched on 13 February 1945 and completed on 5 July; MTB 525 completed in October. With the ending of the war in Europe three units, 534, 535 and 536, were cancelled while bulding but two units, ex-531 and 537, were altered and modified for conversion to controlled target boats, stripped of armament and fitted with a petrol-engined winch. These two postwar conversions are represented by the general arrangement drawings of CT 44.

Two other units were authorised in 1945, both experimental designs. The first, MTB/MGB 538, was one of the twenty orders previously mentioned, but was a completely different Vosper hull design, and did not complete until August 1948. The other, MTB 539, was ordered on 25 August 1945 and was an experimental alloy hull built by Saunders-Roe and completed in 1950 to become the prototype for the postwar 'Dark' Class fast patrol boats.

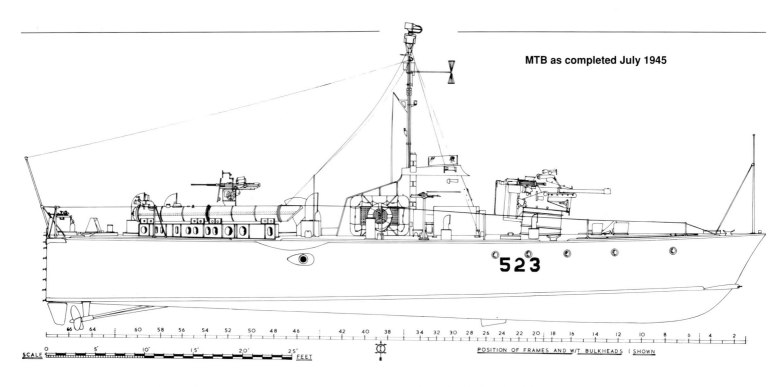

MTB as completed July 1945

SCALE | 0 | 5' | 10' | 15' | 20' | 25' | FEET

POSITION OF FRAMES AND W/T BULKHEADS | SHOWN

523

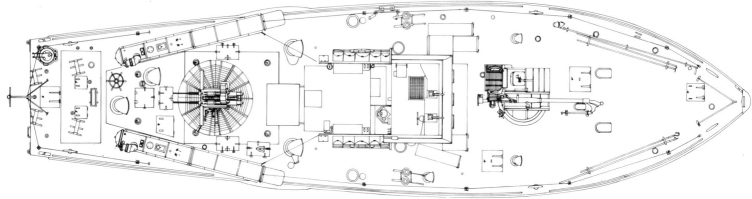

**General arrangement and detail
MTBs 523–530, 532**

1 Packard petrol engines
2 Cooler
3 Generator
4 Pool petrol tank (40gal)
5 Fuel tanks (220gal)
6 Centre fuel tank (970gal)
7 Wing fuel tanks (550gal)
8 Radar office
9 Gyro repeater
10 W/T office
11 Galley
12 Hinge-down cots
13 Folding table
14 Twin 0.303in Vickers guns
15 Life float
16 Flag locker
17 Whip aerial
18 Compass
19 Companion
20 Bullet-proof door

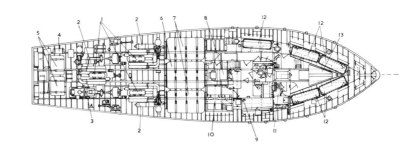

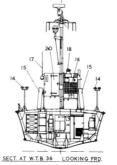

SECT. AT W.T.B. 36 LOOKING FRD.

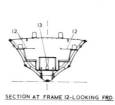

SECTION AT FRAME 12-LOOKING FRD.

SECT. AT FRAME 48 LOOKING FRD.

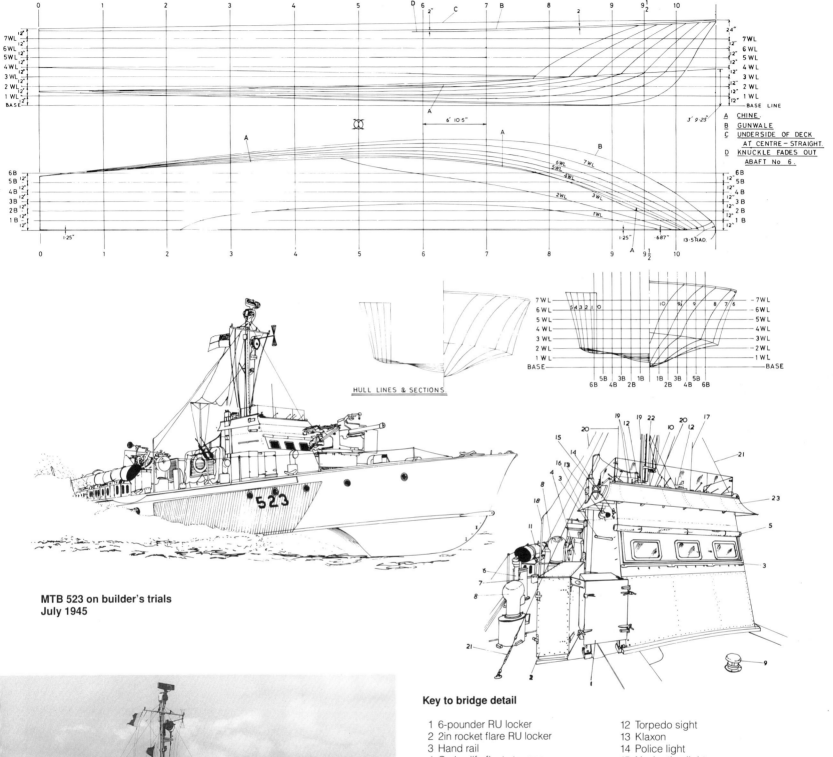

HULL LINES & SECTIONS

A CHINE.
B GUNWALE
C UNDERSIDE OF DECK AT CENTRE – STRAIGHT.
D KNUCKLE FADES OUT ABAFT No 6.

**MTB 523 on builder's trials
July 1945**

Key to bridge detail

1 6-pounder RU locker
2 2in rocket flare RU locker
3 Hand rail
4 Carley life float stowage
5 Rolled canvas screen
6 Twin-0.303in Vickers GO gun pedestal
7 0.303in RU ammunition bin
8 Cowl ventilator
9 Mushroom ventilator
10 Loud-hailer training handwheel
11 18in torpedo tube
12 Torpedo sight
13 Klaxon
14 Police light
15 Navigation light
16 Aerial trunk
17 Whip aerial
18 Aerial spreader
19 Signal halyard
20 Aerial
21 Mast stay
22 Mast
23 Wind deflector

MTB 524 (Type II) on trials, postwar and back to an all grey paint scheme.
Beken & Son, Cowes

CT 44 (ex MTB 531) as completed
in September 1947, side profile,
plan and lines

EXTERNAL PROFILE

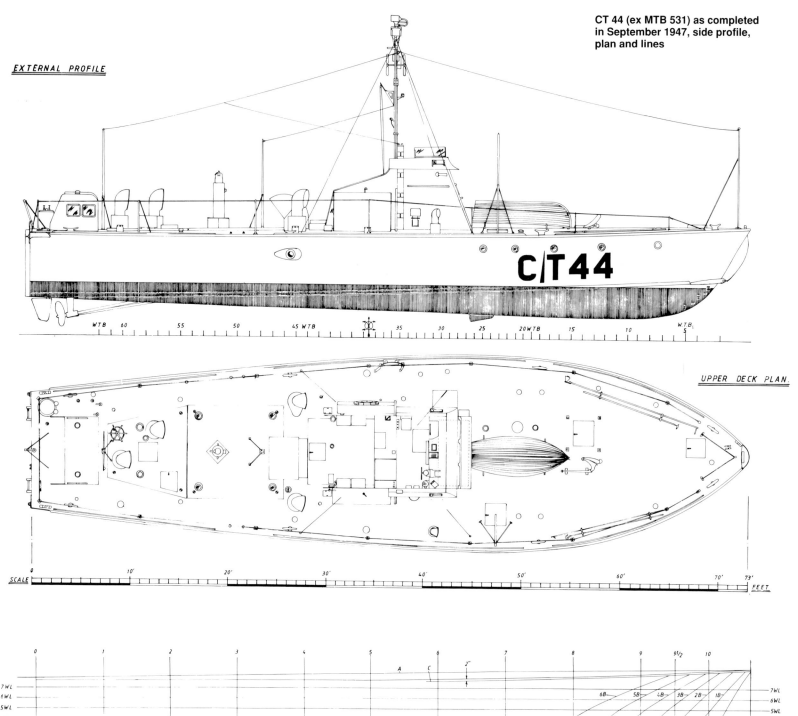

C/T 44

WTB 60 55 50 45 WTB 35 30 25 20 WTB 15 10 WTB S

UPPER DECK PLAN.

SCALE 0 10' 20' 30' 40' 50' 60' 70' 73' FEET

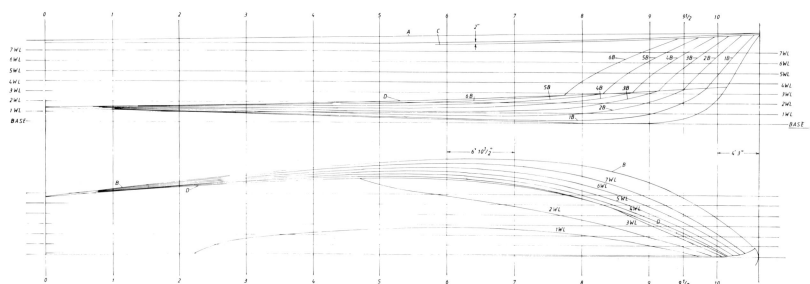

MTB 1024 (ex-524) in 1949, minus her forward gun but with 2in rocket flare launcher. Note that her centre rudder is clear of the water.
Courtesy D H MacDonald

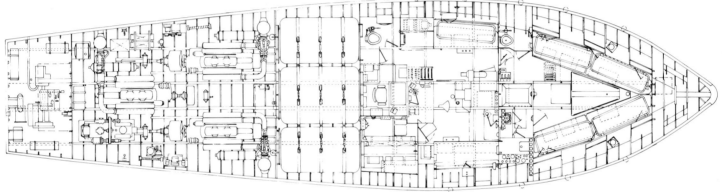

CT 44 plan view of accommodation

The US-built MTB 407 in the Mediterranean in 1945. This vessel is fitted with US SO radar, whip aerial and twin 20mm forward.
Courtesy Geoffrey Hudson

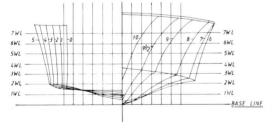

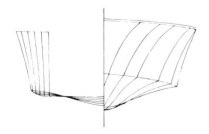

**Experimental 73ft MTB 379 as
completed January 1944**

379

| FRAMES | 64 | 62 | 58 | 54 | 50 | 47 | 44 | 42 | 40 | 36 | 32 | 28 | 24 | 20 | 17 | 14 | 10 | 8 | 6 | 4 | 2 | FRAMES |

| SCALE | 0 | 5' | 10' | 15' | 20' | 25' | 30' | 35' | 40' | 45' | 50' | 55' | 60' | 65' | 70' | 73' | FEET |

*1030 (ex-530) as an MGB in February 1950.
She mounts a short 4.5in gun forward (see
Volume I) and the new twin 20mm manual
Mark 12 mounting aft.*
Wright & Logan

Vosper MTBs 379, 380–395

1 Watertight hatch
2 CQR anchor
3 Ready use ammunition locker
4 Boat hooks etc
5 Crew's companion
6 Rocket flare box
7 Rocket flare projector
8 Backstay eyeplate
9 Inhibitor tube
10 Fire extinguisher
11 Fresh water filling under step
12 Sounding pipe
13 Pad for hydrophone gear
14 Torpedo impulse charge box
15 Portable cover over deck glands
16 0.303in twin Vickers machine guns
17 Washdeck connection
18 Petrol filling pipe
19 Petrol sounding pipe
20 Breathing apparatus stowage box
21 CSA container
22 Oil filling and sounding pipe
23 Towing fitting
24 Stern light
25 Navigation light
26 Overtaking light
27 Radar aerials
28 Twin 20mm Oerlikon mounting
29 Transom rungs
30 Hatch to engine room
31 18in torpedo tubes
32 Bullet-proof door
33 Fresh water tank (45gal)
34 Scuttle canopy
35 12in cowl vents
36 6in cowl vents
37 Folding cot (port and starboard)
38 Settee berth (port and starboard)
39 Folding table
40 Four hinge-down cots
41 Dumbflow silencer
42 Pool petrol tank
43 Packard engine
44 Lubricating oil tanks
45 Loud-hailer
46 Grenade box
47 Horn
48 Hand rail
49 Lifebelt
50 Vent pipe
51 Stool
52 Compass
53 Fairlead
54 Cleat
55 Liferafts
56 Galley
57 W/T office
58 Cooler
59 Generator
60 V-drive
61 Platform
62 Flag locker
63 WC
64 Radar office
65 Mast stay
66 Torpedo chocks
67 Fuel tanks

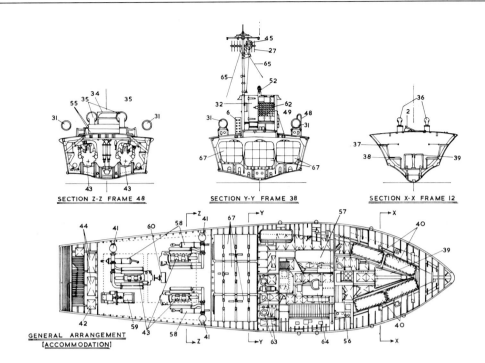

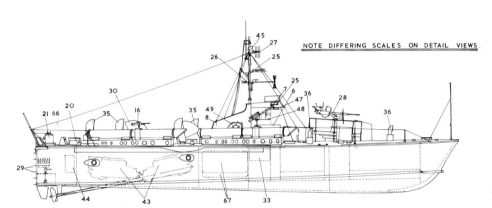

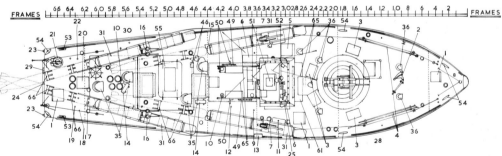

Vosper construction

In designing a hull to meet certain operational requirements, which in this case would entail the carriage of a load across the sea at high speed, one of the most important problems to solve was that of producing a structural system which would allow for the desired hull form to be achieved and maintained while at the same time making provision for the mounting and installation of the necessary armaments or other specialised fittings or accommodation.

Strength combined with light weight was to be an essential feature, and the design called for rather more careful and precise limits than was usually the case with slower and less specialised types of craft. Assuming the hull was to be formed by the bottom skin and sides covered in by a deck, it was clear that the structure would have to hold the skin together and retain its shape whilst underway and being pounded by seas from every direction.

The main members fulfilling this function are the frames which constitute the transverse strength of the craft, and are fashioned to the shape of the bottom and sides and hold the skin in position.

This may be carried out directly by laying the heel of the frame adjacent to and touching the skin. Longitudinal girders also fulfil a function in contributing to the strength in a longitudinal sense.

The lateral or transverse strength lay mainly in the system of framing as well as in the transverse bulkheading. The main longitudinal strength of the hull considered as a girder came from the two sides which were conveniently planked diagonally, and were further stiffened by the side frames, which, with the longitudinal girders running forward and aft inside the hull, form the 'webs'. The flange or 'fibre' strength of the 'girder' consisted in bottom and decking with associated deck beams considerably fortified by good continuous sheer strakes as well as deck stringer plates fore

The 70ft boats 20, 21 and 23 building. They were sold to Romania.
Vosper Thornycroft (UK) Ltd

and aft. It is clear that the decking had much significance long-itudinally and it was desirable to avoid permanent openings for engine hatches etc as much as possible. As an addition, there was pillaring throughout, especially in way of deck loads such as guns, torpedoes, etc and where large areas without support from bulkheading had to be contended with.

The stressing of an MTB was well beyond what can be imagined by those who have only an academic outlook on the problem. The bottom, where it breaks the surface of the water forward, that is to say at about a third of the length from forward, required consider-able additional stiffening due to severe stressing. It was usual prac-tice to halve the framing spacing for some distance along the hull in way of this region. The gunwale member was also very highly stressed. A deck stringer plate was of great value in this connection.

When the vessel was being driven at high speed towards an on-coming series of waves a much localised loading seemed to be expe-rienced in the region where the chine breaks the surface. As the

The Greek Navy's T3 under construction. Note the fine workmanship in the forward frames.
Vosper Thornycroft (UK) Ltd

boat plunged down towards the next wave ahead it was checked suddenly in its descent so that the bow tended to carry on down, especially if heavy weights were located in this region. There was also a tendency for the forward portion to shear itself from the remaining two-thirds of the hull, and there was then set up a tend-ency to break or strain the top fibre of the girder. If any weakness existed, this would show about this point, by starting of fastenings in way of the gunwale or by the top of the side planking pulling away from the gunwale member. The decking might also be pulled away from the gunwale in this region, and general weakness could cause a buckling even of the side planking or skin near the gunwale.

The MTB would not be strong enough to stand up to such conditions if the structure were designed only to fulfil the require-ments stated above; mostly because of acceleration forces due to pitching in the forward sections and as a result of the impact load-ing. The stresses set up in the course of running through a system of waves at high speed, and slamming, were very high indeed and

did occasionally cause problems to inexperienced commanders.

It was considered that the structural scheme with which this type of craft ended the war period was as light as could be, having regard to the materials available and used at the time. In most cases, failures occurred in the prototype and development stages which had to be put right during the course of production, so that the inference was that strength was by no means excessive. Most of the failures experienced were of the stress raiser type — that is, though the majority of the structure was adequate, special cases would give trouble.

A great deal was learned by the company during the sea trials of their Private Venture 68ft MTB, Job 1763, and a great deal of redesign was undertaken to strengthen the hulls of the following production 60ft and the wartime 70ft units. It is obvious that lessons had been learned as examination of the drawings shows that

MTB 59 – a view of her transom, cavitation plates and twin rudders. Her propellers are not yet fitted. Note that only two rudders are fitted; later three rudders were standard.
Vosper Thornycroft (UK) Ltd

hull framing was wider and more substantial, and spaced closer together over the length of the boat. The whole framing of the hull was braced to prevent the hull working. The unit that became MTB 102 had only four watertight bulkheads and the production 70ft units had five.

The drawings

Drawing 9716, which is the construction plan for MTBs 57–66, ordered on 26 February 1940 under the 1939 War Programme, has been redrawn.

Nominally known as 70ft MTBs, they were in fact 70ft 6½in hull length. The hull was divided by the five watertight bulkheads, from forward to aft as follows: forepeak 7ft 10½in long, the first frame being 2ft ½in from the bow, the remaining four frames being spaced 1ft 2in apart; crew space was 11ft 8in long with nine frames spaced 1ft 2in apart; through the next watertight bulkhead is the 18ft 4in accommodation where the twenty-one frames were spaced

10in apart; aft again, the tank space is 8ft 9in long and the seven frames are 1ft 2in apart; the next compartment, the largest, was the engineroom, being 21ft 0in long, with seventeen frames spaced 1ft 2in apart; the final compartment, the after peak, was 3ft 8in long with the two frames 1ft 2in apart; the final bulkhead is frame 67, the transom. The only watertight bulkhead to have an opening is 16, which has an opening for a watertight door, just 3ft 6in high. (These are the dimensions shown on the drawing, which are at variance with the drawings of the hull lines – see below.)

The deck planking was double skin mahogany. The inner skin was 6in × ¼in laid at 45° diagonal; the outer skin was 6in × ³⁄₁₆in laid fore and aft with oiled calico between the skins; the outer skin being lightly caulked and filled with Seamflex. The topside planking was double skin mahogany. The inner skin 6in × ¼in laid diagonally at 65°; the outer skin 6in × ³⁄₁₆in was laid diagonally at 45° with oiled calico between the two skins. The bottom planking was triple skin mahogany; outer skin ⁷⁄₁₆in laid fore and aft; the two inner skins ¼in were laid on opposite diagonals with oiled calico between the skins.

All steelwork was zinc-sprayed. The girders were of glued construction and not drilled for bolts except at the frame brackets as shown in the detail drawings. The bulkhead stiffeners were to be secured by 7G copper clench nails and No 14 brass wood screws, alternately. To the rear of the upper deck break (frame 22) was a bollard chock 1½in oak with a ⅛in MS plate under and flanged 1½in all round and secured to the gunwale and beams. The wheelhouse cockpit was ⅜in mahogany waterproof three-ply. Two-inch diameter pillars were fitted to take deck weights. The 6in-wide stem was fitted with a Delta metal stemband. Unlike in the later US built Vospers, side scuttles were fitted. The forward towing bollard was secured to the first watertight bulkhead. (Between frames 20 and 23 there was a chock for an A/S gland, for the fitting of Asdic if required.)

As an alternative, from the same period, Vosper Drawing 9879 has been redrawn. This shows the one-off MTB 103, built at the Admiralty's request for a trials MTB with stepped hull. Ordered on 10 December 1938, she had five watertight bulkheads in an overall length of exactly 70ft. All sixty frames were spaced at 1ft 2in centres. She was designed to carry two Isotta-Fraschini engines but her engineroom space was redesigned to accommodate two Packards. Drawing 9424, which shows the engine seats for the Packard installation, was unfortunately too faint to redraw.

The odd-numbered frames were main type framing whilst the even-numbered frames were the intermediate type framing except for frame 48. The centre of gravity was at about frame 30 with the frames on the aft side of the frame line aft of that and on the forward side of the frame line forward. The bottom frames throughout were 1⅛in sided mahogany, the side frames in the engineroom 1¼in sided mahogany, and the side frames elsewhere 1in sided mahogany above the chine brackets. The stem was 6in wide varying from up to 8in in thickness, with a Birmabright stemband.

Deck planking was double skin mahogany, the inner skin ¼in worked diagonally and the outer skin ½in worked forward and aft with oiled calico between skins and the outer skin lightly caulked with Seamflex. The deck beams were 1in sided mahogany and the deck stringers 2in × 1in Canada rock elm.

The topside planking was double skin mahogany – the outer skin ½in thick laid on diagonals 45° to the horizontal rising forward and the inner skin ¼in thick laid on diagonals 60° to the horizontal rising aft, with oiled calico between the skins.

The bottom planking was triple skinned mahogany. The outer skin was ½in thick laid fore and aft and the two inner skins were ¼in thick laid on opposite diagonals with oiled calico between the skins.

It will be seen from the plan views in both of these drawings that there were slightly differing shapes forward, the first being more pointed. But performance-wise there can be little comparison, one having only two Packard engines and the other, three, although the stepped hull design was reputed to be very very fast.

Drawing 9359 shows detailed construction of the torpedo troughs built in the 70ft boats, which by quirk of fate was right in the area of weakness described above. The trough planking was triple skin mahogany, the inner skin ³⁄₁₆in laid at 45°, the middle skin ¼in laid at 60° and the outer also ¼in laid at 60° opposing diagonals, and again with oiled calico between the skins. There was also considerable local strengthening. The fastenings were 2½in × 10 gauge brass screws to gunwales and frames and 12 gauge copper nails with ⅜in rooves through the planking.

MTB 97 – engineroom looking forward, showing engine beds and already a collection of debris building up in the bilges. This would be removed as she is fully fitted out. Note that the main frames are numbered in chalk.
Vosper Thornycroft (UK) Ltd

The next subject is detail of the cavitation plates, Job 1137/40 – a total of 130. These were ¼in brass plates, two per boat and added to help reduce propeller cavitation or slip, directly above the two rudders on 4ft centres. All connections to transom planking were of naval brass and no dissimilar metals were to be used. The plate and brackets were to be portable and secured to the transom angles by ⅜in diameter naval brass bolts to facilitate the removal of the rudders if and when required. The two per boat was increased to three when a third centreline rudder was fitted to improve the turning circle.

The development of bridge, wheelhouse and instrumentation has been covered as a separate subject due to the changes undertaken during the war period, and next comes the rigging plan for the 70ft boats. Initially the PV and 60ft units had an inverted Y type mast. The simple mast was positioned on the starboard side of the bridge wing, and little changed apart from the fitting of radar (see Volume I).

The twin 0.5in Mark V turret was fitted in the centre of the boat above frame 48 with two 2in diameter pillars below, and was to be parallel to the static load waterline. The 1½in × 1½in × ³⁄₃₂in flanged mild steel plate was box ended and bolted to the hatch beams. The coaming was to be supplied by the boatbuilder and the guns and turret were to be provided by the Admiralty. As far as Vosper was concerned it had to supply the coaming of ⅛in mild steel finished with two coats of red lead.

The next drawing is for a wooden bandstand for a twin 20mm Oerlikon gun (Mark IX) on the 1940 programme MTBs. The bandstand was to be made in four portable sections as shown. Brackets at each end of sections were fastened together with ⁵⁄₁₆in diameter snap head mild steel bolts with washers. All bolts were 3½ in long and worked through the framing – the ½in ply platforms to framing with 1¼in × No 10 countersunk brass screws; the ⁵⁄₁₆in ply curtains to the framing with 1in × No 10 countersunk brass screws and the ³⁄₁₆in ply tread strips to the framing with ⅝in × No 8 countersunk brass screws, and the whole bandstand was to be cemented throughout with Beetle A cement. This mounting replaced the twin 0.5in mounting from 1944 as production improved. A single 20mm Oerlikon was also fitted forward on many Vospers MTBs of the period, with the added weight penalty in the area of high stress.

Frequently mines or depth charges were carried on operations and the later 70ft boats had a standard layout for either mines or depth charges. The mine or depth charge chutes were supplied by the Admiralty and fitted parallel with the static waterline. The combined deck strip to take the mine and depth charge chute was constructed of mild steel, handed with four pairs per ship as shown, and with hardwood packing both above and below the deck for strengthening as shown. The drawing is modified to 7 July 1942 as follows: the bolt holes were elongated in the flanges of the portable mine chocks 19 February 1942; schedule numbers were added for Jobs 2187–2202, 20 May 1942; a covering board added and rubber was altered 3 June 1942 and lastly a revised gunwale stiffening and covering board was added 7 July 1942. The units this applied to were MTBs 57–66, 79–88, 89–91 and 360–362.

Dimensions

There has always been some discrepancy regarding the correct dimensions of the 'short' 70ft MTBs as Vosper boats are known, and, having checked all Vosper hull drawings these are the authors' conclusions:

Drawing 8282 for 60ft MTBs Jobs 1983–84 (Swedish) and 2018–21 (Norwegian). The hull length 60ft 0in and the maximum breadth 15ft 0in. Frames are spaced 1ft 2in from the transom. The ordinates are 6ft 0in apart. The deck camber is 4½in on 15ft 0in breadth. The bottom planking is ⅞in thick and the topside planking ⅝in thick.

Drawing 8357 for MTBs 20–23, contract CP BR 8/23940/38. Jobs 1942–45 (MTBs 21, 20, 22 and 23) and 2023–24 (MTBs 29 and 30 – built by Camper & Nicholson to replace units sold to Romania). Hull length 70ft 3¼in with a maximum breadth of 16ft 0in. Frames spaced 1ft 2in apart, the ordinates 7ft 0in apart. The deck camber is 4½in at maximum breadth. The bottom planking is 1in thick and topside planking ¾in thick.

Drawing 9077 (dated 16 April 1940). Contract CP B8/45405/39 for MTBs 31–40. Hull length 71ft ½in. Maximum breadth 16ft 9in; the ordinates spaced 7ft 0in apart.

Drawing 9116 Jobs 2069–78 (70ft MTBs Admiralty 1939s) and 2081–94, 2095–2106, 2115–21, 2122–24, 2153–56, 2157–60, 2161–64, and 2165–66 (70ft MTBs Admiralty 1940s) for Admiralty numbers 57–66, 73–86, 87–98, 222–228, 229–231, 243–242, 232–235, 236–239 and 240–241. Hull length 71ft ½in with a maximum

breadth of 19ft 7in. The frames spaced 1ft 2in apart, the ordinates 7ft 0in apart. The camber of the main and raised deck is 6in in 19ft 0in breadth. From 2094 (MTB 86) onwards the bottom planking was changed from three skins ¼in × ¼in × ½in to two skins ½in × ½in.

Drawing 89179, the general arrangement for MTBs 347–362, contract CP 35093/42. Hull lines for these were not available, but the general arrangement gives a hull length of 70ft ½in and a maximum breadth of 19ft 6in, with frame spacing of 10in. This has caused some problems as accurate drawings of the torpedo tubes show them as 24ft 1½in length overall, which according to the scale are even longer, but it does tend to confirm that there were no hulls built at 72ft 6in.

Drawing 11245 (dated 25 November 1943) for jobs 2225, 2239–48 and 2249–54 (MTBs 379 (prototype), 380–389 and 390–395 – the so-called 73ft type I) have a hull length of 72ft 11in and a maximum breadth of 18ft 9in. The offsets to the outside of hull planking are:

MTB 351 forward messdeck, starboard side looking aft.
Vosper Thornycroft (UK) Ltd

camber of deck 8in in 19ft 0in breadth (this camber was maintained from the transom to No 8 ordinate but varied forward to suit the gunwale heights given in the offsets tables (not shown)); the planking is shown as topsides ¼in × ⁷⁄₁₆in, bottom ⁷⁄₁₆in × ½in, deck and transom ½in ply. The ordinates are spaced 6ft 10½in apart, and the waterlines and buttocks 12in apart. The same hull applied to the later Type II 73ft units.

Drawing 9854 for Vosper's only 'long' design, MTB 510, gives a length of 100ft 6in, a maximum breadth of 22ft 4in and a deck camber of 8in in 23ft 0in of breadth. Her ordinates were spaced 10ft 0in apart.

Vosper's two experimental units were numbered in the Admiralty block for experimental designs 100–200. MTB 102 (Vosper PV) has a length of 68ft 0in with a maximum breadth of 14ft 0in. Her frames were spaced 2ft 4in apart and her ordinates 7ft 0in apart. Her loaded draught displacement was 31.16 tons and her light draught displacement 18.59 tons.

Drawing 8548 for MTB 103 (later CT 05) gives a hull length of 70ft 0in and a maximum breadth of 18ft 3in. Her frames were spaced 1ft 2in apart from her transom, and the ordinates spaced 7ft 0in apart. The deck camber was 5in at the maximum breadth. Her side planks were ¾in and bottom planks 1in thick.

As a point of interest, measurement was made of a number of the general arrangement views to include the cavitation plates which provide the same variations, but if the dimensions are taken of the construction detail of the cavitation plates (Drawing 9525) the length of the actual plate as fitted to the transom is exactly 18in, therefore if the boat hull is 71ft long, the extra length including the plate is 72ft 6in (although in fact it is 72ft 6½in). The drawing details it as Job 1137–40 for a total of 130 plates or 65 units. The boat numbers are detailed as Nos. 2081–94 (MTBs 73–86), 2095–2106 (MTBs 87–98), 2115–21 (MTBs 222–228), 2122–24 (MTBs 229–231, 2153–56 (MTBs 243–5, 242), 2157–60 (MTBs 232–235) and 2161–66 (MTBs 236–241). As this is only some 45 units, it is assumed that cavitation plates were retro-fitted to earlier boats, as well in later orders.

This briefly outlines some of the problems Vosper had to solve with their high speed MTBs, and examination of the drawings helps illustrate how the high standard of workmanship and design helped to achieve this, as opposed to the slightly less demanding stresses encountered by the generally larger and slower Fairmile designs covered in Volume I.

MTBs 390 and 391 under construction at Wivenhoe. The 73ft Type I. The high standard of workmanship continues. Note that planking has commenced on 391.
Vosper Thornycroft (UK) Ltd

70ft MTBs construction detail

Hull steelwork

Items	Scantlings
Floor lugs to hog	1½in × 1¼in × ⅛in
Deck stringer	1½in × 1½in × ⅛in
Deck stringer lugs to beams	3in × 1½in × 14 gauge double
Stringer and carling brackets	14 gauge
Engine girder top angles	1½in × 1½in
Engine girder bottom angles	1½in × 1¹⁄₁₂in
Engine girder plates	½in
Engine girder diagonal struts	1in × 1in × ½in
Girder brackets to frames	14 gauge
Vertical lugs to above	1½in × 1½in × ⅛in
Deep floors under engines	14 gauge
Raised deck diaphragm plates	14 gauge
Carling lugs to beams	3in × 2in 14 gauge double
Chine lugs	1½in
Gunwale lugs	14 gauge

Timberwork

Items	Materials	Scantlings
Sternpost	Oak	3in sided × 4in to 3in
Transom framing	Oak	3¼in × 3¼in rabbeted for planking
Breasthook	Oak	3½in sided
Gunwale and chine knees	Oak	2¼in sided moulded as shown
Raised deck knees	Oak	2in sided moulded as shown
Samson posts	Oak	4in square
Stem	Elm	Laminated and sided and moulded as shown
Hog	Elm	6in × 3½in aft to 6in × 4in forward of scarf increased to 7½in × 3½in at hog
Main gunwale	Elm	4½in × 3in tapered at ends
Raised deck gunwale	Elm	3½in × 3in
Chine	Elm	3in × 3in aft 3½in × 3½in mids 5in × 2½in forward
Rubbers	Elm	2¾in × 1¾in at gunwale 3in × ¾in at chine
Bottom frames	Birch	Sided 1in moulded. 6in at hog 5½in at chine

Side frames aft from frame 40	Mahogany	Sided 1in moulded 5½in at chine 5in at gunwale
Side frames forward from frame 39	Mahogany	Sided ⅞in moulded 5½in at chine 5in at gunwale
Bulkhead beams	Mahogany	Sided 1in moulded 6in at ctr 5in at gunwale
Beams aft from frame 40	Mahogany	Sided 1in moulded 6in at ctr 5in at gunwale
Beams forward from frame 39	Mahogany	Sided ⅞in moulded 6in at CTR 5in at gunwale
Strong beams 63, 48, 34 and 22	Mahogany	Sided 2in
Engineroom hatch carling	Mahogany	5½in × 2in reduced to 5½in × 1½in abaft F
Tank hatch carling	Mahogany	6in × 1½in
Wheelhouse carling	Mahogany	3in × 2in
Wheelhouse cants	Mahogany	3in × 2in
Bottom planking	Mahogany	⁷⁄₁₆in × ½in × ¼in
Topside planking	Mahogany	⁷⁄₁₆in × ¼in
Deck planking	Mahogany	⁷⁄₁₆in × ¼in
WT bulkheads	Mahogany	¼in × ³⁄₁₆in laid opposite 45° diagonal
Bulkhead stiffeners	Mahogany	3in × 1¼in except where otherwise stated
Transom stiffeners	Mahogany	4in × 1½in
Scuttle fore and aft	Mahogany	3in × 1in
Intercostal chocks	Spruce	Sided 1½in
Bulkhead frames	Birch multiply	Sided as detailed
Girders	Birch multiply	As detailed
Deck stringers	Columbia pine	2in × 1in
Beam knees and struts	Birch 5-ply	⅞in thick double
Chine brackets	Birch 5-ply	⅞in thick double
Floors and girder brackets	Birch 5-ply	⅞in thick as detailed

Note: All steelwork to be zinc-sprayed; girders to be of glued construction and must not be drilled for bolts except at frame brackets as shown in detail. Bulkhead stiffeners to be secured by 7g copper clench nails and No 14 brass wood screws, alternately. Topside planking double skin mahogany. Inner skin 6in × ¼in laid diagonally at 60°, outer skin 6in × ³⁄₁₆in laid diagonally at 45°. Oiled calico between skins. Bottom planking triple skin mahogany outer skin ⁷⁄₁₆in laid fore and aft, two inner skins ¼in laid on opposite diagonal. Oiled calico between skins.

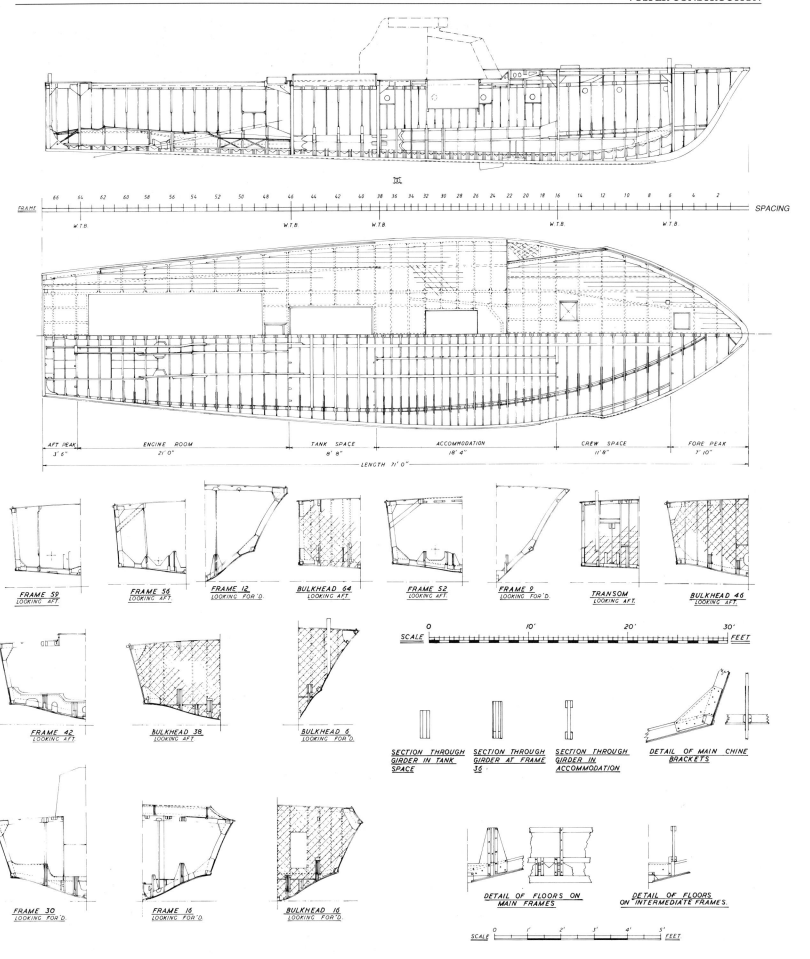

FRAME | 66 64 62 60 58 56 54 52 50 48 46 44 42 40 38 36 34 32 30 28 26 24 22 20 18 16 14 12 10 8 6 4 2 | SPACING

W.T.B.   W.T.B.   W.T.B.   W.T.B.   W.T.B.

AFT PEAK	ENGINE ROOM	TANK SPACE	ACCOMMODATION	CREW SPACE	FORE PEAK
3' 6"	21' 0"	8' 8"	18' 4"	11' 8"	7' 10"

LENGTH 71' 0"

FRAME 59
LOOKING AFT.

FRAME 56
LOOKING AFT.

FRAME 12
LOOKING FOR'D.

BULKHEAD 64
LOOKING AFT.

FRAME 52
LOOKING AFT.

FRAME 9
LOOKING FOR'D.

TRANSOM
LOOKING AFT.

BULKHEAD 46
LOOKING AFT.

FRAME 42
LOOKING AFT.

BULKHEAD 38
LOOKING AFT.

BULKHEAD 6
LOOKING FOR'D.

SCALE   0   10'   20'   30'   FEET

SECTION THROUGH
GIRDER IN TANK
SPACE

SECTION THROUGH
GIRDER AT FRAME
36

SECTION THROUGH
GIRDER IN
ACCOMMODATION

DETAIL OF MAIN CHINE
BRACKETS

FRAME 30
LOOKING FOR'D.

FRAME 16
LOOKING FOR'D.

BULKHEAD 16
LOOKING FOR'D.

DETAIL OF FLOORS ON
MAIN FRAMES

DETAIL OF FLOORS
ON INTERMEDIATE FRAMES.

SCALE   0   1'   2'   3'   4'   5'   FEET.

95

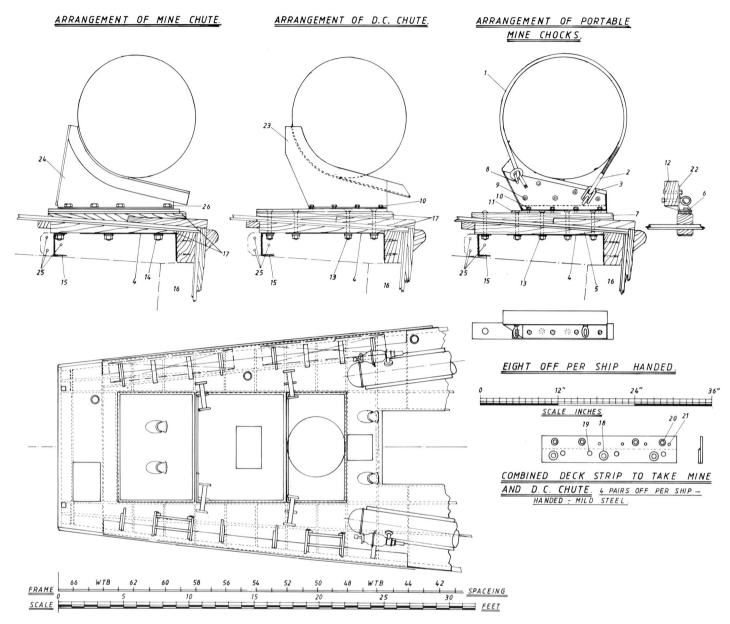

ARRANGEMENT OF MINE CHUTE.   ARRANGEMENT OF D.C. CHUTE.   ARRANGEMENT OF PORTABLE MINE CHOCKS.

EIGHT OFF PER SHIP HANDED.

SCALE INCHES

COMBINED DECK STRIP TO TAKE MINE AND D.C. CHUTE. 4 PAIRS OFF PER SHIP – HANDED – MILD STEEL.

Arrangement of mine and depth charge chutes

1 1½in circular Manila strop
2 Thimble – Admiralty Pattern 5083
3 ⅜in dia shackle – Admiralty Pattern 5441
4 ⅛in mild steel washer plate
5 Hardwood packing ⅜in minimum thickness
6 ¾in × ⅜in elongated holes in flange
7 Hardwood packing to compensate for camber and sheer of deck
8 ½in diameter eyebolt
9 ⅜in diameter galvanised mild steel bolts
10 ⅜in diameter mild steel set screws tapped into deck strip
11 2in × ⅜in mild steel deck strip
12 Teak chock
13 ½in diameter countersunk mild steel bolts with nuts, washers and grommets

14 ⅝in diameter countersunk mild steel bolts with nuts, washers and grommets
15 ⅛in mild steel plate flanged 2in and secured to beams by ⅛in plate welded on
16 2in × 12 gauge brass screws
17 Hardwood packing 4in wide × ⅜ in minimum thickness above deck packing rabbeted 2in wide × ¼in deep for mild steel strip. Top and bottom surfaces of packing horizontal
18 Holes for ⅝in diameter countersunk bolts (D to J)
19 Holes for ⅝ diameter mild steel set screws (D to J)
20 Holes for ½in diameter countersunk bolts (D to J)
21 Holes for ⅜in diameter mild steel set screws (D to J)
22 ⅛in mild steel plate bracket with

end webs welded on
23 DC chute – supplied by Admiralty
24 Mine chute – supplied by Admiralty
25 ⁵⁄₁₆in diameter bolts
26 ⅝in diameter mild steel set screws tapped into deck strip

(D to J) = drilled to jig

Note: Chutes parallel to static WL

Modifications:
Bolt holes elongated in flanges of portable mine chocks – 19 February 1942.
Schedule Nos added for jobs 2187–2202 – 20 May 1942.

Covering board added and rubber altered – 3 June 1942.
Revised gunwale stiffening and covering board added – 7 July 1942.

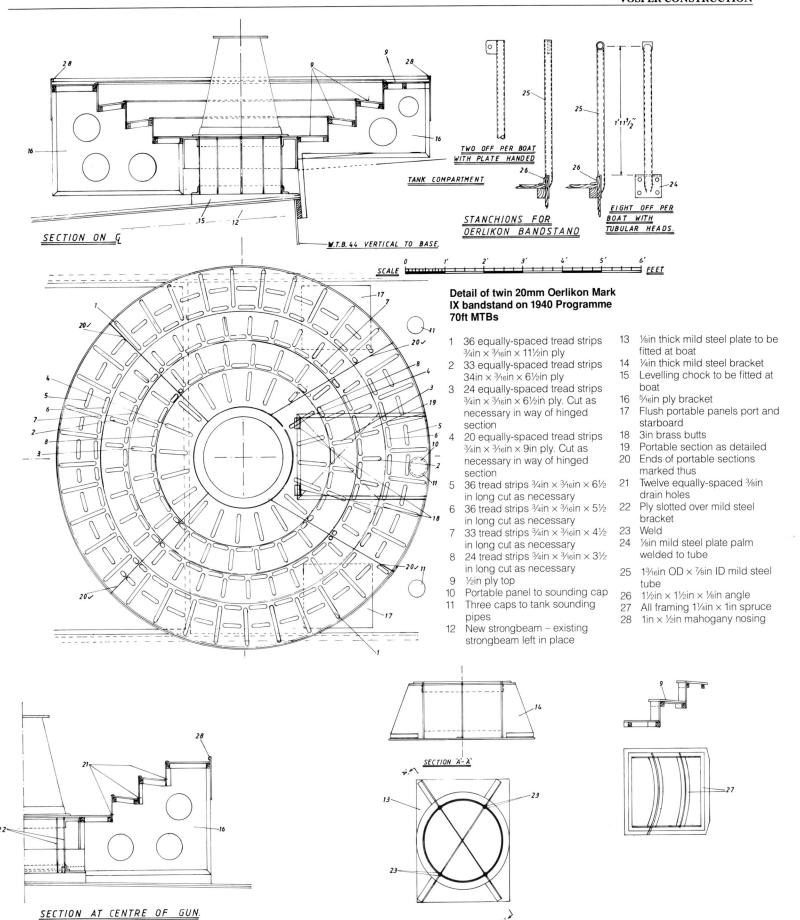

SECTION ON ⊈

TWO OFF PER BOAT
WITH PLATE HANDED

TANK COMPARTMENT

STANCHIONS FOR
OERLIKON BANDSTAND

EIGHT OFF PER
BOAT WITH
TUBULAR HEADS.

W.T.B. 44 VERTICAL TO BASE.

SCALE 0 1' 2' 3' 4' 5' 6' FEET

1'11½"

**Detail of twin 20mm Oerlikon Mark
IX bandstand on 1940 Programme
70ft MTBs**

1 36 equally-spaced tread strips
$\frac{3}{4}$in × $\frac{3}{16}$in × 11½in ply
2 33 equally-spaced tread strips
34in × $\frac{3}{16}$in × 6½in ply
3 24 equally-spaced tread strips
$\frac{3}{4}$in × $\frac{3}{16}$in × 6½in ply. Cut as
necessary in way of hinged
section
4 20 equally-spaced tread strips
$\frac{3}{4}$in × $\frac{3}{16}$in × 9in ply. Cut as
necessary in way of hinged
section
5 36 tread strips $\frac{3}{4}$in × $\frac{3}{16}$in × 6½
in long cut as necessary
6 36 tread strips $\frac{3}{4}$in × $\frac{3}{16}$in × 5½
in long cut as necessary
7 33 tread strips $\frac{3}{4}$in × $\frac{3}{16}$in × 4½
in long cut as necessary
8 24 tread strips $\frac{3}{4}$in × $\frac{3}{16}$in × 3½
in long cut as necessary
9 ½in ply top
10 Portable panel to sounding cap
11 Three caps to tank sounding
pipes
12 New strongbeam – existing
strongbeam left in place

13 $\frac{1}{8}$in thick mild steel plate to be
fitted at boat
14 $\frac{1}{4}$in thick mild steel bracket
15 Levelling chock to be fitted at
boat
16 $\frac{5}{16}$in ply bracket
17 Flush portable panels port and
starboard
18 3in brass butts
19 Portable section as detailed
20 Ends of portable sections
marked thus
21 Twelve equally-spaced $\frac{3}{8}$in
drain holes
22 Ply slotted over mild steel
bracket
23 Weld
24 $\frac{1}{8}$in mild steel plate palm
welded to tube
25 $1\frac{3}{16}$in OD × $\frac{7}{8}$in ID mild steel
tube
26 1½in × 1½in × $\frac{1}{8}$in angle
27 All framing 1¼in × 1in spruce
28 1in × ½in mahogany nosing

SECTION AT CENTRE OF GUN.
LOOKING FOR'D.

SECTION 'A'-'A'

DETAIL OF GUN PEDESTAL.

Rigging plan for 70ft MTBs

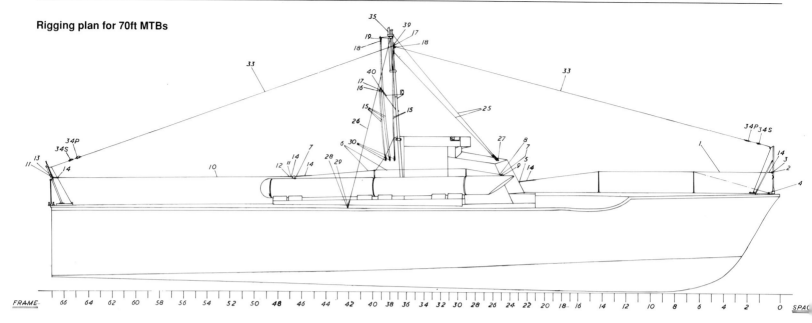

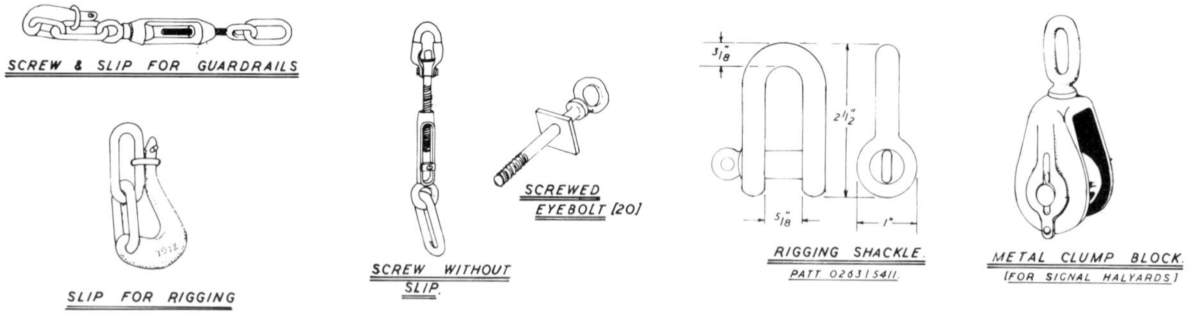

SCREW & SLIP FOR GUARDRAILS

SLIP FOR RIGGING

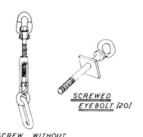

SCREW WITHOUT SLIP

SCREWED EYEBOLT [20]

RIGGING SHACKLE.
PATT 026315411.

METAL CLUMP BLOCK.
[FOR SIGNAL HALYARDS]

Rigging warrant (per boat)

No	Item	Material	Length	Size	No off	Supply	Remarks
1	Lifeline forward	FSWR galvanised	5 fathoms	¾in 617	1	Vosper (bought out)	
2	Lifeline forward – thimbles	Mild steel galvanised	–	1in	1	Vosper (bought out)	
3	Lifeline forward – shackle	Mild steel galvanised	–	⅜in straight	1	Vosper (bought out)	
4	Lifeline forward – eyebolt	Mild steel galvanised	–	⅜–2¼in shank	1	Vosper (bought out)	Alternative position of lifeline on deck
5	Lifeline forward – eyebolt	Mild steel galvanised	–	⅜in	1	Vosper (bought out)	Fitted to wheelhouse front
6	Lifeline torpedo tubes	FSWR galvanised	9 fathoms	¾in 617	2	Vosper (bought out)	
7	Lifeline torpedo tubes – thimbles	Mild steel galvanised	–	1in	4	Vosper (bought out)	
8	Lifeline torpedo tubes – shackles	Mild steel galvanised	–	⅜in straight	2	Vosper (bought out)	
9	Lifeline torpedo tubes – eyeplates	Mild steel galvanised	–	¼in	2	Vosper (bought out)	Fitted to forward end of torpedo tubes
10	Lifeline aft	Manilla	9 fathoms	2in	2	Vosper (bought out)	4½ fathoms ~ each
11	Lifeline aft – thimbles	Mild steel galvanised	–	Round	4	Vosper (bought out)	
12	Lifeline aft – shackles	Mild steel galvanised	–	½in straight	2	Vosper (bought out)	Fitted to aft end of torpedo tubes
13	Lifeline aft – shackle	Mild steel galvanised	–	½in bow	1	Vosper (bought out)	Fitted to transom staff
14	Lanyards and lashings	Cod hambro line	10 fathoms	½in 3 strand	–	Vosper (bought out)	
15	Signal halyards	Plaited line	24 fathoms	No 4	–	Vosper (bought out)	For masts and stayes
16	Blocks	Gunmetal	–	1¼in	5	Vosper (bought out)	Single sheave for halyards
17	Block shackles	Gunmetal	–	⅛in straight	5	Vosper (bought out)	
18	Blocks	Mild steel galvanised	–	2in	2	Vosper (bought out)	Double for W/T aerial
19	Block shackles	Mild steel galvanised	–	¼in straight	2	Vosper (bought out)	
20	Flag swivels Inglefields	Gunmetal	–	2½in	5 prs	Vosper (bought out)	For halyards (not shown)
21	Marline	–	2lbs	Fine yacht		Vosper (bought out)	(Not shown)
22	Yard lifts	FSWR	1 fathom	½in 6112		Vosper (bought out)	
23	Yard lifts screw eyes	Brass	–	12G	2	Vosper (bought out)	
24	Screw eyes	Brass	–	12G	3	Vosper (bought out)	2 for yard blocks. 1 for gaff block
25	Forestays	FSWR	6 fathoms	½in 6112	2	Vosper (bought out)	Fitted to mast. 1 upper, 1 lower
26	Backstays	FSWR	14 fathoms	½in 6112	2	Vosper (bought out)	Fitted to mast port and starboard
27	Forestay eyeplate	Mild steel	–	–	1	Vosper made	Double fitted to wheelhouse top
28	Backstay eyeplates	Mild steel	–	½in	2	Vosper (bought out)	Fitted over gunwales
29	Rigging screws	Gunmetal	–	4in	4	Vosper (bought out)	Fitted to mast stays
30	Cleats	Canadian rock elm	–	6in long	9	Contractor	5 for halyards. 4 for W/T aerial
31	Lashings (not shown)	Cod hambro line	2 fathoms	½in. 3 strand	–	Vosper (bought out)	For yard lifts and insulator strops
32	Outhauls (not shown)	Cod hambro line	7½ fathoms	½in. 3 strand	–	Vosper (bought out)	
33	W/T aerial	–	–	–	2	Admiralty	1 port, 1 starboard
34	W/T aerial insulators	Glass	–	–	6	Admiralty	
35	RDF mast (if fitted)						
36	Twin aerial leading forward						
37	Wood cleats to hold stays						
38	Raised tank hatch coaming						
39	3ft 0in yard						
40	CAFF						

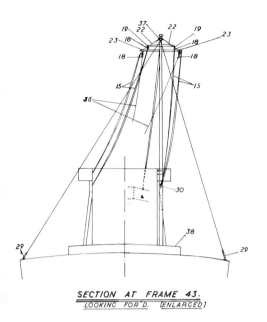

SECTION AT FRAME 43.
LOOKING FOR'D. [ENLARGED]

THIMBLE EYE.

EYEPLATE.

**Vosper 008
Typical construction**

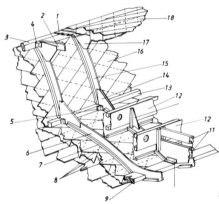

1 Gunwale shelf
2 Box lugs
3 Gunwale
4 Deck beam
5 Chine lugs
6 Bottom frame
7 Frame cant
8 Triple skin mahogany planking
   with oiled calico between skins
9 Hog or false keel
10 Hog lugs
11 Deep floor
12 Longitudinal girder
13 Chine
14 Chine brackets
15 Side frame
16 Double diagonal mahogany
   planking with oiled calico
   between skins
17 Bracket or gusset
18 Double skin deck with oiled
   calico between skins

**Vosper 70ft MTBs construction
detail of cavitation plates**

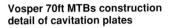

1 ³⁄₁₆in brass plate
2 ¼in brass plate
3 3in × 1in chock
4 1¼in × 1¼in × ³⁄₁₆in brass angle
5 Web
6 Transom
7 Angles secured permanently to
   transom
8 2in 24 gauge brass countersunk
   wood screws
9 24 gauge brass countersunk
   head screws in this hole.
   Remainder ³⁄₈in brass bolts with
   heads burred over on to nuts
10 ³⁄₈in brass bolts
11 ³⁄₈in brass rivets
12 Holes to clear (bolt and screw
   heads)
13 Holes for 24 gauge 2in long
   countersunk head screws
14 Holes for ³⁄₈in brass bolts
   countersunk heads brass
   washers to be used inboard side
15 ³⁄₁₆in clear between cavitation
   plate and rudder
16 ³⁄₁₆in brass brackets
17 Holes for ³⁄₈in n-brass bolts

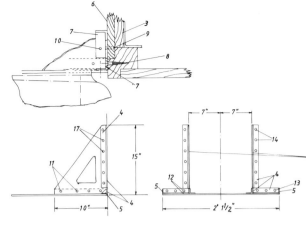

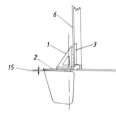

DETAIL

UNDER HULL.

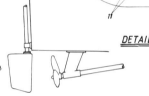

HUNG ON TRANSOM.

ON TRANSOM WITH CAVITATION
PLATE.

VOSPER RUDDER DEVELOPMENT
[OR WHY THE 70' M.T.B. BECAME
THE 72' 6" M.T.B.]

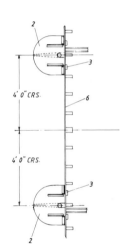

ARRGT. OF CAVITATION PLATES

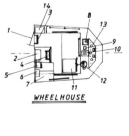

WHEELHOUSE

**General arrangement (as fitted)
MTBs 69 and 70 sections and
wheelhouse**

1 Dashboard
2 Compass lamp
3 Engine throttles
4 Magnetic compass
5 Voice pipes
6 Wheelhouse wheel
7 Folding chart table cupboard
   under
8 Steering gear
9 Telegraph operator
10 Lockheed valves
11 Handrails
12 Ladder – up
13 Ladder – down

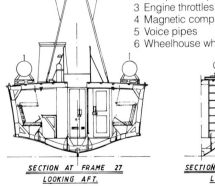

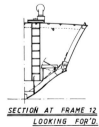

SECTION AT FRAME 48
LOOKING FOR'D.

SECTION AT FRAME 27
LOOKING AFT.

SECTION AT FRAME 12
LOOKING FOR'D.

**Vosper 70ft MTB construction
torpedo trough**

1 Raised deck
2 Footrail 1½in × 1¼ c pine
3 2ft 3¾in radius
4 3½in × 3in elm gunwale
  dovetailed to bulkhead frame
5 1¼in × ½in elm nosing
6 2in × 1in Columbia pine stringer
7 3in × 2in mahogany – rabbeted
  for planking
8 1in × ⅝in elm stringers
9 Main deck
10 2½in moulded oak knees each
   side of beam
11 2in × ½in mahogany bulkhead
   cant
12 2in × 1⅜in mahogany packing
   piece
13 2in sided mahogany strong beam
14 ⅜in plywood brackets each side
   of frame with 1in strip
15 Double ⅜in plywood brackets –
   not cut for deck
16 1½in × 1½in mahogany cant to
   take deck. Bolted to deck beam
   aft side
17 Mahogany frame
18 ½in plywood bulkhead
19 Single ⅜in plywood bracket on
   fore side
20 Double lugs 1½in × 1½in × ³⁄₁₆in
   mild steel angles – galvanised
21 ¼in diameter mild steel
   galvanised bolts
22 2in diameter hole
23 14 gauge galvanised mild steel
   bracket secured by 1¼in × 1¼in ×
   1⅛in lugs and ¼in diameter bolts
   and ⅞in × ¼in double convex
   stiffeners
24 Centreline of torpedo tube 7½
   degrees to centreline of boat
25 2in moulded oak grown knees
26 Rubbers from 2½ × 1¾in elm
   faired to shape of torpedo trough
27 Stringers to be cutaway 1in × ⅜in
   elm
28 21in torpedo tube

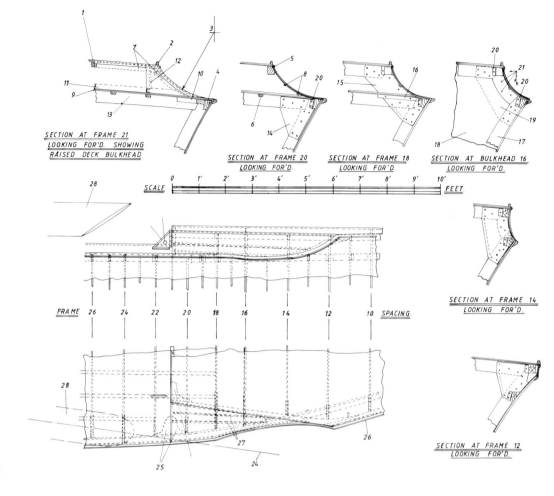

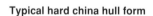

Typical hard china hull form

**Stress loadings on a typical hull
driven at high speed into short
head seas**

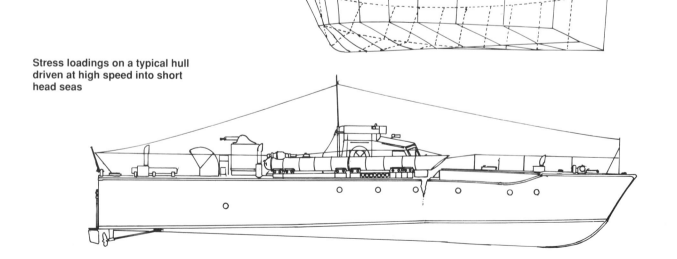

General arrangement of 70ft MTB from Drawing 8663

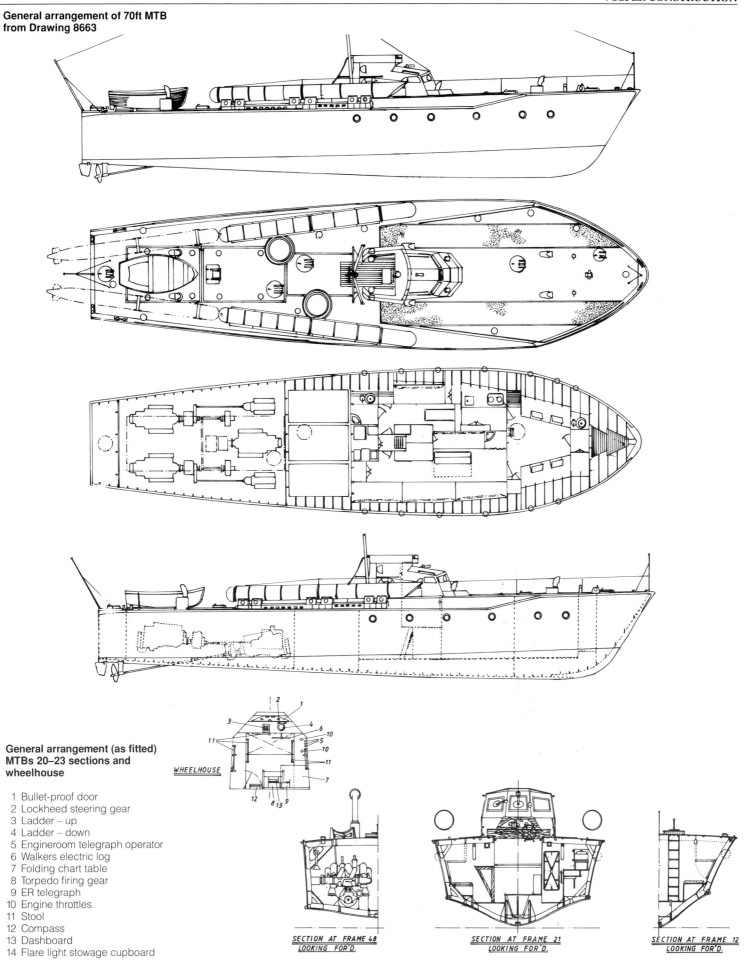

General arrangement (as fitted) MTBs 20–23 sections and wheelhouse

1 Bullet-proof door
2 Lockheed steering gear
3 Ladder – up
4 Ladder – down
5 Engineroom telegraph operator
6 Walkers electric log
7 Folding chart table
8 Torpedo firing gear
9 ER telegraph
10 Engine throttles
11 Stool
12 Compass
13 Dashboard
14 Flare light stowage cupboard

WHEELHOUSE

SECTION AT FRAME 48
LOOKING FOR'D.

SECTION AT FRAME 21
LOOKING FOR'D.

SECTION AT FRAME 12
LOOKING FOR'D.

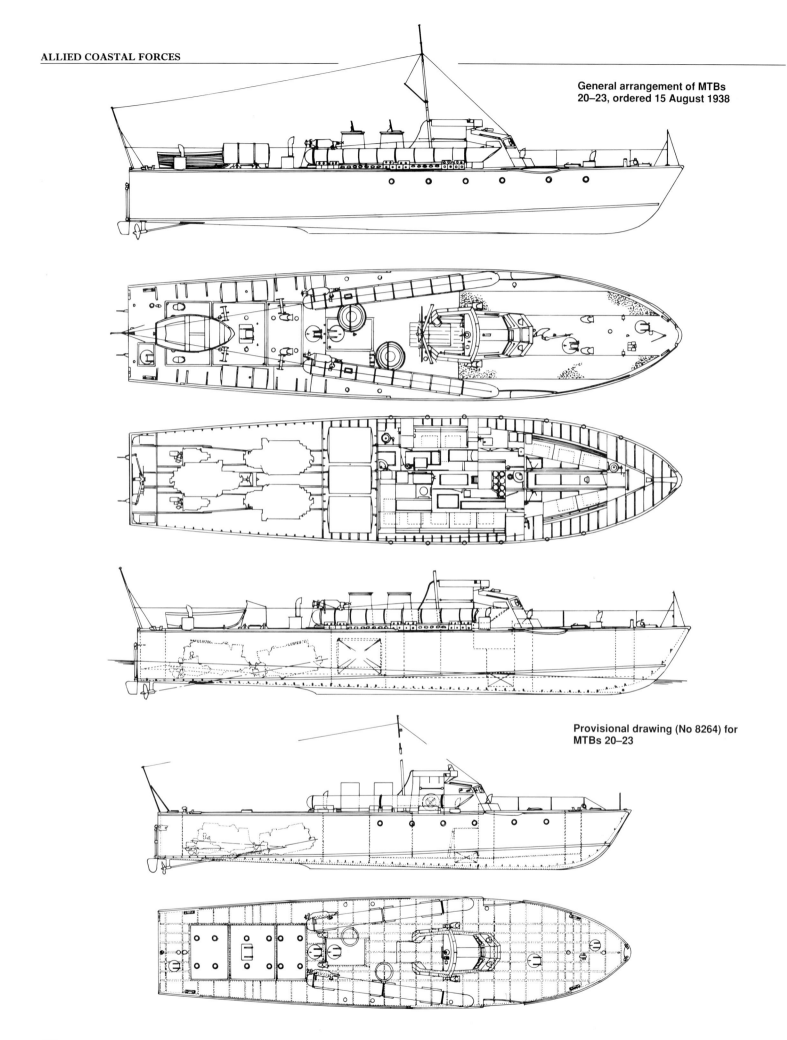

General arrangement of MTBs
20–23, ordered 15 August 1938

Provisional drawing (No 8264) for
MTBs 20–23

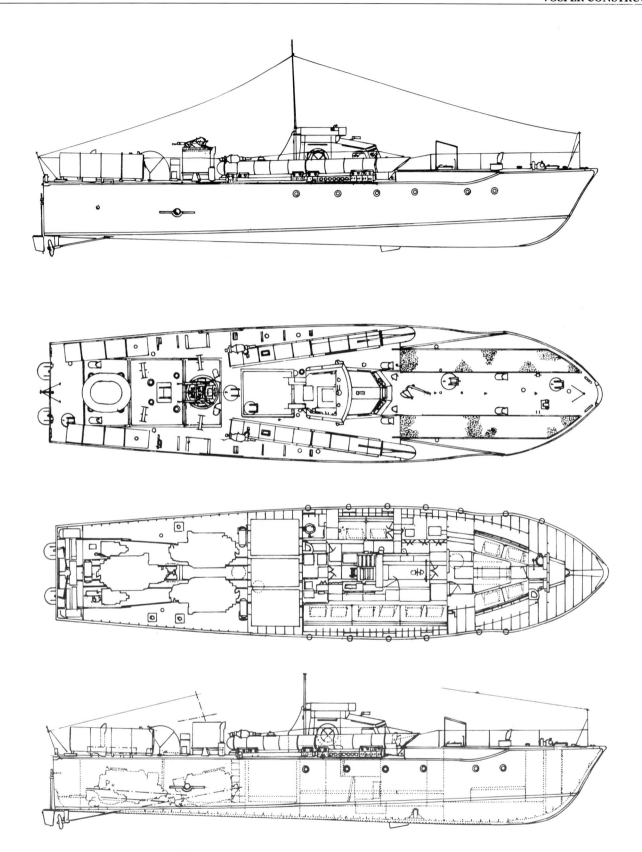

**General arrangement of MTBs
31–40, ordered 27 September 1939**

The Elco 70ft PT

The origins of the 70ft Elco can be traced directly to Hubert Scott-Paine's British Power Boat Company (BPB) 70ft private venture (PV70) MTB design of 1938. Designed by George Selman, PV70 was developed in response to growing competition from Vosper for MTB contracts. The boat was markedly different from both her contemporaries and earlier BPB designs (to be covered in Volume 3 of this series) in a number of aspects. The hard-chine, stepless hull was the result of extensive tank testing and incorporated a system of bonded structures reinforced by copper fasteners. A series of frames and watertight bulkheads were overlaid by two layers of mahogany planks laid diagonally to each other, between which was sandwiched a layer of marine-glue-impregnated aircraft fabric.

In profile, PV70 displayed a graceful reverse sheer and an s-shaped stem, the former being a point of contention between Scott-Paine and Selman. Scott-Paine liked the shape, comparing it with a greyhound at top speed; Selman argued that the reduced height of the frames would weaken the hull structure. Operational experience with the BPB 70ft MGBs would prove Selman correct, as frames and gunwales cracked at the sheer, necessitating the addition of a clamp under the gunwale running from the transom to just aft of the Vickers turrets. Interestingly, this clamp was not added to 70ft Elcos, which were direct descendants of the PV70 design, but could be found on both the 77ft and 80ft Elcos.

The superstructure consisted of a small enclosed pilothouse to which was attached a long, low trunk cabin, running perhaps half the length of the boat and surmounted by two domed, power-operated machine gun turrets. Unlike subsequent prototype and production boats, the sides and top of PV70's trunk cabin met in a rather unattractive sharp angle. Later trunk cabins incorporated

well-radiused junctures.

Completing PV70's departure from other British designs were her trainable 18in torpedo tubes for the standard Mark VIII Royal Navy torpedoes. In practice, these tubes were trained fore and aft until needed; then they were cranked outboard. Two 21in tubes could be fitted in lieu of the four 18in tubes.

Power was provided by three marinised 1000hp Rolls-Royce Merlins which produced a top speed in excess of 44 knots.

Construction of PV70 began in May 1938 and Scott-Paine began actively to seek foreign contracts for his new boat. At about the same time, the US Navy issued a request for proposals from civilian contractors for the design of several motor torpedo boats and submarine-chasers. In January 1939, Henry Sutphen (Elco's executive vice-president) decided to enter the competition. Rather than develop a new type locally, he opted to explore the possibility of building an already-developed European design under licence. After reviewing several designs from Thornycroft, Vosper, and BPB, he decided on the PV70 design. In March 1939 a contract was awarded for the construction of a 70ft prototype motor torpedo boat based on PV70. Upon completion, the new boat was transported to the United States on board the steamer *President Roosevelt*, arriving in New York on 4 September 1939. The boat was then lightered to the Electric Boat Company plant at Groton, Connecticut. Preliminary trials were held off New London on 9 and 10 October 1939, with Scott-Paine at the helm. The trials were successful, but the Navy withheld a contract pending rough-water

PT 10, first of the 70ft PTs, on trials. Elco

*PT 17 during trials in the Caribbean.
Transferred to the Royal Navy as MTB 266,
she was assigned to the 10th MTB Flotilla in
the Mediterranean.* USN

trials on 1 November 1939. Following this second series of trials, the Inspection Officer wrote:

> As a sea boat, PT 9 has my unqualified approval and I have such confidence in the boat after observing her in rough water that I would not hesitate to take her any-where under any conditions.
>
> I started the trials frankly skeptical about the claims I have heard made for this boat during the past year, and I asked for every condition which I thought might bring out any weaknesses in the boat's performance.
>
> I feel that any seagoing officer would share my original doubts in the claims for this boat, but I also feel that any experienced officer would agree with me after witnessing the performance that I saw yesterday. On the seaward run I do not believe that a destroyer could have maintained the speed which PT 8 held with complete comfort for all on board; on the other hand, the seas which bothered PT 9 would have caused no discomfort for a larger ship.

Despite this glowing recommendation, the Board was sceptical and required a second rough-water trial, which PT 9 again passed easily. As a result, on 7 December 1939 Elco was awarded a contract for the construction of twenty-three 70ft boats (eleven PTs and twelve PTCs) of similar design. The prototype was to be placed in service as PT 9, while the new construction were to be numbered PT 10–20 and PTC 1–12. Ultimately, only ten of the original eleven PTs were built, as PT 20 became the prototype 77ft boat.

Prior to construction, however, the Elco yard discovered that the plans it had purchased were not complete; they were for three different boats. Additionally, the jigs, templates and scrive boards which had been shipped from Hythe in November 1939 somehow ended up in Halifax, Nova Scotia. Consequently, Elco retained the prototype as a pattern from which to develop their own plans. As might be expected, the boats which resulted from this process were not exact copies of PT 9. The sinuous hull shape was retained, but the trunk cabin, armament, and machinery installations were modified to meet US Navy requirements. The resulting boats, with the obvious exception of the main armament configuration, were outwardly identical, however.

The Elco hull retained the graceful shape and general structure of its predecessor. The hull proper consisted of sixty-one laminated frames, seven of which were bulkheads, attached to a spruce keel and oak stem. Sides and bottom were double diagonally planked with mahogany, as was the deck. This diagonal deck planking, along with the exposed king plank, was unique to the 70ft boats. Nominal deck planking size was 4in × ³⁄₁₆in.

The major deviations from the original design occurred at deck level and above. The streamlined trunk cabin remained, but the cockpit section was enlarged and raised. The 0.303 calibre machine gun turrets were replaced with similar but larger units mounting twin 0.50 calibre weapons. The trunk cabin was built in three sections: a forward section, containing the pilothouse and cockpit; a midships section, containing the hydraulically operated Dewandre turrets and an access hatch; and an aft section which served as the engineroom canopy. Each section could be removed independently of the other two. Cabin construction followed existing aircraft practice: thin sheets of plywood were glued and screwed to light frames and covered with fabric. Insulation and sound-deadening was provided by a layer of Onazote installed on the interior of the canopy.

The pilothouse was enlarged and faired into the trunk cabin, providing improved wind and spray deflection and better visibility. An alloy boot was fitted to the front of the pilothouse below the Perspex windows and was used for stowage. Access to the boot storage was provided by two small hinged hatches. The cockpit (dustbin) was enlarged and made of aluminium sheet. Grab rails were mounted along the top of the pilothouse and short coachroof aft. Throttles, a compass, warning buzzers, torpedo director, firing keys for the torpedoes, and a combination searchlight/fog bell were located near the helm. A companionway on the starboard side of the cockpit led down into the pilothouse, which contained a duplicate set of controls. A large rectangular window was let into the

Completed 70ft pilothouse shells. Elco

port side of the cockpit bulkhead just above the helm, providing the helmsman with a clear view into the pilothouse.

The midsection contained the two power-operated turrets designed by the Belgian firm of Dewandre. The guns were trained and elevated hydraulically and were enclosed in framed Perspex turret domes. Each turret was fitted with a folding platform on which the gunner would stand. Unlike the later Mark 17 turrets with their integral ammunition boxes, the Dewandres required the ammunition boxes to be mounted directly on the guns. This arrangement was much criticised, as each magazine held only 167 rounds.

The engineroom canopy section contained four deadlights and a trapezoidal hinged hatch for access from above. To facilitate engine removal, a removable rectangular hatch section was fitted on either side of the canopy at its aft end. Two deadlights and a cowl vent were mounted on each hatch section.

In place of the Rolls-Royce engines, three 4M2500 Packard V-12 petrol engines were fitted. Initially developing 1100shp each, these engines were later uprated to 1200shp. The centre engine was direct drive, while the two wing engines were coupled to vee drives.

The primary difference between the PT and the PTC versions was the main armament. The PTs were intended as surface ship killers; as such, they mounted four trainable 18in torpedo tubes. These tubes were near copies of those fitted to PT 9 and were intended to launch the 17.7in Mark 7 Bliss-Leavitt torpedoes, of which there was an ample supply.

The PTCs, on the other hand, were intended as anti-submarine craft. Provisions were made for the installation of sonar equipment beneath the pilothouse. Depth charges were carried on long rails bolted to the deck which led aft to two loading devices which served a pair of Y guns. Additionally, two four-charge racks were mounted on the stern.

Upon delivery, the ten PTs, along with PT 9, were formed into PT Squadron Two under the command of Lt Earl Caldwell. During winter 1940–41, the boats engaged in rough-water trials off Miami and Cuba, experiencing a number of mishaps, including groundings and striking submerged objects. The American co-author's father, who was the helmsman on PT 18 during the trials, noted that his boat struck a submerged object off Fort Lauderdale in January or February 1941. As a result, the props and struts were damaged and the lazarette began to fill with water. Eventually, they were towed into Miami by a Gulf Oil Co tanker. PT 11 had a harder time of it, running aground on a bar near the Isla de Pinos (Isle of Pines) off southwest Cuba. The boat was refloated only after being stripped of most of her topside weight, but was repaired.

In March, the squadron was ordered back to New York where the boats were to be transferred to the Royal Navy as MTB 258–268. Prior to the actual transfer, however, the Royal Navy decided to allocate PT 9 to the Royal Canadian Navy. Stripped of her torpedo tubes and engines, she was towed to Montreal, arriving on 23 August 1941. There, most likely at the Canadian Power Boat Company plant, ex-PT 9 was refitted. Unfortunately, only two 550hp engines (V-12 Kermath Sea Raider) were installed, reducing her top speed to 22 knots. The two domed turrets were retained and two single depth charge racks were installed along either side of the deck edge aft. Intended to function in the ASW role, she was also fitted with type 134A asdic. Commissioned 25 September 1942 as SO 9, she operated out of Halifax, Gaspe, Quebec, and Toronto before being returned to the US Navy at New York in June 1945. A

Another view of PT 10 on trials. Elco

newspaper clipping from the *Boston American* listed her for private sale on 5 September 1946.

The ten 70ft Elco PTs, however, were allocated to the 10th MTB Flotilla and were modified to Royal Navy requirements prior to transfer. These modifications included the replacement of the four trainable 18in tubes with two 21in fixed Royal navy pattern tubes, removal of the domes covering the turrets, and installation of a 20mm Mark 4 on the stern. In addition, two twin 0.303 Lewis machine guns were mounted on pedestals forward of the cockpit and a single depth charge track was added on either side of the Oerlikon aft. When in Royal Navy service, additional modifications were made as necessary. A photograph of MTB 265 taken on 9 August 1943 shows her with three Breda 12.7mm machine guns in place of the twin Lewis guns forward and the 20mm aft.

The first boats to be shipped were MTB 259 and MTB 260, leaving New York in November 1941. Taking a long route around Cape of Good Hope, the boats arrived at Port Said on 20 January 1942 and, two weeks later, at Alexandria after transitting the Suez Canal in 3 hours 23 minutes. The other boats arrived in pairs at short intervals and soon joined their sisters.

Originally, the 10th MTB Flotilla was to have been assigned to Malta, but in February MTB 259–262 proceeded to Tobruk under the command of Lt Cdr Noakes to support Allied efforts in that

The former PV70 as PT 9. Note the extreme similarity between this boat and the 70ft Elcos. The most notable differences are the short pilothouse and small turret domes. Elco

area. There, they spent a number of months doing patrol work and attempting to find targets for their torpedoes with little success.

A series of notes written in July 1945 by Lt Cdr Max Henzell, the flotilla's engineering officer, provides some interesting insights into flotilla operations from that point, as attested by the following excerpts:

> The procedure there [Tobruk] was to find and lay alongside a good wreck, from the large selection available, and drop a camouflage net on the boat during the day.
>
> Our mother ship was the trawler *Unlee* but she was near-missed and very unhappy in the exposed anchorage.

This photograph, taken in 1941 at Miami, shows to good effect the interior of the cockpit. No instruments were fitted in the cockpit and the window provided the helmsman with a view of those fitted in the pilothouse. Elco

> In fact, after a month of daily bombing and 100 miles each way to Derna patrols at night, the crews were getting tired and we returned to Alex for slipping. While at Tobruk, 260 had a narrow shave while fuelling and had 23 holes put in her and the fuel dump on the jetty set on fire. 263 did a good job by saving a tanker that had been torpedoed and set on fire.
>
> On the way to relieve us 263 ran ashore at Mesa Lukk about 15m from Tobruk at some 35 knots. We had a job getting her off as she was high and dry on a sandy beach. However, with the aid of a South African armoured car regiment we got all the gear out and shipped it to rail head at Fort Caputtzo. The hull was patched, filled with 4 gal tins and towed 300 miles to Alexandria.

Prior to the fall of Tobruk in June 1942, the 10th MTB was joined by the 77ft Elcos (MTB 307–316) of the 15th MTB Flotilla under Lt Denis Jermain and the two commenced combined operations. During the evacuation of Tobruk the Elcos had some harrowing moments. As MTB 260, under the command of Lt Martin Solomon, was leaving the harbour, the schooner *Kheyr-el-Din* carrying troops was hit and set ablaze at the harbour entrance. Solomon wheeled about, laid smoke, and engaged a number of German tanks and mortar crews firing on the schooner. Henzell credits MTB 260

with the rescue of 102 soldiers during the action.

Following the disastrous raid on Tobruk in September 1942 (detailed in the section on the 77ft boats), the survivors of the 10th and 15th flotillas were combined into the new 10th MTB Flotilla and operated in the Strait of Messina. Following the Sicily campaign, the boats were transferred to the Aegean Sea, where they engaged in covert operations and attacks on shipping.

The 70ft boats were well-liked in Royal Navy service. Commander Noakes, former commander of the 10th MTB Flotilla, described them as the best of the Elcos and credited them with great manoeuvrability and the ability to sustain 45 knots under just about any circumstance. In October 1945, he wrote to Preston Sutphen that '. . . 265 and 268 (stripped of everything) were doing 52 knots right up to the time they 'paid off' last month . . .'.

Of the twelve PTCs built, only four saw service with the US Navy. In March 1941 PTCs 1–4, under the command of then Lt Robert Kelly, headed for Key West to run trials with their experimental sound units, each boat being fitted with a different design. In a 1981 letter to the author, Kelly described the cruise:

> The division departed Bayonne, NJ in late March for the Washington Navy Yard. There, the sonar gear in-

A Dewandre turret unit prior to being installed in a 70ft boat. The original photograph was badly yellowed, affecting clarity, but the operating cylinders can be made out to the left. Elco

stallations were completed for each of the four boats. PTC1 had an experimental sound gear which had been developed by the Naval Research Laboratory. The transducer was located within a cumbersome cylinder, about 30 inches in diameter, which was lowered through the hull, piercing the keel directly beneath the radio room. For the life of me, I can't recall what mechanism was used to raise or lower it. All I know is that it was not difficult. The cylinder projected about two feet beneath the hull. In order to support the hull, heavy steel plates about 10 feet long and 4 feet wide surrounded the aperture.

Experimental sonars developed by RCA and by the Submarine Signal Company of Boston were installed on two of the other boats of the division. The fourth boat had a modified British asdic sonar similar to that used aboard their destroyers.

We were probably at the Washington Navy Yard about 10 days to 2 weeks. We then headed south via the coastal route in easy stages, travelling only by day. Ports of call en route were Norfolk, VA; Moorhead City, NC; Charleston, SC; St Augustine, FL; and Miami, FL. This trip served as our shakedown cruise. For the most part, it was uneventful except for some engine trouble. We had a Tech Rep from Packard with us and on occasion he had to phone Detroit and have the company air express parts for some of the engines.

While we were en route from St. Augustine to Miami on a bright sunny afternoon, we passed through about fifty large turtles on the surface basking in the sun. As a result, PTC1 nicked one of its propellers on a turtle which didn't dive quite deep enough or quick enough. So, we all spent a couple of days in Miami while PTC1 got its prop straightened at the Miami Boat Company's shipyard.

While in Key West, I believe we were under the operational control of the East Coast Sound School

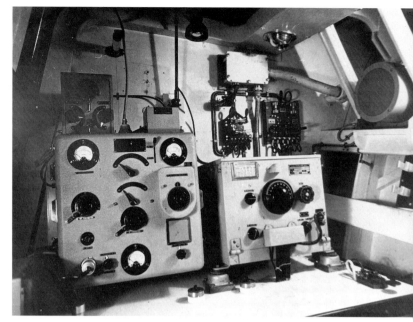

Radio room of a 70ft boat. Elco

which was located there. However, our tests were conducted under the direction of the representative from the Naval Research Lab. During much of our stay at Key West we encountered rather heavy seas – for us. Frequently, the waves were six feet and greater, and our 70 footers bounced around like corks.

The sea conditions, while uncomfortable, proved ideal in proving the fallacy of the concept of PTCs. We soon found out that our sonar signals got lost in the troughs of the waves either going toward a target or returning since the signals wouldn't pass through air.

During the trials, one of the boats lost the head of its transducer. I believe it was the RCA unit. It had a small 8 to 10 inch head attached to the end of a 2–3 foot sword

Packards in the engineroom of a 70ft boat. Elco

Throttle quadrant used on the 70ft and 77ft Elcos. Elco

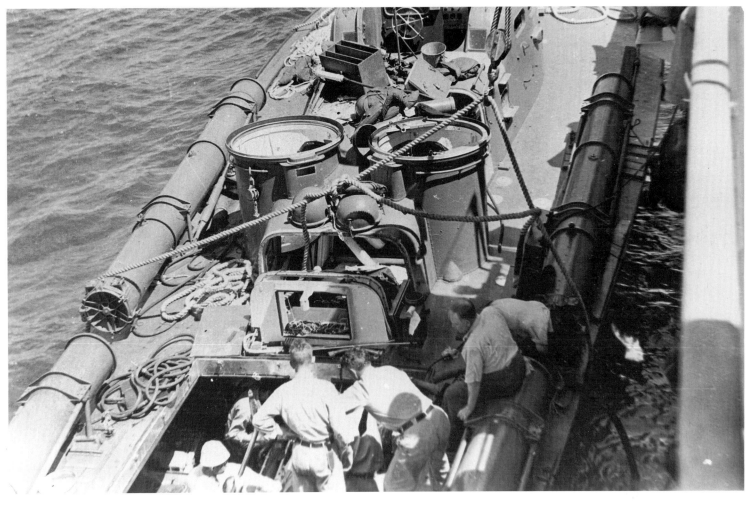

PT 11 aground on the Isle of Pines, off Cuba.
She is being stripped for refloating. PTBM

that projected through the hull and could be raised or lowered for securing or operation. I don't recall what the other two looked like.

Needless to say, since the chief evaluator was from the Navy Research Lab, their gear received the highest grades. However, it was unanimously agreed by all of us that the Electric Boat Company's dream of motor-boat subchasers becoming the modern day counterpart of the World War I subchasers was strictly a pipe dream and would never come to pass.

During the latter part of June, PTC DIV 1 retraced its path up the coast and returned to Bayonne, NJ (Elco's) where the squadron was decommissioned and the boats were turned over to the British for use as motor gunboats (minus the sonar gear).

Like their PT sisters, all twelve of the PTCs were modified and transferred to the Royal Navy as MGBs. Reconfiguration for the MGB role included the removal of all anti-submarine warfare equipment and the fitting of a 20mm Mark 4 and a depression rail on the stern. Unlike the PTs, however, the converted PTCs initially retained their Perspex turret domes. Later, the turrets were removed, the coachroof faired over, and a Vickers Mark V turret was mounted on the deck on either side of the cockpit. In this latter configuration they closely resembled the 70ft British Power Boat Company MGB 50–67. Assigned to the 5th and 7th MGB flotillas, the boats operated out of Lowestoft.

General Characteristics
Builder Electric Boat Company, Bayonne, NJ
Length 70ft 0in
Beam 19ft 11in
Draught 4ft 6in
Displacement 32 tons (design)
Machinery 3 × 4M2500 Packard V-12 petrol engines at 1200shp = 3600shp
Armament
PT
2 × twin 0.50 calibre Browning machine guns
4 × 18in torpedoes
PTC
2 × twin 0.50 calibre Browning machine guns
24 × depth charges
2 × Y guns
2 × stern racks
MTB
2 × twin 0.50 calibre Browning machine guns
2 × twin 0.303 Lewis machine guns
1 × 20mm Oerlikon
2 × 21in torpedoes
2 × depth charges
MGB
2 × twin 0.50 calibre Browning machine guns*
1 × 20mm Oerlikon
2 × depth charges
Note *replaced by (2) twin Vickers 0.5in machine guns in Mark V turrets fitted at a later date.

Seventy-foot Elcos of RON 1 at the Washington Navy Yard in January 1941. PT 9 is against the pier in the second trot and can be distinguished by its smaller turret domes and low pilothouse. NHC

Chronology of major events – 10th and 15th MTB flotillas

Date	Boats involved	Event
14.6.42	259	Suffered heavy weather damage while in tow on passage from Alexandria to Malta. Sank while under tow back to Alexandria 14.6.42
18.6.42	260	Rescued soldiers from burning schooner during evacuation of Tobruk
30–31.8.42	311, 312, 315	Surface attack on convoy off Crete. Sustained hour-long attack by Ju 88s
14.9.42	260, 261, 262, 263, 266, 267, 268, 307, 308, 309, 310, 312, 314, 315, 316	Combined operations with commandos against Tobruk, resulting in loss of MTBs 308, 310, 312 and 314
9.42	260, 261, 262, 263, 264, 265, 266, 267, 268, 307, 309, 311, 313, 315, 316	10th and 15th MTB flotillas combined to form new 10th MTB flotilla
1–2.10.42	307, 309, 311, 316	Attack on Rhodes
13.12.42	260, 307, 315	Unsuccessful attack on motor vessel en route from Malta to Bone
19–20.1.42	260, 264, 313	Attack on shipping off Tripoli. The Italian submarine *Santorre Santarosa* was scuttled on 20.1.43 after being torpedoed by 260; damaged three tugs
30–31.1.42	260, 311, 316	Gunnery attack on S-boats off Bone
24.2.43	262	Bombed and sunk off Cape Serratt
12–13.3.43	265, 316	Damaged (one) S-boat off Zambreta Island, Tunisia

Chronology of major events – 10th and 15th MTB flotillas

Date	Boats involved	Event
22–23.3.43	265, 311	Torpedoed and sank (one) 'F' lighter off Plane Island, Tunisia
31.3–1.4.43	266, 311	Torpedoed and sank (two) steamers (total 6912grt) in escorted convoy off Cani Rocks, Tunisia
2.4.43	267	Lost in heavy weather en route from Benghazi to Malta
26–27.4.43	265, 311	Torpedoed and sank (one) motor vessel off Cani Rocks, Tunisia
2.5.43	311	Mined and sunk between Bone and Bizerta
10.5.43	264	Mined and sunk off Sousse
6–7.6.43	263, 268	Supported commando landing on Lampedusa Island
16–17.6.43	260, 313, 315, 316	Unsuccessful torpedo attack on *Scipione Africano* in Strait of Messina off Reggio; MTB 316 lost to gunfire
17.6.43	313	Damaged by bombs at Casteloriso
19–20.10.43	307, 309, 315	Torpedoed and sank (one) 'F' lighter and (one) motor vessel off Kos Island
15–16.11.43	266, 315	Sank by gunfire (one) landing craft and (one) barge off Leros Island
13–14.12.43	266, 315	Sank by gunfire (one) tug and (two) caiques off Rhodes
12–13.1.44	260, 309	Sank by gunfire (one) caique off Piscopi Island
8.10.44	307	Torpedoed and sank (one) tanker, probably sank (one) motor vessel, possibly damaged (one) lighter off Psara Island
15–16.4.45	307	Torpedoed and sank (one) armed merchant vessel

Construction list

Boat number	Keel laid	Launched	Placed in service	Squadrons (in order of assignment)	Fate
PT					
10	26. 2.40	20. 8.40	7.11.40	2 (USN) 10th MTB (RN)	To RN as MTB 259 11.4.41. Damaged in heavy weather on passage to Malta, and lost when returning to Alexandria 14.6.42
11	1. 4.40	7.10.40	12.11.40	2 (USN) 10th MTB (RN)	To RN as MTB 260 11.4.41. Returned USN 16.3.45
12	9. 4.40	18.10.40	14.11.40	2 (USN) 10th MTB (RN)	To RN as MTB 261 11.4.41. Paid off 12.44 at Alexandria. Sank after 3.45 and destroyed as obstruction 26.8.45
13	17. 4.40	25.10.40	26.11.40	2 (USN) 10th MTB (RN)	To RN as MTB 262 11.4.41. Bombed and sunk off Cape Serratt, Tunisia 24.2.43
14	26. 4.40	7.11.40	29.11.40	2 (USN) 10th MTB (RN)	To RN as MTB 263 11.4.44. Returned USN at Alexandria 16.3.46
15	6. 5.40	15.11.40	5.12.40	2 (USN) 10th MTB (RN)	To RN as MTB 264 11.4.41. Mined off Sousse, Tunisia 10.5.43
16	13. 5.40	23.11.40	31.12.40	2 (USN) 10th MTB (RN)	To RN as MTB 265 11.4.41. Returned USN 16.3.46
17	24. 5.40	2.12.40	16.12.40	2 (USN) 10th MTB (RN)	To RN as MTB 266 11.4.41. Damaged by gunfire and destroyed 17.4.44
18	31. 5.40	9.12.40	30.12.40	2 (USN) 10th MTB (RN)	To RN as MTB 267 11.4.41. Sunk in heavy weather on passage from Benghazi to Malta 2.4.43
19	7. 6.40	16.12.40	31.12.40	2 (USN) 10th MTB (RN)	To RN as MTB 268 11.4.41. Returned USN 16.3.45
PTC					
1	13. 6.40	3. 1.41	6. 3.41	PTCRON 1 (USN)	To RN as MGB 82 15.7.41. Returned USN 3.9.45. Laid up England to 3.46
2	20. 6.40	11. 1.41	6. 3.41	PTCRON 1 (USN)	To RN as MGB 83 15.7.41. Returned USN 16.5.45. Laid up England to 3.46
3	26. 6.40	20. 1.41	3. 3.41	PTCRON 1 (USN)	To RN as MGB 84 15.7.41. Returned USN 21.7.45. Laid up Gillingham to 12.47
4	2. 7.40	25. 1.41	11. 3.41	PTCRON 1 (USN)	To RN as MGB 85 15.7.41. Returned USN 21.7.45. Laid up Gillingham to 12.47
			Completed		
5	9. 7.40	1. 2.41	17. 2.41	PTCRON 1 (USN)	To RN as MGB 86 4.4.41. Returned USN 21.7.45. Laid up Gillingham to 12.47. Being restored at Hoo 1991
6	15. 7.40	8. 2.41	20. 2.41	PTCRON 1 (USN)	To RN as MGB 87 4.4.41. Returned USN 21.7.45. Laid up Gillingham to 12.47.
7	23. 7.40	15. 2.41	7. 3.41	PTCRON 1 (USN)	To RN as MGB 88 4.4.41. Returned USN 19.6.45. Laid up Gillingham to 1.48
8	26. 7.40	21. 2.41	8. 3.41	PTCRON 1 (USN)	To RN as MGB 89 4.4.41. Returned to USN 3.4.45. Laid up Poole to 3.46
9	1. 8.40	3. 3.41	14. 3.41	PTCRON 1 (USN)	To RN as MGB 90 4.4.41. Lost in accidental fire at Portland 16.7.41
10	7. 8.40	5. 3.41	20. 3.41	PTCRON 1 (USN)	To RN as MGB 91 4.4.41. Returned USN 6.7.45. Laid up Poole to 12.47
11	13. 8.40	12. 3.41	27. 3.41	PTCRON 1 (USN)	To RN as MGB 92 4.4.41. Lost in accidental fire at Portland 16.7.41
12	23. 8.40	20. 3.41	28. 3.41	PTCRON 1 (USN)	To RN as MGB 93 4.4.41. Returned USN 13.9.45. Laid up Poole to 11.46

Close-up of the depth charge rails fitted to the PTCs. The superstructure is identical to that of the PT. Elco

PTC 1 on trials. PTBM

Y guns and depth charge tracks on one of the PTCs. Elco

On the PTCs, the depth charges were slid aft along the rails to these lifts, then hand-cranked up to the Y guns. Elco

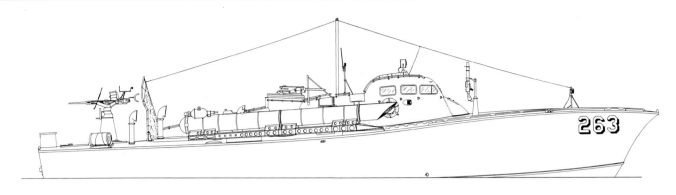

MTB 263 upon completion. She still carries the US Navy-style shaded pennant numbers on her bow and transom. After serving with the 10th MTB Flotilla, she was returned to the US Navy at Alexandria in March 1946.

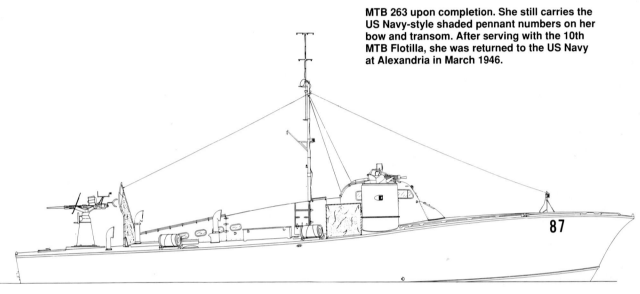

MGB 87 (ex-PTC 6) following modification by the Royal Navy. The Dewandre turrets have been replaced by two Vickers Mark V turrets abeam the cockpit, making it look very much like a 70ft British Power Boat Company MGB.
David Curry (CFVA)

Armament

USN boat number PT	Armament as built	Modifications while in service
10–15, 17–19	2 × twin 0.50 Browning M2 in Dewandre turrets 4 × 18in Mk 7 torpedoes in TT	as RN MTB – 2 × twin 0.50 cal, 2 × twin 0.303 Lewis, 2 × 21in TT, 2 × depth charges
16	as above	as RN MTB – 2 × twin 0.50 cal, 2 × twin 0.303 Lewis, 2 × 21in TT, 2 × depth charges. Lewis and 20mm replaced by single 12.7mm Breda mgs before 8.43
PTC		
1–12	2 × twin 0.50 Browning M2 in Dewandre turrets 2 × 0.303 Lewis forward 32 × depth charges 2 × depth charges 2 × Y guns and 2 × four charge depth charge tracks aft	Prior to transfer to RN, depth charge tracks and Y guns removed; 1 × 20mm Mk 4 added aft. Dewandre turrets later removed and replaced by 2 × twin 0.50 Vickers in Mk V turrets abeam cockpit

Twin 0.303 Lewis machine guns mounted on the Lend-Lease 70ft boats. Elco

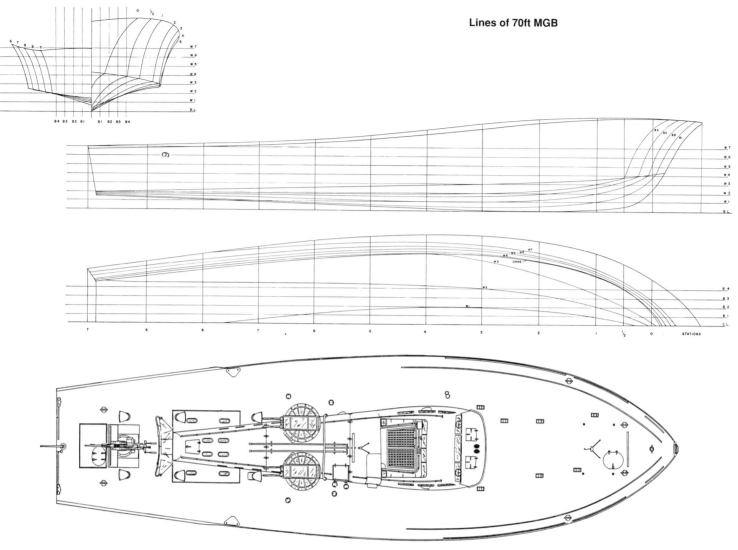

Lines of 70ft MGB

Initial arrangement – 70ft MGB with original
Dewandre turrets.

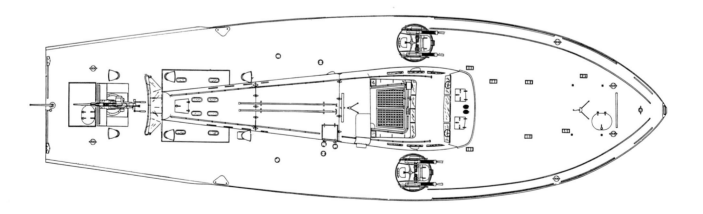

Modified 70ft MGB with Vickers Mk V turrets.

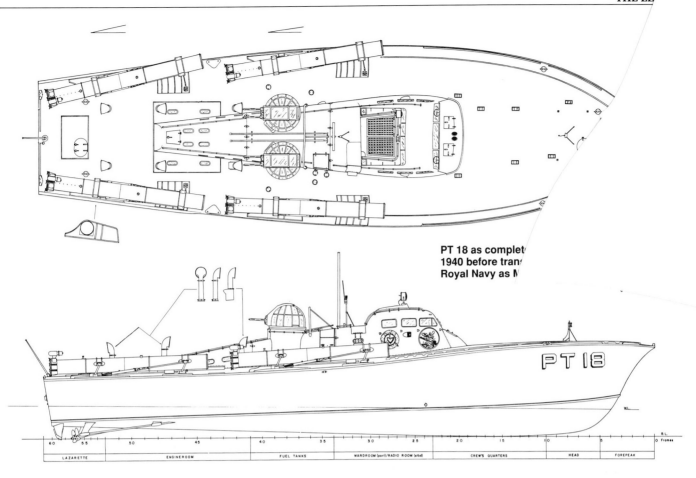

PT 18 as comple
1940 before tran
Royal Navy as M

LAZARETTE | ENGINEROOM | FUEL TANKS | WARDROOM (port)/RADIO ROOM (stbd) | CREW'S QUARTERS | HEAD | FOREPEAK

Stern view of PT 14 after modification to Royal Navy MTB 263. Compare this view with those of the PTs at the Washington Navy Yard. Elco

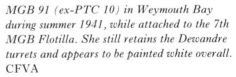

MGB 91 (ex-PTC 10) in Weymouth Bay during summer 1941, while attached to the 7th MGB Flotilla. She still retains the Dewandre turrets and appears to be painted white overall. CFVA

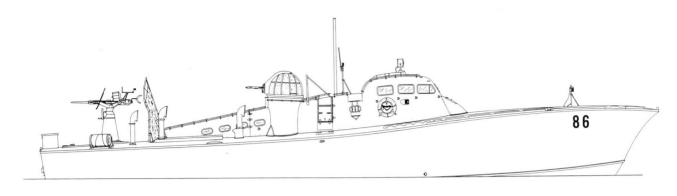

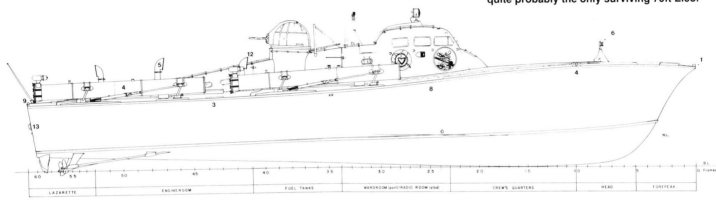

MGB 86 as completed. This boat is still in existence and is being restored (1993) by her current owner at Gravesend. She is quite probably the only surviving 70ft Elco.

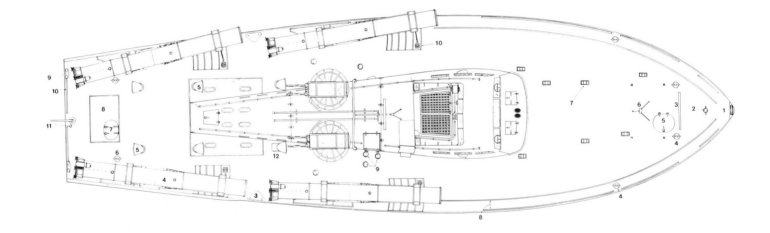

Aft section details

1. Forward torpedo tube foundation
2. Fuel fills
3. Boarding ladder pad
4. 18in torpedo tube
5. Cowl vent
6. 9in bitt
7. Scuttle to lazarette
8. Main lazarette hatch
9. Chock
10. Toe rail
11. Stern light
12. Blower/vent
13. Exhaust pipes
14. Fuel tank vents

Forward section details

1. Bow fairlead
2. Samson post
3. Rail for hatch dodger
4. 9in bitt
5. Hatch
6. Bow light
7. Deadlight
8. Toe rails
9. Fuel fills
10. Torpedo training gear

The Elco 77ft PT

The 77-foot Elco PTs were the direct descendents of the earlier experimental 70-foot types and were the result of a Bureau of Ordnance recommendation in July 1940 that production PTs carry four 21in torpedo tubes. On 23 August 1940 the General Board agreed and recommended that future PTs be about 80ft in length, have a range of 500 miles at 20 knots, a top speed of 40 knots, and mount four 21in torpedo tubes. They were also to carry two twin 0.50 calibre machine guns with 5000 rounds per barrel, smoke generator, radio, and provisions for five days. On 25 September 1940, the Navy awarded Elco a contract for twenty-four 77ft boats based on the original 70ft design. These were ordered as PT 21–32 and PTC 13–24, but the latter were redesignated PTC 33–44 in March 1941. This contract was again amended on 24 March 1941 by the Secretary of the Navy, who directed that the PTCs were to be completed as PTs after trials with the 70ft boats had shown the PTC concept to be unfeasible. Plans were made to build an additional twenty-four boats (PT 45–56 and PTC 25–36), but these were redesignated PT 45–48 and BPT (British PT) 1–20 in the contract received by Elco on 10 April 1941. The BPTs were again redesignated PT 49–68 in December 1941 and PT 49–58 were transferred to the Royal Navy as MTB 307–316.

As a result of the new specifications, the last of the originally-ordered 70ft boats, PT 20, was redesigned and emerged as the prototype 77ft boat. As the prototype, PT 20 was unique among her 77ft sisters in that she retained several features of the 70ft boats. For example, the cockpit section was that of the first series 77ft boats, but the turrets and engineroom canopy were those of the 70ft boats. Initially, she also had provisions for cranking the aft tubes outboard from inside the engineroom canopy.

PT 20 also introduced plywood decking. A review of the factory drawings indicates that the $\frac{3}{16}$in mahogany planks of the 70ft boats were superseded by a layer of $\frac{3}{8}$in mahogany plywood to improve stiffness.

There were two basic series of 77ft boats. The first series comprised PT 20–44 and was built to the original design. Combat experience led to the second series, PT 45–68, which differed from the first series primarily in the shape of the cockpit, armament configuration, and hull stiffness.

The most apparent differences between the two series can be found in the shape of the cockpit. Like the earlier boats, the trunk cabin on both 77ft series was built in three sections, the two after sections being virtually identical on both series. The cockpit sections, however, were quite different in shape. The initial cockpit design retained the boot fitted to the front of the pilothouse and ended in a nearly vertical bulkhead containing a deadlight. The later series dispensed with the boot, incorporated a shallow 'V' into the face of the pilothouse, and replaced the earlier flat rear panel with a sweeping curve that faired into the coachroof aft. The later version also incorporated a small platform aft of the open cockpit, on which was often mounted a whip antenna. On some of the Royal Navy boats, a hinged armour plate was added to the platform to protect the cockpit from astern fire.

The turret section was redesigned somewhat, a locker being attached to the roof of the turret section immediately aft of the turrets and the turret domes being deleted. Later, the entire Dewandre turrets were replaced by the standard Mark 17 mounts enclosed in a combination sprayshield-depression rail.

Hull stiffness had been a weak point in both the 70ft and first series 77ft boats. The boats had a tendency to pound heavily, even in moderate seas, resulting in cracked frames and hull planking, sheared fastenings, loose fittings, and working of the deck and hull sides. These problems first appeared in the 70ft boats during their

PT 32 on trials. The pronounced flare of the bow is very evident. USN

cruise to Key West and, later, in the 77ft boats during the two 'Plywood Derbies' of 1941. These problems were largely overcome by frame strengthening and the addition of an external sheer clamp in the first series 77ft boats. From PT 45 on, external deck stiffeners running fore and aft along both sides of the superstructure and aft deck were installed at the factory. Several of the surviving first series 77ft boats are known to have been retrofitted with the deck stiffeners, as well.

Like their 70ft sisters, the 77ft Elcos were powered by three 4M2500 Packard petrol engines driving three-bladed screws. The centre engine was direct drive, while the two wing engines were connected to vee drives. Rated at 1200shp (later 1350shp), the Packards gave a top speed of about 41 knots with a clean bottom. After a few months in action, top speed dropped radically due to bottom fouling, added weight from soakage and equipment, and general wear and tear on the engines. Sabotage added to the boats' running problems. During the opening months of the Pacific war, the boats of RON 3 in the Philippines had to contend with fuel sabotaged with dissolved wax, requiring it to be filtered through chamois during refuelling.

The early boats were built with the hydraulically-powered, Plexiglas-domed Dewandre turrets, but combat experience demonstrated that the domes fogged up when the guns were fired; additionally, the hydraulic training and elevating mechanisms of the Dewandre mounts were found to be too slow to track modern aircraft and prone to damage. Consequently, the domes were removed and the hydraulics bypassed on surviving boats. A 20mm Mark 4 was also fitted aft on the second series boats.

Both series of 77ft PTs could carry either four 21in torpedoes in tubes, or two tubes and eight Mark 6 depth charges. The torpedoes were fired either electrically from the cockpit, or by percussion at the tube should the electrical firing circuit fail. Late in the war, the tubes of several surviving boats (PT 48 for one) were replaced by the Mark 1 roll-off racks and Mark 13 torpedoes normally fitted to the 80ft Elco and 78ft Higgins PTs.

One of the more interesting modifications applied to the 77ft boats was the conversion of PT 59, 60 and 61 to motor gunboats during summer 1943. Torpedo targets in the Pacific were becoming scarce, and the PTs were being diverted to interdict the large numbers of Japanese barges used to supply their beleaguered garrisons in the islands. As these barges were generally armoured against the 0.50 calibre machine guns carried by the PTs, heavier firepower was required to sink them. Consequently, the three old 77-footers were stripped of their torpedo tubes and fitted with a single

PTs were normally transported by tanker. This photo appears to show the six boats of RON 3 aboard Esso Guadalupe, *on their way to the Philippines in September 1941.* USN

shielded 40mm fore and aft, as well as additional shielded single 0.50 calibre machine guns along the deck. An SO radar mast was mounted on the trunk cabin just aft of the turrets and its associated scope installed in the open cockpit just above the companionway to the charthouse. One of these gunboats, PT 59, was skippered by John F Kennedy, following the loss of his 80ft Elco, PT 109.

The 77ft Elcos first saw combat at Pearl Harbor on 7 December 1941. Six boats of RON 1 (PT 20–25) were moored alongside their tender, a converted barge, at the submarine base when the attack began. Six other boats (PT 26–30, 42) were across the harbour,

PT 34, 31, 35, and 41 in the well deck of a tanker, September 1941. PTBM

being loaded on the tanker USS *Ramapo* (AO 12) for shipment to the Philippines where they were to join the six boats of RON 3 (PT 31–35, 41). Almost immediately, the deficiencies in the PTs' armament became apparent. On the RON 1 boats, the Plexiglas turret domes fogged up during firing. Things were worse for the other boats. Because they were being shipped, their fuel tanks had been emptied and purged with carbon dioxide; consequently, the crews could not run the compressor which drove the pump for the turrets. The hydraulic lines were cut and the turrets were manned by a gunner, two men to slew the turret manually, and an officer for fire direction.

On 10 December 1941, the boats of RON 3, which had been shipped to Cavite Navy Yard in September 1941, got their first taste of combat when Manila was bombed. For the next four months the squadron, under the command of Lt John Bulkeley, was in constant combat. The squadron's exploits, which were immortalised in William L White's book (and the 1945 John Wayne movie) *They Were Expendable*, included an attack on the Japanese light cruiser *Kuma* and a major part in General MacArthur's escape from the Philippines. By 15 April 1942, however, the squadron ceased to exist, all six boats having been lost by that time. PT 31, 32, 33, and 35 were destroyed by their crews to prevent capture; PT 34 (of which the American author's father was coxswain) was set afire and lost during an air attack by four flying boats; PT 41, which had been transferred to the US Army for use as a gunboat on Lake Lanao, was destroyed to prevent capture while being transported overland.

The 77ft boats were in action again in June 1942, when the boats of RON 1 made the 1400-mile trip from Pearl Harbor to Midway under their own power. There, they were involved in the 4 June Battle of Midway, enduring several air attacks and searching for the surviving Japanese carriers.

In July a second RON 3 was commissioned (Lt Cdr Alan R Montgomery commanding), acquiring its boats from RON 2, which was operating in Panama. The first four boats (PT 38, 46, 48, and 60) were transported to Noumea by the tankers *Lackawanna* (AO 40) and *Tappahannock* (AO 43), arriving on 19 September. Following several tows and a final 300-mile leg under their own power, they arrived at Tulagi on 12 October. The remaining four boats (PT 37, 39, 45 and 61) arrived in similar fashion on 25 October. While at Tulagi, under the command of Lt Hugh Robinson, RON 3 (2) operated against Rear Admiral Raizo Tanaka's 'Tokyo Express'. In December RON 3(2) was joined by the 77ft and 80ft boats of RON 2, both squadrons continuing to be actively engaged throughout the Solomons campaign.

While most of the 77ft boats operated in the warm waters of the South Pacific, four of RON 1's boats (PT 22, 24, 27, and 28) had to endure the rigours of the Aleutian climate. On 30 July, 1942, the four boats left Pearl Harbor aboard the steamer *Irvin Macdowell*, arriving at Seattle, Washington, on 11 August. At Seattle, each boat was fitted with a 20mm aft, apparently the first time this weapon was mounted on the early 77ft boats. Leaving Seattle on 20 August, the boats covered the 2500 miles to Dutch Harbor in 12 days. There, PT 28 was fitted with an aircraft radar, another apparent first. For the next four months, the already-stressed boats operated in the harsh Alaskan climate, enduring the cold, wind, collisions, and groundings. Finally, during a three-day storm at Dora Harbor in mid-January, all four boats were badly damaged and PT 28 was driven ashore and broke up. After the storm, the remaining three boats were surveyed and it was determined that PT 24 and PT 27 could be repaired locally; PT 22, however, could not and was to be shipped stateside for repairs. Fate intervened, however, and PT 22 was dropped from the crane while being loaded aboard a Liberty ship, becoming a constructive total loss.

PT 20, first of the 77ft boats, on trials. USN

By summer 1944, most of the surviving 77ft boats were worn out. A number were reclassified as small boats and served as squadron 'hacks' or VIP transports, while others appear to have been transferred to the US Army in New Guinea for clandestine operations. A few of the 77ft boats operated with RON 4, the training squadron at Melville, Rhode Island, where PT 39, 40, and 59 were eventually used for hull repair training; PT 39 was extensively modified while at Melville. In the photograph showing her during a War Bond Rally parade in New York City, she looks very different from her original form. She has the superstructure and deck stiffeners of a second-series 77ft PT, smoke generator and roll-off racks of an 80ft PT, and a 20mm Mark 10 mount in place of the Mark 4. Apparently an engineroom explosion had destroyed the original superstructure and it was replaced by a complete second-series unit, which raises an interesting question. Did this unit come from another boat, or did Elco produce spares?

The ten boats in Royal Navy service, MTB 307–316 (ex-PT 49–58), differed from their US Navy counterparts primarily in armament and minor fittings. In place of the four torpedo tubes and twin turrets, the Royal Navy MTBs mounted only two 21in torpedo tubes at a fixed angle and a single Vickers Mark V turret on the centreline of the coachroof; the 20mm aft was retained. A single depth charge on a roll-off rack was fitted on either side of the deck edge, aft of the Oerlikon mount. Some boats, including MTB 315, mounted two single 0.50 calibre Brownings on tripods forward of the pilothouse.

The ten RN Elcos were assigned to the 15th MTB Flotilla in the Mediterranean and were shipped at about the same time as the 70ft boats of the 10th MTB. The 15th MTB came under the command of Lt Denis Jermain and, in May, moved to Tobruk, where it operated with the 10th MTB, under Noakes. When Tobruk fell in June 1942, the boats moved to Alexandria, from where in August they conducted an unsuccessful attack on a convoy. On 13–14 September, the 15th and 10th MTB took part in the disastrous 'Operation Agreement', a simultaneous assault by combined forces against Tobruk and Benghazi. The Germans were ready for them and, in the ensuing confusion, three of the 15th's boats (MTB 308, 310, 312) were lost in attacks by Italian aircraft, while MTB 314 grounded and was captured. Ironically, following repairs, ex-MTB 314 operated as the German Navy patrol boat RA 10, eventually being sunk by the RAF!

Beautiful builder's model of PT 41 in 1/16 scale currently on display at the MacArthur Museum. MacArthur rode the 41 boat during his escape from the Philippines in 1941. USN

Following the Tobruk debacle, the 15th MTB was dissolved and the surviving boats joined the 10th MTB under Jermain at Alexandria. From there, they took part in the battle for El Alamein; then, in December, moved to Malta for operations against Tripoli and Sicily. In January 1943 the 10th moved to Bone for the Tunisian campaign. During a sweep off Cani Rocks on May 2, MTB 311 hit a mine and had to be sunk by gunfire. In July the flotilla moved across to Augusta for operations in the Strait of Messina. On 17 July, MTB 260, 313, 315, and 316 engaged the Italian light cruiser *Scipione Africano* with the loss of MTB 316, which was apparently hit by a broadside from the cruiser and blew up. By the autumn of 1943 the 10th had been transferred to the Aegean, operating from Casteloriso until 28 November, when the base was evacuated due to German successes in the area. For the next ten months, the flotilla maintained a nomadic existence, operating from advanced anchorages until September 1944 when it moved to Khios. Operations continued throughout the Aegean until the end of the war, at which point the remaining boats were returned to the US Navy for disposal.

77-foot Elco PT data
Length overall   77ft 0in
Beam   19ft 11in
Draught   5ft 3in
Displacement   46 tons
Machinery   3 × 4M2500 Packard petrol engines, 1350shp at 2500rpm = 4050shp
Speed   41 knots
Cruising radius   1400nm
Armament
   PT 20–44
   2 × twin 0.50 calibre Browning M2 machine guns
   4 × 21in torpedoes
   or
   2 × 21in torpedoes
   8 × Mark 6 depth charges
   PT 45–48, 59–68
   2 × twin 0.50 calibre Browning M2 machine guns
   1 × 20mm Mark 4
   4 × 21in torpedoes
   or
   2 × 21in torpedoes
   8 × Mark 6 depth charges
   MTB 307–316
   1 × twin 0.5in Vickers Mark V mount
   1 × 20mm Oerlikon
   2 × 21in torpedoes
   2 × depth charges

Armament

USN boat number PT	Armament as built	Known modifications while in service
20, 21, 23, 25, 26, 29	2 × twin 0.50 Browning M2 in Dewandre turrets	single 0.30 cal on tripod added forward
36–40, 42–44	4 × 21in Mk 8 Mod 3 torpedoes in Mk 18 Mod 1 TT	
22, 24, 26, 27	as above	single 0.30 cal on tripod added forward, 20mm added aft 8.42
30	as above	undetermined
31–35, 41	as above	2 × single 0.303 Lewis on pipe mounts added forward before 9.41
45	2 × twin .50 Browning M2 in Mk 17 mounts 1 × 20mm Mk 4 aft 4 × 21in Mk 8 Mod 3 torpedoes in Mk 18 Mod 1 TT	single 0.30 cal on tripod added forward
46–48	2× twin 0.50 Mk 17 1 × 20mm Mk 4 aft 1 × 0.30 Browning forward 4 × 21in Mk 18 TT	single 0.30 cal on tripod added forward
49–58	1 × twin 0.50 Vickers Mk V amidships 2 × 0.303 Lewis forward 2 × 21in TT RN pattern	undetermined
59–61	2 × twin 0.50 Browning M2 in Mk 17 mounts 1 × 20mm Mk4 aft 4 × 21in Mk 8 Mod 3 torpedoes in Mk 18 Mod 1 TT	tubes removed, 2 × 40mm Mk 3 added fore and aft, 6 × twin 0.50 added alongside superstructure
62–65, 67, 68	as above	undetermined
66	as above	1 × 0.50 cal added at forecastle, 2 × 21in Mk 18 TT, 4 × depth charges; none as small boat

Looking aft on a first-series 77ft boat. The engineroom hatch and escape scuttle are in the centre of the photo. USN

Construction list

Boat number	Keel laid	Launched	Placed in service	Squadrons (in order of assign-ment)	Fate
PT					
20	14.10.40	14. 3.41	20. 6.41	2, 1	To RON 1 13.8.41. Stricken as obsolete 22.12.44. Sold
21	2.12.40	11. 4.41	21. 6.41	1, 3(2)	To RON 3(2) 22.12.42; to RON 2 27.9.43. Stricken as obsolete 11.10.43. Sold
22	10.12.40	18. 4.41	21. 6.41	2, 1	To RON 1 13.8.41. Damaged in storm Dora Harbor, Alaska 12.1.43. Scrapped 11.6.43 *in situ*
23	14.12.40	24. 4.41	25. 6.41	1, 3(2), 2	To RON 3(2) 22.12.42; to RON 2 27.9.43. Reclassified as small boat C 55047 6.10.43
24	27.12.40	30. 4.41	26. 6.41	2, 1	To RON 1 13.8.41. Reclassified as small boat 12.12.44. Stricken 14.7.47
25	6. 1.41	5. 5.41	26. 6.41	1, 3(2), 2	To RON 3(2) 22.12.42; to RON 2 27.9.43. Reclassified as small boat C 55048 6.10.43
26	30. 1.41	10. 5.41	18. 6.41	1, 3(2), 2	To RON 3(2) 22.12.42; to RON 2 27.9.43. Reclassified as small boat C 55049 6.10.43
27	12. 2.41	15. 5.41	27. 6.41	1	Reclassified as small boat 9.12.44
28	20. 2.41	20. 5.41	30. 6.41	2, 1	To RON 1 13.8.41. Wrecked in storm Dora Harbor, Alaska 12.1.43
29	28. 2.41	24. 5.41	2. 7.41	1	Stricken as obsolete 22.12.44. Sold
30	7, 3.41	28. 5.41	3. 7.41	2, 1	To RON 1 13.8.41. Stricken as obsolete 6.3.44. Sold 3.1.47
31	13. 3.41	2. 6.41	8. 7.41	1,3	To RON 3 12.8.41. Destroyed to prevent capture, Subic Bay 19.1.42
32	19. 3.41	6. 6.41	10. 7.41	2, 3	To RON 3 12.8.41. Destroyed to prevent capture, Tagauayan, Philippines 13.3.42
33	25. 3.41	10. 6.41	11. 7.41	1, 3	To RON 3 12.8.41. Aground and destroyed to prevent capture, Cape Santiago, Philippines 26.12.41
34	29. 3.41	14. 6.41	12. 7.41	2, 3	To RON 3 12.8.41. Lost to Japanese aircraft off Cauit Island, Philippines 9.4.42
35	3. 4.41	19. 6.41	16. 7.41	1, 3	To RON 3 12.8.41. Destroyed to prevent capture, Cebu City, Philippines 12.4.42
36	8. 4.41	21. 6.41	27. 8.41	2, 3(2)	To RON 3(2) 11.11.43. Reclassified as small boat C 73994 15.4.44
37	12. 4.41	25. 6.41	18. 7.41	1, 2, 3(2)	To RON 2 13.8.41; to RON 3(2) 27.7.42. Sunk by Japanese destroyer *Kawakaze* off Cape Esperance, Solomons 1.2.43
38	17. 4.41	28. 6.41	18. 7.41	2, 3(2)	To RON 3(2) 27.7.42. Reclassified as small boat C 68730 16.2.44

Boat number	Keel laid	Launched	Placed in service	Squadrons (in order of assign- ment)	Fate
39	22. 4.41	2. 7.41	21. 7.41	1, 2, 3(2)	To RON 2 13.8.41; to RON 3(2) 27.7.42; to MTB Squadrons Training Center, Melville, RI, for training repair personnel 7.8.44. Reclassified as small boat 14.10.44. To Bureau of Ordnance for destruction 1.45
40	25. 4.41	7. 7.41	22. 7.41	2, 3(2)	To RON 3(2) 11.11.43. Reclassified as small boat C 73995 15.4.44
41	30. 4.41	8. 7.41	23. 7.41	1, 3	To RON 3 12.8.41; to US Army 13.4.42. Destroyed to prevent capture on road to Lake Lanao, Mindanao 4.42
42	5. 5.41	12. 7.41	25. 7.41	2, 1	To RON 1 13.8.41. Stricken as obsolete 22.12.44. Sold
43	14. 5.41	16. 7.41	26. 7.41	1, 2	To RON 2 13.8.41. Damaged by Japanese warships, beached Guadalcanal and destroyed to prevent capture 11.1.43
44	17. 5.41	18. 7.41	31. 7.41	2	Destroyed by Japanese warships off Guadalcanal 12.12.42
45	21. 5.41	6. 8.41	6. 9.41	2, 3(2)	To RON 3(2) 27.7.42. Reclassified as small boat 15.4.44
46	21. 5.41	6. 8.41	6. 9.41	2, 3(2)	To RON 3(2) 27.7.42. Reclassified as small boat C 74095 15.4.44
47	4. 6.41	14. 8.41	9. 9.41	2, 3(2)	To RON 3(2) 11.11.43; to MTB Squadrons Training Centre, Melville, RI, for training repair personnel 7.8.44. Reclassified as small boat 14.10.44. For disposal 21.3.47
48	6. 6.41	21. 8.41	15. 9.41	2, 3(2)	To RON 3(2) 27.7.42; to MTB Squadrons Training Center, Melville, RI, for training repair personnel 7.8.44. Reclassified as small boat 14.10.44
			Completed		
49	6. 6.41	21. 8.41	20. 1.42	15th MTB Fl, 10th MTB Fl	Built for RN as PT (BPT) 1, transferred 4.2.42 as MTB 307. Returned USN 3.10.45
50	17. 6.41	26. 8.41	22. 1.42	15th MTB Fl	Built for RN as PT (BPT) 2, transferred 31.1.42 as MTB 308. Bombed by Italian aircraft Tobruk 14.9.42
51	23. 6.41	3. 9.41	9. 2.42	15th MTB Fl, 10th MTB Fl	Built for RN as PT (BPT) 3, transferred 11.2.42 as MTB 309. Returned USN 10.9.45
52	26. 6.41	8. 9.41	10. 2.42	15th MTB Fl	Built for RN as PT (BPT) 4, transferred 20.2.42 as MTB 310. Bombed by Italian aircraft Tobruk, 14.9.42
53	1. 7.41	12. 9.41	23. 2.42	15th MTB Fl, 10th MTB Fl	Built for RN as PT (BPT) 5, transferred 17.2.42 as MTB 311. Mined off Bone, Algeria 2.5.43
54	7. 7.41	16. 9.41	23. 2.42	15th MTB Fl	Built for RN as PT (BPT) 6, transferred 21.2.42 as MTB 312. Bombed and sunk by Italian aircraft Tobruk 14.9.42

The second-series 77ft boats incorporated deck stiffeners running alongside the trunk cabin, as seen here on PT 66. At this time, PT 66 had been reclassified as a small boat and was operating as a VIP transport. USN

Boat number	Keel laid	Launched	Placed in service	Squadrons (in order of assign-ment)	Fate
55	10. 7.41	22. 9.41	28. 2.42	15th MTB Fl, 10th MTB Fl	Built for RN as PT (BPT) 7, transferred 28.2.42 as MTB 313. Returned USN and sold at Alexandria 2.47
56	15. 7.41	25. 9.41	28. 2.42	15th MTB Fl (RN), 6th Raumboot Fl (KM)	Built for RN as PT (BPT) 8, transferred 28.2.42 as MTB 314. Damaged in attack on Tobruk and captured 14.9.42. German RA 10, 6th Raumboot Flotilla. Sunk by RAF off La Goulette 30.4.43
57	18. 7.41	30. 9.41	7. 3.42	15th MTB Fl, 10th MTB Fl	Built for RN as PT (BPT) 9, transferred 7.3.42 as MTB 315. Returned USN 10.9.45
58	22. 7.41	3.10.41	10. 3.42	15th MTB Fl, 10th MTB Fl	Built for RN as PT (BPT) 10, transferred 14.3.42 as MTB 316. Sunk by Italian cruiser *Scipione Africano* in Strait of Messina 17.7.43
			Placed in service		
59	26. 7.41	8.10.41	5. 3.42	4, 2, 3(2)	To RON 2 7.5.42; converted to motor gunboat 10.43; to RON 3(2) 11.11.43; to MTB Squadrons Training Center, Melville, RI, for training repair personnel 7.8.44. Reclassified as small boat
60	30. 7.41	11.10.41	25. 2.42	4, 2, 3(2)	To RON 2 7.5.42; to RON 3(2) 27.7.42. Converted to motor gunboat 10.43. Stricken as obsolete 21.4.44
61	2. 8.41	15.10.41	19. 2.42	4, 2, 3(2)	To RON 2 7.5.42; to RON 3(2) 27.7.42. Converted to motor gunboat 10.43. Reclassified as small boat C 68371 16.2.44
62	6. 8.41	20.10.41	10. 2.42	4, 5	To RON 5 15.4.43. Stricken as obsolete 20.1.45. Sold
63	9. 8.41	23.10.41	7. 2.42	4, 5	To RON 15.4.43. Lost by accidental fire while refuelling at Emirau Island 18.6.44
64	13. 8.41	28.10.41	28. 1.42	4, 5	To RON 5 15.4.43. Stricken as obsolete 20.1.45
65	16. 8.41	31.10.41	24. 1.42	4, 5	To RON 5 15.4.43. Stricken as obsolete 20.1.45. Sold
66	20. 8.41	5.11.41	22. 1.42	4, 8	To RON 8 1.10.42. Reclassified as small boat 23.2.45
67	23. 8.41	8.11.41	19. 1.42	4, 8	To RON 8 1.10.42. Lost by accidental fire while refuelling at Tufi, New Guinea 17.3.43
68	27. 8.41	13.11.41	13. 1.42	4, 8	To RON 8 1.10.42. Aground Vincke Point, New Guinea and destroyed to prevent capture 1.10.43

Note: PT 49–58 did not enter service as PTs.

Note: Date of completion and entry into service were usually the same. There were only a few exceptions.

Good clear view of the pilothouse on PT 28. A single 0.30 calibre Browning machine gun on a tripod is fitted forward. RON 3 boats carried two single 0.303 Lewis guns on pipe stands forward instead. USN

Lines and frames

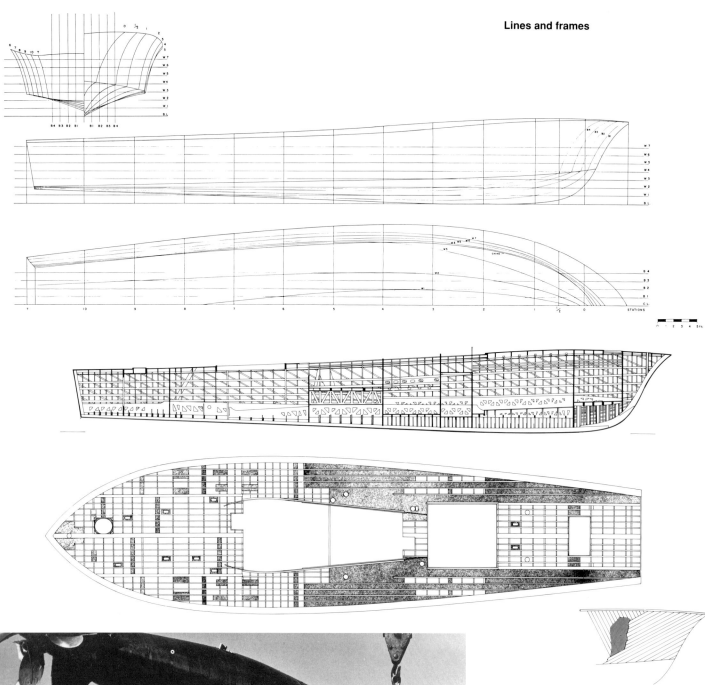

A torpedo being loaded on PT 64, probably at Melville. The portion of the tube next to the trunk cabin has been painted black or dark grey. USN

**General arrangement, side profile
and deck plan PT 20 series**

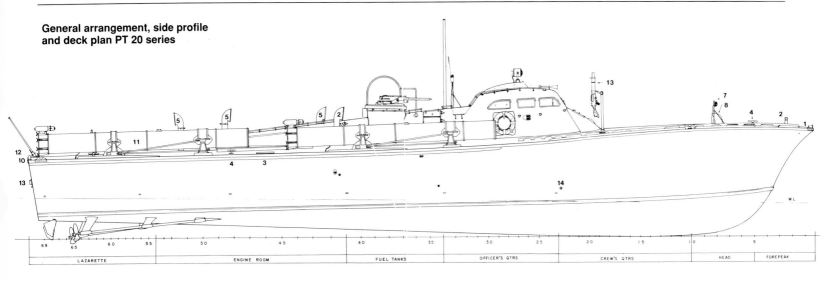

LAZARETTE | ENGINE ROOM | FUEL TANKS | OFFICER'S QTRS | CREW'S QTRS | HEAD | FOREPEAK

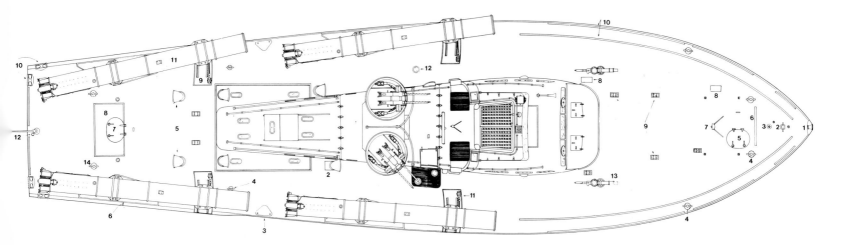

Aft section details

1 Fuel fill
2 Blower vent
3 Boarding ladder pad
4 5in bitt
5 Cowl vents
6 Deck guard extension
7 Scuttle to lazarette
8 Main lazarette hatch
9 Torpedo tube training gear
10 Chocks
11 Mk 18 torpedo tube
12 Stern light
13 Exhaust pipes
14 9in bitt

Forward section details – PT 20

1 Bow fairlead
2 Samson post
3 Flagstaff socket
4 9in bitt
5 Hatch
6 Rail for hatch dodger
7 Bow light
8 Vent
9 Deadlights
10 Toe rails
11 Torpedo training gear
12 Fuel fill
13 0.303 calibre Lewis machine
   gun

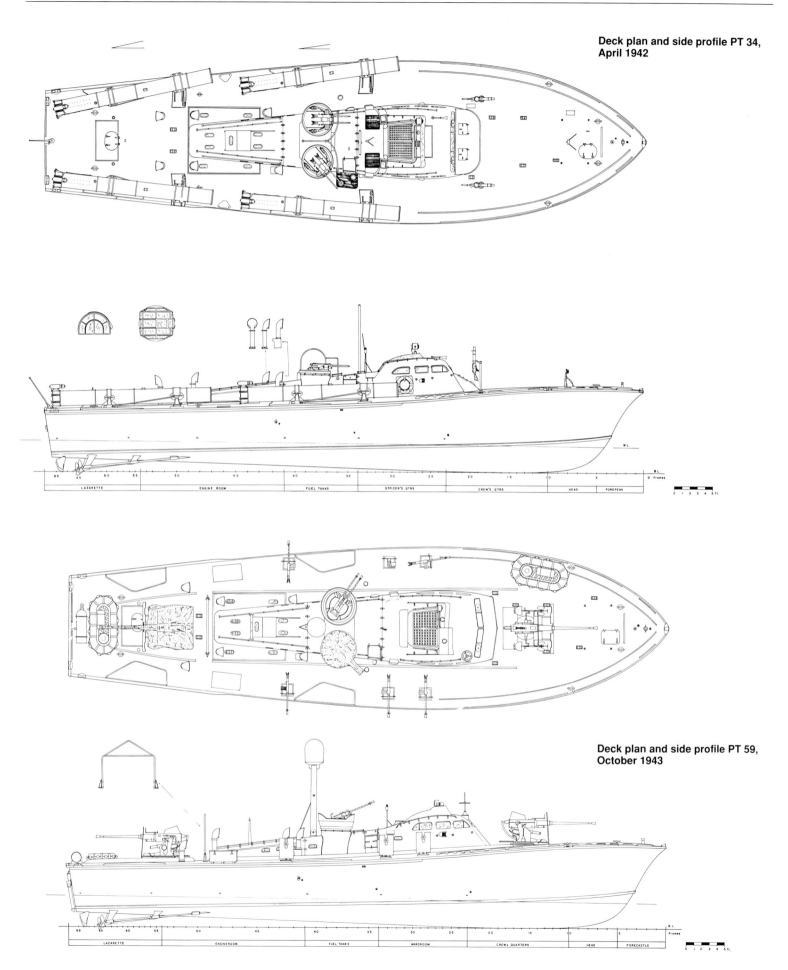

**Deck plan and side profile PT 34,
April 1942**

LAZARETTE | ENGINE ROOM | FUEL TANKS | OFFICER'S QTRS | CREW'S QTRS | HEAD | FOREPEAK

**Deck plan and side profile PT 59,
October 1943**

LAZARETTE | ENGINEROOM | FUEL TANKS | WARDROOM | CREWs QUARTERS | HEAD | FORECASTLE

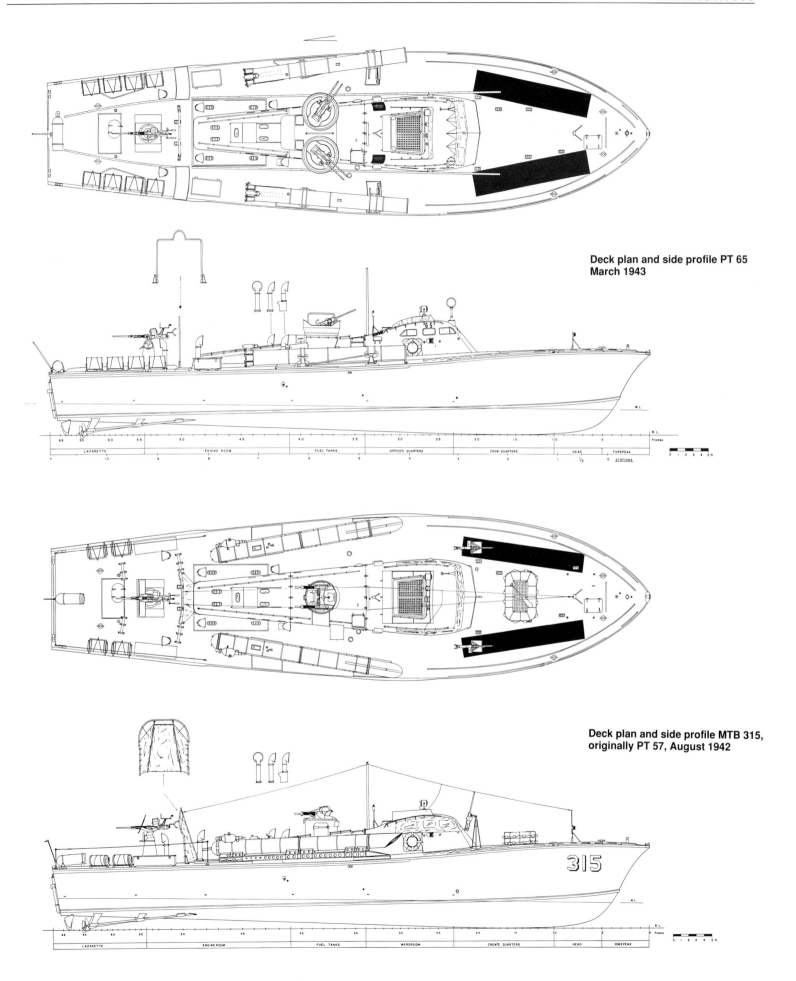

**Deck plan and side profile PT 65
March 1943**

LAZARETTE • ENGINE ROOM • FUEL TANKS • OFFICER QUARTERS • CREW QUARTERS • HEAD • FOREPEAK
STATIONS

**Deck plan and side profile MTB 315,
originally PT 57, August 1942**

315

LAZARETTE • ENGINE ROOM • FUEL TANKS • WARDROOM • CREW'S QUARTERS • HEAD • FOREPEAK

Inboard profile and plan

1   Chain locker
2   Hatch to forecastle
3   Sliding door to crew's WC
4   Locker
5   Pipe berth
6   Settee berth
7   Dish rack
8   Pilot house floor
9   Pilot house helm
10 Drop windows
11 Cockpit floor
12 Cockpit helm
13 0.50 calibre turret
14 Vent
15 Fuel tanks
16 Engineroom canopy hatch
17 Fixed windows
18 Ladder
19 Fresh water tanks
20 Workbench
21 Water closet
22 Sinks
23 Stove
24 Ladder
25 LUX tanks
26 Folding table
27 Radio room
28 Sink

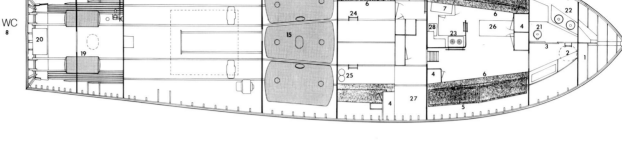

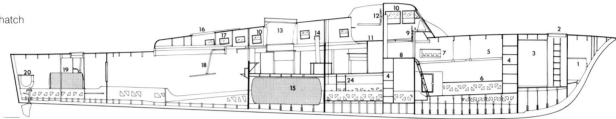

Sections

1   Grab rail
2   Mirror
3   Danforth anchor
4   Sink
5   Sliding hatch to crew's quarters
6   Shelf
7   Water closet
8   Hanging locker
9   Clothing lockers
10 Pipe berth
11 Settee berth
12 Stateroom sink
13 Helm
14 Clear-screen motor
15 Charthouse throttle
16 Charthouse instrument panel
17 Companion to crew's quarters

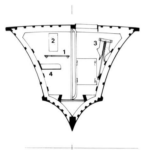

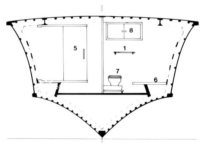

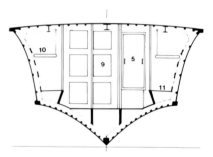

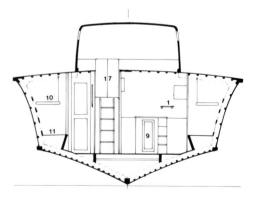

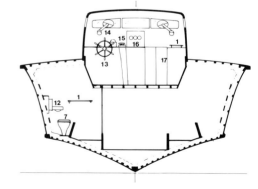

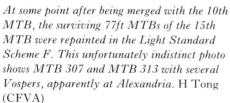

At some point after being merged with the 10th MTB, the surviving 77ft MTBs of the 15th MTB were repainted in the Light Standard Scheme F. This unfortunately indistinct photo shows MTB 307 and MTB 313 with several Vospers, apparently at Alexandria. H Tong (CFVA)

Joiner section

1 King plank – mahogany
2 Decking – ⅝in mahogany plywood
3 Deck beam – African mahogany
4 Gusset – plywood
5 Covering board – mahogany
6 Rubbing strip – white oak
7 Side planking – mahogany
8 Chine – white oak
9 Bottom planking – mahogany
10 Removable deck plates – ⅜in aluminium/balsa ply
11 Keel – Sitka spruce
12 Seat top – ¼in plywood

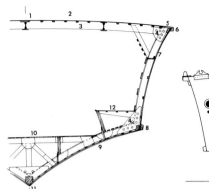 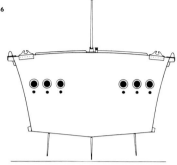 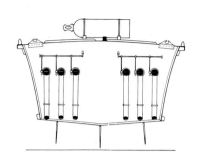

Superstructure rear view

1 Searchlight/fogbell
2 Grabrail
3 Binnacle
4 Throttle quadrant
5 Torpedo director base
6 Radar scope (PT 59–61 as gunboats)
7 Sprayshield/depression rail (PT 45–48, 59–68)
8 Vickers Mk V turret (MTB 307–316)
9 Locker (MTB 307–316)
10 Locker (PT 44–48, 59–68)

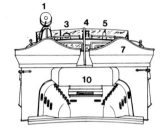 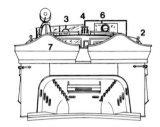 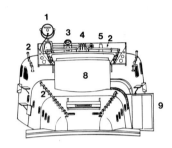

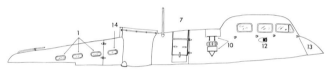

PT 10-19, PTC 1-12

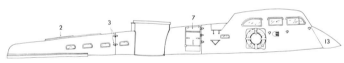

PT 20-44

Differences in 70ft and 77ft superstructures – side view

1 Drop windows
2 Engineroom canopy hatch
3 'Fishtail' plates fastening superstructure sections
4 Boat hook
5 Locker
6 Depression rail for 0.50 calibre machine guns
7 Turret section hatch
8 Access to Vickers Mk V ammunition boxes
9 Locker
10 Steps
11 Radio direction finder (RDF)
12 Sidelight
13 Alloy boot
14 Fixed window
15 Hinged armour plate (RN boats only); platform on US boats

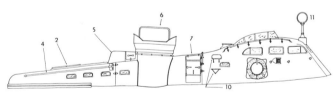

PT 45-48, 59-68

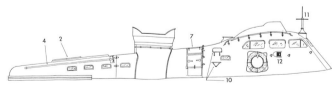

PT 59-61 AS AN MGB

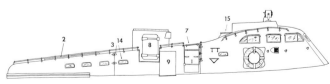

MTB 307-316

An RC model built by Wayne Traxel illustrates the changes made to PT 48. In place of the four tubes, she carries only two Mark 13 torpedoes and four depth charges. W Traxel

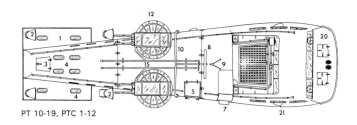

PT 10-19, PTC 1-12

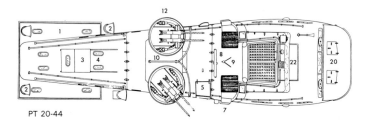

PT 20-44

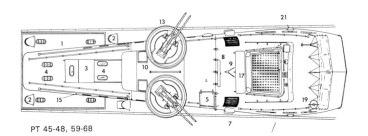

PT 45-48, 59-68

**Differences in 70ft and 77ft
superstructures – top view**

1   Main engineroom hatch
2   Cowl vent
3   Engineroom canopy hatch
4   Deadlights
5   Turret section hatch
6   Locker (RN boats only)
7   Steps
8   Telescoping mast
9   Anchor light
10 Depression rail
11 SO radar
12 Dewandre turret
13 Mk 17 turret
14 Vickers Mk V turret
15 Boat hooks
16 'Fishtail' plates
17 Platform
18 Armour plate (RN boats only)
19 Radio direction finder (RDF)
20 Alloy boot
21 Sidelight
22 Water tank access hatch
23 Deck stiffeners
24 Cutout for access to Vickers Mk
    V turret

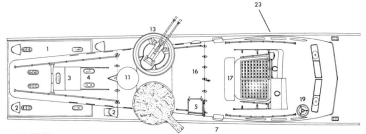

PT 59-61 AS AN MGB

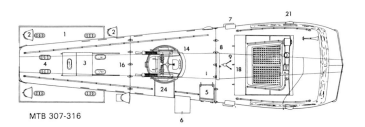

MTB 307-316

The Elco 80ft PT

During the summer of 1941, the US Navy conducted two series of trials to gather collective data on existing PT types. The results of these trials, which became known as the 'Plywood Derbies', would be used to establish a standard production design. The first 'Plywood Derby' was held during 21–24 July 1941 off New London, Connecticut, and involved boats from Higgins, Huckins, Elco, and the Philadelphia Navy Yard. Huckins entered one boat, PT 69; Higgins entered three, PT 6, PT 70 and a 69ft boat (MRB–1) built for the Royal Navy; the Philadelphia Navy Yard entered the aluminium-hulled PT 8; Elco entered five 77ft boats, PT 20, 21, 26, 30, 31 and 33. The second 'Derby' was held on 12 August 1941, and involved only PT 8, 21, 29, 69, 70 and MRB–1.

Based on the results of the two 'Derbies', the Navy indicated that a heavier, more powerful boat was required. The new specifications, issued in autumn 1941, required a boat between 75 and 82 feet in length, powered by three muffled Packard engines, and capable of sustaining 40 knots for at least an hour at full load displacement. Accommodation was to be provided for one officer and eight to ten men, with provisions for 48 hours.

The new design would have to be capable of being mass-produced and was not to incorporate any novelties or features which could not be easily replicated in boat yards other than the original designer's. This requirement was prompted by the Board's knowledge of the effects of bombing on industry in Europe. Captain Cochrane, head of the Board, stated

> . . . we don't want to be put in a position where having once developed the type, something happens to the plant – it may run into fire casualty or something like that – something which has happened abroad in a good many places, and we don't want to be stuck until that plant can build a new plant . . . henceforth, we'll be able to, or must be able to, order boats of any one of the designs built this time from any of the yards . . .

To avoid duplicating the structural weaknesses inherent in the 77ft design, the board was very specific in its recommendations:

The keel stem and stern post frames, deck beams, longitudinals, clamps, shelves, and chine shall be securely through-bolted or riveted and not screwed. Deck longitudinals and side keelsons shall be run continuously the entire length of the boat, as early as possible, with adequate butt joints, and no discontinuities. The arrangement of the engine hatches and opening for trunk cabin house shall be made to suit the deck longitudinals. The side and bottom planking shall be made in two layers of mahogany with muslin between. The decking shall be laid in two layers with the upper courses running fore and aft, with muslin between.

These specifications effectively eliminated the jogged longitudinal of the earlier Elco design, placing less stress on the frames and decking. The Board also stipulated that only a single, outside steering position was required (earlier designs, including most European types, incorporated a steering position in the charthouse) and that the torpedo tubes be easily removed to facilitate the fitting of depth charges if the tactical situation required.

The Elco, Higgins, and Huckins companies were invited by the Navy to submit designs meeting the new specifications. This invitation resulted in major contracts being awarded to Higgins and Elco, with Huckins receiving only a minor contract for six boats (eighteen were eventually built). Despite receiving its contract after Higgins and Huckins, Elco's boats were in squadron service months before their competitors. On 31 January 1942, the General Board adopted the 80ft type as the standard for further construction.

Elco apparently had a winner in its 80ft design. A survey of experienced PT skippers conducted by the Commanding Officer of the Motor Torpedo Boat Squadron Training Center (MTBSTC) in September 1942, indicated a definite preference for the Elco over the Higgins and Huckins boats. Interestingly, the second-series 77ft boats (PT 45–48, 59–68) were considered by many of the officers to be at least equal in some aspects to the 80ft boat! The 77ft

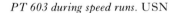

PT 603 during speed runs. USN

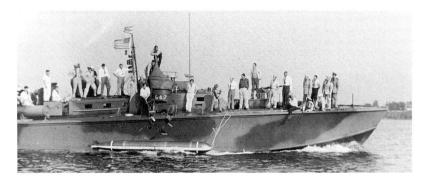

PT 547 retrieving a torpedo during practice firing. This is an interesting shot, as it shows her with a Mark 1 roll-off rack forward and a Mark 18 torpedo tube aft. Camouflage is Measure 31/5P. USN

PT 596 during summer 1945. USN

An excellent view of the instrument panel of a late 80ft Elco, taken 11 April 1945. The bracket in the centre is for the Mark 8 rocket sight. USN

boat was lighter, several knots faster, had a shallower draught and lower silhouette, had a longer cruising radius, and could actually out-accelerate the 80ft type. The 80ft boat was the ultimate choice, however, as it was stronger, rode easier, had better ahead firepower, a smaller turning circle, better interior arrangement, and was more capable of absorbing the inevitable weight increases due to increased armament.

Accommodation, layout, and compartment access on the 80ft boat were considered outstanding for such relatively small craft. Watertight bulkheads separating the compartments were fitted with watertight doors, allowing access to all compartments from within. On the Higgins and Huckins boats, it was necessary to go on deck to move from one compartment to another. The bilges were easily accessed for cleaning and inspection, as well.

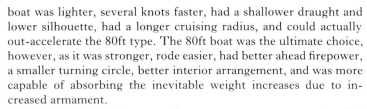

Bow view of PT 596, taken August 1945. The two Mark 50 rocket launchers have been swung outboard to firing position. USN

Mufflers on an 80ft Elco. USN

Test firing a torpedo from the Mark 19 tube on PT 731, one of the Soviet Elcos. Elco

PT 601 was sold to Norway in 1951 and served under the name Hai. *Marinemuseet*

Eighty-foot PTs of RON 24 and 25 in 1944, variously armed and camouflaged. PT 340, in the foreground, has a twin 0.50 calibre mount in front of the forward torpedo, while PT 336, moored alongside, had a Mark 8 rocket launcher in the same position. USN

Although only 3ft longer than her 77ft predecessor, the 80ft boat was an entirely different design and actually much larger. The hard chine hull, constructed of two layers of mahogany set diagonally to each other, was sleek, graceful, and yet deadly in appearance. The superstructure consisted of an angular chart house and day cabin, on each of which was mounted a Mark 170.50 calibre turret, *en echelon*. The forward turret was mounted on the charthouse to starboard, while the aft turret was fitted to port on the aft corner of the day cabin. This arrangement gave a wider firing arc than the earlier Elcos and the current Higgins boats. Abaft the day cabin was the engineroom hatch, on which were mounted four cowl vents and an access hatch.

The size and placement of the turrets and the access hatch are the primary identifying features between the two series of Elco PTs. On the first series (PT 103–196, 314–367), the forward turret was mounted about three feet forward of the aft bulkhead of the chart house, while the access hatch was only slightly raised above the engineroom hatch. On the second series (PT 372–383, 486–563, 565–622), the turret was moved to the aft bulkhead of the chartroom and the access hatch greatly enlarged to double as a vent.

Power was provided by the usual three 4M2500 Packard V-12 petrol engines, initially rated at 1350shp, and eventually at 1500shp. To feed these petrol-hungry engines, each boat carried 3000 gallons of 100 octane in fuel tanks amidships. Needless to say, fire was a constant threat and a number of boats were lost in this manner.

The internal arrangement of the 80ft boats was not unlike that of the earlier 70ft and 77ft types, with crew's WC and quarters forward; wardroom, fuel tanks, and engineroom amidships; and lazarette aft. The superstructure varied considerably from that of the earlier boats, however. The charthouse was quite small internally and provided space for only one or two crew members. An examination of the charthouse of the restored PT 617 revealed how little room there actually was, particularly between the latter leading below and the bulkhead. Along with the charts and other navigation aids, the charthouse contained the radar scope and radio gear.

The day cabin provided a 'lounge' of sorts for the crew and incorporated several berths. Internal access to the day cabin was through a watertight door on the starboard side forward, a companionway into the engineroom aft, and a hatch in the overhead. A

PT 504, RON 34, during a visit by King George VI. She carries a 40mm aft and only two roll-off racks. USN

A view of PT 109 as deck cargo on the steamer
Joseph Stanton, *taken at Norfolk, VA, on 20*
August 1942. USN

Close-up of the forward turret, launching rack
and rocket magazine on PT 588, April 1945.
USN

Close-up of a RON 34 boat during an
inspection by King George VI. USN

PT 140 operating with RON 4, the training squadron. The censor has painted out the radar mast, but missed the radar mast support on the aft portion of the day cabin roof. USN

The depression rail on the late 80ft Elcos were also used to lock the 40mm barrel in place when not in use. Note that the 40mm has the camouflage pattern, Measure 31/20L. USN

hatch was also fitted to the aft turret, opening into the day cabin, for ammunition passing. The sides of the day cabin were fastened to the deck, but the top was a separate unit and could be lifted off for fuel tank removal.

Armament varied considerably on the 80ft boats, particularly as the war progressed. As designed, they carried two twin 0.50 calibre

An overall view of PT 588 at the Elco plant in early April 1945, displaying the starboard side of the Measure 31/20L paint scheme. The deck is Deck Green (20–G). USN

machine guns in Mark 17 mounts, a single Mark 4 20mm aft, and four 21in Mark 18 torpedo tubes. Like their earlier 77ft sisters, provision was made for the replacement of the aft tubes by four depth charges. During 1943, the torpedo tubes were replaced by the much lighter roll-off racks for the 22.5in Mark 13 torpedo. This drastic reduction in weight allowed an increase in the size and number of automatic weapons carried. This was particularly important as targets worthy of a torpedo diminished and the PTs took on the role of motor gunboat, especially in the southwest Pacific, where the primary mission of the PTs had moved from sinking capital ships to 'barge busting'. As an example, by 1945, the standard configuration of a Pacific boat was:

- one 20mm Mark 14 forward, to port
- one 37mm M4 or M9 forward, on the centreline
- two twin Mark 170.50 calibre mounts
- two eight-barrelled, 5in spin stabilised rocket launchers forward
- four 22.5in Mark 13 torpedoes in roll-off racks
- one 40mm Mark 3 mount aft

In another variation, four RON 29 boats (Mediterranean) carried a single Thunderbolt, while the remainder retained the 40mm aft. Perhaps the most unusual modification was that fitted to the boats built specifically for the Soviet Navy (PT 731–760). In place of the four Mark 1 roll-off racks, the Soviet Elcos mounted a single, fixed Mark 19 torpedo tube and two type C depth charge racks on either side. The Mark 19 tubes are notable in that they were the same as those fitted to the early Higgins PTs, and launched their torpedoes by compressed air rather than by ignition of a black powder charge.

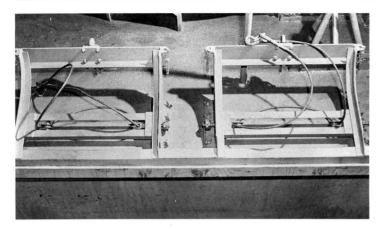

Depth charge racks on PT 731. USN

Stern view of a 600 series boat. Note the extreme aft position of the roll-off racks. The low box in front of the forward rack is for rocket storage. USN

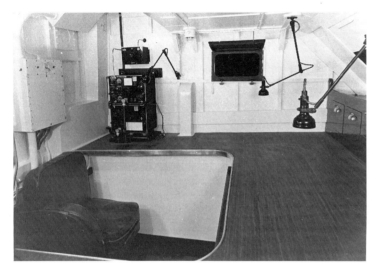

Interior of the chart house. Notice the fine finish on the chart table. Elcos were known for their superior construction and finish. Elco

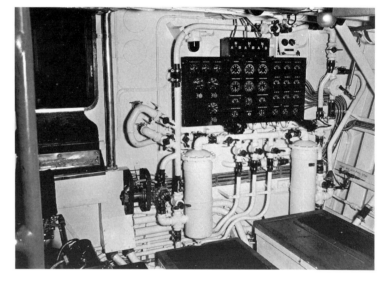

Main instrument panel, engineroom, 80ft Elco. Elco

Engineroom of an 80ft Elco, looking forward. Elco

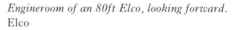

Inside the day cabin, looking aft. The aft turret is to the right of the photo, which shows the ammunition passing hatch. Underneath the deck were 3000 gallons of petrol. Elco

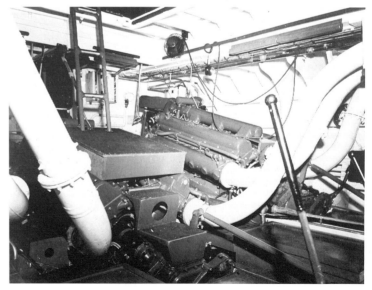

The most likely reason the tubes were fitted in place of the racks was that the tubes provided better protection from the elements for the torpedoes and the Soviet boats would have been operating in harsh climates.

Based on photographic evidence the 80ft Elcos seem to have had more weapons added than any of the other types. Additional 0.30 calibre, 0.50 calibre, and 20mm guns were often fitted wherever space allowed. Experiments were carried out with the 75mm M4 cannon (normally fitted to a B–25H) on the stern of PT 334 in early 1944. Other boats carried 57mm recoilless rifles, 60mm mortars, and a sextuple 2.36in rocket launcher. The latter, designated Mark 13, consisted of six tubes attached to a modified 0.30 calibre mount and was mounted on top of the day cabin on RON 25 boats. Photographs of the Mark 13 mount suggest it may have been made from a pair of triple launchers used by the USAAF at about the same time. Specific changes to the boats' armament, as near as could be determined, are provided in the accompanying tables.

Radar was important to the success of the PT and the first sets were fitted to the Elcos in 1943. A number of the RON 8 boats initially carried US Army SCR-517C units, easily identified by the large, segmented 'beehive' mounted on a short framework on the day cabin. Later, two units designed especially for the PTs were fitted: SO and SO3. Both units were mounted on a 13ft hinged, bipod mast fitted on the forward end of the day cabin. The two are easily distinguished: the SO had the familiar dome, while the SO3 was shaped more like a football, with the antenna exposed. Further details of the radar units will be provided in Volume III.

Most of the 80ft boats served in the Pacific, but two squadrons (RON 34, 35) operated in the English Channel and one (RON 29) in the Mediterranean. Conducting combined operations with RN Coastal Forces units, they faced quite different opponents than their Pacific counterparts. Most operations were against German minesweepers, Raumboats, Schnellboats, trawlers, and Flak lighters, as few major targets were left by this time. A comprehensive history of PT operations in all theatres is contained in the classic *At Close Quarters*.

80-foot Elco PTs data

Length overall   80ft 3in
Beam   20ft 7in
Draught   5ft 0in
Displacement   50 tons
Machinery   3 × 4M2500 Packard petrol engines, 1500shp at 2500rpm = 4500shp
Speed   44 knots
Cruising radius   1400nm

PT 174 was one of the few 80ft Elcos to carry a 40mm forward. In its original form, the gun was mounted within a spray shield and did not have the gunshield shown here. USN

Armament

USN boat number	Armament as built	Modifications while in service	USN boat number	Armament as built	Modifications while in service
PT			169	as above	1 × 37mm M4 forward, 4 × Mk 13 torpedoes in Mk 1 roll-off racks by 1.44
103–108, 110–114, 116–128, 130–137, 139–142, 144–148, 150–153, 155–156, 158, 159, 162–166, 170–173, 175–177, 179–186, 314–329, 332, 333, 335–342, 344–348, 350, 351, 353, 356–361	2 × twin 0.50 Browning M2 in Mk 17 mounts 1 × 20mm Mk 4 aft 4 × 21in Mk 8 Mod 3 torpedoes in Mk 18 TT	undetermined	174	2 × twin 0.50 Browning M2 in Mk 17 mounts 1 × 20mm Mk 4 aft 1 × shielded 40mm forward 4 × 21in Mk 8 Mod 3 torpedoes in Mk 18 TT	TT replaced by Mk 13 torpedoes and Mk 1 roll-off racks by 1944
109	as above	1 × 37mm M3 added forward 29.7.43 (see notes)	178	2 × twin 0.50 Browning M2 in Mk 17 mounts 1 × 20mm Mk 4 aft 4 × 21in Mk 8 Mod 3 torpedoes in Mk 18 Mod 1 TT	2 × twin 0.50 Mk 17, 1 × 37mm M4 and 2 × 20mm Mk 14 forward and 1 × 40mm Mk 3 aft, 4 × 22.5in Mk 13 torpedoes with Mk 1 roll-off racks
115	as above	1 × 20mm Mk 12 replaced 0.50 in forward turret, 4 × 22.5 Mk 13 torpedoes with Mk 1 roll-off racks 5.44	187–192	as above	3.43: 1 × 20mm Mk 12 replaced forward twin 0.50 Mk 17 mount; 1 × 20mm Mk 14 forward and 1 × 20mm Mk 10 aft
129	as above	2 × twin 0.50 Mk 17, 1 × 37mm M4 and 1 × 20mm Mk 14 forward, 1 × 40mm Mk 3 aft, 2 × gravity-fed rocket launchers forward, 4 × 22.5in Mk 13 torpedoes with Mk 1 roll-off racks	193, 194	as above	3.43: 1 × 20mm Mk 12 replaced forward twin 0.50 Mk 17 mount. 1 × 20mm Mk 14 forward and 1 × 40mm Mk 3 aft
138	as above	Thunderbolt with 0.50 and 20mm added lated 1942	195	as above	3.43: 1 × 20mm Mk 12 replaced forward twin 0.50 Mk 17 mount. 1 × 20mm Mk 14 forward and 1 × 40mm Mk 3 aft 9.44 (see notes)
143	as above	2 × twin 0.50 Mk 17, 3 × Mk 14 and 1 × 37mm M9 forward, 1 × 40mm Mk 3 aft, 4 × 22.5in Mk 13 torpedoes with Mk 1 roll-off racks, 1 × 60mm mortar, 4 × depth charges	196	2 × twin 0.50 Browning M2 in Mk 17 mounts 1 × 20mm Mk 14 forward 1 × 40mm Mk 3 aft 2 × 21in Mk 8 Mod 3 torpedoes in Mk 18 TT	undetermined
149	as above	2 × single 0.50 Browning M2 forward			
154	as above	1 × twin 0.50 Mk 17 in aft turret, 1 × 37mm M9 and 1 × 20mm Mk 14 forward, 1 × 20mm Mk 12 in forward turret, 1 × 40mm Mk 3 aft, 2 × 22.5in Mk 13 torpedoes with 4 × Mk 1 roll-off racks, 2 × depth charges aft	330	2 × twin 0.50 Browning M2 in Mk 17 mounts 1 × 20mm Mk 4 aft 4 × 21in Mk 8 Mod 3 torpedoes in Mk 18 Mod 1 TT	2 × twin 0.50 Mk 17, 1 × 37mm M4 and 1 × 20mm Mk 14 forward, 2 × single 0.50 amidships, 1 × 40mm Mk 3 aft, 4 × 22.4in Mk 13 torpedoes, 2 × depth charges in Type C racks forward
157	as above	20mm Mk 12 in forward turret 1943	331	as above	1 × 37mm M4 on tubular tripod forward and 1 × 20mm Mk 14 to port forward 1943
160	as above	Thunderbolt 11.42			
161	as above	1 × 37mm M4 and 1 × 20mm Mk 14 forward, 2 × twin 0.50 Browning M2 in Mk 17 mounts, 1 × 40mm Mk 3 aft, 4 × 22.5in Mk 13 torpedoes in Mk 1 roll-off racks	334	as above	experimentally fitted with 75mm M4 aft 1944
			343	as above	2 × twin 0.50 Mk 17, 2 × 20mm Mk 14 and 1 × 37mm M9 forward, 1 × 40mm Mk 3 aft, 2 × 22.5in Mk 13 torpedoes with 4 × Mk 1 roll-off racks, 2 × depth charges
167	as above	1 × 37mm M4 forward			
168	as above	1 × 37mm M4 and 1 × 57mm recoilless rifle added forward, TT replaced with Mk 13 torpedoes	349	as above	2 × twin 0.50 Mk 17, 1 × 20mm Mk 14 and 1 ×

USN boat number	Armament as built	Modifications while in service
		37mm M9 forward, 2 × rocket launchers forward, 2 × 22.5in Mk 13 torpedoes with Mk 1 roll-off racks, 2 × depth charges, 2 × 0.30 cal 1944: 2 × twin 0.50 Mk 17, 2 × 20mm Mk 14 forward, 2 × 22.5in Mk 13 torpedoes and 4 × Mk 1 roll-off racks, 1 × 40mm Mk aft, 2 × gravity-fed 4.5in rocket launchers forward, 2 × depth charges aft
352	as above	
353, 354	as above	mid-1943: 1 × 40mm replaced 20mm aft
362–373	2 × twin 0.50 Browning M2 in Mk 17 mounts 1 × 20mm Mk 4 aft 4 × 21in Mk 8 Mod 3 torpedoes in Mk 18 Mod 5 TT	undetermined
374–377	as above	autumn 1943: 1 × 40mm Mk 3 replaced aft 20mm
378–383	as above	undetermined
486–490, 492–497, 505, 522, 524, 526–532, 545–551	2 × twin 0.50 Browning M2 in Mk 17 mounts 1 × 20mm Mk 14 forward 1 × 20mm Mk 10 aft 4 × 22.5in Mk 13 torpedoes in Mk 1 roll-off racks	undetermined
491	as above	1 × 37mm M4 and 1 × 20mm Mk 14 added forward, 1 × 40mm Mk 3 probably added aft undetermined (USSR)
498–504, 507, 508, 510, 511, 513, 514, 516, 518, 521	as above	
506	as above	1944: 2 × twin 0.50 Browning M2 in Mk 17 mounts, 1 × 20mm Mk 14 forward, 1 × 40mm Mk 3 aft, 2 × 22.5in Mk 13 torpedoes in Mk 1 roll-off racks, 2 × depth charges; undetermined (USSR)
512	as above	2 × twin 0.50 Browning M2 in Mk 17 mounts, 1 × 20mm Mk 14 forward, 1 × 40mm Mk 3 aft, 2 × 22.5in Mk 13 torpedoes in Mk 1 roll-off racks, 2 × depth charges (USN); undetermined (USSR)
515	2 × twin 0.50 Mk 17 1 × 40mm Mk 3 aft 1 × 20mm Mk 14 forward 2 × 22.5in Mk 13 torpedoes in Mk 1 roll-off racks 2 × depth charges	37mm M9 added to port forward mid-1944
517	2 × twin 0.50 Browning M2	2 × twin 0.50 Mk 17, 1 ×

USN boat number	Armament as built	Modifications while in service
	in Mk 17 mounts 1 × 20mm Mk 14 forward 1 × 20mm Mk 10 aft 4 × 22.5in Mk 13 torpedoes in Mk 1 roll-off racks	37mm M9 to port forward, 1 × 40m Mk 3 aft, 2 × 22.5in Mk 13 torpedoes with Mk 1 roll-off racks, 2 × depth charges
519	as above	mid-1944: 37mm M9 added to port forward, 1 × 40mm Mk 3 aft, 2 × 22.5in Mk 13 torpedoes in Mk 1 roll-off racks, 2 × depth charges
520	as above	37mm M9 added to port forward mid-1944; undetermined (USSR)
523	as above	2 × twin 0.50 Browning M2 in Mk 17 mounts, 1 × 37mm M9 forward, 3 × 20mm Mk 14 forward (2 port, 1 starboard), 2 × single 0.30 Browning in cockpit, 1 × 60mm mortar forward, 1 × 60mm mortar forward, 1 × 40mm Mk 3 aft, 2 × 22.5in Mk 13 torpedoes with 4 × Mk 1 roll-off racks
525	as above	forward 20mm mount fitted with bracket and single 0.50 on either side
533–544	as above	two aft roll-off racks removed, additional 20mm Mk 14 fitted starboard, forward
552–555	as above	Spring 1944: 40mm Mk 3 replaced 20mm aft undetermined (USSR)
556	2 × twin 0.50 Browning M2 in Mk 17 mounts 1 × 20mm Mk 14 forward 1 Thunderbolt aft 2 × 22.5in Mk 13 torpedoes in Mk 1 roll-off racks	
557–559	as above	undetermined
560–563	2 × twin 0.50 Browning M2 in Mk 17 mounts 2 × 40mm Mk 3	undetermined (USSR)
565–622	2 × twin 0.50 Browning M2 in Mk 17 mounts 1 × 37mm M9 and 1 × 20mm Mk 14 forward 4 × 22.5in Mk 13 torpedoes in Mk 1 roll-off racks 2 × Mk 50 5in rocket launchers forward	undetermined
623, 624	as above	none
731–760	2 × twin 0.50 Browning M2 in Mk 17 mounts 1 × 20mm Mk 14 forward 1 × 20mm Mk 10 aft 2 × 21in Mk 19 TT	undetermined (USSR)

Construction list

Boat number	Hull number	Keel laid	Launched	Placed in service	Squadrons (in order of assignment)	Fate
103	3355	24.1.42	16. 5.42	12. 6.42	5, 18	To RON 18 15.2.45. Out of service, stripped, and destroyed 1.11.45
104	3356	29. 1.42	30. 5.42	19. 6.42	5, 18	To RON 18 15.2.45. Out of service, stripped, and destroyed 1.11.45
105	3357	5. 2.42	4. 6.42	26. 6.42	5, 18	To RON 18 15.2.45. Out of service, stripped, and destroyed 1.11.45
106	3358	12. 2.42	9. 6.42	1. 7.42	5, 24	To RON 24 15.2.45. Out of service, stripped, and destroyed 6.11.45
107	3359	16. 2.42	12. 6.42	3. 7.42	5	Lost by accidental fire while refuelling at Emirau Island 18. 6.44
108	3360	27. 2.42	17. 6.42	7. 7.42	5, 10	To RON 10 15.2.45. Out of service, stripped, and destroyed 11.11.45
109	3361	4. 3.42	20. 6.42	10. 7.42	5, 2	To RON 2 22.9.42. Rammed and sunk by Japanese destroyer *Amigiri* in Blackett Strait 2.8.43
110	3362	11. 3.42	24. 6.42	14. 7.42	5, 2, 8	To RON 2 22.9.42; to RON 8 1.6.43. Lost in collision Ablingi Harbour, New Guinea 26.1.44
111	3363	17. 3.42	27. 6.42	16. 7.42	5, 2	To RON 2 22.9.42. Destroyed by Japanese warships off Guadalcanal 1.2.43
112	3364	21. 3.42	3. 7.42	18. 7.42	5, 2	To RON 2 22.9.42. Destroyed by Japanese warships off Guadalcanal 11.1.43
113	3365	25. 3.42	3. 7.42	23. 7.42	5, 2, 8	To RON 2 22.9.42; to RON 8 1.4.43. Damaged by grounding on Veale Reef, Tufi, New Guinea 8.8.43. Scrapped
114	3366	30. 3.42	6. 7.42	25. 7.42	5, 2, 8	To RON 2 22.9.42; to RON 8 1.4.43. Out of service, stripped, and destroyed 28.10.45
115	3367	3. 4.42	9. 7.42	29. 7.42	6, 25	To RON 25 29.5.44. Out of service, stripped, and destroyed 9.11.45
116	3368	7. 4.42	13. 7.42	30. 7.42	6, 10	To RON 10 6.5.44. Out of service, stripped, and destroyed 11.11.45
117	3369	10. 4.42	15. 7.42	4. 8.42	6	Destroyed by Japanese aircraft at Rendova Harbor 1.8.43
118	3370	14. 4.42	18. 7.42	6. 8.42	6	Aground off Vella Lavella and destroyed to prevent capture 7.9.43
119	3371	22. 4.42	21. 7.42	8. 8.42	6	Destroyed by fire in port, Tufi, New Guinea 17.3.43
120	3372	22. 4.42	23. 7.42	12. 8.42	6, 8	To RON 8 1.4.43. Out of service, stripped, and destroyed 28.10.45
121	3373	25. 4.42	25. 7.42	27. 8.42	6, 8	To RON 8 1.4.43. Destroyed by Australian aircraft at Bangula Bay, New Britain 27.3.44
122	3374	28. 4.42	28. 7.42	15. 8.42	6, 8	To RON 8 1.4.43. Out of service, stripped, and destroyed 28.10.45
123	3375	2. 5.42	31. 7.42	18. 8.42	6	Destroyed by Japanese aircraft off Guadalcanal 1.2.43
124	3376	6. 5.42	3. 8.42	20. 8.42	6, 10	To RON 10 6.5.44. Out of service, stripped, and destroyed 11.11.45
125	3377	9. 5.42	6. 8.42	16. 8.42	6, 10	To RON 10 6.5.44. Out of service, stripped, and destroyed 11.11.45
126	3378	13. 5.42	10. 8.42	27. 8.42	6, 9	To RON 9 29.5.44. Out of service, stripped, and destroyed 24.11.45
127	3379	16. 5.42	13. 8.42	4. 9.42	7, 12	To RON 12 15.2.45. Out of service, stripped, and destroyed 26.10.45
128	3380	21. 5.42	17. 8.42	4. 9.42	7, 21	To RON 21 15.2.45. Out of service, stripped, and destroyed 10.11.45
129	3381	26. 5.42	19. 8.42	4. 9.42	7, 8	To RON 8 15.2.45. Out of service, stripped, and destroyed 28.10.45
130	3382	30. 5.42	22. 8.42	7. 9.42	7, 8	To RON 8 15.2.45. Out of service, stripped, and destroyed 28.10.45
131	3383	3. 6.42	26. 8.42	9. 9.42	7, 21	To RON 21 15.2.45. Out of service, stripped, and destroyed 10.11.45
132	3384	6. 6.42	28. 8.42	11. 9.42	7	To RON 21 15.2.45. Out of service, stripped, and destroyed 10.11.45
133	3385	10. 6.42	31. 8.42	16. 9.42	7	Destroyed by Japanese shore battery near Cape Pus, New Guinea 15.7.44
134	3386	13. 6.42	2. 9.42	17. 9.42	7, 25	To RON 25 15.2.45. Out of service, stripped, and destroyed 9.11.45
135	3387	17. 6.42	4. 9.42	21. 9.42	7	Aground near Crater Point, New Britain and destroyed to prevent capture 12.4.44
136	3388	20. 6.42	7. 9.42	23. 9.42	7	Aground Malai Island, New Guinea and destroyed to prevent capture 17.9.43
137	3389	24. 6.42	10. 9.42	25. 9.42	7, 33	To RON 33 15.2.45. Out of service, stripped, and destroyed 28.10.45
138	3390	27. 6.42	12. 9.42	29. 9.42	7, 33	To RON 33 15.2.45. Out of service, stripped, and destroyed 28.10.45
139	3391	30. 6.42	15. 9.42	13.10.42	4	Out of service 16.1.46. Sold 9.10.46
140	3392	3. 7.42	17. 9.42	10.10.42	4	Out of service 28.1.46. Sold 9.10.46
141	3393	7. 7.42	19. 9.42	10.10.42	4	Out of service 16.1.46. Sold 9.10.46
142	3394	9. 7.42	22. 9.42	10.10.42	8	Out of service, stripped, and destroyed 28.10.45
143	3395	13. 7.42	25. 9.42	13.10.42	8	Out of service, stripped, and destroyed 28.10.45
144	3396	15. 7.42	28. 9.42	15.10.42	8, 2, 8	To RON 2 1.43; to RON 8 1.6.43. Out of service, stripped, and destroyed 28.10.45
145	3397	18. 7.42	14.10.42	17.10.42	8, 2, 12	To RON 2 1.43; to RON 12 1.6.43. Aground Mindiri, New Guinea and destroyed to prevent capture 4.1.44
146	3398	21. 7.42	3.10.42	20.10.42	8, 2, 12	To RON 2 1.43; to RON 12 1.6.43. Out of service, stripped, and destroyed 26.10.45
147	3399	24. 7.42	6.10.42	23.10.42	8, 2, 18	To RON 2 1.43; to RON 18 1.6.43. Aground Teliata Point, New Guinea and destroyed to prevent capture 20.11.43
148	3400	27. 7.42	9.10.42	27.10.42	8, 2, 18	To RON 2 1.43; to RON 18 1.6.43. Out of service, stripped, and destroyed 1.11.45
149	3401	30. 7.42	12.10.42	29.10.42	8	Out of service, stripped, and destroyed 28.10.45
150	3402	1. 8.42	15.10.42	2.11.42	8, 12	To RON 12 10.5.43. Out of service, stripped, and destroyed 26.10.45
151	3403	5. 8.42	17.10.42	4.11.42	9, 12	To RON 12 10.5.45. Out of service, stripped, and destroyed 26.10.45
152	3404	7. 8.42	20.10.42	6.11.42	9, 12	To RON 12 10.5.45. Out of service, stripped, and destroyed 26.10.45
153	3405	10. 8.42	23.10.42	10.11.42	9	Aground near Munda Point, New Georgia and destroyed to prevent capture 4.7.43
154	3406	13. 8.42	27.10.42	13.11.42	9	Out of service, stripped, and destroyed 24.11.45
155	3407	15. 8.42	30.10.42	20.11.42	9	Out of service, stripped, and destroyed 24.11.45
156	3408	19. 8.42	2.11.42	18.11.42	9	Out of service, stripped, and destroyed 24.11.45
157	3409	21. 8.42	4.11.42	20.11.42	9	Out of service, stripped, and destroyed 24.11.45

Boat number	Hull number	Keel laid	Launched	Placed in service	Squadrons (in order of assignment)	Fate
158	3410	24. 8.42	7.11.42	23.11.42	9	Aground near Munda Point, New Guinea and destroyed to prevent capture 5.7.43
159	3411	27. 8.42	10.11.42	24.11.42	9	Out of service, stripped, and destroyed 24.11.45
160	3412	29. 8.42	13.11.42	7.12.42	9	Out of service, stripped, and destroyed 24.11.45
161	3413	2. 9.42	16.11.42	28.11.42	9	Out of service, stripped, and destroyed 24.11.45
162	3414	4. 9.42	19.11.42	2.12.42	9	Out of service, stripped, and destroyed 24.11.42
163	3415	7. 9.42	21.11.42	4.12.42	10	Out of service, stripped, and destroyed 11.11.45
164	3416	9. 9.42	24.11.42	8.12.42	10	Destroyed by Japanese aircraft at Rendova Harbour 1.8.43
165	3417	12. 9.42	27.11.42	11.12.42	10	Lost in transit 24.5.43 when transport torpedoed by Japanese submarine *I17* and sunk 100 miles south of Noumea, New Caledonia
166	3418	15. 9.42	30.11.42	22.12.42	10	Destroyed by USAAF B-25s in error off New Georgia 20.7.43
167	3419	18. 9.42	3.12.42	17.12.42	10	Out of service, stripped, and destroyed 11.11.45
168	3420	21. 9.42	5.12.42	22.12.42	10	Out of service, stripped, and destroyed 11.11.45
169	3421	24. 9.42	8.12.42	23.12.42	10	Out of service, stripped, and destroyed 11.11.45
170	3422	26. 9.42	14.12.42	28.12.42	10	Out of service, stripped, and destroyed 11.11.45
171	3423	29. 9.42	14.12.42	30.12.42	10	Out of service, stripped, and destroyed 11.11.45
172	3424	2.10.42	17.12.42	2. 1.43	10	Aground off Vella Lavella and destroyed to prevent capture 7.9.43
173	3425	5.10.42	20.12.42	2. 1.43	10	Lost in transit 24.5.43 when transport torpedoed by Japanese submarine *I17* and sunk 100 miles south of Noumea, New Caledonia
174	3426	7.10.42	23.12.42	6. 1.43	10	Out of service, stripped, and destroyed 11.11.45
175	3427	9.10.42	26.12.42	20. 1.43	11	Out of service, stripped, and destroyed 11.11.45
176	3428	13.10.42	29.12.42	20. 1.43	11	Out of service, stripped, and destroyed 11.11.45
177	3429	16.10.42	31.12.42	20. 1.43	11	Out of service, stripped, and destroyed 11.11.45
178	3430	19.10.42	2. 1.43	20. 1.43	11	Out of service, stripped, and destroyed 11.11.45
179	3431	21.10.42	5. 1.43	20. 1.43	11	Out of service, stripped, and destroyed 11.11.45
180	3432	24.10.42	7. 1.43	22. 1.43	11	Out of service, stripped, and destroyed 11.11.45
181	3433	27.10.42	9. 1.43	26. 1.43	11	Out of service, stripped, and destroyed 11.11.45
182	3434	30.10.42	13. 1.43	30. 1.43	11	Out of service, stripped, and destroyed 11.11.45
183	3435	2.11.42	15. 1.43	2. 2.43	11	Out of service, stripped, and destroyed 11.11.45
184	3436	5.11.42	19. 1.43	4. 2.43	11	Out of service, stripped, and destroyed 11.11.45
185	3437	7.11.42	21. 1.43	6. 2.43	11	Out of service, stripped, and destroyed 11.11.45
186	3438	11.11.42	23. 1.43	9. 2.43	11	Out of service, stripped, and destroyed 11.11.45
187	3439	13.11.42	26. 1.43	18. 2.43	12, 6, 9	To RON 6 10.5.43; to RON 9 29.5.44. Out of service 24.11.45. Sold 5.46
188	3440	17.11.42	28. 1.43	18. 2.43	12, 6, 8	To RON 6 10.5.43; to RON 8 29.5.44. Out of service, stripped, and destroyed 28.10.45
189	3441	19.11.42	30. 1.43	19. 2.43	12, 6	To RON 6 29.10.44. Out of service, stripped, and destroyed 28.10.45
190	3442	21.11.42	2. 2.43	19. 2.43	12	Out of service 26.10.45. Sold 5.46
191	3443	25.11.42	5. 2.43	24. 2.43	12	Out of service 26.10.45. Sold 5.46
192	3444	27.11.42	8. 2.43	25. 2.43	12	Out of service, stripped, and destroyed 26.10.45
193	3445	30.11.42	11. 2.43	27. 2.43	12	Aground Noemfoor Island, New Guinea and destroyed to prevent capture 25.6.44
194	3446	3.12.42	13. 2.43	3. 3.43	12	Out of service, stripped, and destroyed 26.10.45
195	3447	5.12.42	17. 2.43	6. 3.43	12	Out of service 26.10.45. Sold 5.46
196	3448	19. 2.42	19. 2.43	3. 5.43	12	Out of service, stripped, and destroyed 26.10.45
314	3449	11.12.42	20. 2.43	11. 3.43	5, 4	To RON 4 15.4.43. Out of service 16.1.46. Sold 23.6.48
315	3450	15.12.42	23. 2.43	15. 3.43	5, 4	To RON 4 15.4.43. Out of service 14.1.46. Sold 8.6.48
316	3451	15.12.42	25. 2.43	18. 3.43	5, 4	To RON 4 15.4.43. Out of service 16.1.46. Sold 29.12.47
317	3452	19.12.42	27. 2.43	19. 3.43	5, 4	To RON 4 15.4.43. Out of service 28.1.46. Sold 8.6.48
318	3453	23.12.42	3. 3.43	23. 3.43	5, 9	To RON 9 15.2.45. Out of service 24.11.45. Sold 5.46
319	3454	26.12.42	5. 3.43	26. 3.43	5, 9	To RON 9 15.2.43. Out of service 24.11.45. Sold 5.46
320	3455	30.12.42	9. 3.43	8. 4.43	21	Destroyed by Japanese aircraft Leyte Gulf 5.11.44
321	3456	2. 1.43	11. 3.43	8. 4.43	21	Aground San Isidro Bay, Leyte, and destroyed to prevent capture 11.11.44
322	3457	6. 1.43	13. 3.43	8. 4.43	21	Aground near Hardenberg Point, New Guinea and destroyed to prevent capture 24.11.43
323	3458	8. 1.43	17. 3.43	8. 4.43	21	Destroyed by Kamikaze, Leyte Gulf 10.12.44
324	3459	12. 1.43	19. 3.43	8. 4.43	21	Out of service, stripped, and destroyed 10.11.45
325	3460	14. 1.43	23. 3.43	10. 4.43	21	Out of service, stripped, and destroyed 10.11.45
326	3461	16. 1.43	25. 3.43	13. 4.43	21	Out of service 10.11.45. Sold 5.46
327	3462	19. 1.43	27. 3.43	15. 4.43	21	Out of service, stripped, and destroyed 10.11.45
328	3463	22. 1.43	31. 3.43	17. 4.43	21	Out of service 10.11.45. Sold 5.46
329	3464	25. 1.43	2. 4.43	21. 4.43	21	Out of service, stripped, and destroyed 10.11.45
330	3465	28. 1.43	7. 4.43	23. 4.43	21	Out of service, stripped, and destroyed 10.11.45
331	3466	30. 1.43	8. 4.43	27. 4.43	21	Out of service, stripped, and destroyed 10.11.45
332	3467	3. 2.43	10. 4.43	10. 5.43	24	Out of service 6.11.45. Sold 5.46
333	3468	5. 2.43	13. 4.43	10. 5.43	24	Out of service 6.11.45. Sold 5.46

Boat number	Hull number	Keel laid	Launched	Placed in service	Squadrons (in order of assignment)	Fate
334	3469	8. 2.43	15. 4.43	10. 5.43	24	Out of service 6.11.45. Sold 5.46
335	3470	10. 2.43	19. 4.43	10. 5.43	24	Out of service 6.11.45. Sold 5.46
336	3471	13. 2.43	22. 4.43	12. 5.43	24	Out of service 6.11.45. Sold 5.46
337	3472	17. 2.43	24. 4.43	14. 5.43	24	Destroyed by Japanese shore batteries Hansa Bay, New Guinea 7.3.44
338	3473	19. 2.43	28. 4.43	18. 5.43	24	Aground Semirara Island, Philippines 27.1.45 and destroyed 31.1.45
339	3474	22. 2.43	1. 5.43	22. 5.43	24	Aground near Pur Pur, New Guinea and destroyed to prevent capture 27.5.44
340	3475	25. 2.43	5. 5.43	25. 5.43	24	Out of service 6.11.45. Sold 5.46
341	3476	27. 2.43	7. 5.43	28. 5.43	24	Out of service 6.11.45. Sold 5.46
342	3477	2. 3.43	11. 5.43	31. 5.43	24	Out of service 6.11.45. Sold 5.46
343	3478	5. 3.43	13. 5.43	1. 6.43	24	Out of service 6.11.45. Sold 5.46
344	3479	8. 3.43	15. 5.43	17. 6.43	25	Out of service 9.11.45. Sold 5.46
345	3480	11. 3.43	19. 5.43	17. 6.43	25	Out of service, stripped, and destroyed 9.11.45
346	3481	13. 3.43	21. 5.43	17. 6.43	25	Destroyed in error by US Navy aircraft near Cape Pomas, New Britain 29.4.44
347	3482	17. 3.43	26. 5.43	17. 6.43	25	Destroyed in error by US Navy aircraft near Cape Pomas, New Britain 29.4.44
348	3483	20. 3.43	28. 5.43	17. 6.43	25	Out of service 9.11.45. Sold 5.46
349	3484	20. 3.43	28. 5.43	18. 6.43	25	Out of service 9.11.45. Sold 5.46
350	3485	25. 3.43	4. 6.43	22. 6.43	25	Out of service, stripped, and destroyed 9.11.45
351	3486	27. 3.43	8. 6.43	25. 6.43	25	Out of service, stripped, and destroyed 9.11.45
352	3487	31. 3.43	10. 6.43	28. 6.43	25	Out of service, stripped, and destroyed 9.11.45
353	3488	3. 4.43	12. 6.43	2. 7.43	25	Destroyed in error by Australian aircraft Bangula Bay, New Britain 27.3.44
354	3489	6. 4.43	16. 6.43	6. 7.43	25	Out of service 9.11.45. Sold 5.46
355	3490	9. 4.43	18. 6.43	8. 7.43	25	Out of service 9.11.45. Sold 5.46
356	3491	12. 4.43	22. 6.43	22. 7.43	27	Out of service 19.10.45. Sold 5.46
357	3492	15. 4.43	25. 6.43	22. 7.43	27	Out of service 19.10.45. Sold 5.46
358	3493	17. 4.43	29. 6.43	23. 7.43	27	Out of service 19.10.45. Sold 5.46
359	3494	21. 4.43	2. 7.43	22. 7.43	27	Out of service 19.10.45. Sold 5.46
360	3495	23. 4.43	6. 7.43	22. 7.43	27	Out of service 19.10.45. Sold 5.46
361	3496	27. 4.43	8. 7.43	27. 7.43	27	Out of service 19.10.45. Sold 5.46
362	3497	16.11.42	4. 5.43	15. 8.43	18	Out of service, stripped, and destroyed 1.11.45
363	3498	30.11.42	5. 5.43	15. 8.43	18	Destroyed by Japanese shore batteries Knoe Bay, Halmahera 25.11.44
364	3499	19.12.42	19. 5.43	15. 8.43	18	Out of service, stripped, and destroyed 1.11.45
365	3500	4. 1.43	20. 5.43	15. 8.43	18	Out of service, stripped, and destroyed 1.11.45
366	3501	18. 1.43	5. 6.43	15. 8.43	18	Out of service 4.11.45. Sold 5.46
367	3502	1. 2.43	7. 6.43	15. 8.43	18	Out of service, stripped, and destroyed 1.11.45
372	3503*	29. 4.43	10. 7.43	3. 8.43	27	Out of service 19.10.45. Sold 5.46
373	3504*	1. 5.43	13. 7.43	5. 8.43	27	Out of service 19.10.45. Sold 5.46
374	3505*	4. 5.43	16. 7.43	6. 8.43	27	Out of service 19.10.45. Sold 5.46
375	3506*	6. 5.43	20. 7.43	10. 8.43	27	Out of service 19.10.45. Sold 5.46
376	3507*	10. 5.43	23. 7.43	12. 8.43	27	Out of service 19.10.45. Sold 5.46
377	3508*	12. 5.43	27. 7.43	14. 8.43	27	Out of service 19.10.45. Sold 5.46
378	3509*	15. 5.43	30. 7.43	30. 8.43	28	Out of service 21.10.45. Sold 5.46
379	3510*	18. 5.43	3. 8.43	30. 8.43	28	Out of service 21.10.45. Sold 5.46
380	3511*	20. 5.43	6. 8.43	30. 8.43	28	Out of service 21.10.45. Sold 5.46
381	3512*	22. 5.43	10. 8.43	30. 8.43	28	Out of service 21.10.45. Sold 5.46
382	3513*	26. 5.43	12. 8.43	30. 8.43	28	Out of service 21.10.45. Sold 5.46
383	3514*	28. 5.43	14. 8.43	1. 9.43	28	Out of service 21.10.45. Sold 5.46
486	3533	27. 7.43	16.10.43	2.12.43	4	Out of service 16.1.46. Reclassified as small boat C 105335 27.8.46
487	3534	29. 7.43	21.10.43	10. 1.44	4	Out of service 28.1.46. Reclassified as small boat C 105336 27.8.46
488	3535	2. 8.43	23.10.43	2.12.43	33	Out of service 24.10.45. Sold 5.46
489	3536	5. 8.43	27.10.43	2.12.43	33	Out of service 24.10.45. Sold 5.46
490	3537	7. 8.43	29.10.43	2.12.43	33	Out of service 24.10.45. Sold 5.46
491	3538	11. 8.43	2.11.43	2.12.43	33	Out of service 24.10.45. Sold 5.46
492	3539	14. 8.43	4.11.43	2.12.43	33	Out of service 24.10.45. Sold 5.46
493	3540	18. 8.43	6.11.43	6.12.43	33	Destroyed by Japanese warships Surigao Strait 25.10.44
494	3541	20. 8.43	10.11.43	9.12.43	33	Out of service 24.10.45. Sold 5.46
495	3542	24. 8.43	12.11.43	13.12.43	33	Out of service 24.10.45. Sold 5.46
496	3543	26. 8.43	18.11.43	14.12.43	33	Out of service 24.10.45. Sold 5.46
497	3544	30. 8.43	20.11.43	18.12.43	33	Out of service 24.10.45. Sold 5.46
498	3545	2. 9.43	20.11.43	31.12.43	34	To USSR 4.3.45. Stricken and destroyed 1954
499	3546	4. 9.43	23.11.43	31.12.43	34	To USSR 30.12.44. Stricken and destroyed 1954
500	3547	8. 9.43	26.11.43	31.12.43	34	To USSR 30.12.44. Scuttled Barents Sea 1956

Boat number	Hull number	Keel laid	Launched	Placed in service	Squadrons (in order of assignment)	Fate
501	3548	10. 9.43	1.12.43	31.12.43	34	To USSR 31.1.45. Stricken and destroyed 1954
502	3549	14. 9.43	4.12.43	31.12.43	34	To USSR 31.1.45. Stricken 1954
503	3550	17. 9.43	8.12.43	4. 1.44	34	To USSR 30.12.44. Stricken and destroyed 1954
504	3551	20. 9.43	13.12.43	11. 1.44	34	To USSR 30.12.44. Stricken and destroyed 1954
505	3552	23. 9.43	14.12.43	13. 1.44	34, 4	To RON 4 29.12.44. Out of service 1.2.46. Sold 25.9.47
506	3553	25. 9.43	17.12.43	15. 1.44	34	To USSR 31.1.45. Stricken 1954
507	3554	29. 9.43	21.12.43	18. 1.44	34	To USSR 4.3.45. Stricken 1954
508	3555	2.10.43	24.12.43	21. 1.44	34	To USSR 31.1.45. Stricken 1954
509	3556	6.10.43	29.12.43	25. 1.44	34	Destroyed by ramming German minesweeper 9.8.44
510	3557	9.10.43	3. 1.44	15. 2.44	35	To USSR 30.12.44. Stricken and destroyed 1954
511	3558	13.10.43	5. 1.44	15. 2.44	35	To USSR 30.12.44. Stricken and destroyed 1954
512	3559	18.10.43	7. 1.44	15. 2.44	35	To USSR 30.12.44. Stricken and destroyed 1954
513	3560	21.10.43	12. 1.44	15. 2.44	35	To USSR 30.12.44. Stricken and destroyed 1954
514	3561	23.10.43	14. 1.44	15. 2.44	35	To USSR 4.3.45. Stricken 1954
515	3562	27.10.43	19. 1.44	17. 2.44	35	To USSR 4.3.45. Stricken and destroyed 1954
516	3563	30.10.43	21. 1.44	24. 2.44	35	To USSR 7.4.45. Scuttled Barents Sea 1956
517	3564	2.11.43	25. 1.44	25. 2.44	35	To USSR 7.4.45. Returned USN 1955
518	3565	5.11.43	28. 1.44	29. 2.44	35	To USSR 7.4.45. Scuttled Barents Sea 1956
519	3566	9.11.43	1. 2.44	1. 3.44	35	To USSR 7.4.45. Scuttled Barents Sea 1956
520	3567	11.11.43	7. 2.44	7. 3.44	35	To USSR 7.4.45. Scuttled Barents Sea 1956
521	3568	15.11.43	8. 2.44	11. 3.44	35	To USSR 7.4.45. Scuttled Barents Sea 1956
522	3569	18.11.43	11. 2.44	3. 4.44	36	Out of service 29.10.45. Sold 5.46
523	3570	22.11.43	15. 2.44	3. 4.44	36	Out of service 29.10.45. Sold 5.46
524	3571	25.11.43	18. 2.44	3. 4.44	36	Out of service 29.10.45. Sold 5.46
525	3572	29.11.43	24. 2.44	3. 4.44	36	Out of service 29.10.45. Sold 5.46
526	3573	2.12.43	29. 2.44	5. 4.44	36	Out of service 29.10.45. Sold 5.46
527	3574	6.12.43	3. 3.44	11. 4.44	36	Out of service 29.10.45. Sold 5.46
528	3575	8.12.43	7. 3.44	17. 4.44	36	Out of service 29.10.45. Sold 5.46
529	3576	11.12.43	14. 3.44	22. 4.44	36	Out of service 29.10.45. Sold 5.46
530	3577	16.12.43	21. 3.44	27. 4.44	36	Out of service 29.10.45. Sold 5.46
531	3578	30.12.43	28. 3.44	4. 5.44	36	Out of service 29.10.45. Sold 5.46
532	3579	23.12.43	3. 4.44	11. 5.44	36	Out of service 29.10.45. Sold 5.46
533	3580	29.12.43	8. 4.44	17. 5.44	37	Out of service 7.12.45. Sold 5.46
534	3581	4. 1.44	14. 4.44	5. 6.44	37	Out of service 7.12.45. Sold 5.46
535	3582	7. 1.44	21. 4.44	5. 6.44	37	Out of service 7.12.45. Sold 5.46
536	3583	12. 1.44	28. 4.44	5. 6.44	37	Out of service 7.12.45. Sold 5.46
537	3584	17. 1.44	5. 5.44	9. 6.44	37	Out of service 7.12.45. Sold 5.46
538	3585	21. 1.44	11. 5.44	15. 6.44	37	Out of service 7.12.45. Sold 5.46
539	3586	25. 1.44	17. 5.44	21. 6.44	37	Out of service 7.12.45. Sold 5.46
540	3587	29. 1.44	23. 5.44	28. 6.44	37	Out of service 7.12.45. Sold 5.46
541	3588	3. 2.44	30. 5.44	5. 7.44	37	Out of service 7.12.45. Sold 5.46
542	3589	7. 2.44	3. 6.44	10. 7.44	37	Out of service 7.12.45. Sold 5.46
543	3590	10. 2.44	9. 6.44	15. 7.44	37	Out of service 7.12.45. Sold 5.46
544	3591	15. 2.44	16. 6.44	21. 7.44	37	Out of service 7.12.45. Sold 5.46
545	3592	19. 2.44	26. 4.44	8. 9.44	4	Out of service 21.10.45. Sold 3.9.45
546	3515	1. 6.43	17. 8.43	3. 9.43	28	Out of service 21.10.45. Sold 5.46
547	3516	3. 6.43	21. 8.43	4.10.43	28	Out of service 21.10.45. Sold 5.46
548	3517	5. 6.43	24. 8.43	7. 9.43	28	Out of service 21.10.45. Sold 5.46
549	3518	9. 6.43	26. 8.43	10. 9.43	28	Out of service 21.10.45. Sold 5.46
550	3519	11. 6.43	28. 8.43	14. 9.43	28	Out of service 21.10.45. Sold 5.46
551	3520	15. 6.43	1. 9.43	16. 9.43	28	Out of service 21.10.45. Sold 5.46
552	3521	17. 6.43	4. 9.43	22.10.43	29	To USSR as TKA 578(?) 7.4.45. Stricken 1954
553	3522	21. 6.43	7. 9.43	22.10.43	29	To USSR as TKA 579(?) 12.4.45. Scuttled Barents Sea 1956
554	3523	24. 6.43	10. 9.43	22.10.43	29	To USSR as TKA 583(?) 8.5.45. Scuttled Barents Sea 1956
555	3524	28. 6.43	14. 9.43	26.10.43	29	Damaged by German mine off Cape Couronne 24.8.44 and sunk by US gunfire 8.9.44
556	3525	1. 7.43	16. 9.43	28.10.43	29	To USSR as TKA 580(?) 12.4.45. Scuttled Barents Sea 1956
557	3526	3. 7.43	18. 9.43	30.10.43	29, 4	To RON 4 23.11.44. Out of service 28.1.46. Reclassified as small boat C 105338 27.8.46
558	3527	7. 7.43	21. 9.43	2.11.43	29, 4	To RON 4 23.11.44. Out of service 28.1.46. Sold 12.3.48
559	3528	10. 7.43	24. 9.43	4.11.43	29, 4	To RON 4 23.11.44. Out of service 28.1.46. Reclassified as small boat C 105339 27.8.46
560	3529	14. 7.43	28. 9.43	6.11.43	29	To USSR as TKA 584(?) 8.5.45. Scuttled Barents Sea 1956
561	3530	16. 7.43	1.10.43	9.11.43	29	To USSR as TKA 581(?) 12.4.45. Scuttled Barents Sea 1956

Boat number	Hull number	Keel laid	Launched	Placed in service	Squadrons (in order of assignment)	Fate
562	3531	20. 7.43	5.10.43	11.11.43	29	To USSR as TKA 585(?) 7.4.45. Scuttled Barents Sea 1956
563	3532	23. 7.43	7.10.43	22.11.43	29	To USSR as TKA 582(?) 12.4.45. Scuttled Barents Sea 1956
565	3623	28. 4.44	20. 9.44	8.12.44	38	Out of service 24.10.45. Sold 5.46
566	3624	9. 5.44	29. 9.44	14.12.44	38	Out of service 24.10.45. Sold 5.46
567	3625	10. 5.44	10.10.44	17.12.44	38	Out of service 24.10.45. Sold 5.46
568	3626	13. 5.44	17.10.44	19.12.44	38	Out of service 24.10.45. Sold 5.46
569	3627	26. 5.44	25.10.44	23.12.44	38	Out of service 24.10.45. Sold 5.46
570	3628	2. 6.44	31.10.44	30.12.44	38	Out of service 24.10.45. Sold 5.46
571	3629	8. 6.44	9.11.44	14. 1.45	38	Out of service 24.10.45. Sold 5.46
572	3630	14. 6.44	15.11.44	16. 1.45	38	Out of service 24.10.45. Sold 5.46
573	3631	21. 6.44	22.11.44	23. 1.45	38	Out of service 24.10.45. Sold 5.46
574	3632	27. 6.44	5.12.44	7. 2.45	38	Out of service 24.10.45. Sold 5.46
575	3633	1. 7.44	11.12.44	7. 2.45	38, 39	To RON 39 28.9.45. Out of service 24.12.45. Sold 5.46
576	3634	7. 7.44	16.12.44	12. 2.45	38, 39	To RON 39 28.9.45. Out of service 24.12.45. Sold 5.46
577	3635	13. 7.44	30. 1.45	21. 2.45	39	Out of service 24.12.45. Sold 5.46
578	3636	19. 7.44	29.12.44	24. 2.45	39	Out of service 24.12.45. Sold 5.46
579	3637	27. 7.44	7. 2.45	2. 3.45	39	Out of service 24.12.45. Sold 5.46
580	3638	5. 8.44	12. 2.45	6. 3.45	39	Out of service 24.12.45. Sold 5.46
581	3639	14. 8.44	16. 2.45	8. 3.45	39	Out of service 24.12.45. Sold 5.46
582	3640	22. 8.44	21. 2.45	13. 3.45	39	Out of service 24.12.45. Sold 5.46
583	3641	31. 8.45	26. 2.45	20. 3.45	39	Out of service 24.12.45. Sold 5.46
584	3642	7. 9.44	2. 3.45	22. 3.45	39	Out of service 24.12.45. Sold 5.46
585	3643	14. 9.44	7. 3.45	28. 3.45	39	Out of service 24.12.45. Sold 5.46
586	3644	21. 9.44	12. 3.45	30. 3.45	39	Out of service 24.12.45. Sold 5.46
587	3645	28. 9.44	16. 3.44	4. 4.45	39	Out of service 24.12.45. Sold 5.46
588	3646	6.10.44	21. 3.45	10. 4.45	39	Out of service 24.12.45. Sold 5.46
589	3647	17.10.44	26. 3.45	13. 4.45	40	Out of service 21.12.45. Sold 5.46
590	3648	26.10.44	30. 3.45	16. 4.45	40	Out of service 21.12.45. Sold 5.46
591	3649	1.11.44	4. 4.45	19. 4.45	40	Out of service 21.12.45. Sold 5.46
592	3650	9.11.44	7. 4.45	21. 4.45	40	Out of service 21.12.45. Sold 5.46
593	3651	16.11.44	11. 4.45	25. 4.45	40	Out of service 21.12.45. Sold 5.46
594	3652	23.11.44	14. 4.45	28. 4.45	40	Out of service 21.12.45. Sold 5.46
595	3653	30.11.44	18. 4.45	4. 5.45	40	Out of service 21.12.45. Sold 5.46
596	3654	6.12.44	21. 4.45	10. 5.45	40	Out of service 21.12.45. Sold 5.46
597	3655	12.12.44	25. 4.45	16. 5.45	40	Out of service 21.12.45. Sold 5.46
598	3656	18.12.44	30. 4.45	21. 5.45	40	Out of service 21.12.45. Sold 5.46
599	3657	23.12.44	3. 5.45	25. 5.45	40	Out of service 21.12.45. Sold 5.46
600	3658	30.12.44	7. 5.45	31. 5.45	40	Out of service 21.12.45. Sold 5.46
601	3659	5. 1.45	11. 5.45	5. 6.45	41	Out of service 1.2.46. Reclassified as small boat C 6083 24.7.52
602	3660	10. 1.45	15. 5.45	8. 6.45	41	Out of service 30.1.46. To Norway and renamed Snogg (P 954) 1951; 15.7.55. Stricken 1.12.61
603	3661	16. 1.45	21. 5.45	28. 6.45	41	Out of service 30.1.46. To Norway and renamed Sel (P 950) 1951. Stricken 1.12.61
604	3662	25. 1.45	26. 5.45	13. 6.45	41	Out of service 30.1.46. To Norway and renamed Sild (P 951) 1951. Stricken 12.62
605	3663	31. 1.45	30. 5.45	18. 6.45	41	Out of service 30.1.46. To Norway and renamed Skrei (P 952) 1951. Scrapped 1959
606	3664	3. 2.45	5. 6.45	23. 6.45	41	Out of service 30.1.46. To Norway and renamed Snar (P 953) 1951, renamed Lyr 15.7.55. Stricken 1.3.62
607	3665	7. 2.45	11. 6.45	4. 7.45	41	Out of service 30.1.46. Sold 14.5.47
608	3666	12. 2.45	16. 6.45	14. 7.45	41	Out of service 30.1.46. To Norway and renamed Springer (P 955) 1951. Stricken 1966
609	3667	16. 2.45	21. 6.45	9. 7.45	41	Out of service 30.1.46. To Norway and renamed Hai (P 956) 1951. Stricken 1966
610	3668	21. 2.45	26. 6.45	19. 7.45	41	Out of service 30.1.46. To Norway and renamed Hauk (P 957) 1951, renamed Laks 15.7.55. Stricken 1966
611	3669	26. 2.45	30. 6.45	25. 7.45	41	Out of service 1.2.46. To Norway and renamed Hval (P 958) 1951. Stricken 1966
612	3670	2. 3.45	6. 7.45	31. 7.45	41	Out of service 1.2.46. To Norway and renamed Hvass (P 959) 1951, renamed Delfin 15.7.55. Stricken 1.12.61
613	3671	20. 1.45	15. 5.45	10. 8.45	42, 4	To RON 4 26.1.46; to Operational Development Force 15.4.46. To South Korea and renamed Olpamei (PT 26) 24.1.52. Lost in shipyard fire 18.9.52
614	3672	8. 3.45	12. 7.45	14. 8.45	42	Out of service 28.1.46. Reclassified as small boat C 105340 27.8.46
615	3673	14. 3.45	18. 7.45	5. 9.45	42	Out of service 28.1.46. Reclassified as small boat C 105341 27.8.46
616	3674	24. 3.45	24. 7.45	11. 9.45	42, 4	To RON 4 26.1.46; to Operational Development Force 15.4.46. To South Korea 1.52 and renamed Kaimaeki (Kalmakeki) (PT 23)
617	3675	29. 3.45	28. 7.45	21. 9.45	42	Out of service 28.1.46. Sold 3.10.47. Acquired by PT Boats Inc 1979 and restored to

Boat number	Hull number	Keel laid	Launched	Placed in service	Squadrons (in order of assignment)	Fate
						museum display Fall River, Massachusetts
618	3676	3. 4.45	3. 8.45	24. 9.45	42	Out of service 4.2.46. Reclassified as small boat 27.8.46
619	3677	9. 4.45	10. 8.45	1.10.45	42, 4	To RON 4 26.1.46; to Operational Development Force 15.4.46. To South Korea and renamed Koroki (Kiroki) (PT 25) 1.52. Hulk acquired by PT Boats Inc 1968 and shipped to Memphis, Tennessee
620	3678	13. 4.43	17. 8.45	5.10.45	42, 4	To RON 4 26.1.46; to Operational Development Force 15.4.46. To South Korea and renamed Ebi (Jebi) (PT 27) 1.52. Scrapped 1964
621	3679	19. 4.45	12. 9.45	12.10.45	42	Out of service 28.1.46. Sold 15.7.47
622	3680	24. 4.45	18. 9.45	20.10.45	42	Out of service 28.1.46. Sold 24.3.47
623	3681	30. 4.45	–	–		Contract cancelled 12.9.45
624	3682	–	–	–		Contract cancelled 12.9.45
				Completed		
731	3593	4. 4.44	4. 8.44	19. 9.44		To USSR 10.44. Scuttled Barents Sea 1956
732	3594	30. 3.44	–	3.10.44		To USSR in kit form 12.44. Returned USN 14.7.55
733	3595	5. 4.44	–	10.10.44		To USSR in kit form 12.44. Returned USN 14.7.55
734	3596	11. 4.44	–	10.10.44		To USSR in kit form 12.44. Returned USN 20.7.55
735	3597	16. 4.44	–	24.10.44		To USSR in kit form 12.44. Returned USN 20.7.55
736	3598	23. 4.44	–	24.10.44		To USSR in kit form 12.44. Returned USN 19.7.55
737	3599	28. 4.44	–	14.11.44		To USSR in kit form 12.44. Returned USN 19.7.55
738	3600	2. 5.44	–	14.11.44		To USSR in kit form 12.44. Stricken 1954
739	3601	8. 5.44	–	21.11.44		To USSR in kit form 12.44. Returned USN 2.7.55
739	3601	8. 5.44	–	21.11.44		To USSR in kit form 12.44. Returned USN 2.7.55
740	3602	12. 5.44	–	21.11.44		To USSR in kit form 12.44. Returned USN 2.7.55
741	3603	18. 5.44	–	25.11.44		To USSR in kit form 12.44. Stricken 1954
742	3604	23. 5.44	–	25.11.44		To USSR in kit form 12.44. Returned USN 9.7.55
743	3605	29. 5.44	–	30.11.44		To USSR in kit form 12.44. Returned USN 14.7.55
744	3606	3. 6.44	–	30.11.44		To USSR in kit form 12.44. Returned USN 9.7.55
745	3607	7. 6.44	–	9.12.44		To USSR in kit form 1.45. Returned USN 9.7.55
746	3608	12. 6.44	–	9.12.44		To USSR in kit form 1.45. Returned USN 2.7.55
747	3609	18. 6.44	–	14.12.44		To USSR in kit form 1.45
748	3610	22. 6.44	–	14.12.44		To USSR in kit form 1.45. Returned USN 2.7.55
749	3611	27. 6.44	–	23.12.44		To USSR in kit form 1.45. Stricken 1954
750	3612	2. 7.44	–	23.12.44		To USSR in kit form 1.45. Returned USN 9.7.55
751	3613	7. 7.44	–	30.12.44		To USSR in kit form 1.45. Returned USN 9.7.55
752	3614	12. 7.44	–	30.12.44		To USSR in kit form 1.45. Returned USN 9.7.55
753	3615	17. 7.44	–	4. 1.45		To USSR in kit form 1.45. Stricken 1954
754	3616	23. 7.44	–	4. 1.45		To USSR in kit form 1.45. Stricken 1954
755	3617	28. 7.44	–	10. 1.45		To USSR in kit form 2.45. Stricken 1954
756	3618	4. 8.44	–	10. 1.45		To USSR in kit form 2.45. Returned USN 14.7.55
757	3619	7. 8.44	–	20. 1.45		To USSR in kit form 2.45. Returned USN 14.7.55
758	3620	12. 8.44	–	20. 1.45		To USSR in kit form 2.45. Returned USN 14.7.55
759	3621	17. 8.44	–	26. 1.45		To USSR in kit form 2.45. Returned USN 14.7.55
760	3622	21. 8.44	–	26. 1.45		To USSR in kit form 2.45. Returned USN 9.7.55
761		19. 3.45	–	–		Contract cancelled 14.8.45, but hull apparently completed
762		10. 5.45	–	–		Cancelled 14.8.45
763		15. 5.45	–	–		Cancelled 14.8.45
764		19. 5.45	–	–		Cancelled 14.8.45
765		24. 5.45	–	–		Cancelled 14.8.45
766		30. 5.45	–	–		Cancelled 14.8.45
767		5. 6.45	–	–		Cancelled 14.8.45
768		11. 6.45	–	–		Cancelled 14.8.45
769		16. 6.45	–	–		Cancelled 14.8.45
770		22. 6.45	–	–		Cancelled 14.8.45
771		28. 6.45	–	–		Cancelled 14.8.45
772		4. 7.45	–	–		Cancelled 14.8.45
773		10. 7.45	–	–		Cancelled 14.8.45
774		17. 7.45	–	–		Cancelled 14.8.45
775		23. 7.45	–	–		Cancelled 14.8.45
776		30. 7.45	–	–		Cancelled 14.8.45
777		3. 8.45	–	–		Cancelled 14.8.45
778		9. 8.45	–	–		Cancelled 14.8.45

Boat number	Hull number	Keel laid	Launched	Placed in service	Squadrons (in order of assignment)	Fate
779	–	–	–	–		Cancelled 14.8.45
780	–	–	–	–		Cancelled 14.8.45
781	–	–	–	–		Cancelled 14.8.45
782	–	–	–	–		Cancelled 14.8.45
783	–	–	–	–		Cancelled 14.8.45
784	–	–	–	–		Cancelled 14.8.45
785	–	–	–	–		Cancelled 14.8.45
786	–	–	–	–		Cancelled 14.8.45
787	–	–	–	–		Cancelled 14.8.45
788	–	–	–	–		Cancelled 14.8.45
789	–	–	–	–		Cancelled 14.8.45
790	–	–	–	–		Cancelled 14.8.45

Note: *PT 372–383 assembled by Harbor Boat from kits supplied by Elco. All others built by Elco in Bayonne, NJ.

Note: PT 623, 624 and 731–790 were not placed in service as PTs.

Note: For vessels up to PT 622, date of completion and entry into service were usually the same. There were only a few exceptions.

An unidentified 80ft Elco, but probably one of the RON 9 boats, with 20mm MK12 mounts in both turrets, an unusual arrangement. USN

Looking down into the cockpit of an 80ft boat in the PT 486–563 range, as determined by the aerofoil fitted to the front of the windscreen. Note the throttles are to the left of the instrument panel. USN

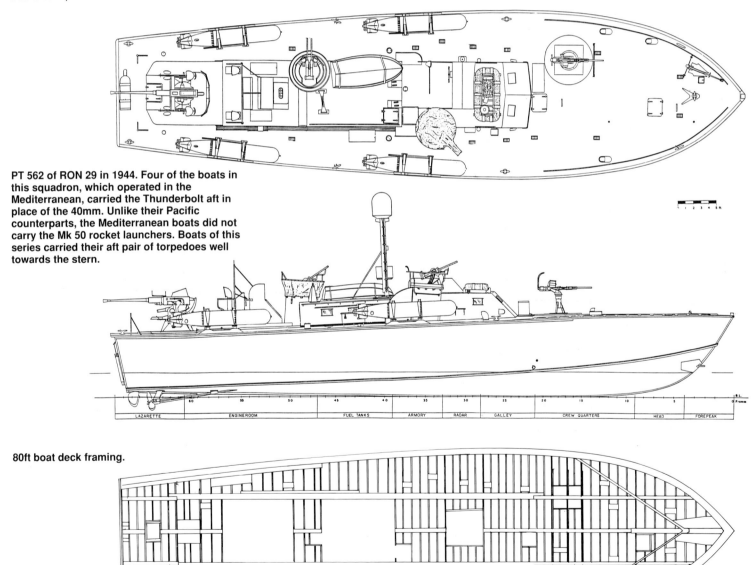

PT 562 of RON 29 in 1944. Four of the boats in this squadron, which operated in the Mediterranean, carried the Thunderbolt aft in place of the 40mm. Unlike their Pacific counterparts, the Mediterranean boats did not carry the Mk 50 rocket launchers. Boats of this series carried their aft pair of torpedoes well towards the stern.

LAZARETTE   ENGINEROOM   FUEL TANKS   ARMORY   RADAR   GALLEY   CREW QUARTERS   HEAD   FOREPEAK

80ft boat deck framing.

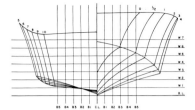

PT 103 series lines

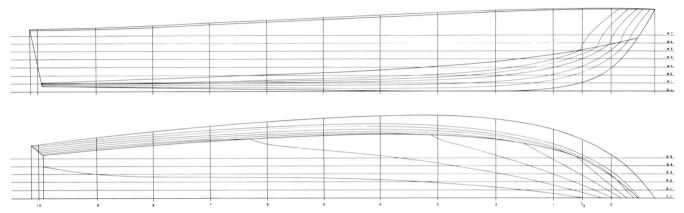

Aft section details – PT 103 series

1   Fuel fill
2   Cleat
3   Deadlight
4   Torpedo tube training gear
5   20mm Mk 4
6   Hatch to lazarette
7   Smoke canister
8   Stern cleat
9   Stern chock
10 Bitt
11 Mk 18 torpedo tube
12 Throttle linkage cover
13 Depression rail
14 Mushroom vent
15 Mufflers
16 LUX pull

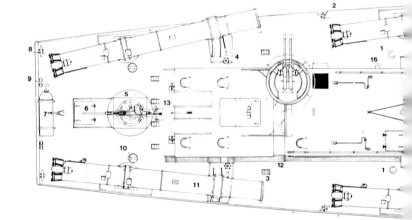

PT 103. Mufflers from astern

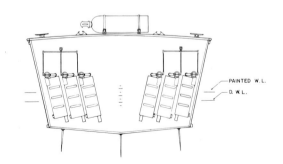

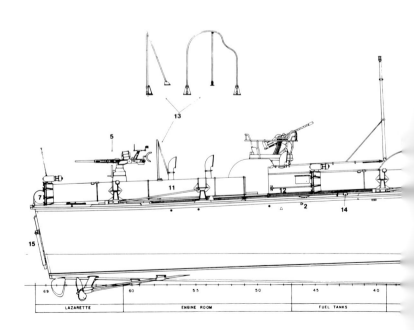

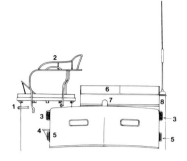

Front of charthouse – PT 103 series

1 Grab rail
2 Depression rail for 0.50 calibre
3 Sidelight
4 Step
5 Vent
6 Windscreen
7 Binnacle
8 Whip antenna

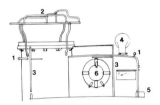

Aft view of day cabin – PT 103 series

1 Grab rail
2 Depression rail
3 Spray shield
4 Cowl vent
5 Throttle linkage cover
6 Life ring

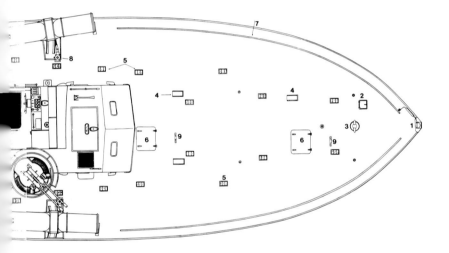

Forward section details – PT 103 series

1 Bow fairlead/light
2 Chain locker hatch
3 Bitt
4 Vent
5 Deadlights
6 Hatch
7 Toe rails
8 Training gear for torpedo tubes
9 Hatch catch
10 Overboard discharge

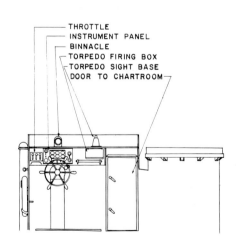

THROTTLE
INSTRUMENT PANEL
BINNACLE
TORPEDO FIRING BOX
TORPEDO SIGHT BASE
DOOR TO CHARTROOM

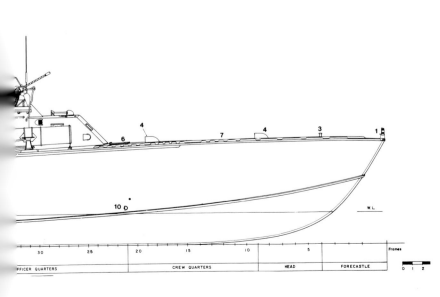

PT 109, August 1943

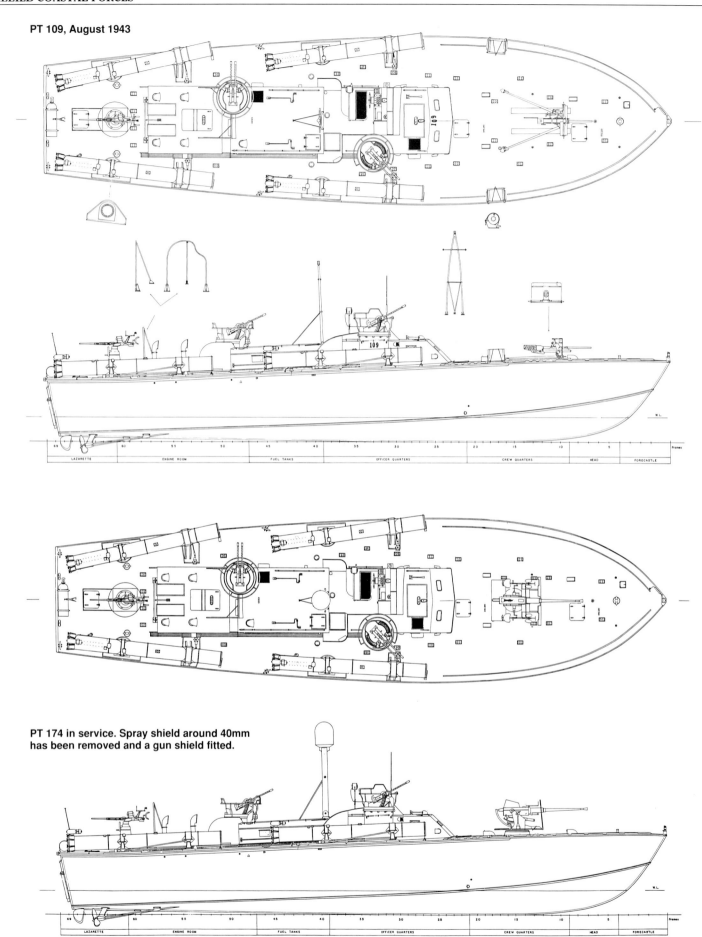

PT 174 in service. Spray shield around 40mm has been removed and a gun shield fitted.

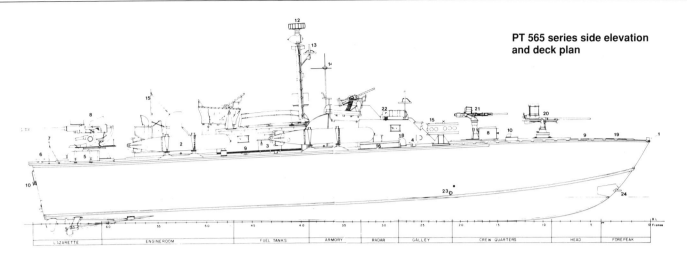

**PT 565 series side elevation
and deck plan**

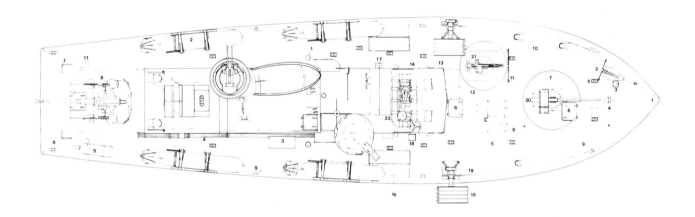

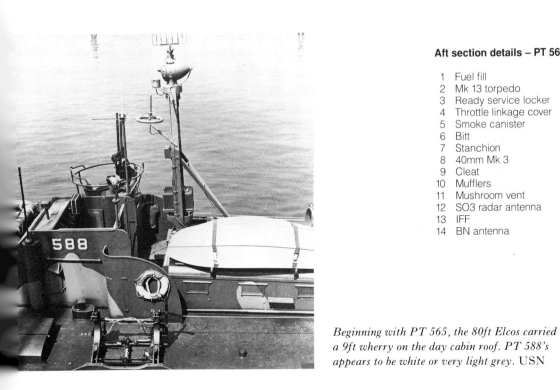

*Beginning with PT 565, the 80ft Elcos carried
a 9ft wherry on the day cabin roof. PT 588's
appears to be white or very light grey.* USN

Aft section details – PT 565 series

1 Fuel fill
2 Mk 13 torpedo
3 Ready service locker
4 Throttle linkage cover
5 Smoke canister
6 Bitt
7 Stanchion
8 40mm Mk 3
9 Cleat
10 Mufflers
11 Mushroom vent
12 SO3 radar antenna
13 IFF
14 BN antenna

**Forward section details – PT 565
series**

1 Bow fairlead/light
2 Danforth anchor
3 Chain locker hatch
4 Bitt
5 Deadlights
6 Hatch
7 Base for 37mm
8 37mm ready service lockers
9 Cleat
10 Vents
11 20mm barrel lock
12 20mm ready service locker
13 Charthouse vent
14 Sidelight
15 Mk 50 rocket launcher
16 Rocket ready service locker
17 Whip aerial
18 Vent
19 Toe rail
20 37mm
21 20mm Mk 14
22 Liferaft
23 Overboard discharge
24 Towing eye

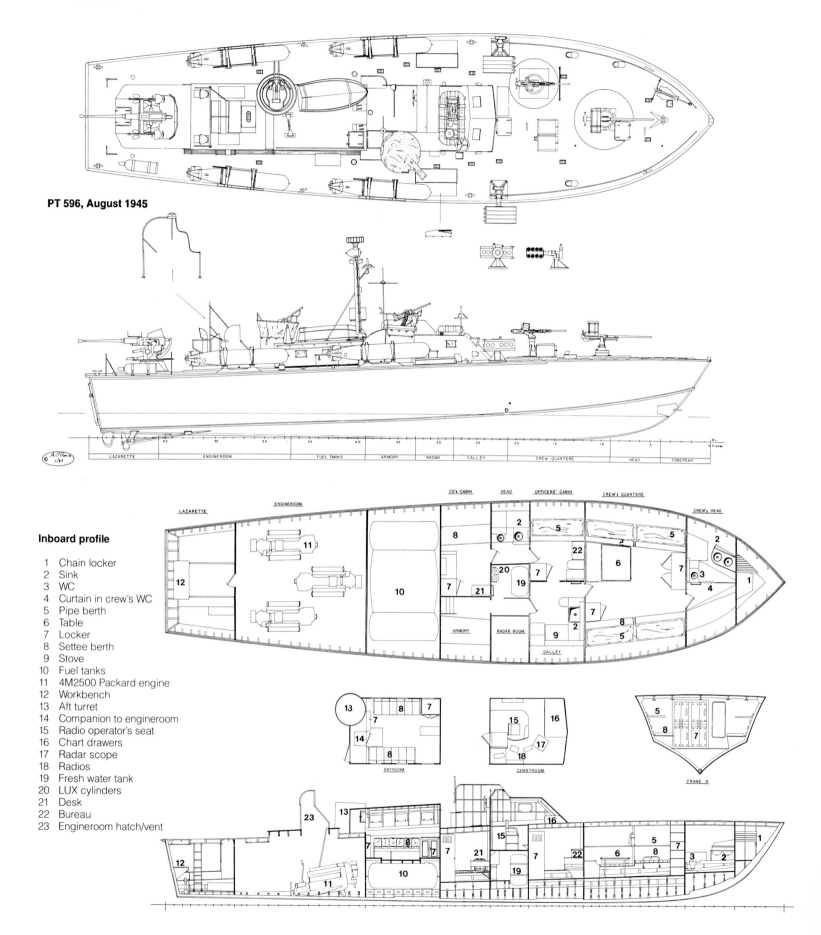

PT 596, August 1945

Inboard profile

1 Chain locker
2 Sink
3 WC
4 Curtain in crew's WC
5 Pipe berth
6 Table
7 Locker
8 Settee berth
9 Stove
10 Fuel tanks
11 4M2500 Packard engine
12 Workbench
13 Aft turret
14 Companion to engineroom
15 Radio operator's seat
16 Chart drawers
17 Radar scope
18 Radios
19 Fresh water tank
20 LUX cylinders
21 Desk
22 Bureau
23 Engineroom hatch/vent

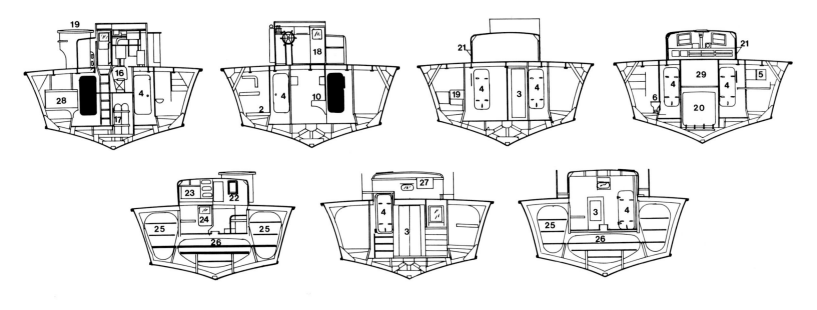

Bulkhead details – PT 565 series

1	Upper berth	16	Radio operator's seat
2	Settee berth	17	LUX tanks
3	Lockers	18	Door to charthouse
4	Watertight door	19	Forward turret
5	Cabinet	20	Freshwater tank
6	Water closet	21	Step
7	Sink	22	Hatch to aft turret
8	Watertight hatch	23	Litter hatch
9	Bureau	24	Hatch to engineroom
10	Desk	25	Wing fuel tank
11	Galley sink	26	Centre fuel tank
12	Refrigerator	27	Flag bag
13	Ladder	28	Officer's mess
14	Table in crew's quarters	29	Radio operator's space
15	Bilge pump		

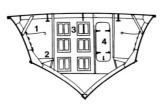

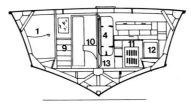
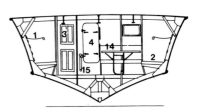

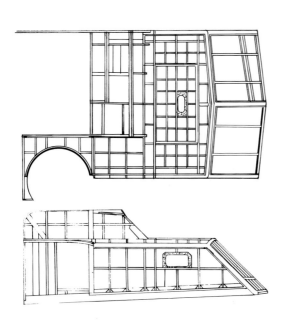
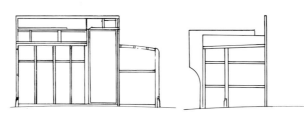
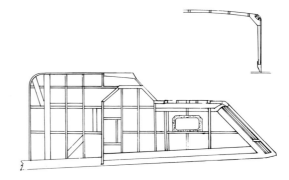

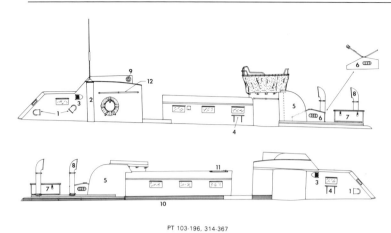

PT 103-196, 314-367

PT 372-283, 486-563, 565-624

PT 372-283, 486-563, 565-624

PT 103-196, 314-367

Differences in superstructures – side view

1 Vents
2 Whip aerial base
3 Sidelight
4 Step
5 Shield
6 Engineroom hatch
7 20mm ready service lockers
8 Cowl vent
9 Searchlight mount
10 Throttle rod cover
11 Dayroom hatch
12 Grab rail
13 40mm ready service locker
14 Locker
15 Boat hook
16 Liferaft locker
17 Light trap (from 565 series)

Differences in superstructures – top view

1 Cowl vent
2 Depression rail
3 20mm ready service locker
4 Main engineroom hatch
5 Engineroom access hatch
6 Throttle rod cover
7 Radar mast support
8 Dayroom hatch
9 Radar mast pivots
10 Torpedo tube training gear crank
11 Step
12 Sidelight
13 Vents

14 Whip antenna
15 Wherry
16 Platform
17 Radio direction finder (RDF)
18 Shield
19 BN antenna (from 565 series)
20 Locker
21 Liferaft locker
22 Light trap (from 565 series)
23 Hatch
24 Armour plate
25 40mm ready service locker
26 Folding mast

Plumbing system

1 Hand pump
2 Sink in crews' WC
3 Sink drain
4 C in crews' WC
5 Drain
6 Galley sink
7 Galley sink drain
8 Officers' WC
9 Fresh water tank
10 Sink in officers' WC

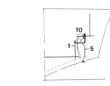
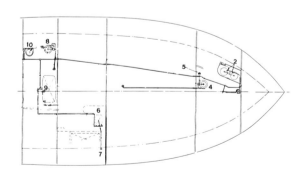
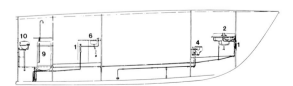

Steering gear

1 Helm
2 Bearing assembly, bulkhead 33
3 Steering shaft
4 Bearing assembly, bottom wing
5 Chain adjuster assembly,
  bulkhead 33
6 Bearing assembly, bulkhead 61
7 Chain adjuster assembly,
  bulkhead 61
8 Lower steering shaft bearing,
  bulkhead 61
9 Steering shaft, 1.25in diameter
10 Backing plate for gemmer gear
11 Rudder post
12 Gemmer gear assembly

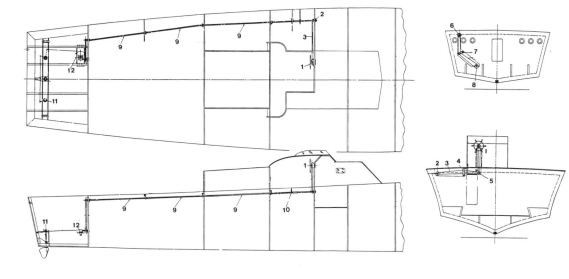

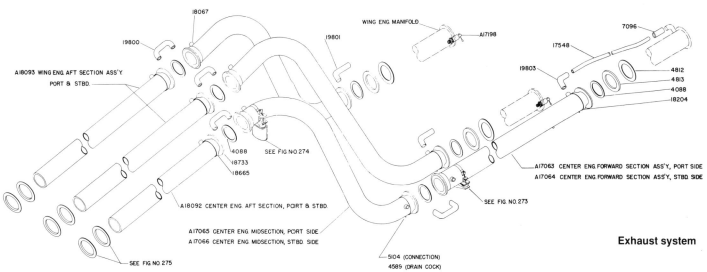

Exhaust system

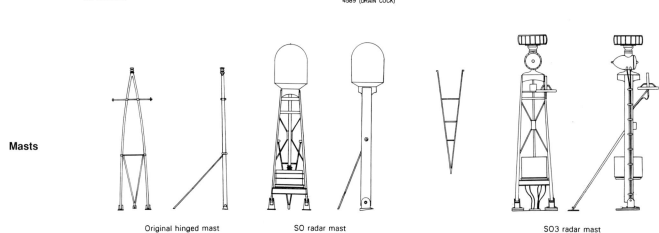

Masts

Original hinged mast   SO radar mast   SO3 radar mast

Starboard view of PT 117 upon completion.
USN

Licence-built Vospers

A large number of various Coastal Forces vessels were acquired from the United States under its Lend-Lease Bill. Finally passed by Congress on 11 March 1941, this Bill requested the appropriation of seven thousand million dollars to produce arms for the fighting democracies.

How did this 'kindness' develop? And how was the United Kingdom to pay for the mass of war material required to carry on the war against the forces of Nazi Germany, which had only recently occupied France and the Low Countries and were only a few miles away across the English Channel?

Britain entered the Second World War with reserves of about $4500 million in currency, gold and in US investments that could be realised. The only way in which these resources could be increased was by new gold production in the British Empire, mainly in South Africa, and by vigorous efforts to export goods, principally luxury goods, such as whisky, fine woollens, and pottery, to the United States. By these means an additional $2000m dollars was procured during the first 16 months of the war. During this period, known as the 'Twilight War', the British Government were torn between a vehement desire to order munitions and aircraft in the United States and the gnawing fear of running out of money, as dollar resources dwindled.

It was clear that UK resources would fail if efforts were not made to resolve the matter of payment. This required elaborate arrangements for eking out the cash reserves. In peacetime Britain had imported freely and made payments in various forms. When war came, however, it was necessary to create machinery to mobilise gold, dollars and other private assets, and to stop the ill-disposed from transferring their funds to countries where they felt they would be safer. It was also necessary to cut out 'wasteful' imports and other non-essentials. In addition to ensuring that money was not wasted, Britain had to see to it that sterling remained an acceptable currency. The countries of the sterling area remained loyal, and with other countries special arrangements were made by which they were paid in sterling – usable anywhere in the sterling area. These arrangements, completed after the spring of 1940, were made originally with Argentina and Sweden, but were extended to

several other countries in Europe and South America.

When the war became hideous reality in May 1940, the British Government under Winston Churchill believed that a new era was dawning in Anglo-American relations. From the time that a new Government was formed, and Sir Kingsley Wood became Chancellor of the Exchequer, a simpler plan was devised, namely, to order everything that was possible and leave future financial problems in the lap of the gods. It was misplaced prudence to worry too much about what would happen when the dollars ran out.

Up to November 1940 Britain had paid for everything that had been received. Already $335m worth of US shares had been sold, and over $4500m in cash. Only $2000m was left, the majority in investments, the greater part of which were not readily realisable, and some had to be kept in hand to carry on daily affairs.

With the re-election of President Roosevelt, and after considerable thought, Winston Churchill sent to him on 8 December a very long letter explaining the prospects for 1941, as seen by the British Government. The letter set out future planning, in particular for shipping, in which the capacity to transport munitions and supplies had priority over the movement by sea of large numbers of military personnel.

However, it was then estimated to take between three and four years to convert the industries of a modern state to war purposes, saturation point being reached when the maximum industrial effort that can be spared from civil needs has been applied to war production. Germany had reached this point by the end of 1939, and the British Empire was only about half-way through the second year of the process. Although much equipment had been ordered it was only the tip of the iceberg. Ships, aircraft, ammunition and modern weapons in particular were required and every effort was made to

MTB 396, licence-built by the Robert Jacob yard, displays her Light Standard Scheme F. Notable differences from British-built Vospers include the type SO radar and the additional sheer clamp. USN

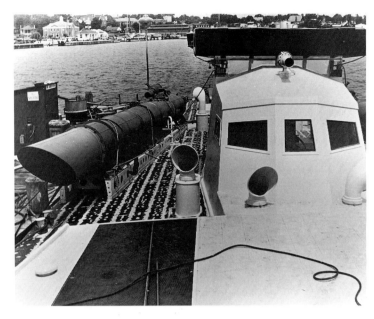

BPT 21 some time after launching. The charthouse has been painted and torpedo tubes have been fitted. The longitudinal deck planking is very evident. R T Miller

Deck view of BPT 21 at launch on 2 May 1942. Note the very dark primer on the hull. The buildings in the background are the US Naval Academy. R T Miller

bring the industrial might of the United States on to a war footing.

In July 1941, once the Lend–Lease programme was under way, Commander Peter Du Cane was flown by Pan Am clipper via Portugal to the United States to help organise the programme started by the Annapolis Boat Co which had negotiated a licence with Vosper to build Vosper boats.

In view of his enterprise in negotiating a licence agreement with Vosper, Mr Chris Nelson, managing director of the Annapolis shipyard, was detailed by the US Bureau of Ships to act as co-ordinator to the remaining boat builders selected. These were Robert Jacobs of Bay City, Herreshoff of Bristol, and one other, not on the original list but investigated by Du Cane. This was Harbor Boat Building Co of Terminal Island, California, which was run by two very capable Italian immigrants who were mostly occupied at that time in the construction of tuna fishing boats.

Other more complicated items, such as main and auxiliary machinery, shafts, vee drives and propellers, were ordered from specialist manufacturers to meet the same specifications as a similar item installed in Britain. The entire electrical installation was produced in the United States to British specifications and distributed to the various yards for installation. The only items actually supplied from the UK were armaments, although some of the twin Mark V mountings may have come from Canada. Much preliminary planning was completed, and detailed drawings provided. The US Bureau of Ships was of infinite help in suggesting which firms were able to provide such items as vee drives, castings for stern tubes, propellers, etc, but there were very tight specifications laid down by the Admiralty in England.

Fifty-eight units were ordered under Lend–Lease in spring 1941 (British MTB 258–301), including sixteen already built and of differing types. Of British Power Boat, Elco and Higgins designs, MTB 258–274 were handed over in April 1941, only a month after

the new Act was passed by Congress.

The first eight US-built Vospers were ordered from the Annapolis Yacht Yard and their keels laid during September and October 1941. The other companies following closely behind. The first units were completed in the autumn of 1942.

Towards the end of November 1942 Commander Du Cane was asked to return and witness the official trials of the prototype Annapolis Vosper (the Royal Navy's MTB 275). This time he crossed the Atlantic in *Queen Elizabeth*, then being used as a high-speed troop carrier. On his arrival at Annapolis the shipyard was a hive of activity, with Dick Miller representing the US Bureau of Ships. The first boat was almost ready to run, but trials were delayed because of ice in the upper reaches of Chesapeake Bay. When the day came for the official trials, Richard Moss, representing the British Director of Naval Construction, Dick Miller and others were present. To the glee of the US element a speed 2 knots in excess of that obtained in the UK was achieved at the same load and with the same power. But for Du Cane it posed the question of how it had come about.

After some weeks of close investigation and measurement of the hull the speed bonus was eventually traced through the draught markings both forward and aft which were secured in the wrong positions on the hull. This gave a false reading for the displacement, which on further investigation was revealed to be some tons lighter than the British Boats, hence the increased speed.

Most early US-built Vospers were destined for the Royal Indian Navy, or the Royal Navy in the Mediterranean. Of sixteen later orders of 22 July 1942, initially for the Royal Navy, eight were diverted to the USSR under Lend-Lease.

MTB 723 has been redrawn from a set of the original Annapolis drawings for PT 661–730 constructed in late 1944 and 1945, supplied by co-author Al Ross. Here can be seen the standard 70ft Vosper hull lines without any deck scuttles but with standard US pattern armament, equipment and SO radar. A unit with a low silhouette and simple whip aerials rather than a mast, she is quite a change from the usual British Vosper MTB. Completed on 14 September 1945, she was built for the USSR but not transferred, being sold in 1948. I think she looks particularly elegant and menacing. There is little to differentiate between the earlier British and US-built Vospers apart from minor detail.

US-built Vospers PT 661–730 data
Displacement   33 tons (US)
Principal Dimensions   Length overall 71ft ½in, war load waterline (WLWL) 66ft 6in, beam over rubbers 19ft 2½in, draught to bottom of propeller 5ft 0in, stem freeboard at WLWL about 7ft 1in, transom freeboard at side 4ft ½in
Machinery   Three shaft Packard petrol engines total 4055hp
Speed   40 knots
Armament   Two 21in torpedoes, two twin 0.5in Browning M2 air-cooled machine guns, single 20mm Oerlikon on Mark 10 mounting, four depth charges (if fitted)
Crew   Twelve
Builder   Annapolis Yacht Yard Inc, Annapolis, Maryland

Port and starboard Packard engines. Note the reverse gear lever on the port transfer case.
R T Miller

Armament

USN boat number BPT	Foreign boat number (navy)	Armament as built	Modifications while in service
21–36	MTB 275–282 (RIN)	1 × twin 0.50 Vickers in Mk V turret	undetermined
29–32	MTB 287–290 (RN)	2 × 21in torpedoes in RN pattern TT	
33–36	MTB 291–294 (RIN)	2 × depth charges	
38–40	MTB 296–298 (RN)		
41–48	MTB 299–306 (RIN)		
49–52	MTB 283–286 (RIN)		
37	MTB 295 (RN); GIS 0018 (Italy)	as above	undetermined
53–55	MTB 363–365 (RN); TKA 221–223 (USSR)	as above	undetermined
56–60	MTB 366–370 (RN); TKA 226–230 (USSR)	as above	undetermined
61, 62	MTB 371, 372 (RN)	as above	undetermined
63–65, 67	MTB 373–375, 377 (RN); GIS 0014, 0015, 009, 0016 (Italy)	as above	undetermined
66	MTB 376 (RN); GIS 0010 (Italy)	as above	1 × 20mm Mk 4 added to forecastle
68	MTB 378 (RN); GIS 0017 (Italy)	as above	1 × 20mm Mk 1 forward, Vickers Mk V turret replaced by twin 20mm Mk IIA
384, 385, 387, 395	MTB 396, 397, 399, 407 (RN)	1 × twin 0.50 Vickers in Mk 5 turret amidships 2 × 21in torpedoes in RN pattern tubes 2 × depth charges	undetermined

USN boat number	Foreign boat number (navy)	Armament as built	Modifications while in service
386, 388–394, 396–399	MTB 398, 400–406, 408–411 (RN); GIS 0012, 001, 002, 004, 003, 0013, 005, 006, 0011, 008, 007, 0028 (Italy)	as above	undetermined
400, 401, 417–429, 436–447, 449	TKA (?) (USSR)	as above	undetermined (USSR)
402–405, 406, 407, 408–413, 414–416, 430–432, 433, 434, 435, 448	TKA 231–234, 243, 244, 235–240, 246–248, 241–243, 249, 240, 251, 252 (USSR)	as above	undetermined (USSR)
661–692	TKA (?) (USSR)	2 × twin 0.50 Browning M2 in Mk 17 mounts 1 × 20mm Mk 10 amidships 2 × 21in Mk 19 TT 2 × depth charges	undetermined (USSR)
693–714		as above	none, not placed in service
715, 716	R41, 42 (Cuba)	as above	unarmed, air/sea rescue (Cuba)
717–730		as above	none, boat not placed in service

Construction list

Boat number	Keel laid	Launched	Completed	Fate
Built by Annapolis Yacht Yard				
BPT				
21	5. 9.41	2. 5.42	2. 3.43	To RIN as MTB 275 2.3.43. Returned USN 16.3.45
22	5. 9.41	16. 5.42	10.11.42	To RIN as MTB 276 10.11.42. Returned USN 17.3.46
23	5.11.41	11. 8.42	10.11.42	To RIN as MTB 277 10.11.42. Returned USN 15.3.46
24	17.11.41	14. 8.42	10.11.42	To RIN as MTB 278 10.11.42. Returned USN 15.3.46
25	19.11.41	14. 8.42	10.11.42	To RIN as MTB 279 10.11.42. Returned USN 16.3.46
26	19.11.41	13. 8.42	26.11.42	To RIN as MTB 280 24.11.42. Returned USN 15.3.46
27	9.12.41	12. 8.42	2.12.42	To RIN as MTB 281 2.12.42. Returned USN 17.3.46
28	11.12.41	11. 8.42	15.12.42	To RIN as MTB 282 15.12.42. Returned USN 15.3.46
Built by Herreshoff				
29	23.12.41	26. 2.42	18. 3.43	To RN as MTB 287 12.3.43. Wrecked in Adriatic 24.11.44
30	24.12.41	9. 3.43	18. 3.43	To RN as MTB 288 26.3.43. Bombed and sunk off Augusta 22.7.43
31	12. 1.42	23. 3.43	12. 4.43	To RN as MTB 289 13.4.43. Returned USN 10.3.45
32	15. 1.42	6. 4.43	12. 4.43	To RN as MTB 290 13.4.43. Returned USN 31.5.45
33	31. 3.42	19. 4.43	10. 5.43	To RIN as MTB 291 10.5.43. Returned USN 15.3.46
34	1. 4.42	3. 5.43	10. 5.43	To RIN as MTB 292 10.5.43. Returned USN 15.3.46
35	8. 4.42	17. 5.43	18. 6.43	To RIN as MTB 293 30.6.43. Returned USN 16.3.46
36	8. 4.42	7. 6.43	8. 7.43	To RIN as MTB 294 9.7.43. Returned USN 15.3.46
Built by R Jacobs				
37	26.12.41	27. 7.42	17. 2.43	To RN as MTB 295 17.2.43. Returned USN 25.9.45. To Italian Navy as GIS 0018 1947. Cannibalised for spares and later scrapped
38	31.12.41	20. 8.42	3. 3.43	To RN as MTB 296 3.3.43. Returned USN 31.5.45
39	8. 1.42	27. 7.42	6. 2.43	To RN as MTB 297 6.2.43. Returned USN 10.9.45
40	13. 1.42	18.11.42	30. 3.43	To RN as MTB 298 30.3.43. Returned USN 25.9.45
41	2. 4.42	20. 8.42	17. 3.43	To RIN as MTB 299 17.3.43. Returned USN 15.3.46
42	2. 4.42	18.11.42	28. 4.43	To RIN as MTB 300 28.4.43. Returned USN 15.3.46
Built by Harbor Boat Building				
43	30.12.41	7. 9.42	10. 2.43	To RIN as MTB 301 10.2.43. Returned USN 17.3.46
44	31.12.41	14.12.42	10. 2.43	To RIN as MTB 302 10.2.43. Returned USN 17.3.46
45	9. 1.42	14.12.42	27. 2.43	To RIN as MTB 303 27.2.43. Returned USN 16.3.46

Boat number	Hull number	Keel laid	Launched	Completed	Fate
46		10. 1.42	6. 1.43	27. 2.43	To RIN as MTB 304 27.2.43. Returned USN 16.3.46
47		11. 2.42	14. 1.43	9. 3.43	To RIN as MTB 305 9.3.43. Returned USN 16.3.46
48		12. 2.42	14. 1.43	31. 3.43	To RIN as MTB 306 31.3.43. Returned USN 17.3.46
Built by Annapolis Yacht Yard					
49		16. 3.42	1. 9.42	3. 4.43	To RIN as MTB 283 3.4.43. Returned USN 17.3.46
50		13. 5.42	2. 9.42	3. 4.43	To RIN as MTB 284 3.4.43. Lost in transit when transport sunk 9.9.43
51		13. 5.42	4. 9.42	3. 4.43	To RIN as MTB 285 3.4.43. Lost in transit when transport sunk 9.9.43
52		22. 5.42	5. 9.42	3. 4.43	To RIN as MTB 286 3.4.43. Returned USN 17.3.46
53		20. 8.42	23. 2.43	30. 9.43	To RN as MTB 363 30.9.43. To USSR as TKA 221 15.2.44. Returned USN at Aitepe, Turkey 1954
54		20. 8.42	24. 2.43	18.11.43	To RN as MTB 364 18.11.43. To USSR as TKA 222 15.2.44. Lost Barents Sea 10.44
55		20. 8.42	25. 2.43	15.12.43	To RN as MTB 365 15.12.43. To USSR as TKA 223 15.2.44. Returned USN at Aitepe, Turkey 1954
56		21. 8.42	26. 2.43	29.11.43	To RN as MTB 366 29.11.43. To USSR as TKA 226 15.2.44. Returned USN 1955
57		21. 8.42	26. 2.43	19.11.43	To RN as MTB 367 19.11.43. To USSR as TKA 227 15.2.44. Returned USN at Aitepe, Turkey 1954
58		7. 9.42	28. 2.43	22.11.43	To RN as MTB 368 22.11.43. To USSR as TKA 228 15.2.44. Returned USN 1955
59		7. 9.42	20. 2.43	22.11.43	To RN as MTB 369 22.11.43. To USSR as TKA 229 15.2.44. Returned USN at Aitepe, Turkey 1954
60		7. 9.42	15. 2.43	29.11.43	To RN as MTB 370 29.11.43. To USSR as TKA 230 15.2.44. Returned USN 1955
61		19. 2.43	15. 5.43	20.10.43	To RN as MTB 371 20.10.43. Scuttled 24.11.44 after grounding at Levrera Island, Adriatic
62		20. 2.43	17. 5.43	30. 9.43	To RN as MTB 372 30.9.43. Sunk by surface craft gunfire off Cape Loviste, Adriatic 24.7.44
63		1. 3.43	14. 6.43	9.10.43	To RN as MTB 373 9.10.43. Returned USN 16.10.45. To Italian Navy as GIS 0014 1947. Cannibalised for spares and later scrapped
64		2. 3.43	15. 6.43	20.10.43	To RN as MTB 374 20.11.43. Returned USN 23.10.45. To Italian Navy as GIS 0015 1947. Cannibalised for spares and later scrapped
65		3. 3.43	15. 6.43	19.11.43	To RN as MTB 375 17.11.43.

Boat number	Hull number	Keel laid	Launched	Completed	Fate
					Returned USN 15.10.45. To Italian Navy as GIS 009 1947. Cannibalised for spares and later scrapped
66		4. 3.43	19. 6.43	2.12.43	To RN as MTB 376 2.12.43. Returned USN 18.10.45. To Italian Navy as GIS 0010 1947. Cannibalised for spares and later scrapped
67		4. 3.43	23. 6.43	2.12.43	To RN as MTB 377 2.12.43. Returned USN 18.10.45. To Italian Navy as GIS 0016 1947. Cannibalised for spares and later scrapped
68		6. 3.43	17. 7.43	15.12.43	To RN as MTB 378 15.12.43. Returned USN 15.10.45. To Italian Navy as GIS 0017 4.4.48. Renumbered GIS 821, then MS 841, then MS 421. Stricken 1958

Built by R Jacobs

PT

Boat number	Hull number	Keel laid	Launched	Completed	Fate
384		15. 5.43	2.10.43	6. 5.44	To RN as MTB 396 6.5.44. Returned USN 10.9.45
385		15. 5.43	9.10.43	13. 5.44	To RN as MTB 397 13.5.44. Returned USN 16.3.46. To Egypt 1.47
386		25. 5.43	15.10.43	25. 5.44	To RN as MTB 398 25.5.44. Returned USN 16.10.45. To Italian Navy as GIS 0012 1951. Renumbered GIS 854, then MS 854, then MS 454. Stricken 31.12.58
387		2. 7.43	5.11.43	1. 6.44	To RN as MTB 399 10.6.44. Returned USN 16.3.46. Sold Egypt 1.47
388		18. 8.43	17.12.43	13. 6.44	To RN as MTB 400 13.6.44. Returned USN 16.10.45. To Italian Navy as GIS 001 24.3.48. Renumbered GIS 811, then MS 811, then MS 461. Stricken 30.6.59
389		17. 8.43	14. 1.44	8. 7.44	To RN as MTB 401 8.7.44. Returned USN 23.10.45. To Italian Navy as GIS 002 1.4.48. Renumbered GIS 812, then MS 812, then MS 462. Stricken 30.4.60
390		14. 9.43	22. 1.44	29. 6.44	To RN as MTB 402 29.6.44. Returned USN 16.10.45. To Italian Navy as GIS 004 1.2.48. Renumbered GIS 814, then MS 814, then MS 464. Stricken 30.6.59
391		14. 9.43	13. 4.44	11. 7.44	To RN as MTB 403 11.7.44. Returned USN 18.10.45. To Italian Navy as GIS 003 1.2.48. Renumbered GIS 813, then MS 813, then MS 463. Stricken 30.4.60
392		18.10.43	9. 3.44	22. 7.44	To RN as MTB 404 22.7.44. Returned USN 7.11.45. To Italian Navy as GIS 0013 4.4.48.

Boat number	Hull number	Keel laid	Launched	Completed	Fate
					Renumbered GIS 822, then MS 822, then MS 422. Stricken 30.9.60
393		18.10.43	13. 6.44	11. 8.44	To RN as MTB 405 11.8.44. Returned USN 10.11.45. To Italian Navy as GIS 005 4.4.48. Renumbered GIS 831, then MS 831, then MS 431. Stricken 31.10.61
394		15.11.43	19. 5.44	2. 8.44	To RN as MTB 406 2.8.44. Returned USN 7.11.45. To Italian Navy as GIS 006 4.4.48. Renumbered GIS 832, then MS 832, then MS 432. Stricken 31.12.61
395		15.11.43	22. 6.44	30. 8.44	To RN as MTB 407 30.8.44. Returned USN 10.11.45. To US Army 1.4.46
396		20.12.43	28. 7.44	9. 9.44	To RN as MTB 408 9.9.44. Returned USN 10.11.45. To Italian Navy as GIS 0011 4.4.48. Renumbered GIS 834, then MS 834, then MS 434. Stricken 30.6.59
397		20.12.43	7. 8.44	11.10.44	To RN as MTB 409 11.10.44. Returned USN 7.11.45. To Italian Navy as GIS 008 4.4.48. Renumbered GIS 823, then MS 823, then MS 423. Stricken 31.12.58
398		26. 1.44	22. 8.44	6.10.44	To RN as MTB 410 6.10.44. Returned USN 7.11.45. To Italian Navy as GIS 007 4.4.48. Renumbered GIS 833, then MS 833, then MS 433. Stricken 31.12.58
399		26. 1.44	1. 9.44	30.10.44	To RN as MTB 411 30.10.44. Returned USN 10.11.45. To Italian Navy as GIS 0028 21.7.48. Renumbered GIS 824, then MS 824, then MS 424. Stricken 30.6.59

Built by Annapolis Yacht Yard

Boat number	Hull number	Keel laid	Launched	Completed	Fate
400		26. 5.43	17. 9.43	17. 1.44	To USSR as TKA (?) 1.44. Returned USN 16.6.54
401		26. 5.43	23. 9.43	17. 1.44	To USSR as TKA (?) 2.44. Returned USN 27.5.54
402		7. 7.43	28. 9.43	20. 1.44	To USSR as TKA 231 2.44. Returned USN 27.5.54
403		8. 7.43	2.10.43	20. 1.44	To USSR as TKA 232 2.44. Returned USN 27.5.54
404		15. 7.43	11.10.43	24. 1.44	To USSR as TKA 233 2.44. Returned USN 27.5.54
405		14. 7.43	13.10.43	24. 1.44	To USSR as TKA 234 2.44. Returned USN 11.8.55
406		23. 6.43	14.10.43	31. 1.44	To USSR as TKA 243 2.44. Returned USN 2.7.55
407		23. 6.43	18.10.43	31. 1.44	To USSR as TKA 244 2.44. Returned USN 14.7.55
408		10. 7.43	21.10.43	4. 2.44	To USSR as TKA 235 2.44. Returned USN 27.5.54
409		9. 7.43	22.10.43	9. 2.44	To USSR as TKA 236 2.44. Returned USN at Aitepe, Turkey

Boat number	Hull number	Keel laid	Launched	Completed	Fate
					27.5.54
410		22. 9.43	27.11.43	23. 2.44	To USSR as TKA 237 3.44. Returned USN 9.7.55
411		22. 9.43	1.12.43	23. 2.44	To USSR as TKA 238 3.44. Scuttled Barents Sea 1956
412		1.10.43	18.12.43	29. 2.44	To USSR as TKA 239 3.44. Sunk by German submarine-chaser UJ 1211 off North Cape 15.7.44
413		1.10.43	27.12.43	29. 2.44	To USSR as TKA 240 3.44. Returned USN 2.7.55
414		27.10.43	14. 2.44	9. 3.44	To USSR as TKA 246 6.44. Stricken 1956
415		27.10.43	26. 2.44	9. 3.44	To USSR as TKA 247 6.44. Stricken and destroyed 1954
416		18.10.43	18. 2.44	14. 3.44	To USSR as TKA 248 6.44. Stricken and destroyed 1954
417		18.10.43	16. 2.44	18. 3.44	To USSR 8.44. Stricken and destroyed 1954
418		26.10.43	22. 2.44	23. 3.44	To USSR 8.44. Stricken and destroyed 1954
419		27.10.43	21. 2.44	23. 3.44	To USSR 8.44. Stricken and destroyed 1954
420		4.12.43	14. 3.44	5. 4.44	To USSR 7.44. Declared unfit for further service, stricken 1954
421		4.12.43	16. 3.44	13. 4.44	To USSR 8.44. Stricken 1954
422		23.12.43	24. 3.44	13. 4.44	To USSR 7.44. Stricken 1954
423		23.12.43	27. 3.44	21. 4.44	To USSR 8.44. Stricken and destroyed 1954
424		28. 2.44	24. 4.44	5. 5.44	To USSR 7.44. Returned USN 5.7.55
425		25. 2.44	28. 4.44	9. 5.44	To USSR 7.44. Returned USN 5.7.55
426		24. 2.44	2. 5.44	16. 5.44	To USSR 7.44. Returned USN 6.7.55
427		24. 2.44	6. 5.44	19. 5.44	To USSR 7.44. Returned USN 6.7.55
428		22. 2.44	13. 5.44	25. 5.44	To USSR 10.44
429		21. 2.44	19. 5.44	31. 5.44	To USSR 10.44

Built by Herreshoff

Boat number	Hull number	Keel laid	Launched	Completed	Fate
430		4. 6.43	24. 1.44	12. 2.44	To USSR as TKA 241 2.44. Returned USN 14.7.55
431		12. 6.43	25. 1.44	26. 2.44	To USSR as TKA 242 3.44. Returned USN 14.7.55
432		15. 6.43	26. 1.44	29. 2.44	To USSR as TKA 243 3.44. Returned USN 14.7.55
433		18. 6.43	26. 2.44	17. 3.44	To USSR as TKA 249 6.44. Stricken and destroyed 1954
434		24. 6.43	3. 3.44	17. 3.44	To USSR as TKA 240 6.44. Lost
435		26. 6.43	4. 3.44	17. 3.44	To USSR as TKA 251 6.44. Stricken 1954
436		1. 7.43	4. 3.44	30. 3.44	To USSR 9.44. Stricken 1954
437		6. 7.43	10. 3.44	30. 3.44	To USSR 9.44. Stricken 1954
438		10. 7.43	27. 3.44	6. 4.44	To USSR 10.44. Stricken and destroyed 1954
439		22. 7.43	29. 3.44	27. 4.44	To USSR 10.44. Returned USN 6.7.55
440		23. 7.43	5. 3.44	13. 4.44	To USSR 8.44. Stricken 1954
441		26. 7.43	7. 4.44	20. 4.44	To USSR 10.41. Stricken and destroyed 1954
442		30.11.43	15. 4.44	27. 4.44	To USSR 10.44. Returned USN 2.7.55

Boat number	Hull number	Keel laid	Launched	Completed	Fate
443		1.12.43	15. 4.44	4. 5.44	To USSR 9.44. Returned USN 6.7.55
444		14.12.43	22. 4.44	4. 5.44	To USSR 9.44. Stricken and destroyed 1954
445		14.12.43	29. 4.44	19. 5.44	To USSR 7.44. Stricken and destroyed 1954
446		20.12.43	10. 5.44	25. 5.44	To USSR 10.44. Returned USN 6.7.55
447		21.12.43	9. 5.44	18. 5.44	To USSR 7.44. Stricken and destroyed 1954
448		30.12.43	24. 5.44	7. 6.44	To USSR as TKA 252 7.44. Returned USN 14.7.55
449		30.12.43	18. 5.44	25. 5.44	To USSR 10.44. Stricken and destroyed 1954

Built by Annapolis Yacht Yard

Boat number	Hull number	Keel laid	Launched	Completed	Fate
661		4. 4.44	14. 8.44	18.11.44	To USSR 12.44. Returned USN 2.7.55
662		1. 4.44	–	18.11.44	To USSR in kit form 12.44. Returned USN 9.7.55
663		1. 4.44	–	18.11.44	To USSR in kit form 12.44. Returned USN 14.7.55
664		1. 4.44	–	18.11.44	To USSR in kit form 12.44. Returned USN 14.7.55
665		1. 4.44	–	18.11.44	To USSR in kit form 12.44. Returned USN 7.9.55
666		1. 4.44	–	18.11.44	To USSR in kit form 12.44. Returned USN 14.7.55
667		1. 4.44	–	18.11.44	To USSR in kit form 12.44. Returned USN 19.7.55
668		1. 4.44	–	18.11.44	To USSR in kit form 12.44. Returned USN 20.7.55
669		1. 4.44	–	18.11.44	To USSR in kit form 12.44. Returned USN 14.7.55
670		1. 4.44	–	18.11.44	To USSR in kit form 12.44. Returned USN 2.7.55
671		1. 4.44	–	18.11.44	To USSR in kit form 12.44. Returned USN 2.7.55
672		1. 4.44	–	18.11.44	To USSR in kit form 12.44. Returned USN 9.7.55
673		1. 4.44	–	18.11.44	To USSR in kit form 12.44. Returned USN 9.7.55
674		1. 4.44	–	18.11.44	To USSR in kit form 12.44. Returned USN 14.7.55
675		1. 4.44	–	18.11.44	To USSR in kit form 12.44. Returned USN 14.7.55
676		26. 8.44	31.10.44	6.12.44	To USSR in kit form 12.44. Returned USN 9.7.55
677		30. 8.44	3.11.44	6.12.44	To USSR 12.44. Returned USN 9.7.55
678		5. 9.44	17.11.44	13.12.44	To USSR 1.45. Returned USN 2.7.45
679		5. 9.44	23.11.44	13.12.44	To USSR 1.45. Returned USN 2.7.55
680		5. 9.44	25.11.44	19.12.44	To USSR 3.45. Returned USN 9.7.55
681		5. 9.44	29.11.44	19.12.44	To USSR 3.45. Returned USN 20.7.55
682		5. 9.44	5.12.44	27.12.44	To USSR 3.45. Returned USN 20.7.55
683		5. 9.44	5.12.44	27.12.44	To USSR 3.45. Returned USN 20.7.55
683		5. 9.44	11.12.44	1. 1.45	To USSR 3.45. Scuttled Barents Sea 1956

Boat number	Hull number	Keel laid	Launched	Completed	Fate
684		2.11.44	10. 1.45	12. 2.45	To USSR 4.45. Scuttled Barents Sea 1956
685		3.11.44	12. 1.45	14. 2.45	To USSR 4.45
686		22.11.44	5. 2.45	23. 2.45	To USSR 4.45. Scuttled Barents Sea 1956
687		30.11.44	6. 2.45	23. 2.45	To USSR 4.45. Scuttled Barents Sea 1956
688		8.12.44	10. 2.45	2. 3.45	To USSR 5.45. Scuttled Barents Sea 1956
689		30.11.44	8. 2.45	3. 3.45	To USSR 5.45
690		8.12.44	14. 2.45	7. 3.45	To USSR 5.45. Scuttled Barents Sea 1956
691		9.12.44	17. 2.45	9. 3.45	To USSR 5.45. Scuttled Barents Sea 1956
692		15. 1.45	2. 3.45	19. 3.45	To USSR 5.45. Scuttled Barents Sea 1956
693		15. 1.45	5. 3.45	21. 3.45	Built for USSR but not transferred. Sold 15.8.46
694		8. 2.45	14. 3.45	5. 4.45	Built for USSR but not transferred. Sold 15.8.46
695		8. 2.45	17. 3.45	5. 4.45	Built for USSR but not transferred. Sold 15.8.46
696		19. 2.45	26. 3.45	14. 4.45	Built for USSR but not transferred. Sold 15.8.46
697		19. 2.45	30. 3.45	18. 4.45	Built for USSR but not transferred. Sold 30.8.46
698		20. 2.45	3. 4.45	21. 4.45	Built for USSR but not transferred. Sold 30.8.46
699		7. 3.45	12. 4.45	1. 5.45	Built for USSR but not transferred. Sold 21.8.46
700		8. 3.45	16. 4.45	3. 5.45	Built for USSR but not transferred. Sold 21.12.46
701		17. 3.45	20. 4.45	9. 5.45	Built for USSR but not transferred. Sold 12.9.46
702		17. 3.45	26. 4.45	14. 5.45	Built for USSR but not transferred. Sold 30.8.46
703		3. 4.45	4. 5.45	22. 5.45	Built for USSR but not transferred. Sold 25.6.46
704		4. 4.45	7. 5.45	26. 5.45	Built for USSR but not transferred. Sold 25.6.46
705		4. 4.45	11. 5.45	30. 5.45	Built for USSR but not transferred. Sold 12.8.46
706		18. 4.45	21. 5.45	8. 6.45	Built for USSR but not transferred. Sold 17.7.46
707		18. 4.45	25. 5.45	14. 6.45	Built for USSR but not transferred. Sold 25.6.46
708		27. 4.45	2. 6.45	23. 6.45	Built for USSR but not transferred. Sold 12.8.46
709		27. 4.45	6. 6.45	27. 6.45	Built for USSR but not transferred. Sold 17.7.46
710		12. 5.45	18. 6.45	4. 7.45	Built for USSR but not transferred. Sold 25.6.46
711		12. 5.45	19. 6.45	11. 7.45	Built for USSR but not transferred. Sold 17.7.46
712		14. 5.45	23. 6.45	18. 7.45	Built for USSR but not transferred. Sold 13.9.46
713		26. 5.45	29. 6.45	19. 7.45	Built for USSR but not transferred. Sold 11.9.46
714		26. 5.45	4. 7.45	23. 7.45	Built for USSR but not transferred. Sold 11.9.46
715		6. 6.45	9. 7.45	29. 7.45	Built for USSR but not transferred. Sold Cuba 8.46 and became R 41. Sunk in hurricane

PT 723 as completed

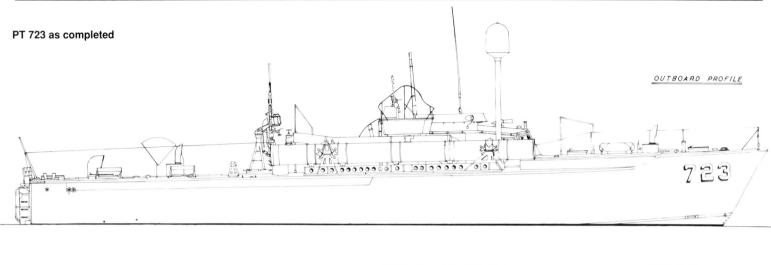

OUTBOARD PROFILE

723

DECK PLAN.

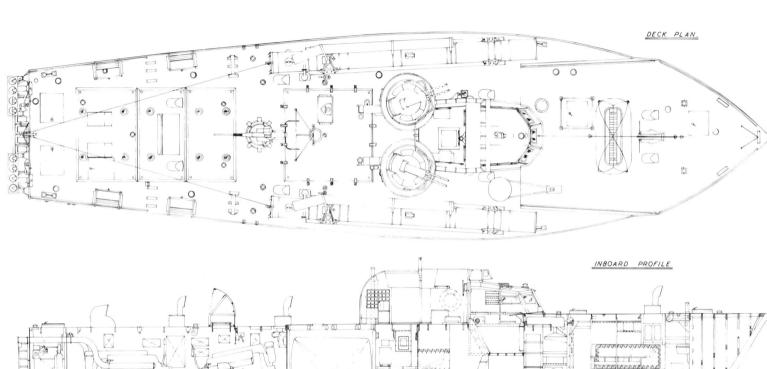

INBOARD PROFILE

ACCOMMODATION PLAN.

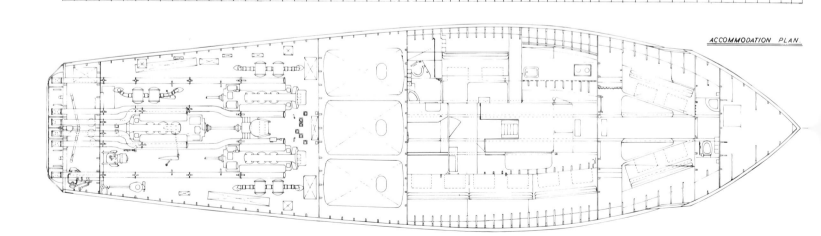

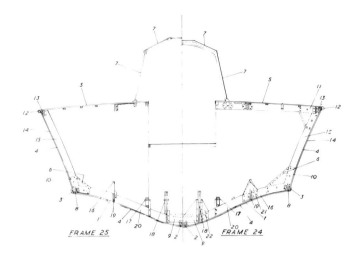

FRAME 25   FRAME 24

United States Licence built PT 723 Lend-Leased to USSR

1 Bottom planking ½in mahogany, inner diagonal
2 Keel 6in sided, laminated white oak, ¾in ply
3 Chine guard ¾in × 3in white oak
4 Muslin oiled between planking
5 Deck planking ⅝in mahogany plywood
6 Chine bracket ⅜in fir plywood
7 Deck house top and sides ⅜in fir plywood
8 Chine piece 3in × 3in aft, 4in × 6in forward, white oak
9 Floor bracket ⅜in fir plywood
10 Filler strip 1in × 1in mahogany
11 Gunwale bracket ⅜in fir plywood
12 Gunwale guard 2½in dia half round white oak
13 Main gunwale 3in × 4½in white oak, tapered
14 Topside planking ⁷⁄₁₆in outer, ¼in inner, mahogany, double diagonal
15 Topside frame 1in sided mahogany, 5½in at chine, 5in at sheer
16 C girder – built up from 10 gauge steel and 1½in × 1½ × ³⁄₁₆ in angle
17 Girder hatch rests ¾in × ⅞in white oak
18 A girder – built up from ½in plywood double and ¾in sided mahogany
19 Intercoastal chocks 1½in sided spruce
20 Bottom frame – 4 and 5 6in at G 5½in at chine, 1in sided mahogany
   Bottom frame – 17 to 43 6in at G 5½in at chine, 1in sided white oak ⅜in laminations
   Bottom frane – elsewhere 6in at G, 5½in at chine, 1in sided mahogany, 1⅛in white oak cap
21 C girder bracket – 14 gauge steel
22 A girder bracket – ⅜in fir plywood

Boat number	Hull number	Keel laid	Launched	Completed	Fate
					5.10.48, salvaged and returned to service as air/sea rescue launch
716		6. 6.45	17. 7.45	2. 8.45	Built for USSR but not transferred. Sold Cuba 7.46 and became R 42. Sunk in hurricane 5.10.48, salvaged and returned to service as air/sea rescue launch
717		22. 6.45	23. 7.45	12. 8.45	Built for USSR but not transferred. Sold 26.6.47
718		22. 6.45	26. 7.45	15. 8.45	Built for USSR but not transferred. Sold 27.6.47
719		22. 6.45	1. 8.45	24. 8.45	Built for USSR but not transferred. Sold 27.6.47
720		5. 7.45	8. 8.45	29. 8.45	Built for USSR but not transferred. Sold 18.6.47
721		5. 7.45	11. 8.45	4. 9.45	Built for USSR but not transferred. Sold 21.7.47
722		16. 7.45	17. 8.45	6. 9.45	Built for USSR but not transferred. Sold 15.8.47
723		16. 7.45	27. 8.45	14. 9.45	Built for USSR but not transferred. Sold 12.4.48
724		31. 7.45	8. 9.45	21. 9.45	Built for USSR but not transferred. Sold 18.7.47
725		31. 7.45	8. 9.45	1.10.45	Built for USSR but not transferred. Sold 18.8.47
726		31. 7.45	14. 9.45	6.10.45	Built for USSR but not transferred. Sold 16.8.47
727		10. 8.45	20. 9.45	13.10.45	Built for USSR but not transferred. Sold 20.6.47
728		10. 8.45	25. 9.45	20.10.45	Built for USSR but not transferred. Sold 18.8.47
729		18. 8.45	29. 9.45	27.10.45	Built for USSR but not transferred. Reclassified as small boat 16.11.45; to operational development force 14.12.45. Stricken 31.3.47
730		18. 8.45	29. 9.45	30.10.45	Built for USSR but not transferred. Reclassified as small boat 16.11.45; to Maritime Commission 18.11.47

Note: The licence-built Vospers were not placed in service as PTs.

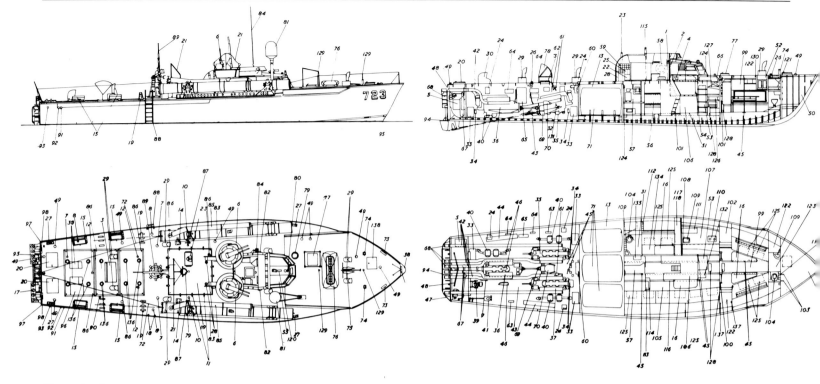

Key to detail

1	Steering column and helm indicator	39	Auxiliary generator	
2	Door and manually operated switch	40	Heat exchanger	
3	Engineroom access hatch	41	Air compressor	
4	Emergency engineroom signal	42	Main engine exhaust pipes	
5	Auxiliary engine fuel tank	43	Engineroom	

1 Steering column and helm indicator
2 Door and manually operated switch
3 Engineroom access hatch
4 Emergency engineroom signal
5 Auxiliary engine fuel tank
6 Twin 0.5in machine gun mounting
7 4in deck plate to lubricating oil tank (30gal)
8 4in deck plate distilled water to main engine
9 Auxiliary bilge pump
10 Fuel filling and sounding pipe
11 Hatch holding-down bolts and pads
12 4in engine lift deck plate
13 Fuel tank compartment
14 Torpedo tube heater
15 Depth charge stowage
16 Drop-leaf table
17 Smoke port unit – port and starboard
18 Boarding ladder fittings
19 Torpedo loading chocks
20 Steering gear access hatch
21 Gun depression rail
22 Recognition lamp stowage
23 Spare 0.5in gun barrel case
24 Water expansion tank
25 Aldis lamp stowage
26 Exhaust blower vent
27 Bollard
28 Fire extinguisher
29 6in ventilator box
30 12in ventilator box
31 Officers' WC
32 V-drive oil tank
33 Lubricating oil tank
34 Lubricating oil filter
35 Port main engine
36 Centre main engine
37 Starboard main engine
38 Stem head plate

39 Auxiliary generator
40 Heat exchanger
41 Air compressor
42 Main engine exhaust pipes
43 Engineroom
44 Battery box
45 Pillars
46 Stern tube
47 Exhaust muffler guard
48 Steering gear
49 Mushroom ventilator
50 Forepeak
51 Floorboards
52 Bosun's locker
53 Food locker
54 Chart rack
55 Deckhouse
56 Officers' bunks
57 Radio room
58 Life buoy
59 Flag locker
60 Instrument panel
61 Throttle control
62 Muffler control
63 Distribution panel
64 Generator regulators
65 Main switchboard
66 Fresh water tank
67 CO_2 cylinders
68 Exhaust muffler
69 V-drive
70 Engineer's seat
71 Fuel tanks
72 Life line – ⅝in Manila
73 Closed fairlead
74 Samson post
75 Danforth anchor
76 Liferaft
77 Crew's hatch
78 Canopy frame
79 12in deck plate
80 Bow light
81 SO radar
82 Navigation light
83 21in torpedo tube

84 Whip aerial
85 Compression chamber
86 Lifting eyes
87 Fuel tank vent
88 Boarding ladder
89 Single 20mm Oerlikon mounting
90 CO_2 pull box
91 Compressor exhaust
92 Generator exhaust
93 Heater exhaust
94 Cavitation plate
95 Towing eye
96 Escape hatch
97 Quarter knee
98 Open fairlead
99 Crew's quarters
100 Watertight door
101 Ladder
102 Oilskin locker
103 Rope hook
104 WC
105 Wardroom
106 Magazine
107 Galley
108 Sliding door
109 Monel metal sink
110 Two burner stove
111 Dishrack (over)
112 Ditty box
113 First aid locker
114 Bookcase (under)
115 Mast
116 Keyboard
117 Wine locker (under)
118 Linen locker
119 Tank hatch
120 Horn
121 Rail
122 Shelf
123 WC
124 Clock
125 Locker (under)
126 Stove
127 Hood

128 Heater
129 Stanchion
130 Alarm
131 Scoop control port and starboard
132 Ice box
133 20mm Oerlikon ready use locker
134 Officers' cabin
135 Locker
136 Deadlights
137 Coat hooks
138 Forepeak hatch

PT 723 lines

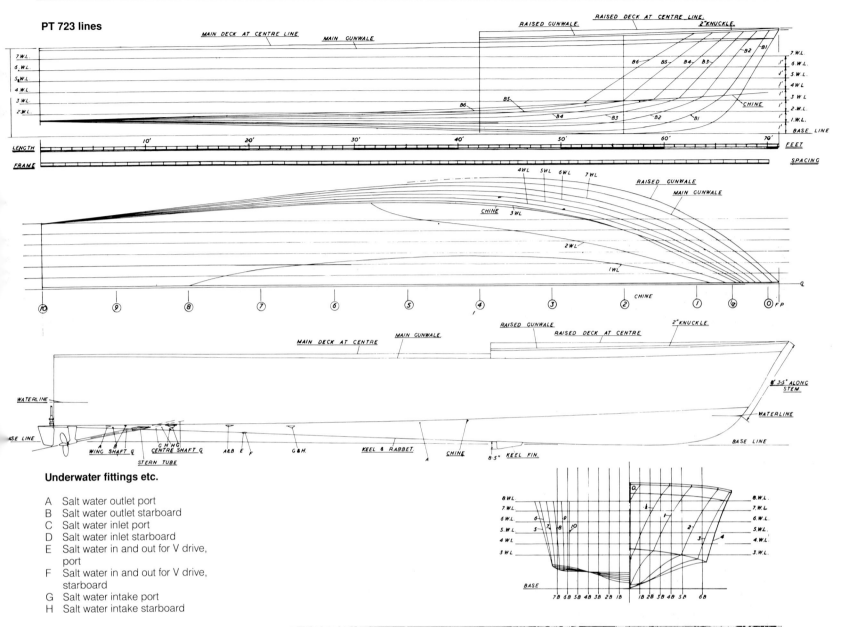

Underwater fittings etc.

A   Salt water outlet port
B   Salt water outlet starboard
C   Salt water inlet port
D   Salt water inlet starboard
E   Salt water in and out for V drive,
     port
F   Salt water in and out for V drive,
     starboard
G   Salt water intake port
H   Salt water intake starboard

*The first series of Annapolis-built Vospers
under construction. The mixture of planking
and plywood is obvious in the construction of
the charthouse.* R T Miller

PT construction

One popular misconception about PT boats is that they were built of plywood. While plywood was used extensively for gussets, superstructures, and, in some boats, decking, the hulls were planked. A wide variety of construction materials were used, including Sitka spruce, white oak, African mahogany, Western red cedar, balsa, fir plywood, stainless steel, brass, aluminium, Monel, glue, and muslin. Drawings and tables in this section, along with text in the sections on each type, will serve to illustrate the differences.

Construction of all three types of Elcos followed the same basic process. Once the hundreds of construction drawings had been completed and the lines had been lofted, the frames were sawn, notched, and then assembled on a scrive board. The scrive board was a large flat surface on to which all of the frame lines had been transferred and which was equipped with slotted guides for positioning the frame components. Each frame component was laid on the scrive board and aligned with its respective outline by the guides. ting edges were trimmed as necessary, the frames were assembled with glue, screws, and plywood gussets, and removed for storage.

The hulls were assembled upside down in specially-designed

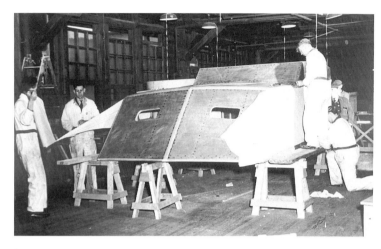

Covering the charthouse of an early 80ft boat with muslin prior to painting. USN

Turning a planked 70ft hull. Elco

170

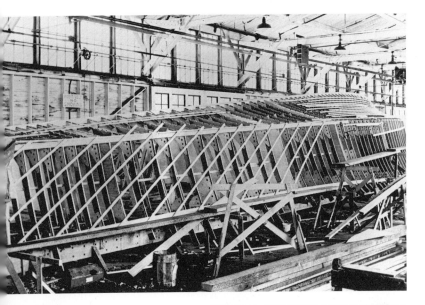

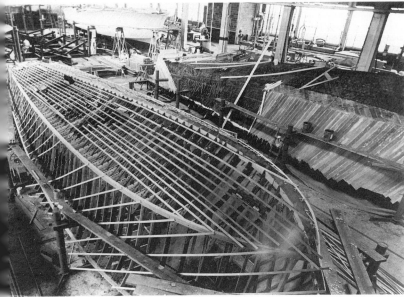

jigs. First, the frames and bulkheads were set in their respective locations and aligned. Then, the preassembled keel and stem were lowered into notches cut into each frame and secured with bolts. After the keel was in place, the chine and sheer plank were installed and faired. Longitudinal battens were then laid in notches in the frame bottoms and diagonal battens attached to the frame sides, followed by an intermediate framing, usually forward.

Once the framing was completed, the first of two diagonally-opposed layers of planking was applied. Each plank was fastened to the frames with Monel screws below, and brass or bronze screws above, the waterline. Headed-over copper nails were used to secure the planks to the diagonals, battens, intermediate frames, and other planks. After the first layer of planking had been completed, a coating of marine glue was applied to the hull and covered with muslin, which was then ironed to ensure that the glue filled the pores of the cloth. The second layer of planking was then laid opposite to the first.

When both layers of planking had been completed, the hull was turned upright and the various girders, clamps, and filler blocks were installed. The covering board and deck longitudinals were installed next, followed by the decking, guard clamps, gunwales, and chine guards. With the hull structure essentially complete, the fuel tanks, engines, and related equipment were then installed.

Construction of the superstructure for each type was essentially the same. Thin sheets of plywood were screwed and glued to a lightweight framework. An insulating material called 'Onazote' was sandwiched between the inner and outer skins and the outer skin was covered with fabric and glue. Turret tubs were constructed of several layers of veneer over a framework.

At any given time, up to twenty boats could be seen under construction in the boat assembly building (Building 21) at Bayonne. Once they had been turned upright, they were placed on wheeled cradles and moved from station to station in production line fashion. As each hull was completed, it was towed out of Building 21 to another building for detailing, then to the huge yard crane for launching. Launching was accomplished by lowering the cradle and boat into the water, the PT floating free and being towed to the wet basin for fitting out.

Various stages of 80ft construction taken between March and April 1943. Elco

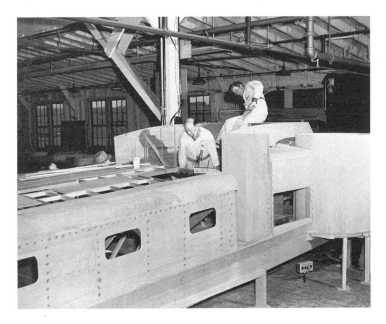

The charthouse and day cabin were built in jigs, to ensure a proper fit. The 3360 scribbled on the day cabin indicates that this unit belongs to hull 3360, PT 108. Elco

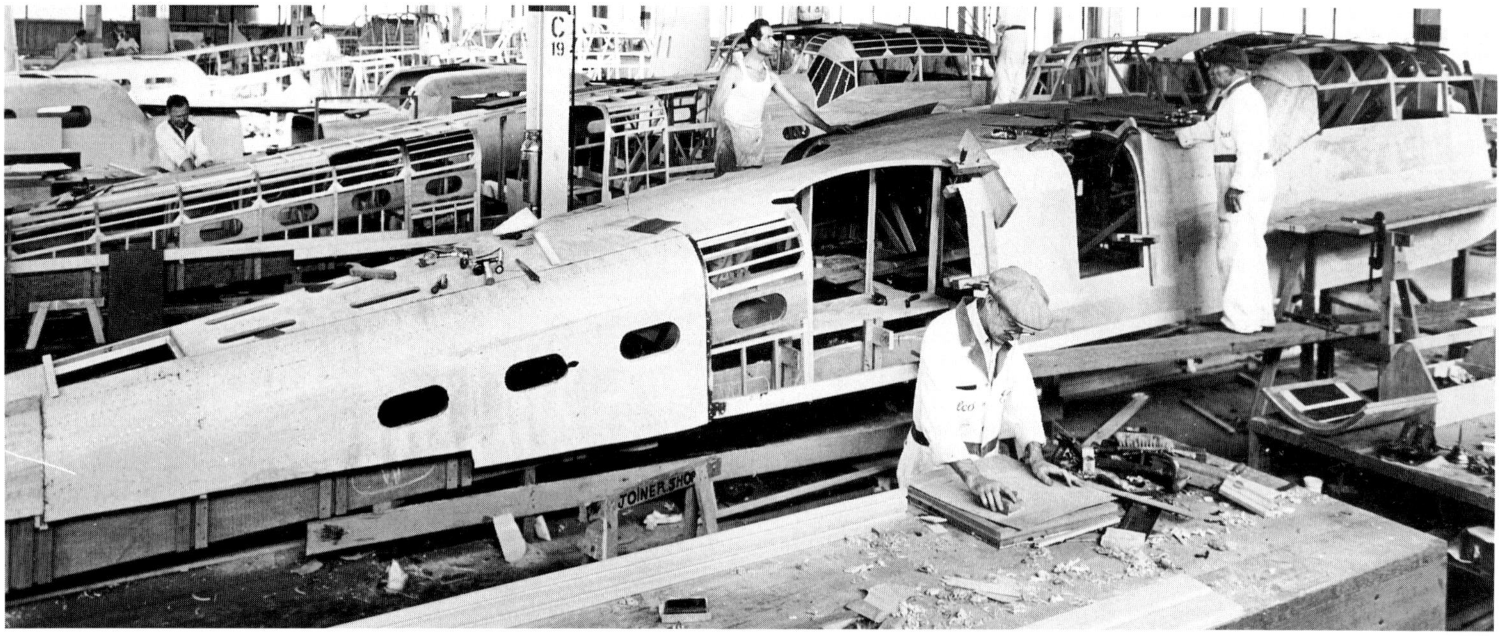

Trunk cabin of a 70ft boat being sheeted over.
Elco

Comparison of major structural components

Decking

PT 10–19, PTC 1–12	70ft	Mahogany planking, inner and outer, 3/16 × 4in
PT 20–44	77ft	Mahogany plywood, 3/8in
PT 45–48, 59–68, BPT 1–10	77ft	Mahogany plywood, 5/8in
PT 103–196, 314–367, 372–383	80ft	Mahogany planking, 3/8in outer, 5/16in inner
PT 486–563, 565–624	80ft	Plywood, 5/16in fir core, 1/20in birch crossbanding, 1/12in mahogany facing

Keel

PT 10–19, PTC 1–12	70ft	Spruce, sided 5 3/4in
PT 20–44	77ft	Spruce, sided 5 3/4in
PT 45–48, 59–68, BPT 1–10	77ft	Spruce, sided 5 3/4in
All 80ft	80ft	Spruce sided 5 3/4in

Longitudinal battens

PT 10–19, PTC 1–12	70ft	Spruce, 7/8in × 1 1/2in
PT 20–44	77ft	Spruce, 7/8in × 1 1/2in
PT 45–48, 59–68, BPT 1–10	77ft	Spruce, 7/8in × 1 1/2in
All 80ft	80ft	Spruce, 7/8in × 1 1/2in

Planking, bottom

PT 10–19, PTC 1–12	70ft	Mahogany, 5/16in inner, 7/16in outer
PT 20–44	77ft	Mahogany, 5/16in inner, 7/16in outer
PT 45–48, 59–68, BPT 1–10	77ft	Mahogany, 5/16in inner, 7/16in outer
All 80ft	80ft	Mahogany, 7/16in inner, 1/2in outer

Planking, top side

PT 10–19, PTC 1–12	70ft	Mahogany, 5/16in inner, 3/8in outer
PT 20–44	77ft	Mahogany, 5/16in inner, 3/8in outer
PT 45–58, 59–68, BPT 1–10	77ft	Mahogany, 5/16in inner, 3/8in outer
All 80ft	80ft	Mahogany, 5/16in inner, 7/16in outer

Stem

PT 10–19, PTC 1–12	70ft	Spruce, sided 5 3/4in
PT 10–19, PTC 1–12	70ft	Spruce, sided 5 3/4in
PT 20–44	77ft	Spruce, sided 5 3/4in
PT 45–48, 59–68, BP 1–10	77ft	Spruce, sided 5 3/4in
All 80ft	80ft	Spruce, sided 5 3/4in

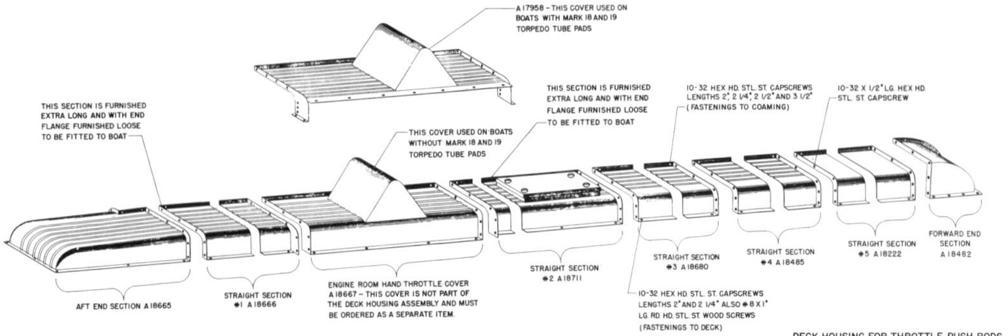

DECK HOUSING FOR THROTTLE PUSH RODS

PT camouflage

United States Navy camouflage during the Second World War is a complex and confusing (no pun intended) subject. Camouflage measures were being developed at a rapid pace, and paint mixing formulae changed while the paint name remained the same. The Bureau of Ships and fleet commanders argued over what measures were most effective, and individual unit commanders often exercised a high degree of personal initiative when interpreting the painting instructions. Consequently, it is very difficult to make general statements about which boat was painted in what measure at any given time. To do so with any degree of accuracy requires dated photographic evidence of each boat throughout its operational life, which is not available. Still, this information is important to the enthusiast and, perhaps more so, to the modeller. This section attempts to deal with this problem by providing a table of camouflage measures applied to each boat upon completion and after assignment to a squadron, and a further table listing paint formulae and related data. These tables are based primarily on photographs, official documents, crew member recollections, BuShips camouflage measure drawings, two fine books on camouflage published by the Floating Drydock, and research conducted by the late Del Palmieri. These tables should not be considered definitive, however, as a certain amount of conjecture was necessary.

Palmieri's work appeared as a series of eighteen articles in *Scale Models* magazine between April 1979 and June 1982 and quite possibly comprises the most comprehensive data on US Navy camouflage published to date. Camouflage enthusiasts would do well to acquire copies of these articles.

There were at least twelve different approved camouflage measures applied to the Elco PTs between 1940 and 1945, as well as a variety of unofficial, field-applied patterns. Most of the boats produced up to early 1943 left the factory in grey and were then repainted as appropriate for their theatre of operations. Pacific boats were generally repainted overall green initially, then one of the multiple green measures. Atlantic boats generally retained an overall grey scheme. As one might expect, though, variations occurred. The Elcos operating in the Aleutians were grey, while the RON 29 boats in the Mediterranean were light blue (Measure 16), despite having left the factory in the greens of Measure 31/5P.

Elco also altered some of the approved BuShips measures, adding to the confusion. David Swasey, a camoufleur at Elco during the Second World War, wrote:

> At around this time [1943], requests began to come to the Navy Department from the South Pacific for schemes in green. The Bureau of Ships' Camouflage Office designed an excellent scheme called 'Measure 31'. An order came through to put it on all boats from now on. We were well suited to handle this job immediately, as by now our layout men and paint crews were in top form. We got permission from Washington to vary this design, while still adhering to the basic principles, and brought out six different patterns of this scheme which we put on the boats, one design following the other, and then back to the first one again, and so on, so that no more than two boats would be alike in each squadron of twelve. This scheme was applied to thirteen squadrons, and admittedly took care of the most serious problem at that time; ie, hiding out.
>
> With 'Measure 31' we developed a green undercoat of great durability to act as a base for wear and tear, and also a green canvas for gun covers, etc, fireproofed and conditioned for all kinds of weather.

One of the patterns altered by Elco was 31/5P, for which BuShips drawings are available. The basic pattern consisted of soft-edged (sprayed), irregular patterns of a dark green over a medium green. Exactly what greens were used is a small problem, as changes to the greens were occurring at the same time that Measure 31/5P was being applied. The BuShips drawing shows Navy Green (5–NG) over Ocean Green (5–OG); however, Outside Green 1, 2 and 3 were being phased in at this time, as well. It is possible that the

Overall starboard view of the Adaptor pattern applied to PT 170. The light blue-grey replaces the white in the third panel from the stern and second panel from the bow. Elco

later boats were Outside Green 3 over Outside Green 2.

Based on Swasey's descriptions and the period, it would appear that the measure listed as 31/? in the tables was another of the variations Elco created. This pattern consisted of hard-edged, vertical wave patterns, most likely Outside Green 3 and 2. As it has not proved possible to locate any BuShips measure drawings identifying this pattern, it is listed as 31/?.

Probably the most well-known green pattern was Measure 31/20L, which was developed in 1944. This pattern consisted of hard-edged, irregular patterns of Outside Green 3, Outside Green 2, and black, the pattern being different on each side. 31/20L first appeared on PT 533 in May 1944 and became standard on most Elcos from PT 565 on. The pattern was supposed to be placed in slightly different locations on each boat in a squadron, so that no two were alike. However, photographic evidence suggests that this was the exception rather than the rule.

The patterns of the various green measures were applied to all vertical surfaces, while decks and all other horizontal surfaces, including the tops of the charthouse and day cabin, were generally painted Deck Green (20–G). Of course, there were exceptions, a number of 31/?-painted boats carrying the patterns over on to the decks. The latter practice was far more common to Higgins PTs, however.

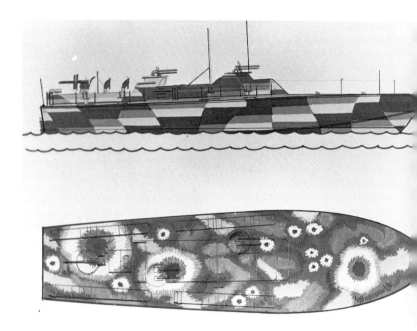

Some of the camouflage schemes experimented with by Elco were rather bizarre. The colours in the side view are pink, green, light blue, and dark grey. The top view colours are blues, greens, and white, simulating shallow-water patterns. Elco

Elco used models to experiment with various schemes before applying them to actual craft. Note the unique pattern on the drawing in the background. Elco

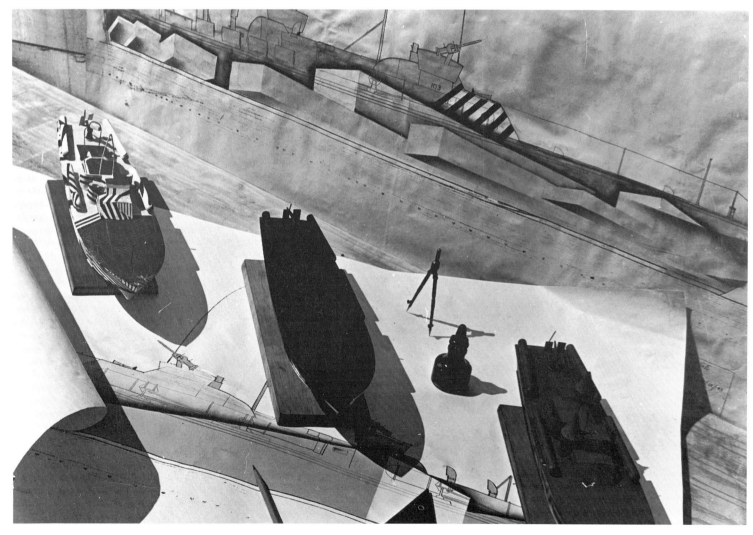

PT 196, the last of the original contract boats, had a series of light grey stripes and a shark's face added to the original Measure 14, along with the nickname 'Elcopuss', upon completion. She reverted to a more normal Measure 31/5P in service. USN

One of the more unusual measures developed was the radical Adaptor, or 'Zebra', system designed as a disruptive rather than low visibility measure. This system consisted of black and white stripes painted on all vertical surfaces, with light blue-grey counter-shading. The intention was to create the impression of a box, thus breaking up the shape of the actual boat. The optimal stripe width was determined to be 4in, although widths up to 12in would be effective. This measure was not used operationally on Elcos, although a variation in which the white was replaced with a yellowish green was applied to PT 163–174 for a short period. The Higgins boats of RON 15 did arrive in the Mediterranean with the black and white version, however.

A single boat might carry several measures over its operational life, depending on when it was built, how often its operating area or mission changed, how long it lasted, and how closely squadron commanders adhered to BuShips directives. The boats of the original Squadron 3 are a prime example of drastic change over a very short period of time. The six 77ft boats (PT 31–35, 41) were placed in service between 8 and 25 July 1941, at which time they were painted overall Navy Gray (No.5) with Outside Dark Gray (No.5–D) decks. Between July and September, when they were shipped to the Philippines, they were repainted in Measure 1 (overall Outside Dark Gray No.5–D). Three months later, following the Japanese attack on Pearl Harbor, they were painted dark green. The American co-author's father was on PT 34 at the time and he noted that they used locally-acquired paint and deck swabs to complete the camouflage!

Sometimes the boats were even repainted between leaving the

PT 66 in the Solomons displays one of the first field-applied green patterns. Contemporary colour photos show that, upon arrival, PT 66 carried Measure 13, with Navy Blue or Sea Blue numbers on the pilothouse. USN

factory and being placed in service. Leo Brown, in his history of RON 37, noted that the boats (PT 533–544) were delivered from Elco to Brooklyn in grey, then sent over to Fyfe's boatyard on Long Island to be painted green prior to acceptance. Photographs of the boats working up in Panama in August 1944 clearly show them in Measure 31/20L.

The boats of RON 29 left the factory in Measure 31/5P but were immediately repainted in a modified Measure 16 (Thayer Blue) when assigned to the Mediterranean.

The area below the waterline on all PTs in US Navy service was generally 'Copperoyd', a brownish-red antifouling paint produced by the Metallic Coatings Corporation of New York.

Each squadron was expected to maintain its own boats, including painting. A BuShips Allowance List for PTs, issued 21 May 1945, assigned each squadron the following quantities of paints to keep the boats in proper shape:

Acid-resisting black	5 gallons
Copperoyd bottom paint	360 gallons
Canvas preservative (blue, grey, or geen)	15 gallons
Deck Blue (20–B)	50 gallons
Deck Green (20–G)	60 gallons
Flat black (13)	300 gallons
Navy Green (5–NG)	30 gallons
Ocean Green (5–OG)	60 gallons

Colour schemes of the Royal Navy Elcos varied as much as the US Navy boats. The 70ft PTCs were completed in overall Navy Gray (No.5) and repainted in 507–C when in Royal Navy service as MGBs. The 70ft PTs, on the other hand, were delivered to the Royal Navy in either Measure 3 or 507–A and carried US Navy-style shaded pennant numbers. The 77ft boats were also delivered in light grey, probably 507–C, and likewise carried the shaded pennant numbers. While operating around Tobruk, they carried an Admiralty disruptive pattern of grey, white, and black.

A photo of MTB 307 and MTB 315 being paid off in 1945 shows them in Light Standard Scheme F (overall light grey with white counter shading and dark grey pennant numbers). The decks and other horizontal surfaces do not appear to have been painted the much darker B–15 normally associated with this scheme.

Initially, the Royal Navy boats appear to have had the 'Copperoyd' bottom paint with which they were originally painted. However, most of the MTBs and MGBs reverted to the more normal black paint used by the Royal Navy on Coastal Forces Craft. Often, the bottom paint did not extend to the bow, terminating at a point which corresponded to the area of the hull normally exposed when the boat was on plane. From this point forward, the bottom was painted the same light colour as the rest of the hull.

Details of Royal Navy camouflage applications, including countershading requirements and paint formulae, are contained in Volume 1 of this series.

Camouflage colour data

Colour name	Colour number	Mixture	Dates in use	Approximate 1929 Munsell number	Colour name	Colour number	Mixture	Dates in use	Approximate 1929 Munsell number
Outside Navy Gray	No. 5	Undetermined	1920–12.40	5 PB 7/2	Tropical Green		Mix 5 parts zinc chromate (Formula 84) with 4 parts tinting paste (5-TMa)	1.43–1944	
Outside Deck Gray	No. 20	Undetermined	1920–12.40	5 PB 3/2	Pale Gray	5-P	Mix 1 part blue-black tinting material (5-TM) with 160 parts white (5-U)	3.43–1945	5 PB 8/1
Light Gray	5-L	Mix 1 part blue-black tinting material (5-TM) with 40 parts white (5-U)	1.41–8.41	5 PB 7/2	Light Gray	5-L	Mix 1 part blue-black tinting material (5-TM) with 40 parts white (5-U)	3.43–1945	5 PB 7/2
Ocean Gray	5-O	Mix 5 parts blue-black tinting material (5-TM) with 40 parts white (5-U)	1.41–8.41	5 PB 5/2	Pale Green	5-PG	Mix 1 part green tinting material (5-GTM) with 120 parts white (5-U)	3.43–1945	5.0 G-Y 8/2
Dark Gray	5-D	Undetermined	1.41–8.41	5 PB 2/2	Light Green	5-L	Mix 1 part green tinting material (5-GTM) with 40 parts white (5-U)	3.43–1945	5.0 G-Y 7/2
Black	82	Premixed	1.41–1945						
Haze Gray	5-H	Mix 2 parts blue-black tinting material (5-TM) with 40 parts white (5-U)	9.41–5.42	5 PB 6/2	Haze Green	5-HG	Mix 2 parts green tinting material (5-GTM) with 40 parts white (5-U)	3.43–1945	5.0 G-Y 5.5/2
Ocean Gray	5-O	Mix 5 parts blue-black tinting material (5-TM) with 40 parts white (5-U)	9.41–5.42	5 PB 5/3	Ocean Green	5-OG	Mix 12 parts green tinting material (5-GTM) with 40 parts white (5U)	3.43–1945	5.0 G-Y 5/2
Sea Blue	5-S	Mix 10 parts blue-black tinting material (5-TM) with 40 parts white (5-U)	9.41–5.42	5 PB 4/4	Navy Green	5-NG	Mix 40 parts green tinting material (5-GTM) with 8 parts white (5-U)	3.43–1945	10 G-Y 2.5/1.5
Navy Blue	5-N	Mix 15 parts blue-black tinting material (5-TM) with 40 parts white (5-U)	9.41–5.42	5 PB 3.4/3	Deck Green	20-G	Mix 32 parts of green tinting material (5-GTM) with 8 parts white (5-U) and 160 parts blue-black tinting material (5-TM)	3.43–1945	5.0 G 2/1.5
Deck Blue	20-B	Mix 20 parts blue-black tinting material (5-TM) with 20 parts untinted deck paint (20-U)	9.41–5.42	5 PB 3/4					
Haze Gray	5-H	Mix 2 parts blue-black tinting material (5-TM) with 40 parts white (5-U)	6.42–3.43	5 PB 6/2	Outside Green 1	Green 1	Undetermined	1944–45	5.0 G-Y 6/3
Ocean Gray	5-O	Mix 5 parts blue-black tinting material (5-TM) with 40 parts white (5-U)	6.42–3.43	5 PB 5/3	Outside Green 2	Green 2	Mix 3 parts Ocean Green (5-OG) with 1 part Navy Green (5-NG)	1944–45	7.5 G-Y 3.5/2
Navy Blue	5-N	Mix 15 parts blue-black tinting material (5-TM) with 40 parts white (5-U)	6.42–3.43	5 PB 3.4/3	Outside Green 3	Green 3	Mix 4 parts Navy Green (5-NG) with 1 part Thayer Blue tint medium (5-BTM)	1944–45	10.0 G-Y 5/2
Thayer Blue	5-B	Mix 1 part blue tinting material (5-BTM) with 40 parts white (5-U)	6.42–3.43	5 PB 8/2					
Deck Blue	20-B	Mix 20 parts blue-black tinting material (5-TM) with 20 parts untinted deck paint (20-U)	6.42–1945	5 PB 3/4					

USN boat number PT	Foreign boat number	Initial measure (factory-applied)	Subsequent measure(s) (field-applied)

Elco 70ft PTs

USN boat number PT	Foreign boat number	Initial measure (factory-applied)	Subsequent measure(s) (field-applied)
PT 10–19	MTB 259–268 (RN)	Navy Gray (No. 5) overall with Dark Gray (No. 5-D) Decks	Measure 3 (USN); probably 507A overall (RN)
PTC 1–12	MGB 82–93 (RN)	Navy Gray (No. 5) overall with Dark Gray (No. 5-D) decks	Probably 507-C overall (RN)

Elco 77ft Pts

USN boat number PT	Foreign boat number	Initial measure (factory-applied)	Subsequent measure(s) (field-applied)
20, 21, 24, 27–30, 37, 39, 42, 43		Navy Gray (No. 5) overall with Dark Gray (No. 5-D) decks	Measure 1, Measure 14
22		as above	Measure 1
23, 25, 26, 36, 38, 40	C 55047, 55048, 55049, 73994, 68730, 73995	as above	Measure 1, Measure 14
31–35, 41		as above	Measure 1. Dark Green overall after 7.12.41
44, 45, 47, 48		as above	Measure 1. 1943: overall Green, possibly variation of Tropical Green System without mottling
46	C 74095	as above	as above
49, 51, 55, 57	MTB 307, 309, 313, 315 (RN)	as above	Admiralty disruptive – broad bands of white, black and light grey (probably G-45); Light Standard Scheme F
50, 52–54, 56, 58	MTB 308, 310–312, 314 (later German RA 10), 316 (RN)	as above	Admiralty disruptive – broad bands of white, black and light grey (probably G-45)
59		as above	Measure 14. 1943: overall Green, possibly variation of Tropical Green System without mottling
60, 62–64, 67, 68		as above	Measure 14
61		as above	as above
65		as above	overall Green, possibly variation of Tropical Green System without mottling
66		as above	Measure 14. Unusual mottled pattern, probably greens, on hull after transfer to RON 8.

(continued) Subsequent measure(s): Overall Dark Green with shark's mouth and eyes as small boat

Licence-built Vospers

BPT

USN boat number PT	Foreign boat number	Initial measure (factory-applied)	Subsequent measure(s) (field-applied)
21–28, 49–52	MTB 275–282, 283–286 (RIN)	Light Standard Scheme 'F'	Light Standard Scheme 'F' (RN)
29–32, 38–40	MTB 287–290, 296–298	probably 507-C overall	probably 507-C overal (RN)
33–36, 41–48	MTB 291–294, 299–306	as above	probably 507-C overall (RIN)
37	MTB 295 (RN), GIS 0018 (Italy)	as above	probably 507-C overall (RN)
53–60	MTB 363–370 (RN); TKA 221–223, 226–230 (USSR)	Light Standard Scheme 'F'	Light Standard Scheme 'F' (RN); unknown (USSR)
61, 62	MTB 371, 372	as above	Light Standard Scheme 'F' (RN)
63–68	MTB 373–378 (RN); GIS 0014, 0015, 009, 0010, 0016, 0017 (Italy)	as above	Light Standard Scheme 'F' (RN); light grey (unknown measure) (Italy)

PT

USN boat number PT	Foreign boat number	Initial measure (factory-applied)	Subsequent measure(s) (field-applied)
384, 395	MTB 396, 407 (RN)	Light Standard Scheme 'F' (RN)	Light Standard Scheme 'F' (RN)
385, 387	MTB 397, 399 (RN)	as above	Light Standard Scheme 'F' (RN); unknown (Egypt)
386, 388–394, 396–399	MTB 398, 401–406, 408–411 (RN); GIS 001, 002, 004, 003, 0013, 005, 006, 0011, 008, 007, 0028 (Italy)	as above	Light Standard Scheme 'F' (RN); light grey (unknown measure) (Italy)
400, 401	TKA (?) (USSR)	unknown, but probably similar to Measure 13 (USSR)	unknown (USSR)
402–405, 406, 407, 408–413, 414–416	TKA 231–234, 243, 244, 235–240, 246–248 (USSR)	as above	as above
417–429	TKA (?) (USSR)	as above	as above
430–432, 433, 434, 435, 448	TKA 241–243, 249, 240, 251, 252	as above	as above
436–447, 449, 661–692	TKA (?) (USSR)	as above	as above
693–714, 717–730		as above	none, not placed in service
715–716	R41, 42	unknown (Cuba)	unknown (Cuba), but photographs suggest light grey or white overall

Elco 80ft Pts

USN boat number PT	Foreign boat number	Initial measure (factory-applied)	Subsequent measure(s) (field-applied)
103–117		Navy Gray (No. 5) hull with Dark Gray (No. 5-D)	Measure 13. Overall Green, possibly variation of Tropical

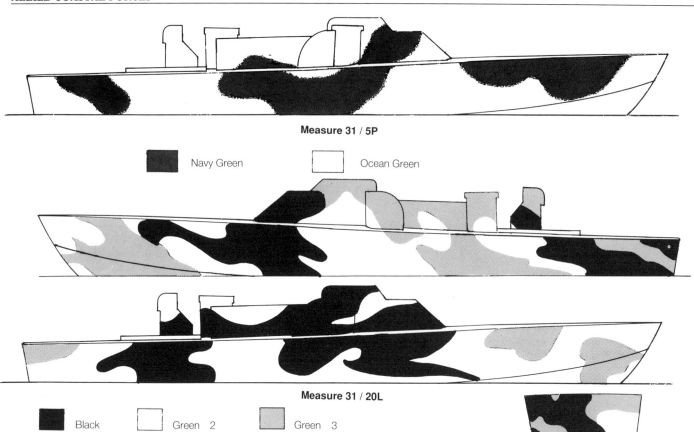

Measure 31 / 5P

Navy Green   Ocean Green

Measure 31 / 20L

Black   Green 2   Green 3

USN boat number PT	Foreign boat number	Initial measure (factory-applied)	Subsequent measure(s) (field-applied)	USN boat number	Foreign boat number	Initial measure (factory-applied)	Subsequent measure(s) (field-applied)
		superstructure	Green System without mottling	314–317		lines of Haze Gray Measure 13	Tropical Green System, Measure 13
118–160, 162, 175–177, 179–186, 318, 319		Measure 13	overall Green, possibly variation of Tropical Green System without mottling	328		Measure 31/5P	Measure 31/20L
				332–342		as above	Measure 31/?
				362–367		Measure 14	Measure 31/5P
				486, 487	C 105335, 105336	Measure 13	Measure 13
163, 164, 168–172, 174		Adaptor pattern (Green)	as above	498–504, 506–508, 510–521	TKA (?) (USSR)	as above	Measure 13 (USN); unknown (USSR)
165–166, 173		Adaptor pattern (Green)	Adaptor pattern (Green)	505, 509, 545		Measure 13	Measure 13
167		Adaptor pattern (Green)	overall Green, possibly variation of Tropical Green System without mottling. Measure 31/20L	552, 553, 554, 556, 560, 561, 562, 563	TKA 578 (?), 579 (?), 583 (?), 580 (?), 584 (?), 581 (?), 585 (?), 582 (?) (USSR)	Measure 31/5P	Modified Measure 16 – Thayer Blue overall with Deck Blue (20-B) decks (USN); unknown (USSR)
178		Measure 13	Measure 31/?	555		as above	Modified Measure 16 – Thayer Blue overall with Deck Blue (20-B) decks
187–195, 320–327, 329–331, 343–361, 372–383, 488–497, 522–532, 546–551		Measure 31/5P	Measure 31/5P	557, 559	C 105338, 105339	as above	Modified Measure 16 – Thayer Blue overall with Deck Blue (20-B) decks (RON 29). Measure 13 (RON 4)
				558		as above	as above
196		Measure 14 much modified – shark's mouth on bow, wavy	Measure 31/5P	565–600, 607, 617–618,		Measure 31/20L	Measure 31/20L

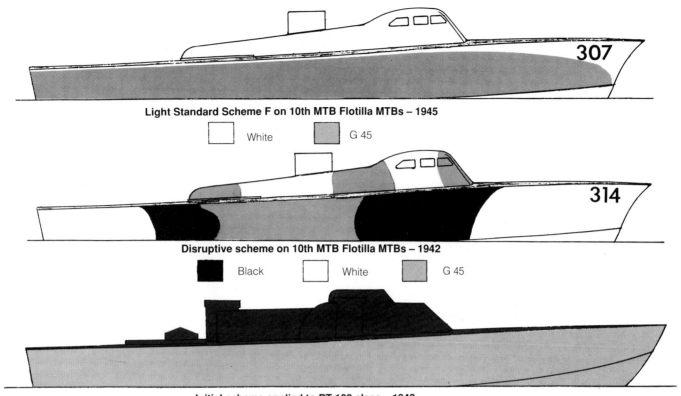

Light Standard Scheme F on 10th MTB Flotilla MTBs – 1945

☐ White   ▨ G 45

Disruptive scheme on 10th MTB Flotilla MTBs – 1942

■ Black   ☐ White   ▨ G 45

Initial scheme applied to PT 103 class – 1942

▨ Navy Gray #5   ■ Dark Gray #5–D

USN boat number	Foreign boat number	Initial measure (factory-applied)	Subsequent measure(s) (field-applied)	Colours associated with Camouflage Measures	
				Measure	**Colours**
621–624				Standard Navy Gray	Navy Gray (No.5),
601	C 6083	as above	as above		Dark Gray (No.5-D)
602–606	*Snogg* (renamed *Knuff*); *Sel; Sild; Skrei; Snar* (renamed *Lyr*) (all Norway)	as above	Measure 31/20L (USN); unknown (Norway)	Measure 1	Dark Gray (No. 5-D)
				Measure 3	Light Gray (5-L)
					Deck Gray (No. 20)
				Measure 13	Haze Gray (5-H)
					Deck Blue (20-B)
608–612	*Springer; Hai; Hauk* (renamed *Laks*); *Hval; Hvass* (renamed *Delfin*) (all Norway)	as above	as above	Measure 14	Ocean Gray (5-O)
					Deck Blue (20-B)
				Measure 16	Thayer Blue (5-B)
					Deck Blue (20-B)
				Tropical Green System	Tropical Green
					Deck Green (20-G)
613, 616, 619, 620	*Olpamei; Kaimaeki* (*Kalmakeki*); *Koroki* (*Kiroki*); *Ebi* (*Jebi*) (South Korea)	as above	Measure 31/20L. Measure 13 postwar (USN); unknown (South Korea)	31/5P	Navy Green (5-N)
					Ocean Green (5-OG)
					Deck Green (20-G)
614, 615	C 105340, 105341	as above	Measure 31/20L	31/?	Navy Green (5-NG)
731–760	TKA (?) (USSR)	overall Gray – possibly Haze Gray, measure unknown (USSR)	unknown (USSR)		Ocean Green (5-OG)
					Deck Green (20-G)
				31/20L	Green 2
					Green 3
761–790		none; boat not completed	none; boat not placed in service		Black
					Deck Green (20-G)
				Adaptor (White)	White
					Black
					Haze Gray (5-H)
					Deck Blue (20-B)
				Adaptor (Green)	Haze Green (5-HG) (?)
					Black
					Deck Green (20-G)

Note: Last colour listed in each measure is deck colour

The Packard 4M–2500 marine engine

During the 1920s Hubert Scott-Paine of the British Power Boat Co had developed the Napier Lion aero engine and modified it for use as a marine power plant. This was so successful that this engine powered the first 60ft MTBs that his company built for the Admiralty. However, he considered that they were not powerful enough, and sought other ideas. He obtained permission to use the new Rolls-Royce Merlin, and with his experience of the Napier conversion he was able to provide the Derby engineers with a detailed specification and suitable ahead and astern gears for the units. These were placed in limited production for foreign orders. None the less, it was thought prudent to consider other sources. Like Peter Du Cane, he was not happy to rely on the Italian Isotta-Fraschini marine engine.

In the summer of 1938 Scott-Paine met with the Engineer-Vice Admiral, Sir George Preece, but they developed a mutual antipathy. Not satisfied with the assurance that a British diesel engine was in the pipeline, Scotty searched for an alternative. On 25 May 1939 a meeting was arranged with a Mr Platt, the Paris representative of the American Packard company. He was told that an English boat builder was interested in purchasing 100 engines. Mr Platt stated that Packard had done no serious selling since 1930, but that they could develop a 1200hp engine of the type that had been used by Gar Wood for racing.

On 30 June the engineering vice-president of Packard wrote to Scott-Paine, stating that they had received authority from the US Navy to export their new 'V'-form 12-cylinder supercharged marine engine, which was in limited production for their experimental PT boats. Scott-Paine also had an interest in selling British Power Boat designs to the US Navy.

'Scotty' resolved to go to America and obtain a sure supply of engines, and set up a deal with Elco for the production of British Power Boat designs. He travelled to America aboard SS *Aquitania*, arriving on 16 September. His Merlin powered PV Boat arrived on the 5th, by then designated PT9. On the 23rd he arrived in Detroit

and was negotiating with Packard. Later an agreement was made and Scotty set to work with Packard's engineers to design modifications to the M-2500 engine. These included the adoption of Scott-Paine's patented assembly rails, as used with the Merlin installation, the adoption of magneto ignition, changes to the water jacket and crankcase material and some redesign. The Packard method of supercharging was replaced by the method used in the Merlin, and modifications were made to the induction pipes and cylinder blocks. Discussions also took place with the Joe Reverse Gear Company for the supply of suitable ahead and reverse gears for use in boats built for the US Navy.

On 19 December a further meeting took place to thrash out a provisional agreement for the new engines that were to substitute for the Rolls-Royce Merlin in the Elco boats. Scotty placed a firm order for 100 engines, and at the same time concluded an agreement for the British Power Boat Company to be the sole agent for the sale of the engine in the British Empire. The agreement gave his company a 10 per cent commission on the sale price of the engine. The basic price of the engine was to be $21,500, plus the 10 per cent commission.

These are the events of the British part taken in the Packard story. During 1940 149 engines were produced, the first 81 going to Elco and the remainder being divided between Britain and Canada. By the end of the war 4,686 Packard marine engines had either been purchased by the British Purchasing Commission or had been made available to Britain under Lend-Lease.

The Packard 4M–2500 marine engine was a 4-stroke cycle, liquid

A Packard engine on a Vosper test bed in 1941.
Note the 'U' tube for boost readings, the water-
cooled exhaust pipes and the brake test
machinery attached to the propeller shaft.
Vosper Thornycroft (UK) Ltd

The centre Hall-Scott Defender petrol engine in MTB 36, which was fitted with three supercharged 900hp engines and capable of only 25–28 knots.
Vosper Thornycroft (UK) Ltd

cooled, supercharged 12-cylinder 60 degree 'V' type unit of 6⅜in bore, 6½in stroke. The total piston displacement was 2490 cu in and the standard compression ratio 6.4 to one. The engine was rated at 1200hp at 2400rpm and 1350hp at 2500rpm. It was normally furnished as a complete marine power plant with a direct connected reverse gear in which was embodied a double cone-type clutch and positive forward drive. The engine and reverse gear weight (dry-net) was 2950lb. They were built by the Packard Motor Car Co, Marine Engine Division of Detroit, Michigan.

The engines were improved and modified during construction as a result of use in service where modifications to small components were incorporated, but apparently no major redesign took place during the war years.

Basically the engine consisted of two banks of six individual closed-end type steel cylinders, with welded-on water jackets, mounted at an angle of 60 degrees on a cast aluminium crankcase. The crankshaft was forged alloy steel, counterweighted, and carried in eight shimless, removable, shell bearings. An harmonic vibration damper was fitted to the supercharger end of the crankshaft. Fork and blade connecting rods and forged aluminium pistons were used. The two exhaust and two intake valves per cylinder were actuated by a single camshaft on each cylinder bank through end-fulcrum-type rocker levers. A gear driven vane-type fuel pump supplied petrol to the down draught, floatless, aviation-type carburettor located on the inlet side of the gear driven centrifugal supercharger.

Regularly furnished accessories in addition to the reverse gear included fuel pump, tachometer drive, carburettor, air cleaner and flame arrester, electrical starter, generator and generator regulator, magneto, distributors, high-tension ignition booster coil and the required wiring and shielding. Optional accessory equipment included 3½hp take-off, 8½hp accessory drive, automatic ignition overspeed cut-out and synchronised auxiliary engine drive.

To avoid confusion when referring to the direction of rotation, right or left hand side, or front and rear of the engine, it was always considered that the engine was viewed from the reverse gear end, and since the engine could be installed with either end forward, reference will be to the supercharger and reverse gear ends, rather than to front and rear.

Rotation The engine is described as of right hand rotation since the crankshaft turns clockwise when viewed from the reverse gear end.

Cylinder banks The cylinder banks are referred to as right or left when viewed from the reverse gear end. The cylinder construction was a composite design in which the six cylinders of each bank and the bolted-on valve housings were considered as a single cylinder block unit and removed and reinstalled as such. Individual cylinders were interchangeable, as were the two blocks of six cylinders.

Cylinders The individual cylinders were consecutively numbered 1–6 in each bank, starting at the reverse gear end, with firing order 1R–3L–4R–5L–2R–1L–6R–4L–3R–2L–5R–6L. The twelve individual closed-end-type cylinders were of all-steel construction including the integral combustion chamber. The outside of each cylinder barrel was plated to resist corrosion and the welded-on water jackets were of stainless steel. Except for synthetic rubber sealing rings used around the connecting water passages, no gaskets were used between the cylinders and the valve housing. The cylinders were provided with flanges located some distance above the lower end of the barrel by which they were bolted to the crankcase. The valve housings were of cast aluminium machined on all surfaces and used interchangeably on the right and left banks. The housings distributed the fuel mixture to the inlet valves, acted as exhaust outlets and carried the valve guides and camshaft bearing pedestals.

Valve mechanism The entire valve operating mechanism was enclosed, with the valve housing covers of cast aluminium carrying mounting pads for the tachometer drive, 3½hp take-off drive and ignition automatic overspeed cut-out, which were driven from the camshafts. There were four valves per cylinder, two inlet and two

The engine-room of MTB 74 looking forward, with the huge exhaust system (no Dumbflow silencers yet) and little spare space. Note the two pyrene (CTC) fire extinguishers clipped to the deckhead.
Vosper Thornycroft (UK) Ltd

exhaust, set in the forged steel cylinder head. The exhaust valve seats were of the inserted types and faced with Stellite, as were the heads of the exhaust valves, their stems being hollow and filled with sodium to aid in cooling.

The valves of each cylinder block were actuated through individual rocker levers by a single camshaft carried in seven unlined, split-type pedestal bearings of aluminium alloy bolted to the top of the valve housing. The camshafts were hollow and carried oil under pressure to the bearings and rocker lever shafts; the camshafts were marked right and left and were not interchangeable.

The valve rocker levers were of the individual end fulcrum type, bronze bushed at the fulcrum end where they pivoted on rocker lever shafts carried by the camshaft pedestals. Each cam follower roller was carried on 34 small rollers assembled without a separator to form a quill bearing. The tappets in the ends of the levers were of the self-aligning type and were threaded into the rocker lever to provide a means for valve clearance adjustment. The camshafts were driven from the supercharger end of the crankshaft through a train of bevel gears. The magneto, distributor, fuel pump and various accessory drives were also driven by the same gear train.

Crankcase The crankcase was of a modified box section composed of two aluminium castings joined below the crankshaft centreline. The main bearing upper halves were carried in the transverse webs of the crankcase upper half. The main bearing lower halves were supported in individual V-shaped forged steel bearing caps, the sides of which were T-slotted to receive the heads of special bolts passing through holes in the transverse webs to the outside of the crankcase. The lower crankcase lower half or oil pan (sump) carried a mounting pad at the supercharger end for the combined pressure and scavenge oil and fresh water pump unit. A screen above the oil pump inlet, extending the full length of the sump, protected the oil pump unit from being damaged by foreign particles carried over in the oil. A scavenge oil line extending to the reverse gear end of the sump and a scavenge oil inlet direct through the pump body kept the crankcase scavenged regardless of which end of the engine was high or the state of the sea.

Crankshaft and main bearings The counterweighted crankshaft was of forged alloy steel machined all over. Starting from about engine No 3140 the crankshaft was nitrided to increase journal life.

MTB 523 (73ft Type II) engine-room looking aft. Note 'Dumbflow' to port and generator to starboard.
Vosper Thornycroft (UK) Ltd

The crankpins and main bearing journals were bored out with large holes and plugged to provide reservoirs for oil; the crankpins received oil from the adjacent main bearings through passages drilled in the cheeks. The supercharger end of the crankshaft was splined internally and externally. The crankshaft vibration damper was carried on the external spline, which received the supercharger drive shaft. The number 8 main bearing at the supercharger end of the crankshaft was a one-piece bushing mounted in a plate bolted to the end of the crankcase. The other seven main bearings were of the split type. The main bearings were steel-backed, lined with a special lead-bronze bearing material and lead-tin plated. End thrust was taken on No 1 main bearing. The bearings were non-adjustable, wear being corrected by renewal of the bearing shells.

Connecting rods The connecting rods were 'I' section steel forgings. The piston pin hole in the upper end of the connecting rods was bronze bushed to carry the floating piston pin, which was lubricated by the mist of oil thrown off the lower connecting rod and main bearings, entering oil holes in the top of the rod.

Pistons The pistons were of forged aluminium internally ribbed for greater strength and heat dissipation. Four piston ring grooves all above the piston pin carried the three compression and one oil ring used per piston.

Lubricating oil system The engine and reverse gear were pressure lubricated as a unit, utilising the dry sump principle. After leaving the engine the oil was cooled by passing through a heat exchanger and returned to the main supply tank for recirculation. Oil drawn from the supply tank was delivered under pressure to the main distribution manifold inside the crankcase and to the pressure relief valve on the oil pump housing, which bypassed into the outlet passage from the scavenger pump, thus returning the excess oil to the main supply tank. The crankcase oil manifold led oil to all of the main bearings, which in turn fed the connecting rod lower bearings through drilled passages in the crankshaft cheeks, the oil under pressure acting as both a lubricating and cooling medium. A bypass thermostat was installed in the oil 'out' line to control oil temperature.

The oil pump assembly was mounted on the bottom of the sump at the supercharger end directly above the fresh water pump which was bolted to it. Both were driven by a common vertical shaft connected to a bevel gear which meshed with the crankshaft gear. An adjustable relief valve was mounted externally on the pump body, which was tapped to receive oil 'in' and oil 'out' temperaure gauges.

Cooling system Because of corrosive action of sea water on aluminium alloys, a closed-circuit distilled water system was used to cool the engine. The details of the system varied with different installations, depending on the size of the boat and engine arrangements. Drawings show the diagrammatic layout, the path of the distilled water being as follows: leaving the discharge side of the fresh water pump under pressure, the water was carried to distribution manifolds at each side of the engine near the base of the cylinders and through individual outlets to the water jackets of each cylinder; directed by baffles, the water flowed around the cylinders and up into the valve housings through connecting passages in the top of the cylinders. After passing through cored passages in the valve housing, it flowed through outlets in the valve housing end covers, at the supercharger end. From the engine outlet, the water could be taken directly to the heat exchanger and cooled by passing around pipes through which sea water was pumped, or returned to the expansion tank and from there to the heat exchanger and then on to the pump inlet. Steam vents from the high points of the piping system to the expansion tank were provided as shown in the systems drawings.

An automatic by-pass thermostat (not supplied as part of the engine) was installed in the engine outlet piping to the heat exchanger to control the temperature of the cooling water. When the temperature of the water was below the desired operating temperature, the thermostat closed, bypassing the water around the heat exchanger and returning it directly to the suction side of the pump. As the temperature of the water increased, the thermostat opened, sending the water through the heat exchanger. By automatically varying the quantity of water being bypassed, the thermostat held the engine operating temperature within close limits, depending upon the sea water temperature in the area of operations.

From the supercharger end of each side of the distribution manifold, warm fresh water was piped to the water jacketed supercharger elbow. After flowing through the elbow, warming it, the fresh water was returned to the outlets at the supercharger end of the valve housings.

On the Packard type W9 and W10 engines the exhaust manifolds were cooled by the fresh water system. Water from the outlet at the reverse gear end of each valve housing was piped to the adjacent exhaust manifold. After flowing through the manifold water jackets, it flowed into a cross header connecting with the outlets at the supercharger end of the engine and thence into the main outlet pipe.

Salt water system   The cooling medium, sea water was taken in through and discharged from scoops on the boat hull and circulated through the heat exchanger to take the heat from the fresh water coolant. On all but types W9 and W10 engines the salt water pump taking sea water from the heat exchanger provided sufficient circulation through the heat exchanger for cooling only when the engine was idling, and was supplemented by some other means, such as scoops on the boat hull to provide the amount of sea water needed to cool the heat exchanger when under way. Sea water

discharged from the salt water pump was circulated through the water jacketed exhaust manifold and then overboard through the exhaust pipe. On Types W9 and W10, the exhaust manifolds were cooled by fresh water from the engine cooling system. The modified centrifugal salt water pump had sufficient capacity for engine cooling needs and the salt water scoop merely directed the water to the pump inlet. Discharge from the pump could be into the exhaust pipes or overboard with a sufficient quantity bypassed into the exhaust pipes to provide cooling of the exhaust gases, or dumbflow silencers.

Fuel and induction system   The petrol intake manifolding was of the true down-draught type, characterised by the use of anti-backfire screens, located between the side manifolds and cylinder blocks. In order to secure the best mixture distribution, the manifold tube which connected the supercharger outlet to the centre intake manifold was cellularly divided to straighten the mixture flow.

Supercharger   The supercharger, together with its gearing, was contained in three aluminium housings attached by studs to a mounting flange on the end of the crankcase opposite the reverse gear. A water-jacketed elbow delivered the petrol/air mixture from the carburettor directly to the impeller, which delivered it through a diffuser and the splitter tube to the centre intake manifold. The supercharger was of the centrifugal type, being driven at 6.53 times engine speed by a train of gears from the crankshaft. The drive was through a quill-type shaft splined in the end of the crankshaft to a spring coupling gear in the supercharger housings. The spring

MTB 385 (73ft Type I), engineroom looking forward. Note the mechanic's seat.
Vosper Thornycroft (UK) Ltd

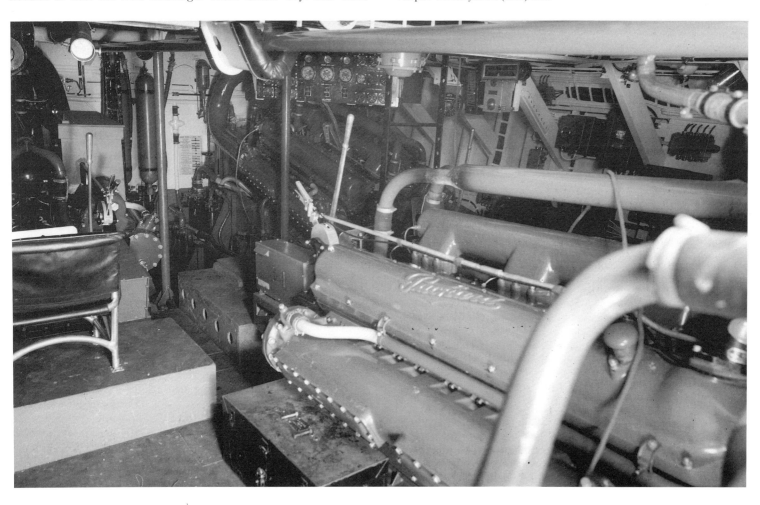

coupling gear drove a two-step intermediate gear which in turn drove the gear on the impeller shaft. All were lubricated from the engine pressure oiling system.

Carburettor Each engine was fitted with a modified Holley model 1685F aircraft-type carburettor of the down-draught type installed on the inlet side of the supercharger.

Fuel pump When the engine was running, the fuel supply for the carburettor was supplied by the engine driven fuel pump, which was of the rotary, 4-bladed, positive displacement type. The unit was equipped with a combination relief and bypass valve, the function of which was to permit control of the delivery pressure and the use of an auxiliary hand pump for starting the engine.

Ignition system This comprised a single high-tension double-spark magneto, two separately driven distributor units, a 24-volt booster coil for use when starting and the required wiring, radio shielding and spark plugs.

Magneto The magneto was a Scintilla model DFLN–4 and operated in conjunction with two separate spark distributing units. Rotation was anticlockwise, when viewed from the drive end, at 1½ times crankshaft speed. The drive was through a synthetic rubber coupling from the upper end of the camshaft centre drive gear.

Spark advance on type W7, W8, W9 and W10 engines was manually controlled and had a range of 20 magneto 13.3 crankshaft degrees. On the earlier types W1 to W6 the throttle lever and spark advance lever were interconnected, and when the engine was idling at closed throttle the magneto breaker was fully retarded. As the throttle was opened the magneto breaker was also advanced, being made to follow the throttle movement by a coil spring. When the throttle was closed the magneto breaker was retarded accordingly by positive action of the interlocking lugs on the levers. Linkage ratios were such that the magneto breaker was moved to its full advance position when the lever on the carburettor throttle shaft had opened 11 degrees.

Distributors The two distributors driven from the camshaft side drive gears received the high-tension current from the magneto and distributed it to the two independent sets of spark plugs. The left hand distributor provided ignition for the spark plugs in the exhaust side of each cylinder, whilst the right hand distributor fired the intake side plugs.

Booster coil A separate battery-operated vibrating type, high tension booster coil was connected to the right hand distributor. The coil supplied a series of sparks which were distributed by a separate electrode on the distributor finger which was 30 degrees retarded with respect to the electrode which distributed the magneto sparks and so assured freedom from 'kick back' during starting.

Battery charging system The engines were fitted with a reverse gear mounted 24-volt generator and a generator regulator or control unit for external mounting on a bulkhead or some other part of the boat structure. Batteries, switches, radio shielding, fuses, ammeters etc were supplied by the boat builders.

Generator The high output (70–75 ampere) DC generators furnished with type W5, W7, W8, W9 and W10 engines were mounted on the reverse gear upper half housing and driven from a gear on the propeller shaft at 2.183 times crankshaft speed. On the earlier type W1, W2, W3, W4 and W6 engines equipped with low output (25–30 ampere) generators, the drive ratio was 1.5 times crankshaft speed. The generator drive was from the driven side of the clutch. The generator only functioned when the boat was under way.

Generator regulators The generator regulator unit consisted of a voltage regulator element, a current or load regulator element and a reverse current or cut-out relay combined in one enclosed unit and mounted externally from the generator. It functioned to control generator operation completely.

Engine starting Each engine was fitted with a 24-volt electrical starter attached to a special flange on the reverse gear upper housing. The electric starting motor drive was through a train of spur gears and a type RK Bendix drive to a ring gear on the outside of the reverse gear clutch drum. Incorporated in the Bendix drive pinion was a friction overload clutch set to slip under a load of 235 to 250 foot pounds.

Starting motor detent A starter motor pinion detent was provided to ensure the engagement of the Bendix pinion with the clutch ring gear in cold weather, when an accumulation of cold oil on the spiral shaft could prevent the pinion from being moved into engagement by its inertia alone. The detent comprised a manually-operated plunger assembled in the reverse gear housing which, when depressed by hand from the outside of the engine, pressed against the pinion and prevented it from turning with the spiral shaft, thus forcing the pinion to travel along the spiral into engagement with the ring gear.

Reverse gear The engine was sold as a complete marine power plant equipped with a built-in reverse gear and clutch. The reverse gear unit was bolted directly to the end face of the crankcase incorporating a double cone clutch and positive forward drive. Special mounting flanges on the upper half of the case carried the double reduction electric starting motor and the battery charging generator. In all engines up to the W7 the clutch friction rings were actuated by means of toggle rods. The W8, W9 and W10 engines employed a design in which the toggles acted directly on the push plate. The W10 was furnished with an auxiliary drive on the reverse gear end cover through which the propeller could be driven by a small auxiliary engine. The auxiliary drive comprised an engine flange through which the auxiliary engine drove a gear on the propeller shaft through a blocker-type synchronising gear clutch. A gear-type oil pump on the underside of the reverse gear case provided lubrication for the auxiliary drive gears and clutch.

A number of engine cooling and lubricating system layouts, for various, early and later engines, are shown. All the tubing sizes specified are outside diameters (O/D) with wall thicknesses of about ³⁄₆₄in to ⁵⁄₆₄in. All the oil and petrol lines were to be thoroughly cleaned before assembly and all the pipe connections were to be flexible to prevent fracture and reduce pipe stresses. All filters fitted were to be cleaned at 10-hourly intervals. The salt water scoops provided all the sea water flow required to cool the fresh water (distilled water) heat exchanger. The salt water pump cooled the engine exhaust manifolds only. The oil screen shown fitted was only temporary, being fitted on the inlet side of the oil pump to prevent any residual dirt in the oil tank, or in the oil lines, from reaching the pump when the engine or tank was first installed. The 'filter screen' was to be removed once the boat was put in commission.

Engine operation

The use of high-octane petrol was fraught with dangers, and starting all petrol engined craft was a time of stress for the commander and crew. Any leak of petrol from the tanks or fuel pipes could cause a build-up of petrol vapour with all the inherent risks of explosion or fire from a spark, and standing orders had built-in safety routines. All engineroom ventilators had to be run long enough to ventilate the engineroom and the bilges thoroughly before engines were started. With the ignition switches in the 'off' position the engine was turned at least two complete revolutions by the use of the electric starter to ensure that the engine rotated freely. All the drain cocks and drain plugs in the exhaust manifold end covers and exhaust pipes, tanks, coolers, filters, pumps, etc which were opened when the engine was previously stopped and secured, were closed. All the water, oil and fuel supply tanks were checked for content (that is, full) and all the valves were turned to the operating position. Except in emergency, the engine, water and oil temperatures were not to be lower than 50°F (13°C) when starting the engine. The use of auxiliary electric heaters was required to maintain this temperature in the engineroom, with the resultant drain on the batteries. After more than one hour's exposure to lower temperatures, the engine, water and oil was to be warmed by maintaining an engineroom temperature in excess of 55°F for at least three hours prior to starting.

Starting For starting it was necessary to remove the cover from the air cleaner on the carburettor and adjust the salt water 'in' and 'out' scoops so that the salt water pump would draw sea water through the heat exchanger. With W9 and W10 engines, with the use of fresh water cooled exhaust manifolds, both scoops were opened. With W7 and W8 engines, if the inlet to the pump was on the out side of the heat exchanger, the 'out' scoop was closed and the 'in' scoop opened. If the inlet to the pump was in the inlet side of the heat exchanger, the salt water 'in' scoop was to be closed and the 'out' scoop opened.

The reverse gear lever was to be in the neutral position. With W10 engines, having auxiliary drive, both the auxiliary drive and auxiliary engine clutches were disengaged. The operation of the throttle was to be checked and the fuel supply line valves opened. The wobble pump pressure had to be at least 5lb but not more than 7lb, registered on the fuel pressure gauge.

If the engine was cold, it was primed with a few strokes of the hand primer pump, which was then closed. (If the engine was warm the primer pump was not required.) The throttle was opened slightly and the magneto advance control lever put in the full retard position; the starter line switch was closed, the ignition switch turned to bring the starting booster coil into operation and the starter used to turn the engine. As soon as the engine started, the switch was turned to the magneto position. To avoid overheating of the booster coil and rapid wear of the contact points, operation on the booster coil was to be kept to the minimum.

Immediately the engine started the oil pressure was checked. The gauge should have shown pressure within five seconds. If pressure was not registered after ten seconds, the engine was shut down and the cause of pressure loss identified or rectified. Oil pressure was not to be allowed to exceed 150lb/sq in. If it exceeded that amount on a cold start, the engine was to be stopped and the oil heated by some means before restarting.

Warming up The engines were not to be idled whilst alongside and no load was to be put on until the water 'out' temperature reached 110°F and oil 'in' 110°F. After the engines were started and idling, the salt water scoops remained in starting position until the boat got under way. However, the exhaust outlet was to be checked to ensure that water was circulating through the exhaust manifolds and cooling pipes.

The engines were warmed up whilst under way whenever possible to shorten the warm-up period and thus reduce the possibility of spark plug fouling. Immediately the boat got under way, salt water 'in' and 'out' scoops were opened, and the thermostats automatically regulated water temperature. The engines were to be operated at moderate speeds – 800rpm to 1000rpm – during the warm-up and at not more than 1000rpm until the oil 'in' temperature reached 130°F. However, in an emergency the engine could be run provided the oil pressure did not exceed 150lb/sq in and held steady.

If operating instructions were complied with, the engines were generally very reliable and daily, 25-hour, 50-hour, 50-hour, 100-hour and 250-hour inspections were suggested. Vosper had some installation problems with early boats when the Packard was first introduced, but with experience in service they were resolved and the engine proved to be an excellent power source for the Allied navies, both the US Navy and the Royal Navy sharing a common high-speed engine unit. The Packard power:weight ratio compared well with other marine power units of the period:

Engine	bhp	weight	lb/bhp
Napier Sea Lion	500	1652lb	3.31
Isotta-Fraschini (CRM)	1100	2699lb	2.45
Rolls-Royce Merlin	1100	2240lb	2.0
Packard 4M–2500	1500	3017lb	2.0

Whilst the Packard was undoubtedly a godsend and was produced in the nick of time, there are those who argue that the lighter Isotta was the better engine.

Packard model 4M-2500 marine petrol engine

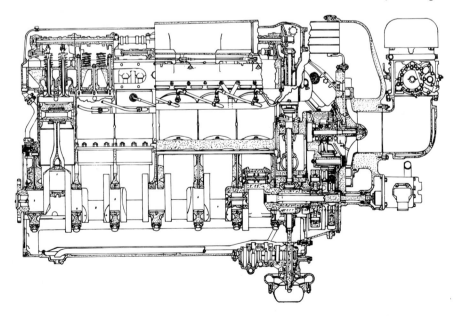
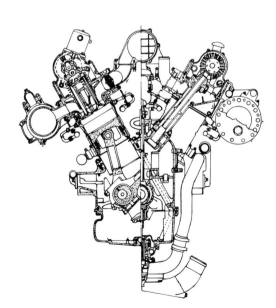

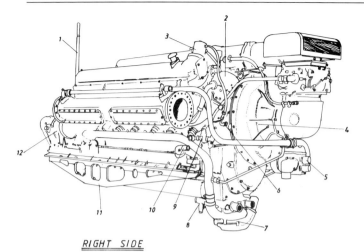

RIGHT SIDE   LEFT SIDE

General Arrangement – Types W7, W8

1   Reverse gear lever
2   Distributor
3   Ignition overspeed cutout
4   Supercharger
5   Salt water pump
6   Booster coil
7   Fresh water pump
8   Oil pumps
9   Fuel pump
10 Oil tank vent
11 Side rail
12 Generator
13 Power take-off
14 Fresh water inlet
15 Sea water inlet
16 Tachometer drive
17 Centre intake manifold
18 Ventilating manifold
19 Cranking motor
20 Reverse unit
21 Exhaust manifold drain
22 Starter detent

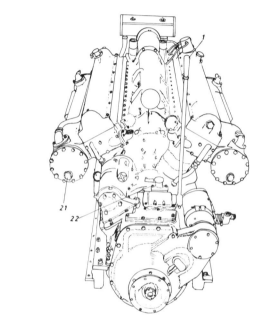

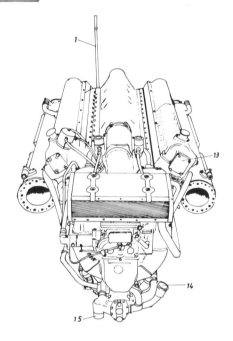

Oil and water cooler units (bolted together as a single assembly)

1   Water heat exchanger
2   Sea water – out
3   Sea water – in
4   Oil cooler
5   Fresh water
6   Vent plug

Pressure oil strainer showing new pressure relief valve bypass tube (starting with engine No 9211)

1   Plug
2   New bypass tube
3   Banjo connection
4   New oil inlet connection

Packard engine fuel system

1   Fuel pump
2   ⅛in OD
3   Fuel tank
4   ³⁄₁₆in OD
5   Shut-off valve
6   ¾in OD
7   Strainer
8   1in OD
9   Primer lines
10 Filter – mounted close to engine
11 Relief valve
12 Wobble pump
13 Primer pump
14 Carburettor
15 ¾in 14 Nat pipe tap
All fittings for fuel lines between engine and hull bulkhead must be of approved flexible aircraft type and installed to prevent vibration

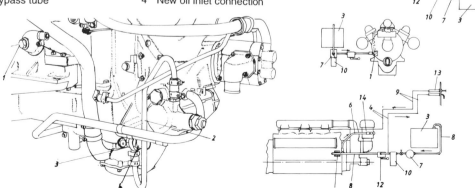

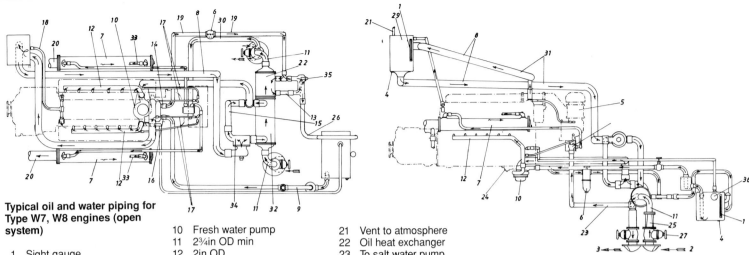

Typical oil and water piping for Type W7, W8 engines (open system)

1 Sight gauge
2 Salt water scoop – in
3 Salt water scoop – out
4 Drain
5 Carburettor
6 Oil filter
7 Exhaust manifold
8 3in OD
9 1¾in OD

10 Fresh water pump
11 2¾in OD min
12 2in OD
13 Bypass 1½in OD
14 Oil – out
15 Bypass 2½in OD
16 Oil – in
17 ½in OD
18 Steam line 1in OD
19 1½in OD
20 5in OD exhaust pipe

21 Vent to atmosphere
22 Oil heat exchanger
23 To salt water pump
24 Oil pump
25 Salt water strainer
26 2¾in OD
27 3in gate valve – quick opening type
28 Salt water pump
29 Fresh water expansion tank
30 Salt water pipe 2in OD to salt water pump

31 Must slant upward to tank
32 Fresh water heat exchanger
33 Overboard through jacketed exhaust pipe 1¼in OD
34 Fresh water thermostat (must be accessible)
35 Oil thermostat (must be accessible)
36 Hand hole cover (to clean tank)

Oil pump – top section (showing path of oil flow)

1 To oil tank
2 From oil tank
3 Down
4 Oil inlet from crankcase to scavenger pump
5 To engine oil manifold
6 Inlet to pressure pump

7 Pressure relief valve
8 To oil outlet temperature gauge
9 Up
10 Outlet from pressure pump
11 Outlet from scavenger pump
12 From scavenger line in CC

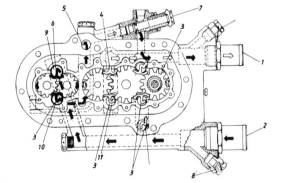

Wiring

1 Six cables 7mm to exhaust plugs
2 Six cables 7mm to intake plugs
3 Exhaust distributor
4 Intake distributor
5 Automatic cutout
6 Ignition booster coil
7 Knife switch 200 Amp.+
8 To starting switch button
9 Tell-tale light + optional by boat-builder
10 Switch terminal
11 24-volt battery
12 9mm cable
13 Exhaust
14 Intake
15 High tension
16 7mm cable
17 Starter
18 Fuse
19 Ammeter
20 Field
21 Battery
22 Boat builder's junction box +
23 Connect to ungrounded side of battery
24 Armature
25 Generator
26 Tee connector

27 Magnetic starting switch
28 These wires must be radio shielded
29 No 16 Insulated cambric cable
30 Battery terminal
31 Magneto

32 Voltage regulator
33 Start
34 Both
35 Intake
36 Exhaust
37 Off

38 No 4 Insulated cable
39 No 12 Insulated cable

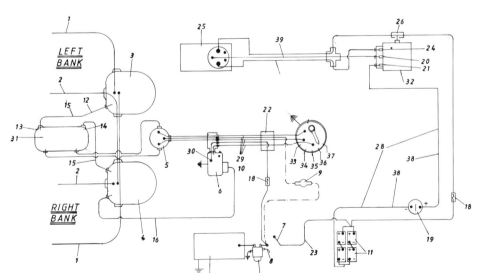

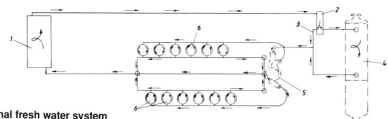

Optional fresh water system

1 Fresh water expansion tank
2 Thermostat
3 Bypass
4 Heat exchanger
5 Fresh water pump
6 Cylinders

Bendix drive and overload clutch assembly – Model RK13

1 Head screw
2 Meshing spring

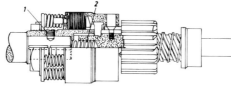

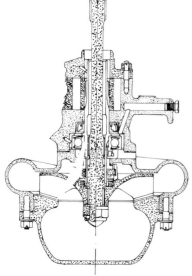

Fresh water pump section.

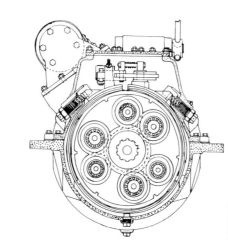

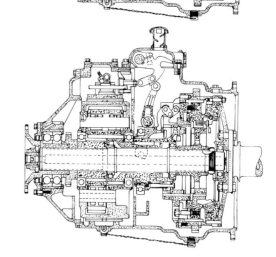

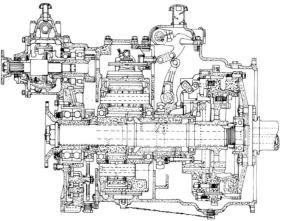

Scintilla type magneto (sparks from which distributed by two separately driven distributors)

1 Breaker cover screw
2 Breaker cam
3 Breaker cam assembly
4 Cam cap
5 Insulating bushing
6 Contact breaker housing
7 Coil cover
8 Coil
9 Condenser
10 Magnet
11 Lock ring
12 Bearing retainer
13 Tapered bushing

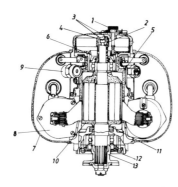

Fresh water pump section.

Typical Pesco fuel pump detail

1 Relief valve diaphragm
2 Relief valve spring
3 Bypass valve disc
4 Bypass disc spring
5 Retainer gasket
6 Spring washer
7 Adjusting screw
8 Adjusting nut
9 Drive shaft
10 Relief valve
11 Lock nut
12 Lock plate
13 Rotor
14 Retainer
15 Spring
16 Seal disc
17 Seal ring

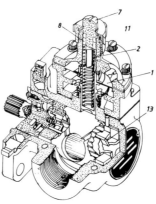

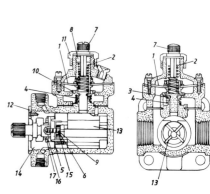

Typical oil and water piping for Type W9, W10 engines (closed vented system)

1 Drain
2 Oil filter-edge type .003in gap
3 Vent to atmosphere
4 Oil pump – 20–24gal per minute
5 Fresh water pump. Capacity about 200–300gal per minute at top speed
6 Salt water priming pump
7 Salt water priming pump sea cock and strainer
8 Vosper type salt water pump, about 120gal per minute. Contains screen
9 Fresh water expansion tank (12gal). At filler level provides 3gal extra space above filler for expansion and condensation
10 Valve – must be accessible for frequent cleaning
11 Salt water strainer – easily removable for cleaning
12 1½in OD drain pipe at low end of manifold
13 Outlet must be away from inlet to prevent short-circuiting of oil through tank
14 1in OD vent tube in line to crankcase so installed that oil will drain to tank or engine
15 Fresh water thermostat (must be accessible)
16 Valve to provide additional sea water flow through cooler at high speed
17 ⅜in soft aluminium spacer if copper exhaust pipe used

18 Total screen area about 20 sq in. 14 mesh .020in diameter brass wire screen. Oil screen must be readily accessible for cleaning
19 Hand hole cover (to clean tank)
20 Oil thermostat (must be accessible)
21 Must slant upward to tank
22 Fresh water heat exchanger
23 3in gate valve – quick opening type
24 Salt water scoop – out
25 Salt water scoop – in
26 To salt water pump
27 Sight gauge
28 Bypass 1½in OD
29 Oil heat exchanger
30 Oil in
31 Oil filter
32 Salt water pump
33 Salt water out
34 Oil out
35 5in OD exhaust pipe
36 Exhaust manifold
37 Salt water in
38 3¼in OD
39 3in OD min
40 2¾in OD min
41 Shut-off cock
42 ½in OD
43 Drain 1in NPT
44 1½in OD
45 2in OD
46 1¾in OD
47 Oil tank
48 Discharge pipe must rise directly from outlet of pump to provide a minimum head of 1ft
49 Carburettor

Note All tubing sizes specified are outside diameters with wall thicknesses of about ³⁄₆₄in to 5/16in.
Oil and petrol lines must be thoroughly cleaned before assembly.
All pipe connections to the engine must be flexible.
All filters to be cleaned at 10-hour intervals.

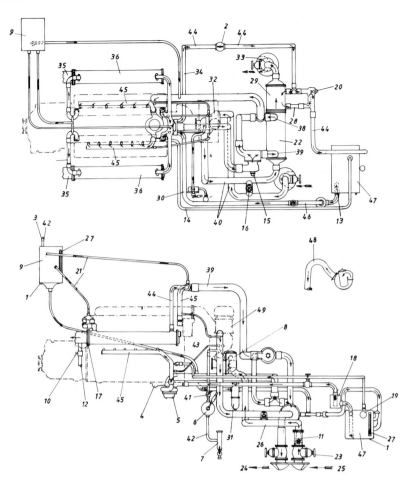

Packard engine detail: diagrammatic side view of engine cooling system and portion of lubricating system

The salt water scoops provide all the sea water required to cool the fresh water heat exchanger. The salt water pump cools the exhaust manifolds only. The oil screen shown was used temporarily on the inlet side of the oil pump to prevent any residual dirt in the oil tank or lines from reaching the pump when the engine or tank was first installed. The filter screen (39) was removed before the boat was put in commission.

1 Outlet to expansion tank
2 ⅜in pipe flushing water for stern tube bearing
3 Fresh water expansion tank (12gal)
4 Overboard through jacketed exhaust pipe
5 Fresh water thermostat – must be accessible
6 1in pipe connection vent line
7 To boat heaters ¾in OD
8 From port engine 1⅜in OD
9 From oat heaters ¾in OD
10 From starboard engine 1⅜in OD
11 To dead engine 1in OD
12 Salt water scoop – out
13 Salt water scoop – in
14 Salt water strainer
15 5in OD exhaust pipe
16 SW pipe 1¾in OD

17 Bypass 1½in OD
18 Bypass 2in OD
19 Salt water – out
20 Salt water – in
21 Oil – out
22 1⅜in OD
23 Salt water pump
24 1¾in OD
25 ½in OD
26 1in OD
27 Oil filter
28 1-1/2in OD
29 Steam line – 1in OD
30 Emergency valve
31 Oil pump
32 Fresh water pump
33 Oil filler cap
34 3½in gate valve
35 Heat exchanger
36 Sight gauge
37 Oil tank
38 Oil thermostat
39 Oil screen
40 2in OD
41 Exhaust manifold
42 Oil in
43 Overboard
44 From coolers
45 To salt water pump
46 Carburettor
47 Valve in closed position
48 Engine and reverse gear c supply tank (25gal)

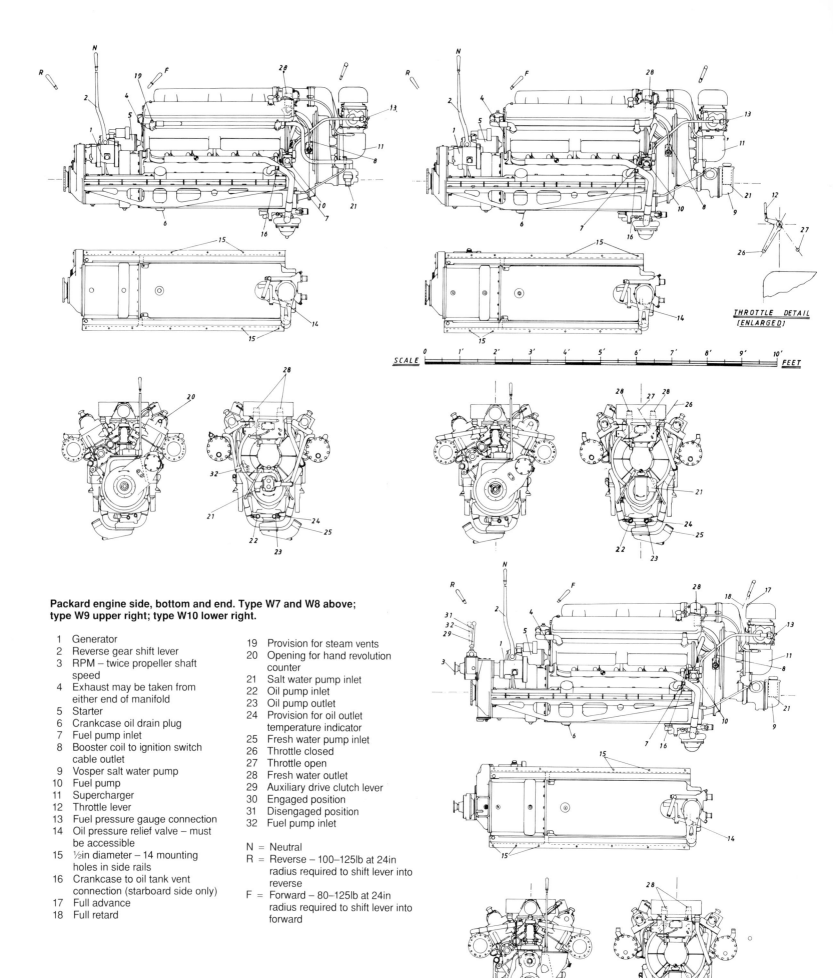

Packard engine side, bottom and end. Type W7 and W8 above; type W9 upper right; type W10 lower right.

1 Generator
2 Reverse gear shift lever
3 RPM – twice propeller shaft speed
4 Exhaust may be taken from either end of manifold
5 Starter
6 Crankcase oil drain plug
7 Fuel pump inlet
8 Booster coil to ignition switch cable outlet
9 Vosper salt water pump
10 Fuel pump
11 Supercharger
12 Throttle lever
13 Fuel pressure gauge connection
14 Oil pressure relief valve – must be accessible
15 ½in diameter – 14 mounting holes in side rails
16 Crankcase to oil tank vent connection (starboard side only)
17 Full advance
18 Full retard
19 Provision for steam vents
20 Opening for hand revolution counter
21 Salt water pump inlet
22 Oil pump inlet
23 Oil pump outlet
24 Provision for oil outlet temperature indicator
25 Fresh water pump inlet
26 Throttle closed
27 Throttle open
28 Fresh water outlet
29 Auxiliary drive clutch lever
30 Engaged position
31 Disengaged position
32 Fuel pump inlet

N = Neutral
R = Reverse – 100–125lb at 24in radius required to shift lever into reverse
F = Forward – 80–125lb at 24in radius required to shift lever into forward

THROTTLE DETAIL (ENLARGED)

SCALE 0 1' 2' 3' 4' 5' 6' 7' 8' 9' 10' FEET

190

The twin 0.5in Vickers machine gun, Mark V mounting

Between the two world wars, the Admiralty had considered a number of options for warship anti-aircraft defence. The contemporary theory was 'hosepiping' – to throw enough metal at the aircraft during its approach to destroy it or cause it to fail to complete its attack. Thus a weapon that could discharge enough ammunition at the target to make it inevitable that the target would be hit was all that was required. Several ideas were considered.

In 1935 a prototype 0.661in gun on a six-barrelled mounting was ordered from Vickers-Armstrongs, but after considerable design effort it was cancelled in 1938. This weapons system was expected to fire at a rate of 300 rounds per gun per minute. The eight barrelled and six barrelled 2-pounder pom-pom mounting was developed for capital ships, cruisers and destroyers, but carried great weight penalties. These multi-barrelled weapons had been slowly improved by Vickers since 1923, with firing trials in 1927, followed by sea trials in 1928. Production of these very complex mountings was slow and they were issued to the Fleet in the early 1930s. The smaller four-barrelled Mark VII mounting was developed later and joined the Fleet from 1936, but both were of no use for small warships.

The 0.5in Vickers Mark III machine gun was the standard last resort anti-aircraft gun prior to the introduction of the 20mm Oerlikon. It had much in its favour. It had been proved in the Great War in the 0.303in version and scaled-up and improved to 0.5in to see service in various marks from 1933. There were three marks in use during the Second World War – III, IV and V, the Mark III being the navy weapon. Marks IV and V were army AFV guns with a lower rate of fire for use in light tanks and armoured cars.

The gun was a recoil operated, water cooled with link-belt fed ammunition and was capable of firing up to 700 rounds per minute.

Here was a weapon that could 'hosepipe', it was already in production, and was a relatively cheap answer to the problem of close-range anti-aircraft fire.

A number of mountings were introduced for small ships. The quadruple Mark I, I**, II, II* and III were introduced in the mid 1930s. The four guns were arranged one above the other, canted at a slight angle and the belts fed in two on each side, the training and laying of the mounting being controlled by handwheels. In large units usually four mountings were fitted, with two aboard destroyers, and early in the war a single quad mounting was found on some 'Flower' class corvettes, fleet minesweepers, and coastal sloops.

Later, a smaller, lighter twin mounting, the Mark IV, was introduced. Here the two guns were side by side, with the ammunition belts fed from each side. Half the weight of the quad mounting, this manually-operated weapon was issued to trawlers, motor minesweepers and many Fairmile MLs. It, too, was turned and trained by handwheel, and required a crew of two, plus loaders to replace the ammunition belts. It weighed 1592lb. Something lighter with easier control was required for MTBs.

The twin 0.5in Vickers Machine Gun power operated gun turret prototype was first produced in 1939 by Marine Mountings Ltd, a company set up by sports car manufacturer Archie Frazer-Nash, and underwent trials aboard Vosper's private venture MTB. As a result of those trials the mounting designated 'Twin 0.5in Mark V

Twin 0.5in power mounting aboard a 77ft Elco
of the MTB 307–316 series.
Imperial War Museum

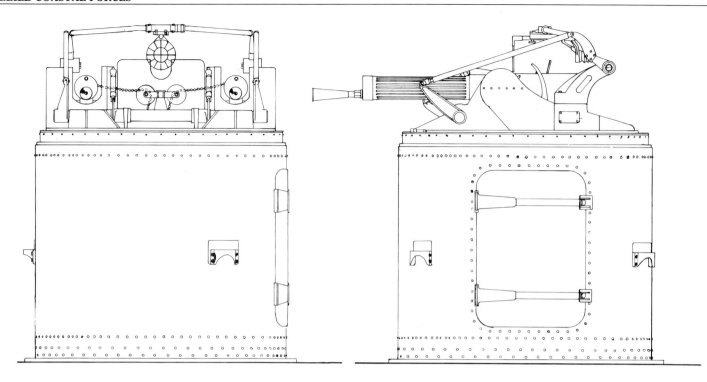

(Power Operated) Mounting' went into series production early in 1940, and was fitted to MTBs from the second half of 1940.

The purpose of this equipment was to provide power operation of a turret containing two 0.5in Vickers machine guns, with accuracy and sensitivity of control and with the least possible fatigue to the gunlayer.

The power used was hydraulic, derived from two variable-flow

The 0.5in Vickers machine gun on 0.5in Twin Mark V powered mounting. An ammunition box for the belted ammunition is shown to the left, one box per gun.
Courtesy Priddy's Hard Armament Museum

pumps. These were belt driven and designed to give a continuous supply of oil under pressure. Two pumps were fitted, usually one on each auxiliary engine. (The pumps for mountings on Thornycroft boats were gear driven and after 1941 were direct coupled.) The variable flow pumps, recuperators, relief valve and drain valve were on the fixed structure; the remainder – valve box, training motor, elevating rams, firing valve and pistons were positioned in the turret. The oil under pressure entered and left the turret through the base junction.

The twin 0.5in guns' rate of fire of about 700 rounds per minute per barrel was quite adequate against aircraft of the period, but was not good against the Axis E-boat, which had its bridge cupola armoured against the relatively light 0.5in round. The gun's automatic action was obtained by the explosion of the shell which drove the recoiling portion of the gun to the rear, and springs which returned it to the firing position with a live round from the breech block. The gun was water cooled for longer periods of sustained firing, and had a steam escape plug and drain plug fitted at the front end and a filling plug at the rear end of the barrel casing. The muzzle passed through a gland which was extended to the front to form a flash eliminator.

The twin Mark V powered mounting weighed 1041lb. The ammunition belt feed ran through hollow inner trunnions, with the ammunition box capacity of 650 rounds per gun being carried on the mounting. This mounting was also produced in the United States for Vosper boats built under licence for the Royal Navy, and was known as the Mark VC. A number of these were adapted to carry the US Navy's water cooled version of the 0.5in Browning M2 gun. These were fitted in many DEMS and some escort vessels. In spite of the shortcomings of the 0.5in round, a number of Royal Navy destroyers carried the Mark V (power operated) mounting on their bridge wings whilst operating against the Japanese, this being due to a shortage of 40mm Bofors guns and 20mm Oerlikons.

The twin 0.5in Vickers machine gun, Mark V mounting data
Calibre 0.5in
Muzzle velocity about 2520fps *(continued page 193)*

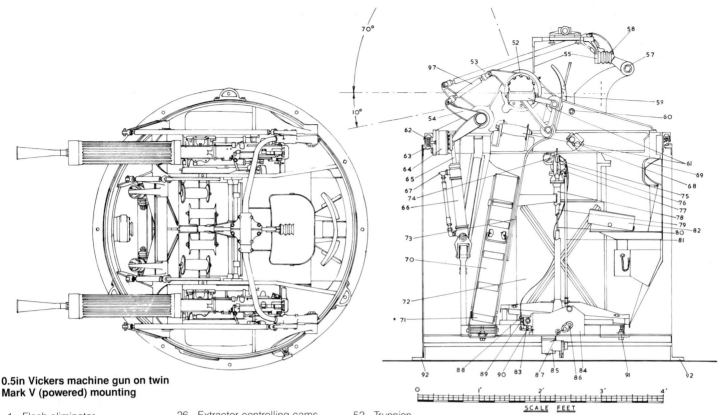

0.5in Vickers machine gun on twin Mark V (powered) mounting

1	Flash eliminator	26	Extractor controlling cams
2	Front gland	27	Rear cover
3	Steam escape plug	28	Trigger bar
4	Drain plug	29	Front cover hinge pin
5	Water jacket	30	Bottom feed lever
6	Steam tube	31	Trunnion block
7	Slide valve	32	Front cover catch
8	Filling plug	33	Front joint pin
9	Feed block	34	Lock
10	Outside plate	35	Side levers
11	Safety stop	36	Connecting rod
12	Crank handle	37	Adjusting nut and washer
13	Check lever	38	Rear joint pin
14	Lanyard bracket	39	Crank
15	Loading and cocking lanyard	40	Bottom plate
16	Rear crosspiece	41	Buffer spring
17	Guard	42	Resistance piece
18	Crank check roller resistance piece	43	T fixing pin
19	Front cover	44	Rear cover hinge pin
20	Safety catch	45	Fuzee
21	Adjusting screw	46	Fuzee spring plunger
22	Firing rod	47	Fuzee spring casing
23	Extractor guides	48	Fuzee spring bracket
24	Shock absorbing spring	49	Fuzee adjusting screw
25	Side plates	50	Front cover catch
		51	Safety stop detail – mounting

52	Trunnion	77	Master valve lever
53	Sight operating rod	78	Control column
54	Gun elevating bracket	79	Training valve operating tube
55	Sights	80	Master valve push rod
56	Sight tube	81	Elevating rod
57	Sight pivot	82	Gun layer's seat
58	Sight eyepiece	83	Pressure from valve box
59	Firing cam	84	Valve box
60	Rear gun pin	85	Base junction
61	Guide rollers	86	From training motor
62	Rack pinion	87	To firing valve
63	Rack	88	Adjuster
64	Training motor	89	Pressure to fire to firing pistons
65	Piston rod	90	Firing valve
66	Elevating ram	91	Surging roller
67	Bleed screw	92	Base ring
68	Firing piston	93	Footsteps
69	Sorbo pad back rest	94	Door clip
70	Ammunition box	95	Door hinge
71	Ammunition box runway	96	Torque tube
72	Box for empty cartridges and links	97	Gun elevating rod
73	Shield	98	Trigger bar lever – (gun)
74	Firing trigger		
75	Quadrant		
76	Handle		

Barrel length   31.11in (62 calibres)
Recoil   about 1.25in
Weight of gun complete (waterjacket empty)   56lb
Weight of gun complete (waterjacket) full, 7pts)   62lb
Gun length overall   about 52in
Rate of fire   about 700rpm
Weight of complete round   about 2.9oz
Cartridge length   4.28in
Bullet weight   1.32oz
Mounting
  Outside diameter of turret base ring   53.5in
  Outside diameter of turret barbette   48in
  Radius swept by gun muzzles at 0° elevation   44in
  Weight of turret without guns or ammunition   917lb

Weight of turret with guns and 1300 rounds   1289lb
Power   hydraulic
Training rate   0°–72° per second
Elevating rate   0°–50° per second
Oil   DTD 44C
In system   2 galls. (approx).
Working pressure – nominal   300psi
Training arc   360° continuous
Elevation arc   −10° to +70°
Guns   two 0.5in Vickers
Ammunition box capacity   650 rounds per gun
Firing mechanism   hydraulic
Gun sight   eyeshooting

193

The 20mm Oerlikon gun in the Royal Navy

It is well known that the majority of navies in the late 1930s lacked an efficient close-range weapon for use against low-flying aircraft. The Royal Navy had studied the problem and had not come up with an effective answer apart from an expensive and heavy multi-barrel 40mm 2-pounder pom-pom, which was totally unsuitable for small warships. The 20mm Oerlikon then proved to be one of the most effective weapons systems, and in its developed version is still in use today. It has a long history dating from just after the First World War.

In 1923, the Magdeburger Werkzeugmaschinenfabrik of Switzerland took over the major share of Schweizerische Werkzeugmaschinenfabrik (Swiss Machine Tool Works), which had been founded in 1906. In January 1924 the new parent company sent Emil Georg Buhrle to Oerlikon to examine the strengths and weaknesses of their recent acquisition and in the summer of that year Buhrle was appointed manager with a staff of eighty. Now that the company was in foreign ownership, the title 'Sch-

weizerische' (Swiss) was dropped, and the company became 'Werkzeugmaschinenfabrik Oerlikon' – Oerlikon Machine Tool Works. Oerlikon, now the parent company, took over development of the 20mm 'Becker gun' from Maschinenbau AG Seebach, then in liquidation, which had been developing the basic idea since the end of the Great War.

Buhrle saw that the new inertia operated blow back system which it used was capable of further development and Oerlikon took over all the patents covering the 20mm Becker gun, the prototype anti-tank gun and the Becker technicians. By Christmas 1924 Oerlikon

A 20mm Oerlikon on Mark IIA mounting on MTB 353, in March 1944, in the Ferry Dock, Dover. Note the splinter mattresses and the blacked-out wheelhouse (chartroom) windows.
Imperial War Museum

had obtained small orders for the new weapon from Finland and Mexico.

In 1929 the first large order was presented – 120 guns for Chiang Kai-shek's National Chinese government. Five years later they received their first large European order, from Lithuania, followed by others from Czechoslovakia, Argentina and Japan.

By 1937, the British Admiralty had become interested. Development work for their order took two years and was to result in the Royal Navy's 20mm Oerlikon Mark I mounting. When war was declared in September 1939 production for the Royal Navy had just commenced. The contract was for 1500 guns, but only 109 were to reach the United Kingdom before the fall of France.

After the Sudeten crisis of 1938, France had placed large orders for the gun and ammunition, as had the Netherlands, and with the additional work load, the parent factory had to increase in size, as well as put work out on sub-contract.

In late 1939, the Swiss Army possessed 36 20mm guns and the production of some 500 guns had been made for 28 different countries. These were very small orders compared with what was to come.

British interest in the gun started in 1935 when Antoine Gazda, who had earlier in the year joined Oerlikon as a salesman, obtained the order for Japan. On his way home he came to England, bringing with him a very impressive film of the 20mm gun in action. The film was seen by Lord Louis Mountbatten, a serving officer in the Royal Navy, who was to become a disciple. Within a week arrangements had been made to have Gazda meet a committee from the Admiralty. He was unfortunately unable to give the accompanying lecture, due to a throat infection, and Lord Louis took over, giving both the talk and the film show.

It is fair to comment that the new 20mm weapon had a drawback that was to prove bad for its image in Royal Navy gunnery circles. Its breech mechanism did not lock and seal before firing, which was contrary to the safety regulations then in force. The British Government was already spending vast sums on new ordnance in the shape of the 2-pounder pom-pom, 0.5in Vickers machine guns, and a new H/A twin 4in Mark XIX mounting was due to enter service.

Lord Mountbatten conducted an almost lone campaign during 1937–38, at over 200 meetings and demonstrations, to get the new 20mm weapon introduced into Royal Navy service. In April 1938 the weapon was fitted aboard Vosper's 78-foot private venture MTB (102) and underwent trials, where it was seen favourably by Admiral Sir Roger Backhouse, the Commander-in-Chief. Thus additional influence was gained and an order placed with Oerlikon for delivery of guns, mountings, and ammunition. The 20mm gun did not stay aboard for long, however, and was soon replaced by the prototype twin 0.5in Vickers power-operated machine gun mounting (later to become the standard Mark V mounting).

Once the Admiralty had made their decision, they sent a gunnery specialist, Stuart Mitchell, to the Oerlikon works. On his arrival in April 1939, he was not surprised to find that the Germans were very interested in the same gun for the *Luftwaffe*. The Oerlikon factory at Zurich was thus turning out guns and ammunition to both potential adversaries. In fact the steel for the gun barrels and recoil springs came from Germany, but no attempt was made to hamper the British contract.

By June 1940 the route for the delivery of the weapons was overrun by the Axis invasion forces. Mitchell was forced to return by way of Turkey, Palestine and eventually via Egypt and within three weeks he was back at the Admiralty. Earlier an agreement had been made to produce the gun and its mounting with the ammunition under licence in Great Britain, and he had brought the required drawings with him, with ideas to implement production.

A factory site in Brighton had been earmarked for production,

but with the fall of France its location on the south coast was considered too vulnerable, and an alternative site at Bangor, North Wales, was suggested.

July passed and nothing had been decided. The Royal Navy was not in possession of any close-range weapon of note, and then a Canadian, Charles Frederick Goodeve, after serving in the Royal Naval Volunteer Reserve, joined the staff of the Director of Scientific Research at the Admiralty. As a result of his considerable string pulling, bluff and the removal of 'red tape', a factory was established at Ruislip, Middlesex, on the site of some new railway running sheds.

Even then there were trade union problems, and although production was delayed, the first British 20mm Oerlikon gun passed its test proofing after seven months. Within a year Ruislip was turning out 750 guns monthly, and by late 1942 monthly production had increased to 1000 with shadow factories producing half as many again.

However, production still did not match demand, and in October 1940 Mitchell had been sent to the United States to arrange production facilities. The United States, still at peace, displayed little interest and only a few companies would accept the manufacture of parts. Mitchell had to convert the drawings from metric to Imperial dimensions.

The parent works at Zurich had attempted to ship a sample to the United States but it fell into German hands at Bordeaux. However, a replacement was urgently shipped in a destroyer from the United Kingdom. Under the provisions of Lend-Lease, no war material could be produced in the United States, unless it was considered to be of use by the US armed forces. Thus the fate of mass-producing the gun there hung in the balance. It was demonstrated to the US Navy Bureau of Ordnance at about the time of the Japanese attack on Pearl Harbor. Backed up by a report from the British Admiralty and a previous visit by Lord Mountbatten, the weapon was ordered for full production in less than 24 hours.

Interestingly, the 20mm Oerlikon gun was not a cheap weapon system to produce. A similar 20mm weapon designed for army use, the 20mm Polsten gun, compares:

	Polsten	Oerlikon
Number of components	119	250
Number of machining operations	900	3000
Cost (estimated)	£60–70	£320

During the war, 44,553 20mm Oerlikons were produced under licence in Great Britain. A further 300,000 were manufactured in the United States with an expenditure of about $3,000,000,000 on mountings and ammunition. With both countries producing a fully-interchangeable standard weapon, a considerable number were supplied by the United States to the Royal Navy. The weapon was fitted to virtually every type of ship. Motor torpedo boats carried single or twin mountings, while battleships carried between seventy and eighty, particularly when the supply situation improved in the last three years of the war.

The gun

The 20mm Oerlikon gun was an automatic gun designed for H/A, close-range anti-aircraft fire with an effective range of 1000–1200 yards. The weapon was operated by the pressure set up by the explosion of the round, the empty cartridge case being blown back against the breech, forcing it to the rear against the resistance of the barrel springs, which then carried the moving parts forward again.

The breech was not locked at the time of discharge, and the round was fired a fraction of an inch before it was fully home in the chamber, the neck of the shell case swelling to form a gas-tight seal. The barrel and casing did not recoil, the whole force of the explosion of the round being utilised to propel the projectile and operate the moving parts.

The Mark I gun was the original type made in Switzerland. The Mark II was also made for the Royal Navy in the United States. For local reasons connected with US Navy procedure, the guns made in the United States were marked either Mark II USN or Mark IV USN. From the user's point of view there were no differences between the three marks, all being completely interchangeable, but there were slight variations. The Mark I had a detachable flash eliminator. The barrel locking lever arrangements were separate from the double loading stop, and the barrel locking lever also locked the barrel sleeve, having three positions. The gun had both single-shot and automatic firing. The Mark II gun had a bell-mouthed barrel, the barrel locking lever and double loading stops being combined in one axis, and the barrel locking lever having only two positions. The gun was only capable of automatic fire.

The sights consisted of an eyepiece and an eyeshooting sight, having 100, 200 and 300 knot rings. The early models had only 100 and 200 knot rings. The Mark V US gunsight was introduced to overcome vibration experienced with the original Admiralty-type open sight. The main features were its compactness, an adjustable backsight, and a small elevation indicator from which the gunlayer could read the angle of sight.

Magazine

Care was necessary in the loading of the magazines, otherwise rounds would topple over in the feed guides and cause jamming. At least three magazines were available in the ready-use lockers, with their springs at full tension. The remaining magazines were left with initial tension only, except in conditions where sustained action was probable, when all would be ready for rapid use. The magazines required maximum protection from sea water and weather. Failures found in the gun had proved to be a result of damage caused to the magazines by rough handling.

The magazine itself comprised a cylindrical drum which contained 60 rounds, driven along a spiral path inside the drum by a clock spring.

Ammunition

Ammunition was of limited Swiss, British and US manufacture, and the Swiss issue was obsolete when the gun was produced in large numbers from 1941. The various types of ammunition were distinguished by the following colours:

	Swiss	British	US
HE tracer	blue	light blue	Filled Tetryl

British ammunition

HE tracer The shell contained a percussion fuse having no moving parts, the detonator of which was fired by the crushing action of the fuse body, which occurred on impact with the target. The shell was divided into two compartments by a septum across the middle. The front portion was filled with the explosive, which was fused to detonate the filling in that portion only upon striking the target.

The tracer composition at the rear was inserted from the base end and pressed in at a pressure comparable with the chamber pressure of the gun. A brass disc was placed over the composition. This was held in place by a steel washer, which was secured into the base of the shell. The tracer composition was ignited directly from the heat of the propellant gasses, and burned during flight of the shell for about 3.75 seconds.

HE non-tracer This shell was fitted with a fuse of the same type as that in the HE tracer, and the HE filling detonation method was identical.

HE incendiary This was similar to the HE type, except that it was filled half with HE and half with incendiary composition. The only external difference was the colour of the shell.

HE incendiary tracer Similar to the HE tracer type, with its HE portion partly filled with incendiary composition. The HE incendiary ammunition was only distinguished by the colour of the shell. The inclusion of the incendiary composition resulted in an extremely high explosive temperature, making this ammunition very effective for the ignition of fuel etc in a target.

Practice tracer This shell was filled with tracer composition only, which was ignited by the propellant gasses, as in the HE tracer shell. In this case the tracer composition burned for a considerably longer period.

Practice non-tracer This was a steel shell hollowed as required to obtain correct weight and length.

Cartridge drill Mark I and Mark II This was solely for magazine loading practice and not to be loaded into the gun.

Bulleted blank This consisted of a leather-board bullet envelope into which a mixture of lead flakes and litharge had been pressed at a suitable pressure load. On firing the gun this projectile travelled along the barrel in the usual way, and imparted the necessary recoil to function the gun mechanism, but on leaving the barrel the centrifugal forces set up were sufficient to burst the leather-board envelope, and cause the lead/litharge to disintegrate a short distance from the muzzle. This ammunition could be fired in harbour for gun crew practice without endangering either personnel or property. It gave erratic firing and was not to be used for testing the functioning of the gun. After use the guns had to be carefully cleaned and oiled.

Fuses British ammunition was fitted with the percussion fuse No. 254 Mark II, which contained no moving parts. The detonator was fired by the crushing action of the fuse body on impact with the target. This fuse unfortunately was not sensitive, not being armed by the rotary motion as it passed through the bore of the gun, as in the case of larger guns. At action ranges the fuse would perforate the skin of an aircraft without functioning, just piercing the skin. It would, however, operate on impact with wing spars, petrol tanks or other heavy structures. This was one of the problems encountered by the US Navy and to a lesser extent by units of the Royal Navy when operating against Japanese kamikaze aircraft in the Pacific. The round was not heavy enough to inflict stopping damage to the approaching aircraft. The British propellant was nitro-cellulose flake (neonite).

The US ammunition was of a similar manufacture to the British, with the exception that the explosive charge was tetryl or pentolite, and the propellant was graphite tubular neonite.

Single 20mm Oerlikon mountings

In late 1941 the following mountings were in Royal Navy service:

Mark I; hand raising gear

Mark IIA; fixed pedestal

Mark IIIA; fixed pedestal with minor differences from mark IIA.

Mark I This mounting was designed so that the height of the gun trunnions above the deck could be varied rapidly and at will to enable the gunlayer to assume the easiest position at any particular angle of sight. At the rear end of the gun cradle there were two boxes filled with lead balance weights. A canvas bag was attached to the cradle to catch the expended cartridge cases.

Mark IIA This mounting had a fixed-height pedestal containing no raising gear. A stepped platform around the mounting provided

A 20mm Oerlikon on a hand raising mounting aboard a British Power Boat MGB, February 1942.
Imperial War Museum

the layer with various steps for easier movements for the various elevations, and a loader's step was attached to the pedestal to assist in loading the fresh magazine. The pedestal head contained a centre pivot roller bearing and two ball thrust bearings. A clock-type balance spring was fitted to the left hand trunnion of the mounting to balance the gun, which would otherwise have been muzzle heavy. The spring tension was adjustable, but once set did not require further setting. A half-full magazine (30 rounds) was mounted on the gun to adjust the balance.

Mark IIIA This was a fixed-pedestal mounting similar in appearance to the Mark IIA, but had greater simplicity in manufacture in that roller and ball bearings had been replaced by a lengthened pivot having a bearing bush at the upper end, and a steel on phosphor-bronze footstep bearing below.

Mark IV US mounting This was of the hand raising type and very similar in design to the Mark I. To cock the gun, the cutsplice lanyard or wire lanyard was attached to a hook at the base of the mounting and the column was raised. A protective gun shield moving only in the horizontal plane was secured to the carriage.

Mark V US mounting This was very similar to the Mark IIA mounting but had a heavy cast-iron pedestal and a shorter pivot. The pivot was cylindrical in shape and rested upon a bearing bush at the upper end, and on a phosphor-bronze block at the lower end. The protective shield was in two parts, leaving a gap through which the gun was elevated. This mounting was also manufactured in Canada, for use aboard Royal Canadian Navy units, but the pedes-

tal was constructed of fabricated steel.

Mark VIIA This mounting superseded the Mark IIA and consisted of a short cylindrical pedestal bolted to the deck by eight securing bolts. The gun and cradle were unevenly balanced (muzzle heavy) in the trunnions in order to give a shorter working radius in elevation to the rear end of the gun. To counteract this uneven balance, to each side of the cradle rear a large cam and chain was secured to, and passed around, the outer periphery of each. The chains were led through the top of the turntable and secured to a crossbar at the top of the lead weight. The function of the cams was to vary the pull of the weight on the cradle according to the angle of elevation of the gun. Friction was reduced by the rollers and by the chains passing over guide rollers fitted with ball bearings.

Limits of elevation were from 15 degrees depression to 85 degrees elevation. Later mountings had the elevation restricted to 75 degrees. A protective splinter shield of ½-inch plating was secured to the carriage and moved only in the horizontal plane. A double shoulder rest was fitted at the rear end of the breech casing. No cartridge case collecting bag was fitted, but the front of the carriage was constructed so as to form a chute which caught the ejected cases, which fell to the front of the gun. The working radius of the gun was 40 inches.

When aboard submarines the mounting was known as the Mark VIIA submarine mounting. The gun shield was omitted, drainage holes were cut in the lower part of the pedestal, and the access hole cover plate was left off. To prevent the formation of rust, the upper bearings and the counterbalance guide rollers were of stainless steel. The rollers were fitted with ball bearings to give easier working, and felt rings which acted as a water excluding device. This mounting was still in use during the Falklands conflict.

Mark VIIIA This was a low-angle, extra light mounting, designed for use in coastal craft. It consisted of a conical-shaped steel pedestal, bolted to the deck by 12 holding-down bolts. In this mounting the gun was capable of elevation from 15 degrees depression to 20 degrees elevation. Again a standard ½-inch thick protective shield was fitted. A cartridge case collecting bag was fitted under the rear end of the breech casing. Photographs of this mounting in service have not been found, probably due to its very restricted use against aircraft.

The 20mm Oerlikon gun data
Calibre 20mm or 0.8in (approx)
Barrel 9 grooves, right hand
Length overall 8ft
Muzzle velocity 2725fps
Rate of fire 465–480rpm
Weight (gun only) about 141lb
With sight and shoulder piece 173lb
Weight of Mark I mounting (hand raised) 10cwt
Weight of Mark IIA mounting (fixed pedestal) 10cwt 26lb
Weight of Mark IIIA mounting (fixed pedestal) 10cwt 26lb
Weight of Mark VII mounting (complete) about 14cwt
Weight of Mark VIII mounting (fixed pedestal) 5.5cwt
Magazine capacity 60 rounds
Full magazine weight 61lb
Empty magazine weight 30lb
Normal allowance (per gun) 8 magazines
Working radius of gun (not Mark VIIA) 45in
Weight (complete gun and shield) Mark I mounting 5.5 tons
Upward lift 1.2 tons
Downward blow 1.5 tons
Maximum range at 45° elevation about 6250yds
Round weight 8½oz

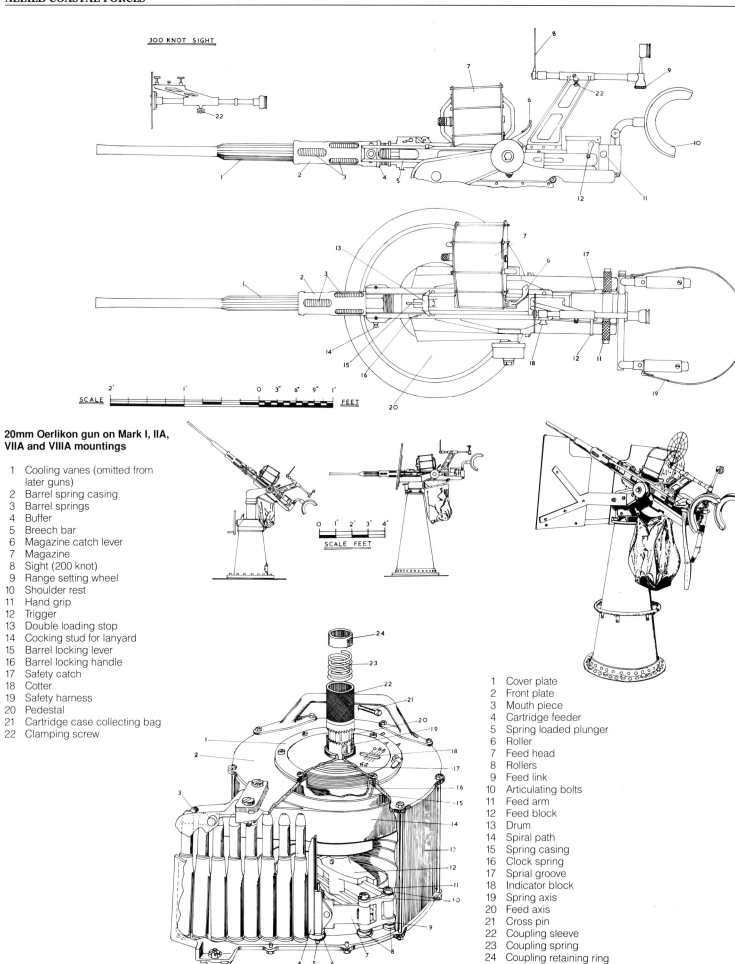

300 KNOT SIGHT

SCALE FEET

20mm Oerlikon gun on Mark I, IIA, VIIA and VIIIA mountings

1 Cooling vanes (omitted from later guns)
2 Barrel spring casing
3 Barrel springs
4 Buffer
5 Breech bar
6 Magazine catch lever
7 Magazine
8 Sight (200 knot)
9 Range setting wheel
10 Shoulder rest
11 Hand grip
12 Trigger
13 Double loading stop
14 Cocking stud for lanyard
15 Barrel locking lever
16 Barrel locking handle
17 Safety catch
18 Cotter
19 Safety harness
20 Pedestal
21 Cartridge case collecting bag
22 Clamping screw

1 Cover plate
2 Front plate
3 Mouth piece
4 Cartridge feeder
5 Spring loaded plunger
6 Roller
7 Feed head
8 Rollers
9 Feed link
10 Articulating bolts
11 Feed arm
12 Feed block
13 Drum
14 Spiral path
15 Spring casing
16 Clock spring
17 Sprial groove
18 Indicator block
19 Spring axis
20 Feed axis
21 Cross pin
22 Coupling sleeve
23 Coupling spring
24 Coupling retaining ring

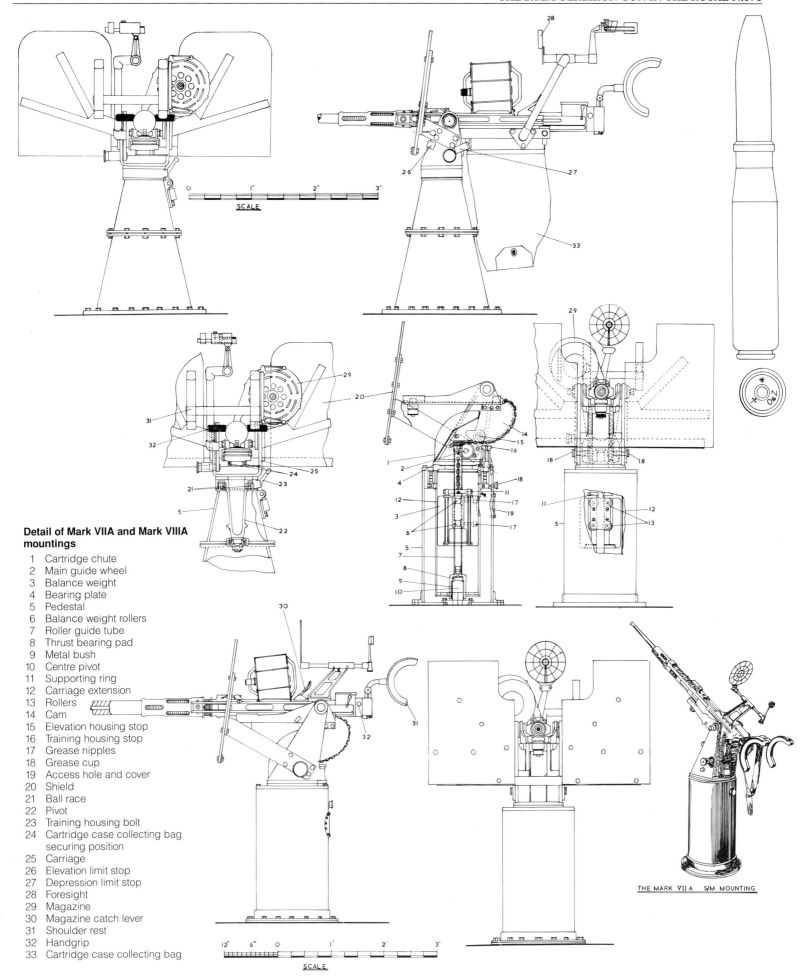

Detail of Mark VIIA and Mark VIIIA mountings

1 Cartridge chute
2 Main guide wheel
3 Balance weight
4 Bearing plate
5 Pedestal
6 Balance weight rollers
7 Roller guide tube
8 Thrust bearing pad
9 Metal bush
10 Centre pivot
11 Supporting ring
12 Carriage extension
13 Rollers
14 Cam
15 Elevation housing stop
16 Training housing stop
17 Grease nipples
18 Grease cup
19 Access hole and cover
20 Shield
21 Ball race
22 Pivot
23 Training housing bolt
24 Cartridge case collecting bag securing position
25 Carriage
26 Elevation limit stop
27 Depression limit stop
28 Foresight
29 Magazine
30 Magazine catch lever
31 Shoulder rest
32 Handgrip
33 Cartridge case collecting bag

THE MARK VIIA S/M MOUNTING

SCALE

The twin 20mm Oerlikon Mark V (power-operated) mounting

The purpose of this equipment was to provide power operation to a turret containing two 20mm Mark II or Mark IV Oerlikon guns, with accuracy and sensitivity of control, and with the least possible fatigue to the gunlayer. It was introduced into Royal Navy service in 1942, and worked on the same hydraulic principle as that previously described with the lighter twin 0.5in Mark V mounting.

The power was hydraulic, derived from a pump designed to give a continuous supply of oil under pressure to a closed-circuit system. In coastal forces craft the pump was usually of the variable-flow type, driven from the main or auxiliary engines, or it may have been either a vane type or gear-wheel type. In larger ships with local drive units either vane type or gear-wheel types were found. These were driven by an off-the-mounting electric motor and fitted with a relief valve set at 300psi.

The mounting power system and power units were of simple and robust construction. Maintenenace was considerably reduced as they were automatic, self-contained and self-lubricated. In the case of C/Fs where the power was from the main or auxiliary engines, the hydraulic pipes were originally run under the deckheads, but in this position they were prone to damage from enemy gunfire, so the pipes were relaid along the keel in new construction.

No less serious was the inability to use the power-operated mountings when the boats were stopped, unless the Ford auxiliary engine was started and the pipelines changed over to another pump, when one turret would be used. When the boat was stopped and listening for enemy E-boats, the running of the auxiliary engine made audible warning of the enemy impossible.

At the front of the mounting, extending under the guns, was a cover plate held down by four wing nuts, giving access to the hydraulic pipe line assembly. The platform on the left-hand side of the mounting was extended outwards to support the gunlayer's seat.

Operation of the firing trigger at the control handles controlled the firing valve in the body by Bowden cable, which had an adjuster. On the trigger being pressed, the Bowden cable operated the firing valve and admitted pressure to the rear side of the firing piston, forcing this outwards and operating the firing cam.

If the guns were trained on a 'dangerous bearing', such as if fired they would hit the ship's structure, then the built-in fire interrupter gear would prevent operation of the firing cam.

Two elevating cylinders were fitted, one each side of the carriage. Each cylinder was anchored at the rear of the platform to pivot brackets which permitted the cylinders to oscillate freely about their lower ends.

The rams were coupled up to the cradle, elevating and depressing the guns according to the direction in which the ram moved when operated by the gunlayer sitting at the universal control valve box. The mounting training motor was situated at the top of the turret between the two guns.

A shield was fitted to the platform and afforded protection to the gunlayer and the universal control valve box. Being rectangular in shape, it was contoured to the left-hand trunnion, to which it was bolted. The shield was also supported by the platform, the top being cut away to permit full depression of the gunsight. A light canvas weather shield was fitted to protect the gunlayer on his left-hand side. (Not much protection if gunfire was being returned!)

The turret revolved on twenty vertical rollers, on the lower roller path with the training rack. Nineteen horizontal rollers were fitted to prevent excessive lateral movement. The sight consisted of an aperture backsight and an eye-shooting foresight. The foresight had three circles – 300, 200 and 100 knots. A stiffener web and bearing tube were welded to the foresight to reduce vibration.

The universal control valve box controlled the volume and direction of oil flow to the training motor, elevating cylinders and firing piston. A back-up manual power unit was fitted to the rear of the mounting. This was a hand-operated pump mounted to the rear tie angle of the gunlayer's platform. The pump was driven by two hand-operated cranks through a double chain drive, and was fitted with suction and pressure ports. There was no pressure gauge fitted as the pressure obtained depended entirely on the manual effort of the rating operating it.

Maintenance

The mounting required regular attention to maintain it in correct working order. Loss of oil through loose joints or unions was a certain source of trouble. If the oil circuit was broken, the open ends of the pipes were to be plugged immediately to prevent the entry of dirt or grit. To save the elevating ram piston rods from exposure and corrosion, guns were usually left elevated so that the rods were housed and protected. It was most important, however, that if the mounting was fitted with a Mark XIV gyro gun sight (by 1944 many mountings fitted in larger units had the design slightly modified to accept this sight, but it was not usually fitted to CFs) the guns be left in the horizontal position. If the guns were left in elevation for an hour or two, then the gyro gun sight would be useless until it had been brought to the horizontal position for a similar period to recover.

The 20mm Oerlikons on twin Mark V power operated mounting aboard a Fairmile 'D' type, in April 1943. It is an early mounting and lacks the additional fittings and armour of later production mountings.
Imperial War Museum

A later twin 20mm Oerlikon Mark V power mounting, also aboard a Fairmile 'D' type. Bullet holes can be seen in the splinter mattress to the rear of the bridge.
Imperial War Museum

Particulars
Weight of turret (with guns and ammunition) 2247lb
Weight of cradle (fitted with gun mounting blocks) 200lb
Maximum angle of elevation 70°
Maximum angle of depression −10°

Arc of training 0–360°
Radius swept by gun breech 56.25in
Power Hydraulic
Working pressure 300psi
Oil used in system DTD 44D
Firing mechanism Hydraulic
Rollers – horizontal 19
Rollers – vertical 20
Gun sights Eye-shooting
Maximum range at 45° elevation about 6250yds
Holding down bolts 12
Distance between guns 13in
Height of mounting 69⅝in
Height of gun trunnions 44⅛in
Downward blow on firing 1.75 tons
Upward lift on firing 0.9 tons
Crew two (gunlayer and loader)

This mounting was fitted to most 'long' C/F designs and British Power Boat short MGBs, where the firepower was a great improvement on the power-operated twin 0.5in Mark V turret, but, with the greater weight penalty and the effect on boat stability, a lighter mounting was required.

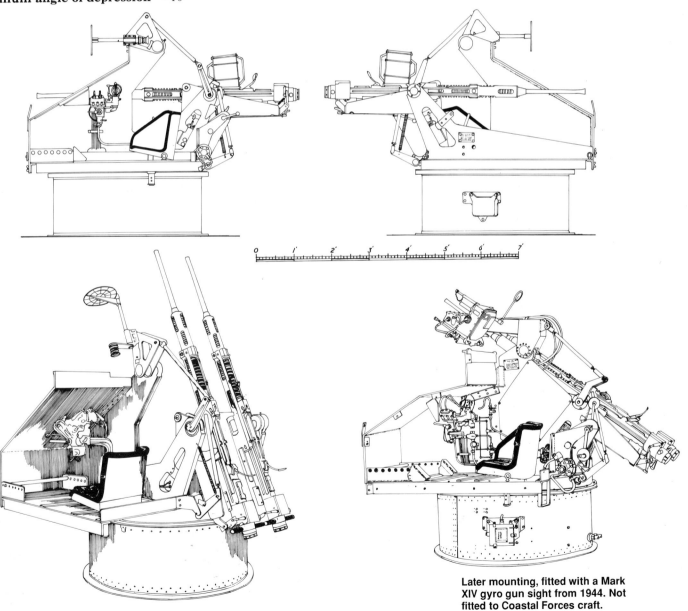

Later mounting, fitted with a Mark XIV gyro gun sight from 1944. Not fitted to Coastal Forces craft.

The twin 20mm Oerlikon Mark T and Mark IX manual mountings

This twin 20mm Oerlikon manually-operated mounting came about as an urgent requirement at the insistence of commanders of British Power Boat motor gunboats, and in particular through the efforts of Lt Cdr Robert P Hitchens RNVR.

Hitchens had already won his first DSC for work during the Dunkirk evacuation, when he was serving in a minesweeper. He later joined Coastal Forces to become commander of the 6th MGB Flotilla based at Felixstowe, with *MGB 64*. He later transferred to work up the new 8th MGB Flotilla with new much improved 71ft 6in British Power Boat MGBs operating from Dartmouth, and went back to Felixstowe with his new worked-up flotilla in September 1942.

He helped put Royal Navy gun boats 'on the map', and through his ideas and operational experience formulated tactics of the time. He worked very closely with British Power Boat Co and the company implemented many of his ideas in the direction of better boats with greater firepower. He felt that MGBs lacked firepower, and, if the opportunity arose to tackle a larger more worthwhile target, they lacked torpedo armament also. On one occasion he said, 'Half our value as offensive craft was wasted through inability to deal faithfully with any target larger than an E-boat, except for the rare and excessively risky chances of delivering a successful depth charge attack. If even one torpedo could be carried we would have a good chance of damaging bigger game when the opportunity occurred. The ultimate ideal for the small fast boat was obviously for the gun boats to carry torpedoes, and the torpedo boats sufficient guns to enable them to tackle E-boats. If this could be achieved there would be a vast saving of boats and personnel. Both types could do either job.'

He went on to say that the difficulties were twofold; the inability to carry extra weight on 'short' boats and the extraordinarily intractible attitude taken up by the authorities immediately responsible for the development of Coastal Forces. This argument lasted many months and waxed bitter as more and more evidence arrived from operational officers who returned in boats damaged and burnt and with crew members killed or injured after operations against enemy E-boats.

The new 71ft 6in gun boats were armed with power-operated turrets driven by oil pressure supplied from pumps in the engine-room. The turrets were excellent, and where they were essential, as in the case of the 2-pounder which could not be controlled from the shoulder, nothing could have been better. But all power-operated guns were heavy, were extremely vulnerable to enemy gunfire, and could not be used when the boat was stopped, since the gun pumps were driven off the wing propeller shafts.

For these and other operational reasons, where automatic guns could be carried without involving the use of a powered turret, crews were most anxious to have them. The 20mm Oerlikon could be controlled just as well, or almost so, from the shoulder, as had been the custom in the earlier boats where the single 20mm was fitted.

A simple but brilliant idea came from HMS *Beehive*'s (Felixstowe) gunnery officer, Lt Woods RNVR, who proposed a dual cradle on the lines of the twin gun cradle in the powered turret, and putting it on the existing single hand-worked mounting, thus doubling the firepower of the 20mm guns carried. Lieutenant Bailey had seen the importance of the idea and had pushed matters on, and

soon after the flotilla's arrival from Dartmouth the first prototype dual cradle was completed and proved satisfactory on sea trials.

In the meantime requests had continued for a lightly constructed hand-worked Oerlikon mounting. The single mounting provided with its cast iron pedestal weighed 1530lb. If one could be built weighing only 300–400lb there would be a considerable saving of weight.

On 2 June 1942, with the arrival of the new boats, it was suggested that if a light mounting were provided it could be placed in the position of the Holman projector aft of the twin 20mm Mark V turret, the latter being moved elsewhere where it could function equally well. It was also suggested that the total weight of the gun and mounting need not exceed 700lb, that no additional ammunition need be carried, and that if the equivalent weight was taken out of the boat in the shape of excess water and other unnecessary equipment, there would be a loss in displacement and perhaps room for a pair of 18in torpedo tubes.

As mentioned above, British Power Boat had been advised of the problems and its design staff had undertaken work to come up with an answer. George Selman has provided a great deal of information and practical help regarding this work. He was able to supply British Power Boat general arrangement drawings of lightweight mounting Mark T (Drawing A33476 of 10 February 1943), with detailed drawings of the machining and welding, details of the trunnion bracket and pivot (A33417 of 22 January 1943) and a drawing of the sub-assembly of the vertical pivot housing (Drawing 33467).

Thus a new lightweight twin 20mm Oerlikon mounting was produced. Known as Mark T mounting by British Power Boat, but soon to join the Service in increasing numbers as the Mark IX (Manual), it gave the same firepower as the power-operated Mark V mounting previously carried on MGBs and was considerably lighter by some 1497lb. The Mark IX mounting solved the problem for British Power Boat and enabled two 18in torpedo tubes to be fitted to its MGBs and they were soon reclassified as MTBs; these will be covered fully in Volume 3.

The estimated weight of the new lightweight mounting, excluding guns and magazines, sights and cartridge collecting bag, was 400lb. The estimated weight of the guns etc was 350lb and the estimated total weight was 750lb. The nominal height of the gun trunnions was 4ft 6in. The 2ft 5in diameter base plate was secured to the deck pad by 16½in BSF bolts. Later a splinter shield was fitted to the front of the mounting. Whilst it was difficult to handle against aircraft in a rough sea, the new mounting proved very popular with 'the troops'.

Another drawing provided by George Selman was A33883 (5 August 1943), showing the detail for fitting the new mounting to MGBs 134–138, in place of the original power-operated mounting. There is stowage for sixteen 20mm magazine drums, a total of 960 rounds (plus the magazines on the mounting), and the gunner has a 15in-wide circular platform around the mounting pedestal. Other bonuses were the reduction of the boat silhouette and no further need for hydraulic pipes to a power-operated mounting aft.

As production increased the new mounting was seen in growing numbers aboard other Coastal Force types, including Fairmile Ds, MLs and later in the war Vosper 70ft boats.

Hitchens was killed in the early hours of 13 April 1943 by a final

burst of enemy fire after a minor engagement had been broken off. He had taken part in 148 operations, of which 14 were actions against the enemy.

Oerlikon 20mm guns on a Mark IX manual mounting aboard HMS Nonsuch *in 1945. Note the quadruple 0.303in Vickers GO mounting on the bridge deckhouse (see Volume I).*
United Press International (UK) Ltd

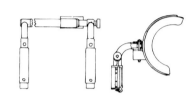

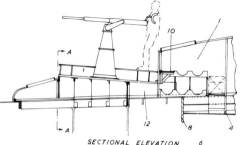

Detail arrangement of twin 20mm Oerlikon on HA LA hand worked mounting for MGBs 134/138. Increased armament drawing No A 33883 5 August 1943

1 20mm magazine fitted with stowage racks for 16 drums
2 Two drums in rack to starboard. 1ft 6in above floor
3 Two drums in rack on floor
4 WT compt bulkhead standard
5 16in wide seat over drum
6 Six drums in rails
7 Engineroom hatch
8 Bulkhead 42
9 Gun platform
10 Hinged step
11 Flushed step
12 Stowage space

Note: This set of drawings has been redrawn from small negatives of the originals kindly provided by George Selman, late chief designer for British Power Boats, Southampton. He has contributed a great deal of information, data and a multitude of drawings which will be redrawn for Volume 3.

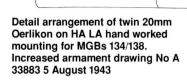

SECTIONAL ELEVATION

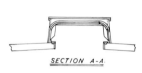

SHOULDER REST MARK I

SECTION A-A.

SCALE 0 1' 2' 3' 4' 5' 6' 7' 8' 9' FEET

ASSEMBLY

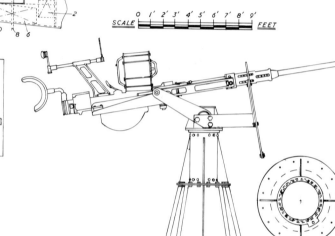

General arrangement and detail of lightweight twin 20mm Oerlikon mounting Mark T

Drawing Reference	Description
1 A 33355	S/A Cradle
2 D 33418	S/A mounting lock pin unit
3 A 33417	S/A trunnion bracket and pivot
4 A 33467	S/A vertical pivot housing
5 A 33461	S/A pedestal
6 A 33355	S/A gun retaining bolt
7 D 33418	As item 2
8	Bolts and nuts ½in diameter BSF × ¾in long
9 D 33474	Trunnion pin
10	Seegar circlip for 1¼in diameter shaft
11	Tecalmit greaser

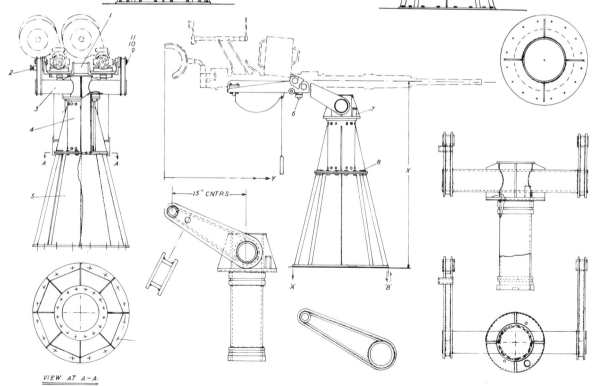

VIEW AT A-A.

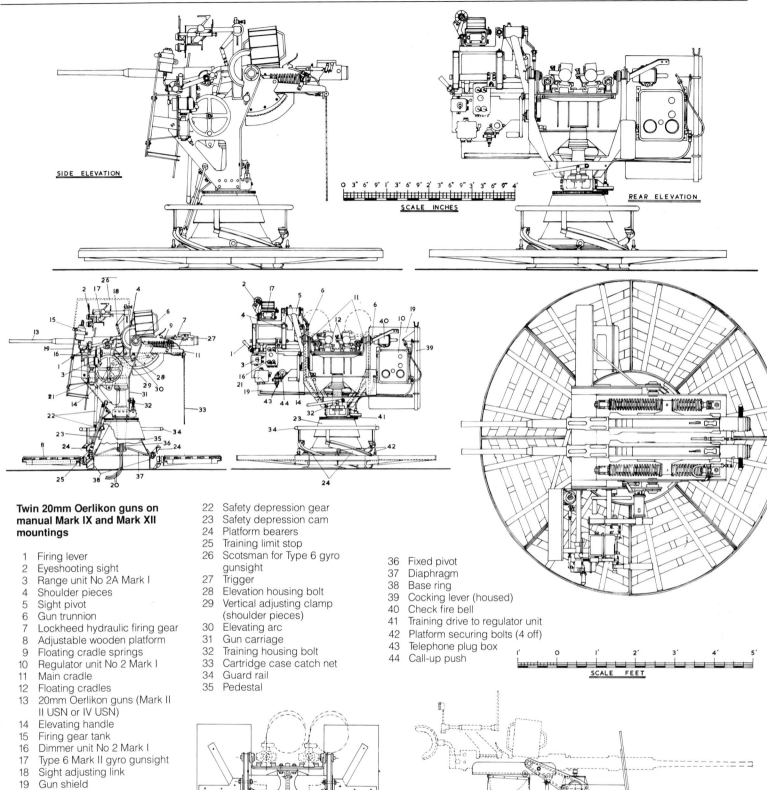

SIDE ELEVATION

REAR ELEVATION

SCALE INCHES

SCALE FEET

Twin 20mm Oerlikon guns on manual Mark IX and Mark XII mountings

1 Firing lever
2 Eyeshooting sight
3 Range unit No 2A Mark I
4 Shoulder pieces
5 Sight pivot
6 Gun trunnion
7 Lockheed hydraulic firing gear
8 Adjustable wooden platform
9 Floating cradle springs
10 Regulator unit No 2 Mark I
11 Main cradle
12 Floating cradles
13 20mm Oerlikon guns (Mark II II USN or IV USN)
14 Elevating handle
15 Firing gear tank
16 Dimmer unit No 2 Mark I
17 Type 6 Mark II gyro gunsight
18 Sight adjusting link
19 Gun shield
20 Power cable leads
21 Low power supply change-over switch

22 Safety depression gear
23 Safety depression cam
24 Platform bearers
25 Training limit stop
26 Scotsman for Type 6 gyro gunsight
27 Trigger
28 Elevation housing bolt
29 Vertical adjusting clamp (shoulder pieces)
30 Elevating arc
31 Gun carriage
32 Training housing bolt
33 Cartridge case catch net
34 Guard rail
35 Pedestal

36 Fixed pivot
37 Diaphragm
38 Base ring
39 Cocking lever (housed)
40 Check fire bell
41 Training drive to regulator unit
42 Platform securing bolts (4 off)
43 Telephone plug box
44 Call-up push

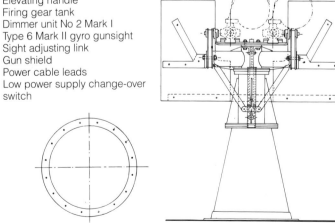

The Lanchester 9mm machine carbine

The Lanchester was notable not for any oddity in its design or construction, but because it was ever made in the form it was. It was nothing more than a direct copy of the German MP28/II designed by Hugo Schmeisser. On close examination there were very few visible changes apart from the stock, which was of similar pattern to that of Rifle Number 1 (SMLE), and it also had a bayonet lug to take the long bayonet Pattern 1907 or Bayonet No.1. Other differences were in the design of the receiver lock catch and the magazine housing, the latter component being of solid brass, in full naval tradition but hardly appropriate in time of war.

This weapon was conceived in some haste at a period in the war when Britain was at a low ebb, but whatever may be said against the copying of a weapon used by the enemy, the MP28 was a proven design of known reliability. The Lanchester followed the same trend. It took its name from its designer and was produced by the Sterling Engineering Co of Dagenham, Essex, exclusively, and somewhat unusually, for the Royal Navy. One of the authors recalls firing one on the range during the 1950s during training, when they were still part of the equipment for Royal Navy boarding parties.

The gun derived its action from the 'blow back' of its moving parts by the pressure of gas developed during the passage of the bullet along the barrel. It originally could fire in single-shot or automatic, being cooled by the air flow between the barrel and barrel casing. A simple, handy and robust weapon, it could be used effectively up to a range of 200 yards. Beyond that the effect of wind on the 9mm round rendered accuracy difficult. Single-shot was normally authorised when used by boarding parties. When fired on automatic the tendency was to throw slightly upwards, especially if fired from the hip. Besides ensuring instant readiness

for close bayonet combat, the extra weight at the nose cap tended to steady the weapon in automatic fire.

There were two versions of the Lanchester Machine Carbine; the original had a large Rifle No I type of rear sight, and a selector switch on the front portion of the trigger-guard as shown in the drawings. The later Mark I*, which was only capable of automatic fire, had a much simplified rear sight and lacked the selector switch. Most Mark I guns were later converted to Mark I* standard.

This weapon was issued in small numbers to coastal forces from 1943, usually one or two per boat, and was normally stowed in the gun rack outside the ward room.

Lanchester 9mm Machine Carbine data
Length of carbine 33.5in
Length of barrel 7.9in
Calibre 9mm (0.354in)
Weight 9lb 4oz
Muzzle velocity 1250fps
Rate of fire 600rpm
Weight of magazine 11oz (empty), 2lb 3oz (full)
Magazine capacity 50 rounds

The 9mm Lanchester machine carbine as fitted
for night fighting postwar.
Imperial War Museum

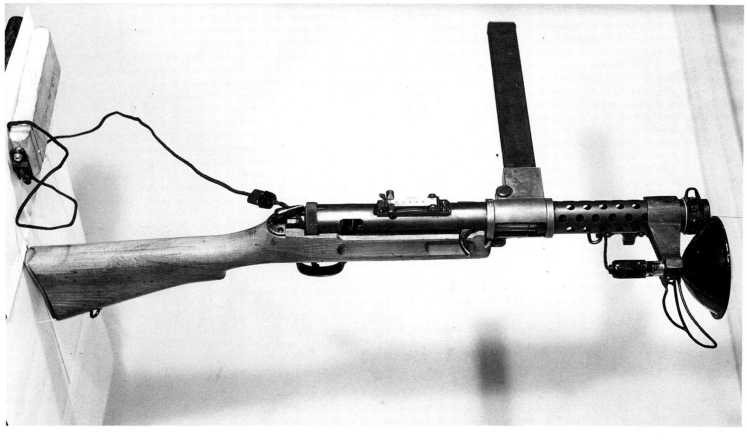

206

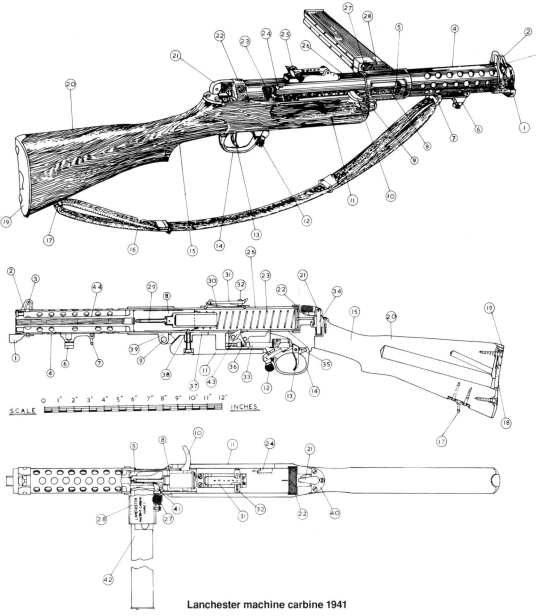

The 9mm Lanchester, as carried by boarding parties of the Royal New Zealand Navy in the 1950s.
Imperial War Museum

SCALE ⊙ 1″ 2″ 3″ 4″ 5″ 6″ 7″ 8″ 9″ 10″ 11″ 12″ INCHES

Lanchester machine carbine 1941

1	Bayonet standard	23	Main spring
2	Foresight guard	24	Safety recess
3	Foresight blade	25	Backsight
4	Barrel casing	26	Bolt casing
5	Extractor	27	Magazine catch thumb piece
6	Bayonet stud	28	Magazine support
7	Upper swivel	29	Firing pin
8	Bolt	30	Backsight leaf spring
9	Hinge screw	31	Backsight leaf
10	Cocking handle	32	Slide
11	Stock	33	Trigger bar
12	Change-over lever	34	Latch pin
13	Trigger	35	Trigger bar extension
14	Trigger guard	36	Sear actuating arm
15	Small of butt	37	Bolt casing support
16	Sling	38	Bent
17	Lower swivel	39	Lug
18	Butt trap	40	Latch plate
19	Butt plate	41	Ejector
20	Butt	42	Magazine
21	Latch	43	Sear
22	Back cap	44	Barrel

18in and 21in torpedo tubes 1939–45

When the first coastal motor boats were built by Thornycroft at Hampton during the First World War, conventional torpedo tubes were far too heavy and a much lighter type had to be devised. About forty years earlier Sir John I Thornycroft had patented special torpedo-dropping and launching gear for the new torpedo launches and second-class torpedo boats that were just coming into fashion. Once again, Thornycroft had to invent something suitable, and the novel idea adopted was of firing the torpedo backwards over the stern of the CMB as the boat was pointed at the target. The firing gear consisted of a long steel ram ending in a bell-shaped head which fitted over the nose of the torpedo. The ram was operated by gas pressure produced in an explosion vessel burning a cordite cartridge. The torpedo was carried on rails fitted into a trough in the after part of the boat and extending well over the stern. A stirrup attachment supported the nose of the torpedo until it was well clear of the boat, so as to protect the firing mechanism. With this astern firing system, the CMB was aimed at the target and, after discharging the torpedo, the boat was promptly turned away from its track. This gave the torpedo the bonus of the speed of the boat on firing, plus the extra speed as the torpedo engine took over.

During the 1920s and '30s there was considerable development of the stepless motor torpedo boat by competing firms, notably British Power Boat Co and Vosper. Although there was some loss of speed as compared with the stepped CMB, the manoeuvrability and sea-keeping qualities were claimed to be better and the hull strength was certainly improved because the loading was distributed more evenly instead of being concentrated largely on the hull step. In both types, which were built at Hampton, the astern firing system was abandoned in favour of light torpedo tubes mounted on the deck to fire ahead at a slight angle to the boat centreline.

In 1937 difficulties in obtaining suitable torpedo tubes for motor torpedo boats ordered by foreign governments (see drawings) led to the decision by Thornycroft to design and produce them in the

The starboard 21in torpedo tube on the Greek MTB T3 in 1939. This vessel was later requisitioned by the Royal Navy as MTB 70.
Vosper Thornycroft (UK) Ltd

firm's own works. The requirement for a lightweight launching tube resulted in considerable investigation of an aluminium tube, but this was later abandoned in favour of thin steel tubes, made of ⅛in welded steel plates fitted with light bronze torpedo guides.

The high pressure air-firing gear used on destroyers and submarines was not suitable for MTBs due to the weight of the necessary air compressors, so powder impulse or cordite impulse was used instead, and here the company's experience with the earlier bomb and depth charge throwers proved of considerable value. A special design of bending side stop was also developed. This patented device was adopted by the Admiralty for about 2000 LC Mark II 18in and 12in torpedo tubes built by various firms, including Thornycroft, with some 170 being built at their Woolston yard. These were all to Admiralty standard designs as shown here for all Royal Navy boats and British boats used by Allied nations; these were also fitted to the units built in the United States for the Royal Navy.

In Vosper 70ft boats the two above-water 21in tubes angled outwards 7½ degrees from the bow. On entering the water the torpedoes turned forward 6½ degrees, giving a spread of 2 degrees or about 120ft at 1000yds range. The tube was fired by a small explosive charge in the combustion chamber or explosion vessel at the rear of the tube. Firing was from the bridge torpedo firing levers, but should the charge not fire, a rating was on standby with a mallet to fire the tube.

The torpedoes of the period, the 21in Royal Naval Torpedo Factory Mark IX, the 21in Mark VIII and the 18in Marks 15 and 17 fitted to long boats are shown to a common scale. (The Mark VIII Torpedo will be detailed in Volume III.) Due to shortages in 1942 some MTBs were fitted with the Mark V torpedo (not drawn), which was rated at 35 knots with a 500lb warhead. It was not in general issue as it was an older type, but it was all that was available at the time. Apparently it was not very reliable. In 1943 the Mark VIII** submarine torpedo was provided, which could make 45

MTB 385 (73ft Type I) in 1945. A view aft from the bridge showing the four 18in tubes.
Vosper Thornycroft (UK) Ltd

knots and had a 750lb warhead. This was a great improvement and preferable in all respects, with a safety range of 100yds, and a contact-only firing pistol.

Torpedo control was achieved by aiming the boat, and the commander firing by remote control when the torpedo sights 'came on'. The optimum boat speed on firing was 12 knots; above or below that speed the torpedoes would dive progressively deeper before achieving their set depths, which was a handicap in shallow water.

All the drawings have been redrawn from official sources and include for comparison tubes provided for foreign orders obtained before the war. Among these is a general arrangement of a close-fit torpedo tube for the 60ft MTBs for Sweden (redrawn from Drawing 8498). These were Vosper numbers 1983 and 1984, and both were handed over on 28 December 1939 as Swedish T 3 and T 4. The tubes were more complex due to the climatic conditions of their home waters. They were fitted for hot water heating and built to take either a long or short torpedo when section 'E' was removed.

Also reproduced is the general arrangement of the 450mm close-fit torpedo tubes for the 60ft MTBs built for Norway (redrawn from Drawing 9241). Of these four units, Vosper numbers 2018–21, two were requisitioned into the Royal Navy as MTBs 71 and 72. These also appear more complex and are easily recognised by the heating jacket and the strong back fitting at the forward end. Presumably in Royal Navy service the tubes were later standardised to normal Admiralty pattern.

The 21in single element torpedo tube which was a one-off, fitted to the mobile torpedo discharge vessel *Bloodhound* is shown. This rather weighty mounting is included as it shows its complexity; this mounting figured in much of the research undertaken on torpedo tube and torpedo firing trials in the late 1930s. The operator sat astride the tube as it was fired, whilst another crewman trained the whole by way of the manual training handle. This was far too heavy for use aboard MTBs and thus rather impractical, but nevertheless useful for trials.

Another foreign order example is shown by the construction detail of the 21in tubes provided for the 70ft MTBs for Greece, and the Admiralty drawings (8746 A–E), which detail tube flanges and individual sections.

This is followed by the Admiralty 21in LC Mark I tube redrawn from Drawing 23951 (16 May 1939) and from a Thornycroft drawing of their 70ft MTBs (to be covered in Volume 3). The weight with firing gear unloaded was about 1350lb and loaded with a Mark VIII torpedo it was about 4550lb. It was, however, to be updated by the design of the LC Mark II as drawn for port tubes (Drawing T3063, of 12 September 1939), and for starboard tubes the cordite gear pocket for the pressure side stops and guiding-in gear to the opposite hand on the tube. There are slight visual differences between the Mark I and Mark II tubes, but the main difference was the reduction in weight. The weight complete with firing gear, unloaded, was 1269lb, and loaded with a Mark VIII Torpedo 4469lb, a reduction of 162lb per pair. This tube remained the standard 21in tube for the rest of the war.

With the smaller and lighter 18in torpedo, suitable for dropping by aircraft, a smaller tube, the 18in LC Mark II, was produced. The earlier type shown here is redrawn from Drawing T3054, and the later improved type is from Drawing T3481 of 1 February 1943, which illustrates slight production changes where welding was used. The estimated weight complete with firing gear unloaded was 748lb and loaded with a Mark XI torpedo 2194lb. The lighter 18in tubes were frequently fitted as two pairs on several 'long' boats such as the Fairmile D, the only Vosper 'long' boat, MTB 510, and the Vosper 73ft Type I. The following Type IIs carried paired 18in tubes with the 6-pounder gun forward. The one-off MTB 74 was fitted with two 18in tubes for a special operation. Other tubes

Unloading an 18in torpedo from a 60ft ex-Norwegian Vosper, either MTB 71 or 72.
Imperial War Museum

designed by British Power Boat Co will be included in Volume 3. The issue of 18in tubes was due to a shortage of 21in torpedoes, with their heavier warhead, which were required for the building programme of Royal Navy submarines, which were built with standard 21in tubes, with additional external tubes being fitted during refits requiring the production of even more torpedoes. As torpedo production improved the 21in tube was retrofitted to post-war MTBs because of the greater destructive power.

During the war the Royal Navy did not introduce the side-launched torpedo, although the US Navy did. This dispensed with the tubes, which were replaced by simple lightweight launching gear (see US section). This was a development introduced in post-war years by the Royal Navy.

An early 70ft boat firing a 21in torpedo for test purposes whilst at HMS Vernon Torpedo School, Portsmouth. Note the quadruple torpedo tube mounting on the jetty.
Vosper Thornycroft (UK) Ltd

Coastal Forces torpedo tubes
1939–45

21in LC Mk 1 torpedo tube

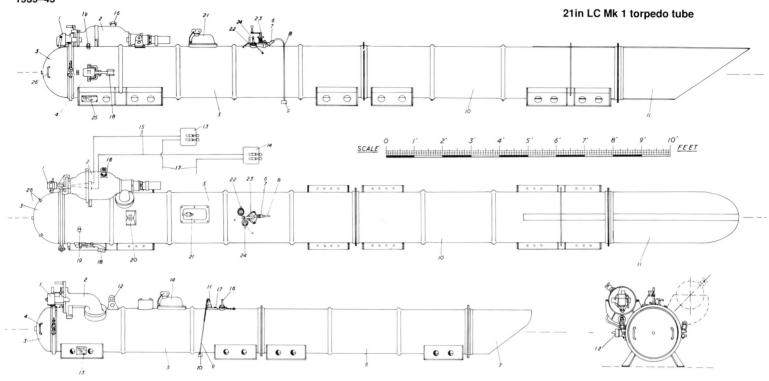

SCALE 0 1' 2' 3' 4' 5' 6' 7' 8' 9' 10' *FEET*

	8	Cable and switch supplied by	15	Exactor controls	23	Depth gear
1 Breech block		shipbuilders	16	Release valve	24	Charging valve
2 Explosion vessel	9	Switch	17	Leads to opposite tube	25	Name plate
3 Rear door	10	Middle length	18	Guiding-in gear	26	Welded handle
4 Side stop (plate type)	11	Lip end	19	Pocket for taking tube pressure		
5 Rear length	12	Side stop – cordite	20	Launching in eye		
6 Lamp holder Pattern 5770	13	Firing position on bridge	21	Latch tripper		
7 Lamp Pattern 666	14	Firing position in wheelhouse	22	Stop valve		

18in LC Mk I torpedo tube –
early type

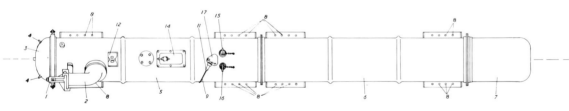

Early Mark 1

1   Breech block
2   Explosion vessel
3   Rear door
4   Welded handle
5   Rear length
6   Middle length
7   Lip end
8   ⅝in dia clearing holes
9   Cable
10 Switch
11 Lamp Pattern 666
12 Launching in eye
13 Name plate
14 Latch tripper
15 Stop valve
16 Charging valve
17 Depth gear
18 Shrouded control panel

18in LC Mark I torpedo tube –
later type

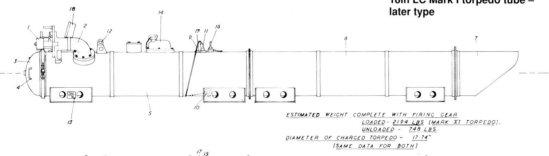

ESTIMATED WEIGHT COMPLETE WITH FIRING GEAR
LOADED - 2194 LBS [MARK XI TORPEDO].
UNLOADED - 748 LBS
DIAMETER OF CHARGED TORPEDO - 17·74"
[SAME DATA FOR BOTH]

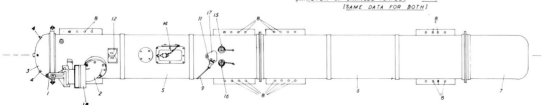

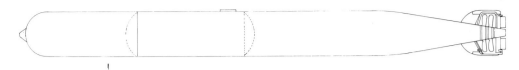

18 INCH MARK 15 & 17 TORPEDO

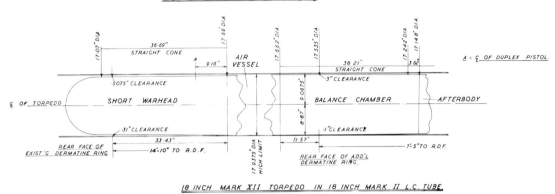

18 INCH MARK XII TORPEDO IN 18 INCH MARK II L.C. TUBE

21in Royal Navy Torpedo Factory torpedo Mark IX

1 Explosion vessel
2 Tommy bar for access fittings
3 Director's seat
4 Foot rest
5 Firing handle
6 Director stand
7 Latch tripper
8 Range spindle
9 Reducing valve
10 Range index
11 Stop valve
12 Charging valve
13 Loading positions
14 Training stop
15 Spring catch
16 Top stop
17 Rollers
18 Clips
19 Stop valve – Mark VIII blowing head
20 Charging valuve – Mark VIII blowing head
21 Starboard 45° forward training position
22 Starboard beam training position
23 Starboard 45° aft training position
24 Port 45° forward training position
25 Port beam training position
26 Port 45° aft training position
27 Training handle

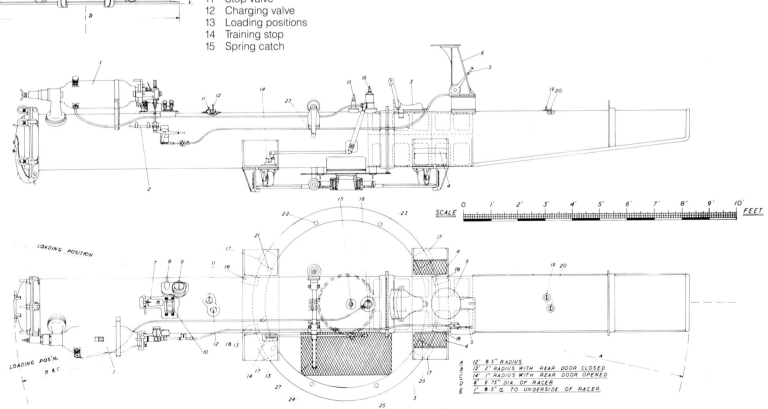

SCALE ——— FEET
0 1' 2' 3' 4' 5' 6' 7' 8' 9' 10'

A 12' 8·5" RADIUS.
B 12' 2" RADIUS WITH REAR DOOR CLOSED.
C 14' 1" RADIUS WITH REAR DOOR OPENED.
D 6' 9·75" DIA. OF RACER.
E 1' 8·5" ℄ TO UNDERSIDE OF RACER.

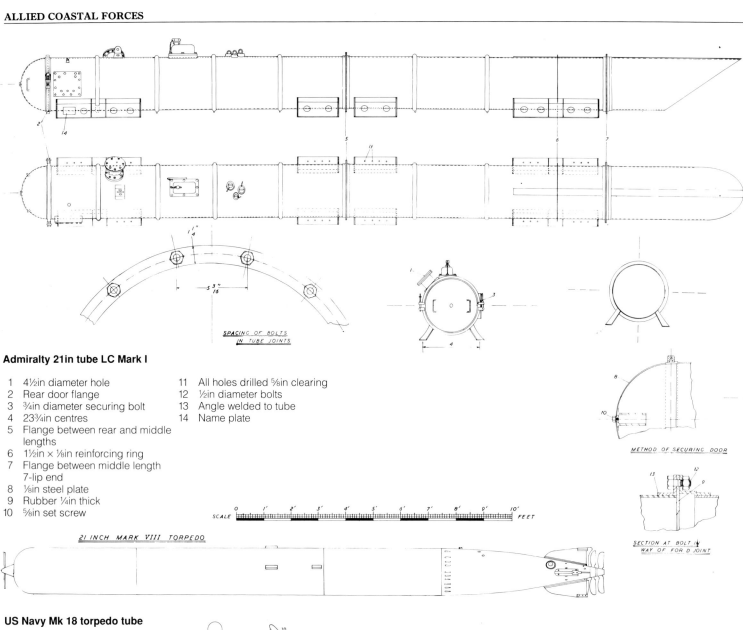

SPACING OF BOLTS
IN TUBE JOINTS

METHOD OF SECURING DOOR

SECTION AT BOLT IN
WAY OF FOR D JOINT

Admiralty 21in tube LC Mark I

1 4½in diameter hole
2 Rear door flange
3 ¾in diameter securing bolt
4 23¾in centres
5 Flange between rear and middle lengths
6 1½in × ⅛in reinforcing ring
7 Flange between middle length 7-lip end
8 ⅛in steel plate
9 Rubber ¼in thick
10 ⅝in set screw
11 All holes drilled ⅝in clearing
12 ½in diameter bolts
13 Angle welded to tube
14 Name plate

21 INCH MARK VIII TORPEDO

SCALE |0   1'   2'   3'   4'   5'   6'   7'   8'   9'   10'| FEET

US Navy Mk 18 torpedo tube

1 Training fitting on saddle
2 Tube lock
3 Training gear assembly
4 Saddle track
5 Bearing assembly for aft saddle
6 Torque rods
7 Safety pin for impulse chamber
8 Percussion 'button'
9 Electrical connection
10 Electrical cable for impulse chamber
11 Clip for electrical cable
12 Butterfly nut for securing breech door
13 Breech door hinge
14 Impulse chamber mount
15 Weld seam
16 Training gear handle
17 Cross-section of webbed breech door

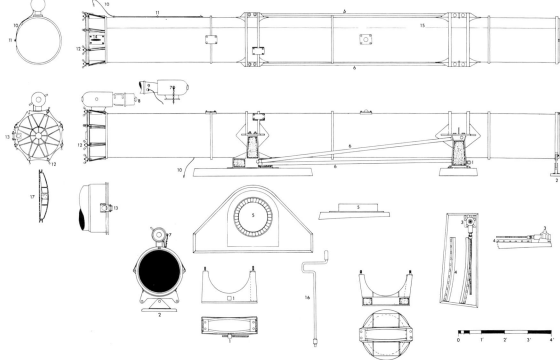

PT torpedo armament

Between 1940 and 1945 Elco PTs were fitted with a variety of torpedoes and launching devices. The original ten 70ft PTs carried four First World War vintage 17.7in Mark 7 Bliss-Leavitt torpedoes in tubes initially designed by the British Power Boat Company for PV70. The 77ft and early 80ft boats normally carried two or four 21in Mark 8 Mod 3 Bliss-Leavitts in Mark 18 Mod 1 or Mod 5 tubes, but could also carry the mark 14 Mod 1 or the Mark 15 Mod 1 torpedoes. From late 1943, two or four lightweight 22.5in Mark 13 aircraft torpedoes in Mark 1 roll-off racks were fitted to new production and retrofitted to most of the surviving earlier boats. Structurally, the various Marks were similar, despite dimensional differences. Each was steam-driven and comprised a warhead, air flask section, afterbody, and tail section. The warhead was hemispherical at the front end and slightly conical at the aft end. A nose piece containing a ring or 'eye' was secured to the forward end of the shell to facilitate handling. Within the warhead shell were a number of reinforcing rings, a tapped ring on the aft end for attaching it to the air flask section, a convex bulkhead, the exploder, and the cast explosive charge. The molten TNT or Torpex was poured into the shell while it was nose down at about a 45 degree angle and allowed to solidify. This put the centre of gravity below the fore and aft axis to provide the desired 'pull-around' stability. The exploder, fitted to the bottom of the warhead shell, was of the contact type. It was armed by the flow of sea water over an impeller after launching.

The 18in and 21in torpedo tubes were similar in appearance and operation, despite the obvious differences in diameter and length. Each unit consisted of a welded steel tube, open at the forward end and sealed by a breech door at the aft end. Along the length of the

Close-up of the Mark 13 mounted on PT 48. The boat alongside also mounts a pair of Mark 13s and is unusual in having a support for the warhead bolted to the deck. W Traxel

The 21in fixed Royal Navy tube on a 70ft Elco. The turret domes have been removed and a pair of twin 0.303 Lewis guns added forward, along with a single 20mm aft. USN

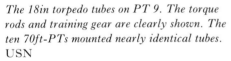

The 18in torpedo tubes on PT 9. The torque rods and training gear are clearly shown. The ten 70ft-PTs mounted nearly identical tubes. USN

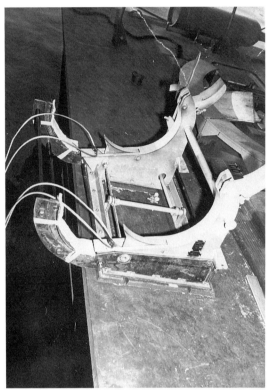

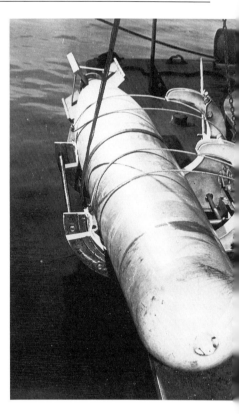

A 21in Mark 18 tube on one of the early 77ft boats, fitted with a muzzle cover to protect the torpedo. The training gear can be seen to the left of the cowl vent. USN

Mark 1 roll-off rack with torpedo loading supports installed. The extreme aft orientation of the rack indicates a very late 80ft Elco. USN

Same rack with a Mark 13 in the process of being loaded. The restraining cables have been attached and need only be tightened once the torpedo is in place. The circle just above the rack is a depression step for the 20mm gunner. USN

tube were several removable plates, secured by either hex nuts or wing nuts, which allowed access to the various depth, speed, and gyro setting controls on the torpedo.

The breech door was attached to the tube by a simple hinge on the inboard side and secured by eight large cast wing nuts. There were two versions of the breech door, one cast, the other welded. Each took the form of a scalloped octagon with U-shaped cut-outs at the outer ends to receive the securing bolts. The two types are easily distinguished, the cast version having reinforcing webs radiating from a central cylinder on the concave surface, while the welded version dispensed with the webbing, having only a simple concave surface. Only the 21in tubes were fitted with the welded door.

Just forward of the breech door, a cylindrical impulse chamber was bolted to a flat on top of the tube. On the 18in tube the impulse chamber could be mounted to left or right of the centreline, but on the 21in tube it was mounted on the centreline. A passage was provided in the mount to allow the gasses created by the ignition of the impulse charge to enter the tube and force the torpedo out of the tube. The forward end of the impulse chamber had an interrupted thread, on to which the canister holding the impulse charge was placed and twisted to lock it in place. A fitting was provided on the inboard side of the canister, to which an electrical ignition cable was attached. This cable was attached to another fitting on the deck and ran below the deck to a firing panel in the cockpit. At the forward end of the canister was a firing pin attached to a large 'button' which allowed percussion ignition of the charge if the electrical ignition failed. Percussion ignition was accomplished by striking the 'button' with a mallet.

At the muzzle end of the tube were three brackets for either an end cap or cable to secure and protect the torpedo during transit. At the lower end of the muzzle of the 21in tube was a bracket with two

holes which was used to secure the tube in train. A triangular plate with a matching hole was fitted to the deck below the muzzle. When aligned, a pin could be inserted into the holes, locking the tube in place.

Two reinforced mounts were welded to the top of the tube. These were bolted to the two saddles when the tube was fitted to the boat. The aft saddle served as a pivot and was mounted on a bearing track bolted to a wooden foundation on the deck. The forward saddle was attached to a curved track which was also on a wooden foundation. The 18in tubes had relatively small saddles with pipe tube mounts and oleo struts. The saddles for the two Mods of the 21in tubes were more robust and varied somewhat. On the Mod 1 version, the two saddles were trapezoidal in profile and were joined and aligned by a pair of torque rods on either side. The Mod 5 version had more rectangular saddles and dispensed with the torque rods.

Attached to the forward foundation of each tube was a training gear assembly. This assembly consisted of a casting which contained a pinion, a universal joint, and a long threaded rod which engaged a threaded fitting on the saddle. To train the tube, a long handle was placed in a fitting on top of the casting and rotated. This caused the threaded rod to rotate within the fitting, moving the tube in the desired direction. The forward tubes would be trained outboard 8.5 degrees off centreline, while the aft tubes would be trained 12.5 degrees.

Torpedoes were loaded into the tubes tail-first through the muzzle. A special winch was attached to the breech end of the tube after the breech door was opened and used to draw the torpedo into the tube.

The Mark 1 roll-off rack for the 22.5in Mark 13 torpedo was developed in 1943 as a lightweight (540lb vs 1450lb) alternative to the earlier tubes. The rack consisted of a rectangular angle-iron base, two curved upright members connected by a tube at the rear, two torpedo restraining cables, and a bell-crank-operated release mechanism. The release mechanism consisted of a lever at the back of the uprights which was connected by a rod to a torque tube in the middle of the base. A bell crank on the front of the torque tube controlled two rods which locked the cradles and restraining cable spools in place.

Loading the rack was accomplished by flipping back the torpedo pads at the top of the uprights and locking the lower cradles, with the torpedo restraining cables attached, in the raised position. The torpedo was lowered on to the cradles, the restraining cables were pulled over the torpedo body and secured by large wing nuts to plates at the rear of each upright, and the steadying pads were pivoted back on top of the torpedo. To launch the torpedo, the turbine was started by pulling a lanyard attached to a toggle on the starting spindle, and the release mechanism lever on the back of the rack was pulled aft. This action released the restraining cable spools and lowered the cradles, allowing the torpedo to roll into the water to begin its run to the target.

Although designed for the 22.5in torpedo, the Mark 1 rack was also approved for the standard 21in unit. This is in direct contrast to the often-made statement that the 21in torpedoes could not be used in the racks as the rolling action at launch would upset their gyros. That the 21in torpedoes were actually mounted in the racks is confirmed by a 1944 photo of one of the RON 29 boats, either PT 552 or 562, at Bastia, Corsica, with four long torpedoes in her racks.

Torpedo data
Mark 7
Builder Bliss-Leavitt
Length 204in
Diameter 17.7in
Weight 1628lb
Propulsion steam turbine
Guidance gyro
Air flask pressure 2000/2500psi
Warhead Mark 7 Mod 5 – 326lb of TNT or Torpex
Exploder Mark 3 Mod 1 Contact
Speed 35kts
Range 3500–6000yds, depending on speed and Mod
Launched from tube

Mark 8 Mod 3
Builder Bliss-Leavitt
Length 256.3in
Diameter 21in
Weight 2600lb
Propulsion steam turbine
Guidance gyro
Air flask pressure 2800psi
Warhead Mark 8 Mod 4 – 456lb of TNT or Torpex
Exploder Mark 3 Mod 2 contact
Speed 36kts
Range 16,000yds
Launched from tube, Mark 18 or Mark 19

Mark 13 Mod 1
Builder Naval Torpedo Station
Length 161in
Diameter 22.5in
Weight 2216lb
Propulsion steam turbine
Guidance gyro
Air flask pressure 2800psi
Warhead Mark 13 – 600lb Torpex
Exploder Mark 8 contact
Speed 33.5kts
Range 6300yds
Launched from roll-off rack Mark 1

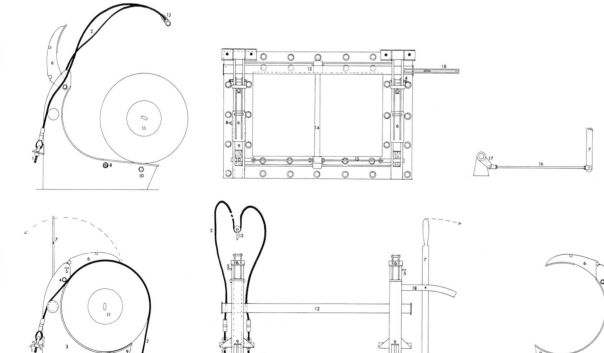

Roll-off rack Mk 1

1 Wing nut
2 Cable
3 Rack frame
4 Pivot pin
5 Ring
6 Frame extension
7 Release lever
8 Cradle pivot
9 Torpedo cradle
10 Cable release pin
11 Mk 13 torpedo
12 3in pipe
13 Pulley
14 Torque tube
15 Release pin linkage
16 Link rod
17 Lever
18 Release lever quadrant

FORWARD

The Dewandre turret

One of the more unique features of Scott-Paine's PV70 (PT 9) carried over to the 70ft and first series 77ft boats was the power-operated Dewandre turret. This unit was quite unusual in that it was enclosed in a framed, Plexiglas dome and was operated through a pneumatic/hydraulic power train. Most contemporary MTB gun mounts were open and manually-operated.

The basic unit consisted of a circular carriage which rotated on a fixed circular track by means of hydraulic cylinders acting through a system of wire ropes and pulleys. A yoke, pivoted aft of the horizontal axis of the carriage, provided an attachment point for the gun mount and was elevated by hydraulic cylinders. The hydraulics were driven by compressed air at about 240psi, supplied from air flasks of about 1 cu ft capacity. The flasks, in turn, were filled by a motor-driven compressor which automatically started when the pressure in the flasks fell below 150psi.

Operation of the turret was very easy for the gunner. He simply moved the guns in the direction he wanted to go and the turret would automatically train and elevate. Holding the guns on target would end the motion in both directions. Interestingly, the guns were not rigidly fixed in their mount but, with the air off, could be trained 12 degrees to either side of the mount centreline and depressed/elevated between −12 degrees and +20 degrees. With the air on, the yoke could be depressed/elevated between −12 degrees

The original Dewandre turret dome on PT 9. Note the relatively small size and the 0.30 calibre guns. USN

Firing practice on MTB 260 prior to transfer. Note the collapsed tubing on the depression rail at the bends. USN

Looking forward at the 77ft turret domes. The pipe depression rail can be seen between the two domes. USN

and +54 degrees, with an additional 31 degrees of elevation available due to the ability of the mount to pivot on the yoke. The carriage could be traversed 165 degrees to either side of the boat's transverse axis. Consequently, a pipe depression rail was fitted between and in front of the turrets to prevent firing into the cockpit and each other. Because of the domes, access to the turrets could only be gained from within the trunk cabin. To maximise internal space, a folding stand was provided for the gunner.

One major shortcoming of the Dewandre turret was the lack of integral magazine storage for the 0.50s. Unlike the later Mark 17 mounts, which had two pairs of curved magazines for each gun mounted directly on the carriage, the magazines were mounted directly on the guns and had a decidedly limited capacity.

The Plexiglas domes used on the 70ft and 77ft boats differed significantly. The original domes fitted to PV70/PT 9 were low, flat-sided, and had relatively few frames, while those fitted to the 70ft Elcos were tall, multi-framed units not unlike contemporary bomber turrets. The increased size and altered design may have been a result of the change from the 0.30 calibre guns of PV70 to the 0.50 calibre Brownings of the production boats. This 'bird cage' dome was also fitted to the first of the 77ft boats (PT 20) on completion, as she was the transition model. Shortly after comple-

The Dewandre turrets on one of the 70ft PTs following modification to an MTB for the Royal Navy. USN

The hydraulically-operated yoke at full elevation on one of the 70ft MTBs. USN

tion, PT 20 was retrofitted with the standard first-series 77ft boats' (PT 20–44) dome which was similar to the original flat-sided dome, but larger. None were fitted to the second series (PT 45–48, 59–68) boats, these having only the open turret initially. Later, a combined spray shield/depression rail was developed and installed on the second series boats.

Combat experience with the turrets at Pearl Harbor and Cavite on 7 and 8 December 1941 immediately demonstrated their shortcomings. The domes fogged up quickly during firing, the guns could not be trained and elevated quickly enough to track contemporary fighter aircraft, and they were useless without compressed air. During the attack on Pearl Harbor, the crews of RON 1 boats had to cut their hydraulic lines and traverse the turrets manually, as they were in the process of being transported as deck cargo and their engines could not be started to run the air compressors. The crews of RON 3 boats in the Philippines cut their hydraulic lines and removed the domes within days of going into action. The domes and hydraulics on the remaining 77ft boats were removed a short time later, although the yoke and gun mounts were retained. Over time, many of the surviving 77ft boats had their yokes replaced by pipe mounts fabricated in the field and, eventually, by the standard Mark 17 mount normally fitted to the 80ft Elcos, Higgins and Huckins PTs, and a myriad of other small craft. The Mark 17 will be detailed in Volume III.

Stripped Dewandre turret on a second-series 77ft PT, taken at Melville. USN

Dewandre turret hydraulics

1 Elevating cylinders
2 Power cylinder
3 Quick-release valve
4 Power cylinder piping
5 Elevating cylinder piping
6 Forward elevating jack
7 Jack piping
8 Piping between valve and quick-action cylinders
9 Piping

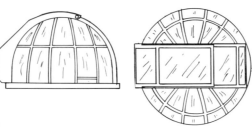

PT 10-19

PT 20-44

Dewandre turret

1 Plexiglas dome
2 Sliding portion of dome
3 Shock absorber pivot
4 Shock absorber/gun cradle
5 Rear gun mount
6 Yoke base
7 Front gun mount
8 Cradle pivot
9 Yoke pivot
10 Turret ring
11 Stationary track
12 Yoke
13 Link
14 Hydraulic cylinders
15 Hydraulic jacks for elevating guns

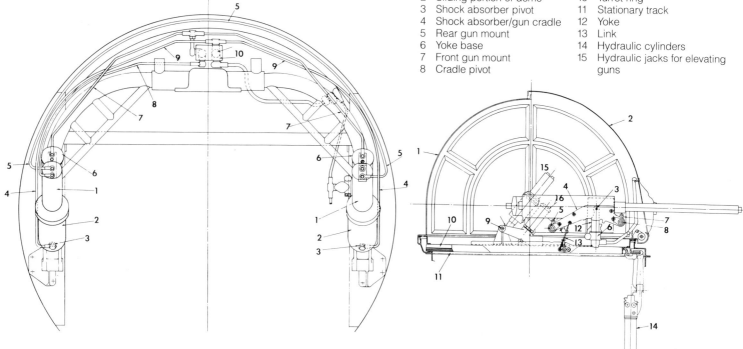

The US 20mm mounts

The 20mm Oerlikon was the standard medium-calibre weapon fitted to Elco PTs, first appearing on the 70ft boats as modified for Royal Navy service. The gun itself was a 20mm/70 calibre weapon consisting of four main groups:

- barrel and breech casing
- breechblock
- recoil and counter-recoil system
- trigger mechanism and locking device.

Designed for automatic firing only, the gun used some of the force developed by the explosion of the propellant to eject the empty cartridge, cock, reload, and fire the next round.

The 20mm fired fixed ammunition from a 60-round magazine at a cyclic rate of about 450rpm. In practice, an experienced crew could maintain a rate of about 300rpm. Usually, every other round or every third round in the spring-loaded magazine was a tracer.

Five different 20mm mounts saw service on the Elco PTs during the Second World War: the single Mark 4, Mark 10, Mark 12, Mark 14 and the quadruple Mark 15 Thunderbolt.

The Mark 4 mount featured a cast pedestal and a variable height trunnion bracket. The pedestal was bolted to the deck, but the pedestal head, through which the column rose, rotated about the top of the pedestal and could be locked in any position by a clamping lever. The column could be raised about 15in by a handwheel mounted on the head. Mounted on top of the column were the trunnion bracket and pivot, which also provided support for the shield, cradle spiral spring, and cradle, to which the gun was bolted. The cradle spring, mounted around the left trunnion, had one end attached to the trunnion and the other to the spring case, thus acting as a counterbalance to the weight of the gun. Adjustable shoulder rests and a ring sight were standard, as was a half-inch-thick shield weighing nearly 250lb, which was usually removed to save weight. The Mark 4 embodied some major disadvantages, especially for relatively small craft like the PT. It was heavy (about 1695lb) and required a three-man crew: gunner, loader, and a third man to raise and lower the column.

The first Elcos to mount the Mark 4 were the former 70ft PTs and PTCs, one mount being fitted aft just prior to transfer to the Royal Navy. The Mark 4 did not become standard equipment on US PTs, however, until the introduction of the second series 77ft boats (PT 45–48, 59–68; BPT 1–10) in 1941. As on the 70ft boats, it was mounted aft between the engineroom canopy and the lazarette hatch. A pipe rail was mounted just aft of the canopy to prevent firing into the superstructure. A similar arrangement was provided on the first series of 80ft Elcos (PT 103–196, 314–367).

The shortcomings of the Mark 4 mount were overcome in early 1943 by the development of the Mark 10 mount, a simpler and much lighter mount than its predecessor. The heavy cast pedestal and variable-height trunnion were replaced by an angle-iron tripod welded to a base ring. The trunnion bracket and pivot were mounted directly on top of the tripod; otherwise, the Mark 10 was similar to the Mark 4. The Mark 10 was considerably lighter than the Mark 4 (850lb vs 1695lb) and dispensed with the shield. The Mark 10 replaced the Mark 4 beginning with PT 372, Elco drawings 3028 and 3032 indicating that, originally, it was to be fitted aft on PT 372–383 and PT 486–563.

The Mark 14 was essentially a shortened Mark 10 mount that lacked the shoulder rests and sights of earlier Marks. These were unnecessary, as the mount was only waist-high and was now mostly used against surface targets. Overall weight of the Mark 14 mount was only 620lb and it was fitted to the same boats as the Mark 10. The standard position was forward, and somewhat to port, of the charthouse, although additional units were often mounted on either side of the charthouse or on the centreline position normally occupied by the 37mm.

A 20mm Mark 4 mount, showing the cradle and spent shell bag. This unit was mounted on the late 77ft and early 80ft boats. USN

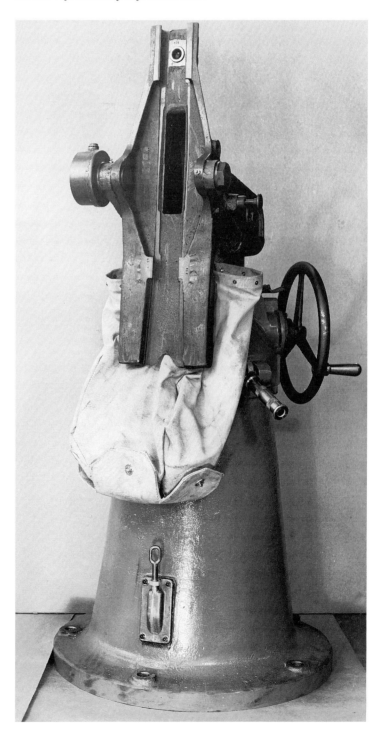

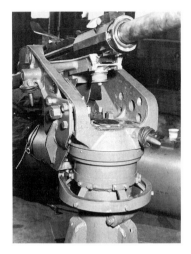

Close up of the Mark 14 gunsight fitted to the 'Thunderbolt'. Elco

Front and rear views of the cradle on a Mark 14 mount on one of the PT 731 series 80ft boats transferred to the Soviets. Elco

The Mark 12 was an experimental mount intended to replace the twin 0.50 calibre Mark 17 turret mounts. The first mounts were Scarff ring units developed by the New York Navy Yard in early 1943 and tested on RON 10 boats, being fitted to the forward turret. These mounts were not successful, but, in April 1943, conversion kits were developed which fitted the carriage stand of the Mark 17 .50 calibre mounts. At 850lb, the Mark 12 was about 100lb heavier than the 0.50 calibre mount it replaced.

The Mark 12 was authorised for boats of RONs 9, 10, 11, and 12; how many boats carried it is another question. Photographs are known showing the Mark 12 mount in the forward turret of PT 157 (RON 9) and PT 195 (RON 12), and in the aft turret of an unidentified RON 9 boat, possibly PT 155.

Probably the most singular 20mm mount fitted to the PTs, however, was the Elco-developed Thunderbolt. The original design, proposed in mid-1942, was to have incorporated a phenomenal combination of six 0.50 calibre machine guns and two 20mm cannon in an electro-hydraulically controlled gondola. Whether this particular configuration was actually developed is unclear. Other configurations, however, were developed and tested, including one with only the six 0.50s and another with three 20mm and a

pair of 0.50s. The first prototype was tested on PT 138 in late 1942, another prototype being fitted at about the same time to PT 160. This second mount incorporated four 20mm and two 0.50s.

Designed as a dual-purpose weapon, the Thunderbolt had an elevation/depression range of +85/−15 degrees and a full 360 degree traverse. To enhance its anti-aircraft capabilities the Mark 14 compensating gunsight was fitted experimentally, although it does not appear to have become standard on production models intended for PTs. At least two units were mounted on battleships [*Massachusetts* (BB59) and *Maryland* (BB46)] to augment their anti-aircraft batteries, and are likely to have retained the Mark 14.

By January 1944 the Thunderbolt had evolved into the production mount, Model C–4, and was fitted to PT 556–559. At this point, the mount consisted of a quadrant-shaped armoured gondola with four 20mm, and was mounted aft in place of the more normal 40mm. The gondola sides and back were constructed of ¼in plate, the front plate being ½in. Attached to the rear of the gondola was a tubular handle which permitted manual elevation and traverse of the mount in the event of an electric or hydraulic failure. A gunner's seat, joystick, and firing treadle were fitted to port, while an oil filter and recuperator were to starboard. Slots were cut in the rear for shell ejection and manual cocking of the 20mm. The gondola pivoted on two vertical yokes, elevation and depression being effected by an hydraulic ram on each yoke. The yokes were attached to a conical base which contained an electrically-driven

A 20mm Mark 4 on one of the first 80ft boats. The shields were removed early on as a weight-saving measure. This particular boat has depth charges in place of the aft torpedo tube. USN

A number of the RON 9 boats, including PT 157, were fitted with the 20mm Mark 12 mount in the forward 0.50 calibre turret, while some others had them aft. PTBM

Four views of the experimental 'Thunderbolt'
mounted on PT 160, taken 5 December 1942.

Unlike production versions, this mount has two
0.50 calibre machine guns in addition to the
four 20mm. Elco

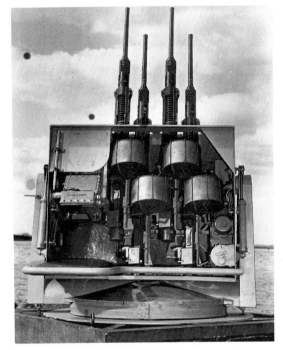

The final version of the 'Thunderbolt', seen here
on 4 October 1943, was designated Model 102–
C–4. This version is fitted with the Mark 14
computing gunsight. Elco

PT 559 was one of four RON 29 boats to carry
the 'Thunderbolt'. This photo of her mount,
taken 18 January 1944, shows that the boat
was still in Measure 31/5P camouflage. Elco

hydraulic traversing motor.

Operational experience with the Thunderbolt resulted in mixed reactions. The first mount carried away in a heavy sea before it could be tested in action. Installation of the mount required deck strengthening and the addition of another 24-volt DC generator, which did not endear it to the Bureau of Ordnance. The Thunderbolt also weighed about the same as the more powerful, but as yet unapproved, 40mm mount. On the other hand, action reports from the Mediterranean indicated that the Thunderbolt was well-liked. Following two gunnery actions between RON 29 boats and German patrol craft on 16 and 18 July 1944, in which two German craft were sunk, the squadron commander, Lt Cdr Stephen Daunis, described the Thunderbolt as '. . . an exceptional weapon . . .'. In early 1945, a few Thunderbolts saw action with RON 10 and RON 21 boats in the southwest Pacific area.

20mm particulars
Barrel weight   150lb
Cyclic   450rpm
Muzzle velocity   2740fps
Maximum altitude   10,000ft at 90 degrees elevation
Maximum range   4800yds at 35 degrees elevation
Elevation limits   varied with mount, but normally −15 degrees
to +90 degrees
Ammunition   HE
Projectile – .0271lb   Case - .190lb
Charge – 27.7 grammes
APT
Projectile – .0268lb   Case – .180lb
Charge – 27.7 grammes

The US 37mm gun

As the war in the Pacific progressed and the number of major surface targets decreased, the role of the PT began to shift to the interdiction of Japanese barge traffic among the islands. The 20mm proved to be relatively ineffective against the armoured barges used by the Japanese, so the search was on for heavier firepower. One solution was to mount the readily-available Army 37mm M3 anti-tank gun on the bow, replacing the single or twin 0.50 calibre Browning often mounted in this position. The M3 was the standard US Army light anti-tank gun of the period and was mounted on an M4 wheeled carriage with shield. It could fire either high-explosive (HE) or armour-piercing (AP) shells and had a nominal muzzle velocity of 2600fps. Trial installations on PTs began in July 1943 and by August 1943 at least four Elcos are known to have mounted the M3: PT 109, 116, 157, and 159. The initial installations were necessarily crude. The gun fitted to 109 on August 1 1943, for instance, was simply bracketed to a couple 2 × 8s spiked to the deck after having its wheels removed. (109 never got a chance to use its 37mm, however; she was sunk by the Japanese destroyer *Amagiri* the very next day.) On other boats, the gun was removed from its carriage and fitted on locally-fabricated mounts. These mounts usually consisted of a U-shaped trunnion support welded or bolted to a plate which pivoted in a simple braced pipe stand bolted to the foredeck, replacing the single 0.50 calibre mounted in that location on many of the boats.

While the anti-tank gun provided a major improvement in firepower, it was slow firing and lacked tracer control. What was needed was an automatic weapon. In September 1943 tests were carried out with the 37mm M4 cannon normally mounted in USAAF P–39 aircraft. Built by American Armament Company, the M4 was light (238lb installed in a P–39), tracer-capable, incorporated an integral 30-round magazine, and had a rate of fire of 150rpm and a muzzle velocity of 2000fps. Initially mounted on locally-produced pedestals of varying design, it was soon determined that, with slight modification, the M4 would fit in the standard Mark 14 20mm mount. Factory production of this mount commenced in mid-1944 and continued until early 1945, when a new mount (Mark 1) was developed specifically for the later M9 version. This mount is easily identified by its broad conical base. The M9 was longer (104in vs 89.5in), heavier (398lb vs 238lb), and had a slower rate of fire (125rpm vs 150rpm) than the M4 it replaced, but compensated with a higher muzzle velocity (2900fps vs 2000fps).

Both versions were normally mounted forward on the centreline; variations, however, were commonplace, particularly among the boats operating in the English Channel and the Mediterranean. Contemporary (1944) newsreel footage shows that the following Elco boats replaced the 20mm Mark 14 mounted to port forward with the 37mm M4:

- PT 509 (RON 34)
- PT 515, 517, 519, and 520 (RON 35)

A number of Higgins boats in the Mediterranean mounted a pair of them forward, as well. Details of these will be provided in Volume III.

Although the 37mm lacked the firepower of the 40mm, it was the preferred weapon in the South Pacific theatre of operations. The primary reason for this preference was that the 37mm gun was lighter than the 40mm and, therefore, did not require the removal of the aft two torpedoes, which was the case when a 40mm was mounted aft. Unlike their southwest Pacific counterparts, the South Pacific boats were still regularly engaging Japanese destroyers and cruisers, and their commanders were loath to give up their torpedoes.

PT 618, one of the very last Elco 80s, displays her factory developed Mark 1 mount for the 37mm. Note how far aft the gun is located compared with earlier boats. USN

Although the 37mm was normally fitted well forward, this was not always the case. The boat in the foreground has reversed the position of the 20mm and 37mm, while the remaining four boats have them in the usual position. USN

Field-developed mounts for the 37mm came in a variety of shapes and sizes. This one is a simple pipe tripod. USN

1 Barrel
2 Receiver
3 Breech block
4 Recuperator
5 Feed box
6 Trunnion
7 Spring housing
8 Charging lever
9 Grip (M-4)
10 Trigger (M-4)
11 Firing pin trip
12 Grip (M-9)
13 Trigger (M-9)
14 Mk 14 mount
15 Mk 1 mount
16 Magazine (M-4, 30 round)
17 Endless belt
18 Magazine (M-9, 30 round)

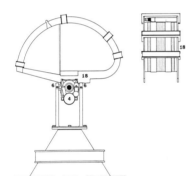

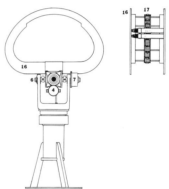

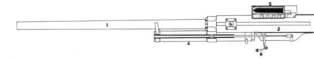

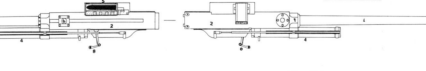

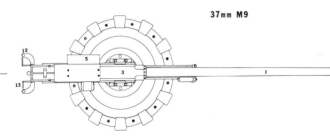

37mm M9

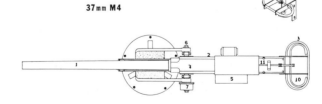

37mm M4

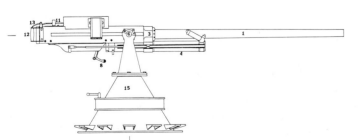

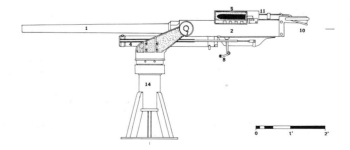

The US 40mm Mark 3 gun

Up to the end of 1942, the heaviest gun carried by the PTs was the 20mm Oerlikon. Squadron commanders, however, were interested in something more powerful. In December 1942 the Bureau of Ordnance ordered the experimental fitting of a single, manually-operated 40mm mount on the foredeck of PT 174, then under construction. The deck was strengthened and a combination splinter-shield and breakwater was fitted forward of the chart-house. The gun was bolted to an octagonal base within the shield. Trials indicated that the bow was not the place for such a large weapon, as this was the area of most violent motion under way and it became difficult to handle. In March 1943 the Bureau conducted further experiments by mounting the 40mm aft in place of the 20mm mount on PT 193–196. This arrangement was an immediate success and the installation became standard on most subsequent Elcos.

As a result, PT 174 was one of the few PTs to have a bow-mounted 40mm, others being three 77ft Elcos (PT 59, 60 and 61), which were converted to gunboats in October 1943. The splinter-shield/breakwater was removed and a simple gunshield was bolted to the mount. Judging by a photograph showing PT 174 later in the war, it appears that the octagonal base may also have been removed, as the gun sits very low, the barrel being perhaps 2ft above the deck. The 40mm on the 77ft gunboats were similarly mounted. A good photograph of the aft mount on PT 59 can be found in Robert Donovan's book *PT 109*. In this instance, the barrel is at waist level.

Designated the Mark 3, the single 40mm was a navalised version of the standard manually-operated US Army M1 anti-aircraft weapon. The basic gun comprised the barrel, breech casing, and breech ring assemblies, breech operating mechanism, a portion of the firing mechanism, automatic loader assembly, automatic loading tray assembly, and recoil mechanism. The gun was supported by trunnions mounted on the sides of the breech casing, on the underside of which was mounted the elevating arc.

The mount comprised the top carriage, platform assembly, elevating mechanism, equilibrators, traversing mechanism, firing mechanism, and roller bearing, which could be bolted directly to a standard 3in/50 foundation, as well as the octagonal base developed specifically for the PTs. Ring sights were provided for both the trainer and pointer, who traversed and elevated the weapon manually.

The Mark 3 could be fired in either automatic or semi-automatic

Left side of the gun, showing the rammer cocking lever in raised position and the trigger trip assembly on the gun cradle. Al Ross

Elevating mechanism. Al Ross

Ring sight. Al Ross

Training mechanism and shell ejection chute. Al Ross

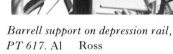

Barrell support on depression rail, PT 617. Al   Ross

40mm crew in action. PTBM

mode, the pointer depressing a firing pedal with his right foot. Ammunition was available in HET and APT rounds, loaded in four-round clips.

Although originally intended as an anti-aircraft gun, the 40mm became the premier 'barge busting' weapon for PTs in the south-west Pacific. It could blow a 12in hole (about four times larger than that of a 37mm hit) in a *Daihatsu* or similar barge. The 40mm was also successfully employed by boats operating against German coastal forces in the English Channel and the Mediterranean. In one such operation on the night of 24–25 August 1944, PT 511, 514, and 520 engaged four S-boats off Le Havre. In the ensuing gun battle, S 91 was so badly shot up that she had to be scuttled by her crew.

The 40mm was also often used to engage targets ashore. On 9 April 1944, for instance, PT 341 engaged a Japanese 3in battery at Cape Gourdon, Saidor, knocking it out after about 50 rounds. In another action during the evening of 24 March 1945, PT 134 and 348 slipped into Cebu City harbour and destroyed two freight wagons and two barges with their 40mm guns.

40mm Mark 3 data
Type   single mount, manual
Barrel weight   296lb
Total weight   2440lb
Oscillating weight   1042lb
Recoiling weight   415lb
Brake load   4800lb
Cyclic   160rpm
Muzzle velocity   2890fps
Max altitude   22,800ft at 90 degrees elevation
Max range   11,000yds at 42 degrees elevation
Elevation limits   −6 degrees to +90 degrees
Ammunition
   AA, AP, T
      Projectile – 1.98lb   Case – 1.89lb   Charge – 315 grammes

40mm Mk 3

1   Flash hider
2   Barrel
3   Recuperator spring cover
4   Recoil cylinder
5   Equilibriator

6   Foot rest
7   Firing pedal
8   Shell ejection chute
9   Elevator's sight
10   Side cover
11   Elevating gear
12   Carriage
13   Firing lever
14   Hand operating lever
15   Elevating arc
16   Safety lever
17   Shell guide
18   Rear chute
19   Ejected shell guide

20   Chute support
21   Training gear
22   Trainer's sight
23   Loader's platform
24   Base ring

1   Clip for 40mm rounds
2   40mm HET round
3   Trunnion
4   Elevating arc
5   Bolt holes for arc
6   Bottom cover
7   Recuperator
8   Recoil indicator
9   Sightbar bracket
10   Extractor release lever
11   Spent shell chute
12   Chute extension
13   Firing pedal linkage

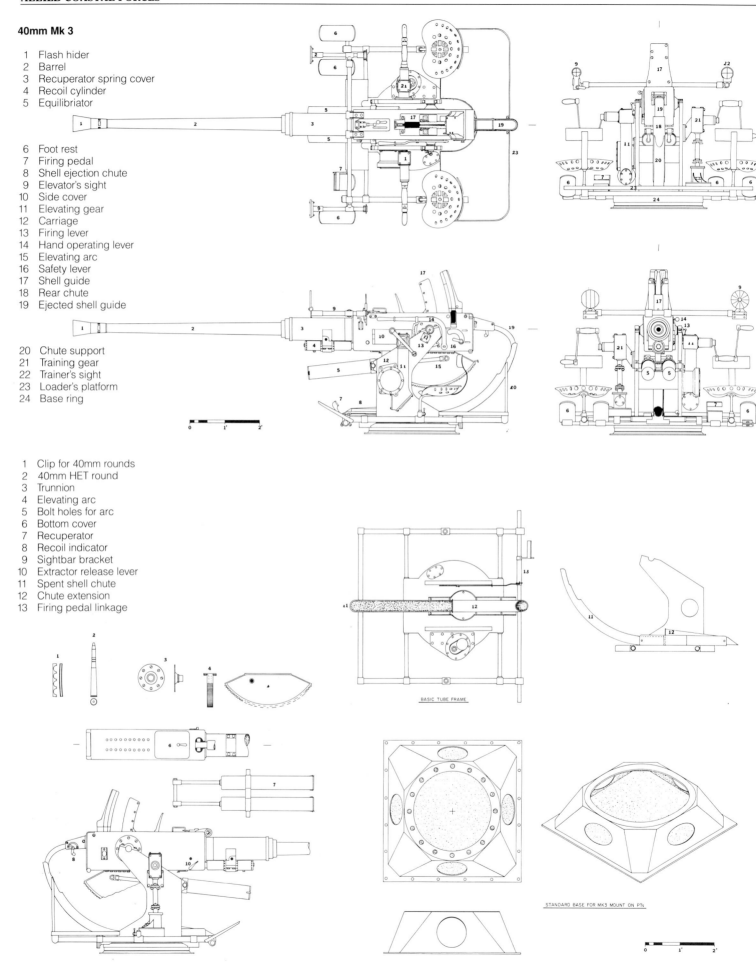

BASIC TUBE FRAME

STANDARD BASE FOR MK3 MOUNT ON PTs

Rocket launchers

Several different rocket launchers were employed on the PTs with varying degrees of success during the war. One of the earliest experiments was the sextuple Mark 13 2.36in launcher developed in 1943. Essentially, this weapon consisted of six Bazooka tubes mounted on a modified 0.30 calibre machine gun mount. A photograph of this mount shows it mounted on the day cabin roof of PT 354, an 80ft Elco, just aft of the radar mast support. Due to the backblast of the rocket, this was probably the safest location for such a weapon.

Several launchers were developed for the 4.5in bombardment rocket during 1944:

- Mark 8 – referred to as the 'Egg Crate', it held nine rounds in a rectangular box-like framework pivoted at the aft end.
- Unknown Mark – a simple, gravity-fed launcher consisting of an upright, two launch rails, and a blast deflector plate. Twelve rounds were carried, six in each column.

Both of these launchers were mounted in pairs on the 80ft Elcos, one on either side, and just forward of, the charthouse.

A third type, not mounted on an Elco, resembled the Mark 20 'Mousetrap' ASW launcher. This type will be detailed in Volume III in the Higgins PT section.

The ultimate wartime launcher was the octuple Mark 50, designed for the 5in spin-stabilised rocket. Developed in late 1944, the Mark 50 consisted of two rows of four tubes attached by an arm to a unique pivoting mount. Like the earlier launchers, the Mark 50 was normally mounted in pairs forward of the charthouse; however, on the very late 80ft boats they were moved back about level with the front of the charthouse. When not in use, the tubes were swung inboard, their muzzles pointing aft. In action, the tubes were swung outboard, cranked to the appropriate elevation, and fired electrically, the backblast being deflected harmlessly into the water alongside. Fire control was through two Mark 1 illuminated sights mounted on top of the windscreen, one for the helmsman and one for the conning officer. The firing panel was mounted on the cockpit bulkhead to the right of the helm.

Two types of rockets were employed: high explosive (HE) with a 5000-yard range and semi-armour piercing (SAP) with an 11,000-yard range. A complete reload for each launcher was carried in ready-service lockers mounted on the deck behind each launcher.

The Mark 50s were first fitted to new production boats in March 1945, commencing with RON 33. Retrofits commenced shortly after, beginning with RON 21, but appear to have occurred only on Pacific boats.

Testing by the Motor Torpedo Boat Squadrons Training Center at Melville indicated that the 5in spin-stabilised rocket could be used with effect against barges, medium coasting vessels, small warships, and shore installations. The bases for these conclusions were published by the CNO in August 1945 and are included here:

I. USE OF ROCKETS AGAINST BARGES

Since the type A barge has been encountered most frequently by PTs its characteristics were selected in studying the effectiveness of the 5-inch rocket against Japanese barges. Its dimensions are approximately: Length 49 feet, freeboard 2 feet, beam 11 feet.

Test firing indicated that one direct hit, unless at the waterline or close enough so that the hole extended below the waterline, would not sink such a barge, but

that it would probably cause such material and personnel damage from shrapnel and blast as to render the barge an easy target for gunfire.

The advantages of rocket fire in this situation appear to be:

(1) Probability of destruction or severe damage by rocket fire is fair.

(2) Probability of shrapnel from near misses causing minor damage and casualties to personnel is good.

(3) Demoralizing effect of rocket fire on personnel in the barge should be substantial. There is a good chance that they would either hit the deck or abandon the barge.

The disadvantages are:

(1) After the first flare or first shot the barge will very probably turn and run, presenting only its stern and maneuvering to offer a very difficult target.

(2) It is very difficult for more than one boat to fire rockets at one barge, or several barges close together. Since the firing boats necessarily converge on the target, if one gets ahead of the other at short range, the

PT 624 just after being cancelled, showing the two Mark 50 rocket launchers not yet in place. The box on either side just forward of the roll-off racks was for rocket storage. USN

former is in danger of being hit by shrapnel from rounds falling short. With the target maneuvering there is also risk that one PT may fire at another.

(3) Rocket fire illuminates the firing boat, making it a clear target for other enemy surface craft and enemy aircraft.

(4) While information on the effect of hits on rockets from various types of small arms fire is not as yet available, it is possible that incendiaries and tracers may set off the motor.

II. SMALL CARGO VESSELS AND MINOR WARSHIPS

The type of target considered would have a length of at least 100 feet and a mean freeboard of 10 feet. Cargo vessels, FCs, DEs, and even DDs may be considered as targets for rockets. These are targets which due to size and draft, or speed and maneuverability, are extremely difficult to hit with a torpedo. Small cargo vessels (sampans, luggers, sea trucks) are being encountered with greater frequency by MTBs and there is reason to anticipate encounters with fast PCs or DEs.

The aim of an attack against this type of target would be to bring as many rocket launchers to bear on the target as practicable. Maximum accurate firing range appears to be about 1,500 yards. Decisive range, i.e., when about one out of three round should hit, appears

to be about 500 yards or less.

Advantages of using rockets against this type of vessels appear to be:

(1) Probability of hitting with about one out of eight rockets appears to be good at 1,500 yards. On a firing run commencing at 1,500 yards and continuing to about 1,000 yards about 20 percent hits should be made.

(2) Even though the hits scored on one run may not sink the target, they should inflict sufficient damage to make it easy prey for either a torpedo or subsequent close range rocket attack.

Disadvantages are:

(1) Even if an undetected approach to firing range is accomplished, return fire may be encountered after the opening round.

(2) Because of the present requirements of rocket control the rocket firing boat cannot zigzag or change speed.

Mark 8 'egg-crate' rocket launchers on PT 131. A simple metal blast shield has been added behind each launcher to prevent damage to the deck and torpedo. USN

III. SHORE BOMBARDMENTS BY PTs EQUIPPED WITH HCSR

The HCSR provides a bombardment weapon which can be used by PTs at a reasonable range with good effect. It is conservatively estimated that at 3,000 yards range about 80 percent of the rounds fired would land in a target area about 350 yards long by 125 yards wide.

Advantages are:

(1) Assuming PTs at night can approach the target area to within 5,000 yards without detection, a quick barrage of rockets should catch a large percentage of personnel above ground.

(2) Small bivouac areas, supply dumps, small harbors, etc., which are not worthwhile targets for fleet bombardment could probably be hit harder with rockets than by the average night bombing.

(3) In amphibious operations, boats equipped with rockets could quickly reach and provide emergency supporting fire against shore installations or areas when other more efficient bombardment vessels were not available for the job.

Disadvantages are:

(1) Due to shore fire it may be impossible to reach proper range and maintain firing course and speed without great risk.

(2) At night, it may be impossible to determine a suitable point of aim.

CONCLUSION

While the final answer on the effectiveness of rockets carried by PT boats will not be known until adequate combat experience has been had, it would appear that the addition of rockets to PT boat armament should do much to fill in the gap between guns and torpedoes, and permit an effective attack to be conducted against any target encountered.

Mark 50 launcher for 5in spin-stabilised rockets trained outboard. PTBM

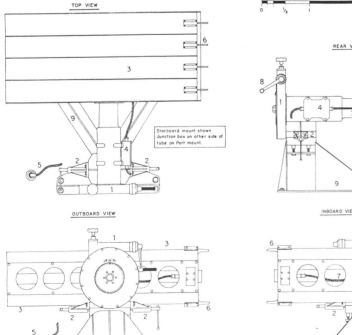

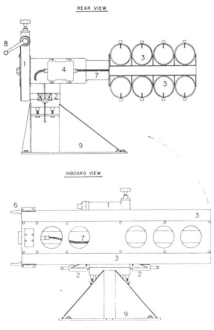

Mk 50

1 Elevating gear
2 Training lock
3 Rocket tube
4 Junction box
5 Deck connector for firing cable
6 Latch
7 Cable
8 Crank
9 Base

Development of bridge and wheelhouse during the Second World War

Vosper drawings illustrate developments undertaken through operational experience gained during the early years of hostilities and technical additions and instrumentation of later war years.

The prewar export orders are shown in the general arrangement drawings and in photographs of the vessels ordered by Greece. Here the bridge and wheelhouse is all metal (a light alloy as far as can be established) with curved windbreak. The mast is of the inverted 'Y' type. Presumably the polished cowl ventilators would be painted over during hostilities. Inside the wheelhouse the instrumentation and layout is very simple – two Kent clear view screens, a voice pipe to the bridge above the wheel, and three flexible voice pipes to starboard. It has proved impossible to make out the instrumentation fitted and the list of engine orders to port is unclear; those legible are in Greek.

The bridge too is rather basic, with a gun tub in the foreground, voice pipe, small engineroom telegraph, bell pushes and a canvas covered spotlight. The base of the mast seems very flimsy and the glass windscreen directly in front of the helmsman would be more useful on a motor boat. However, that was the limit of these earlier Vosper designs.

Two photographs show an early Royal Navy MTB which is believed to be MTB 30, of the early group ordered on 27 September 1939. Again the layout is rather basic, with three engine levers, main telegraph and a rather small flag locker. The wheelhouse again is rather sparse and the starboard clear view screen drive cover is missing. There is little instrumentation.

Vosper Drawing 8226 from the 1938 Programme for Boats No 1942–5 – MTBs 20, 21, 23 and 22 – has been redrawn. Here the bridge and wheelhouse are more sophisticated than the early 60ft units. The instrumentation on the wheelhouse dashboard is still relatively basic, but at least steps were being taken to improve instrumentation and improve control. The mast is still the inverted 'Y' type (not drawn) and the only protection is retaining straps for bullet-proof screens in the wheelhouse. These units, initially built for the Royal Navy, were sold to Romania shortly after completion, but lack later developments brought about by operational knowledge learned the hard way.

Vosper Drawing 9351 (MTBs 74–92 and 222–241) shows the construction of the wheelhouse and bridge for 70ft MTBs. While the open bridge is of what seems to be ply, it is in fact ⅜in non-magnetic bullet-proof plating, which extends into the wheelhouse; the whole structure is on mahogany framing. The box-like bridge top is of 4mm plywood and the wheelhouse roof, while bullet-proof, is covered with canvas and painted. The two vertical side windows slide open and the forward windows are fixed. The door to the wheelhouse is faced with ⅜in non-magnetic bullet-proof plating.

Handrails, or 'grabrails' as they were known in the United States, are located inside and outside the bridge and the whole was made as a single component, lowered on to the hull and bolted down.

Redrawn from Vosper Drawing 9462, the bridge and wheelhouse detail is for MTBs 35, 36, 38 and 218–221. These drawings are particularly detailed and require little explanation, but show the early design standard for boats that joined the service in the spring of 1941.

Vosper Drawing 9562 is also self explanatory and is typical of the

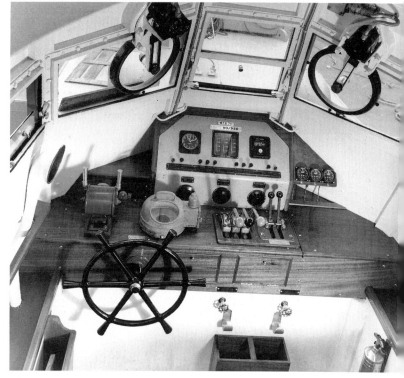

The wheelhouse of MTB 73 in October 1941. This is more sophisticated, with better instrumentation, clock, revolution counters, engine boost gauges, remote torpedo firing levers, magnetic compass and telegraphs, etc (see drawings for detail).
Vosper Thornycroft (UK) Ltd

large group of MTBs 73–98 ordered on 14 May 1940. With the help of a first class photograph of MTB 73's wheelhouse, and another of MTB 97's bridge, one of the first advances noted is two torpedo firing levers in the wheelhouse, and the mast on the starboard side of the bridge wing. As can be seen, a great deal of additional equipment has been added to the earlier basic structure, including additional electrical work, telephones, more 'buzzers', echo-sounder and remote control to engineroom fire extinguishers. The drawing shows the modifications carried out up to the end of 1941.

Drawing 10454 relates to MTBs of the 1939 extension programme. These sixteen later units, numbered 347–362, were ordered on 17 April 1942. Not all were built at Portchester or Wivenhoe, some being sub-contracted to Harland & Wolff, Belfast and Morgan Giles, Teignmouth. In these there are many changes. For the first time access can be gained to the bridge from below, through the chartroom. There is no lower wheel in what was the wheelhouse – now the charthouse. The ship's wheel is now a substantial pedestal and all bridge controls are under the bridge shelf, with seemingly an overall less cramped layout. The drawing is backed up by a photograph of MTB 351's wheel and instruments, and together these illustrate the developments up to the spring of 1943. Note the comprehensive telegraph order control for each

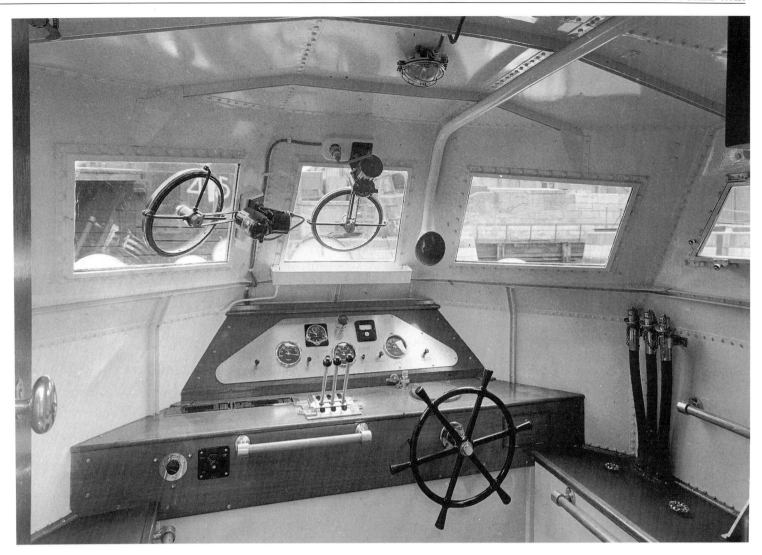

main engine – 'stand by to maximum', 'start gun pump', 'action station', 'make smoke', 'conning tower throttle control', etc.

The next development was for the sixteen units ordered on 10 March 1943, MTBs 380–395, which were known as the 73ft Vosper Type I. MTB 379 was the prototype of this improved design, which was the first Vosper combined MGB/MTB and carried a much heavier armament in the shape of four 18in torpedo tubes. The bridge had been completely redesigned, with a greatly simplified but more comprehensive layout. There is no access to below deck apart from the companionway on the port side, but the cable leads are plainly visible, with the mast mounted to port. The drawing, redrawn from Vosper 10977, is modified up to the summer of 1944. There are three photographs taken aboard MTB 385.

The final subject is redrawn from Drawing 11503A, which shows the arrangement of the bridge instruments for the 1944 Type II 73ft design, MTBs 523–536. It also covers the two target boats produced postwar, in which no armament was fitted. With a wider 'boxy' appearance, it was packed with a mass of technical aids, and bears little resemblance to the bridge/wheelhouse at the commencement of hostilities. Navigation aids were much in evidence, and radar and radio required much additional electrical power. The voicepipes are well padded, but the torpedo sight is little changed. The ship's wheel is now smaller with a single handle to aid with rapid changes of course. There is a morse key adjacent to it. Gunnery control is more sophisticated, with a power operated 6pdr mounted forward, but the torpedo armament has been reduced to two 18in tubes.

The wheelhouse of a Greek 70ft MTB, which was very basic. There are two clear-view screens, simple instrumentation, a clock and voice pipes.
Vosper Thornycroft (UK) Ltd

The bridge of MTB 97 in September 1942. A simple uncluttered layout compared with later Vosper designs.
Vosper Thornycroft (UK) Ltd

ELEVATION LOOKING FROM ₵ TO PORT

8 1/8" RAD.

1' 3" RAD.

SCALE
0   5'   10'   15'
FEET

5" RAD.

PLAN AT BRIDGE TOP

PLAN AT DECK

SECTION AT BULKHEAD

TYPICAL SECTION

3' 4 1/2" RAD.

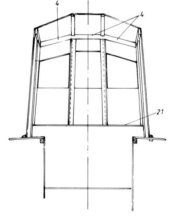

SECTION AT FOR'D END

Construction of wheelhouse and bridge – Vosper 70ft MTBs

1   4mm plywood
2   1/8in 5-ply
3   3in × 2in beam
4   3in × 1¼in mahogany
5   ¾in mahogany platform
6   2½in × 1½in mahogany
7   Roof to be covered with canvas and painted
8   1in × 1in mahogany with ⅜in 5-ply double
9   4¼in × ½in brass bolts with nuts and washers
10 Door faced with ⅜in non-magnetic bullet-proof plating
11 Handrail, port and starboard inside and outside
12 2-1/2in × 1¼in Birmabright
13 Buttstrap
14 ⅜in non-magnetic bullet-proof plating
15 Handrail to form stiffener
16 Vertical sliding window
17 Fixed window
18 5/8in × 1in strip
19 ¾in 5-ply brackets double
20 Air hole
21 Instrument shelf
22 Corner posts – 4in × 2in mahogany
23 ⅜in 5-ply
24 Raised deck
25 5/16in diameter × 3in long galvanised mild steel bolts, nuts and washers
26 Quicktho opening window
27 Quicktho fixed window
28 Mahogany cant 1½in × 1½in oiled and screwed to ply
29 Filling
30 1½in × 12 countersunk head wood screws
31 Space for compass
32 1½ × ⅞in cant
33 Sponge rubber sealing strip

Redrawn from Vosper Drawings 9351 for MTBs 74, 76, 87–92, 222–245.

38 Switch helm indicator
39 Panel light dimmer
40 Steering control valve
41 Sockets for throttle locking bar
42 Changeover switch for navigation lights, anchor and shaded stern lights
43 Navigation light dimmer
44 Retaining straps for bullet-proof screen
45 Canvas awning stanchion socket
46 Sockets for NUC masthead and anchor lights
47 Hydraulic torpedo firing controls
48 Cover over hydraulic steering gear
49 Plug for Aldis lamp (12 volt)
50 Switch wheelhouse light
51 Switch for Aldis lamp (12 volt)
52 Switch chart table light
53 Inspection door for bevel gear
54 Cupboard

55 Chart table with hinged flap
56 Morse signal key
57 Hydraulic throttle controls
58 Buzzer
59 Walker Excelsior electric log
60 Telephone Admiralty Pattern M318
61 Engineroom buzzer push button
62 Marco loudspeaker Admiralty Pattern M317
63 Fire extinguisher
64 Shaded light for chart table
65 Mast mounting
66 Sponge rubber mat
67 Stool
68 Panel giving access to compass correctors
69 Log
70 W/T aerial lead
71 Hatch
72 Horn

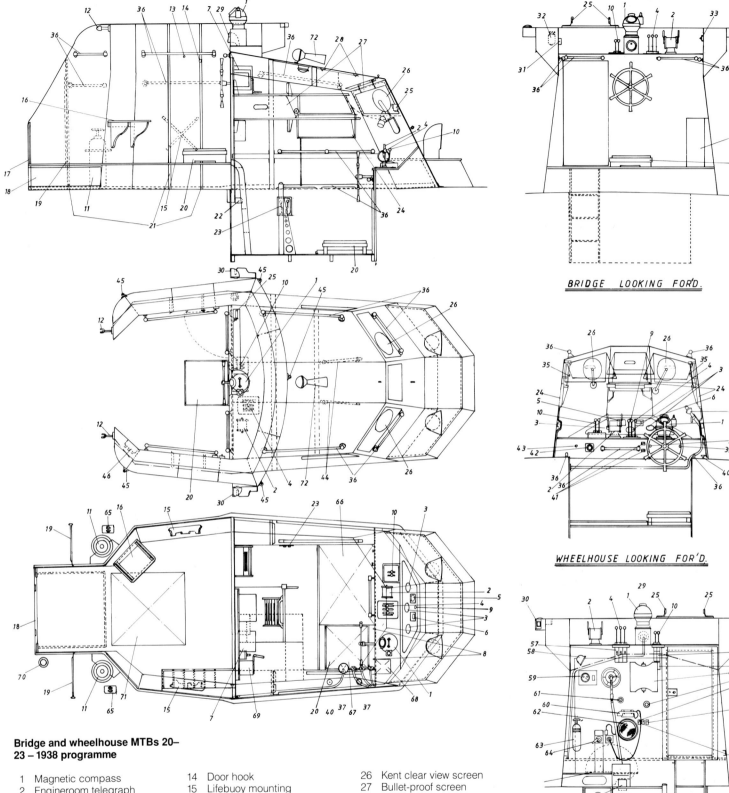

BRIDGE LOOKING FOR'D.

WHEELHOUSE LOOKING FOR'D.

WHEELHOUSE LOOKING AFT

Bridge and wheelhouse MTBs 20–23 – 1938 programme

1	Magnetic compass	14	Door hook	26	Kent clear view screen
2	Engineroom telegraph	15	Lifebuoy mounting	27	Bullet-proof screen
3	Engine revolution counters	16	Seat	28	Strap eyes
4	Engine throttles	17	Brace	29	Voicepipe to wheelhouse
5	Clock	18	Drawer	30	Navigation light box
6	Helm indicator	19	Stay	31	Junction box
7	Engineroom order telegraph	20	Portable stool with sponge	32	Lockheed fluid reservoir
8	Switches		rubber top	33	Signal horn (push button)
9	Dash light	21	Stiffener	34	Signal locker
10	Torpedo firing controls	22	Buffer	35	Stops
11	Fire extinguishers	23	Fire extinguisher remote control	36	Handrail
12	Mast socket	24	Drip trough	37	Voicepipes to bridge, wardroom,
13	Door stop	25	Torpedo director mounting		W/T Office and forecastle

70ft MTBs arrangement of bridge and wheelhouse

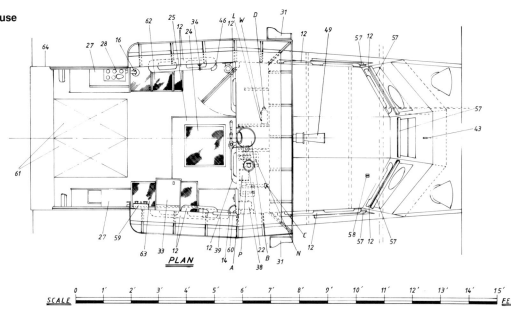

PLAN

SCALE

| 0 | 1′ | 2′ | 3′ | 4′ | 5′ | 6′ | 7′ | 8′ | 9′ | 10′ | 11′ | 12′ | 13′ | 14′ | 15′ |

FEET

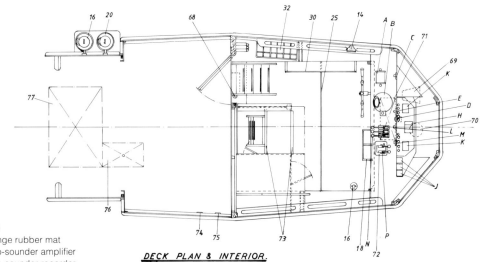

DECK PLAN & INTERIOR.

	Fittings and instruments	*Supply*
1	Spy hole and cover	Admiralty
2	Engineroom orders telegraph illumination socket	Vosper bought out
3	Inspection hole – 'Exactor' gear	Admiralty
4	Engineroom orders telegraph	Vosper bought out
5	Engineroom orders push reply and change switch	Vosper bought out
6	Chart table light	Vosper bought out
7	Loudspeaker – Admiralty pattern M317	Admiralty
8	Switch – wheelhouse roof light	Vosper bought out
9	Roof light switch door operated	Vosper bought out
10	Fire extinguisher remote control	Vosper bought out
11	Junction box electric wiring	Vosper bought out
12	Handrails	Contractor
13	Kent clear view screen	Vosper bought out
14	Voicepipe mouthpiece	Vosper
15	Drip trough	Vosper bought out
16	Fire extinguisher	Admiralty
17	Telescope clips	Contractor
18	Binocular stowage	Vosper
19	Lockheed valves (steering gear)	Vosper bought out
20	Torpedo director lugs	Vosper
21	Telegraph handset	Admiralty
22	Torpedo director socket	Admiralty
23	Life buoy stowage port and starboard	Contractor
24	Helmsman's stool	Vosper
25	Rubatex mats	Vosper
26	Foam extinguisher stowage	Vosper
27	Signal locker	Vosper
28	Recognition pistol rack	Vosper
29	Bookshelves	Vosper
30	Chart stowage	Vosper
31	Bow light boxes	Vosper
32	Lewis gun ammunition rack	Vosper
33	Folding seat (bridge)	Vosper
34	Door catch	Vosper
35	Pencil rack	Vosper

36 Push for gun turret buzzer
37 Inspection door
38 Pushes for horn and alarm
39 Stowage for telephone handset
40 Clip for telephone handset
41 Locker seat
42 Fresh water tank
43 Eyebolt for life line
44 Handrail and stiffener
45 Quicktho opening window
46 Sponge rubber door stop
47 Holes in deck for access to throttles, compass correctors and electric wiring
48 Door for access to Lockheed steering transmitter

49 Horn
50 Sponge rubber mat
51 Echo-sounder amplifier
52 Echo-sounder recorder
53 Roof light
54 Canvas blind
55 Lockheed fluid header tank
56 Aldis lamp socket
57 Canvas blinds fitted to outside of all windows for darkening ship
58 Eyeplate for mast forestay
59 Plugs for mast anchor NUC and recognition lights switch for NUC and recognition lights in centre
60 Rubatex padding round voicepipe
61 Hatches for stowage of signal cone and ball and access to fresh water stop valve
62 Locker seat
63 Portable locker seat with stowage under for 6in number recognition lights
64 End section of bridge platform to be made portable to facilitate tank space hatch removal
65 Buzzer
66 Chart table flap
67 Cupboard
68 Drain to bilges
69 Deck cut away for Lockheed steering transmitter

70 Hole in deck for access to electric wiring
71 Opening in deck
72 Deck and beam cut away for exactor transmitters. Beam to be cut only as required
73 1in × 16 gauge brass strip
74 Fresh water vent pipe
75 Fresh water vent pipe as fitted to MTB 73 only
76 Hatch for access to fresh water stop valve – MTB 73 only
77 As 61 – as fitted on MTB 73 only

Modifications

21.8.41 – Internal handrail. Port side, cut away to clear fire extinguisher remote control
21.8.41 – Drain to bilges moved inboard
17.9.41 – Bridge compass raised on 1in cock
25.9.41 – Holes in deck at forward end of wheelhouse added
25.9.41 – Access door Lockheed steering added
25.9.41 – Pencil rack added (35)
25.9.41 – Cover plate to No 3 made to open upwards
4.11.41 – Fire extinguisher added on port locker

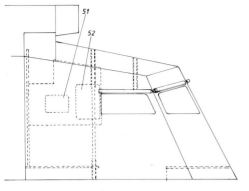

ELEVATION SHOWING ECHO SOUNDING GEAR.

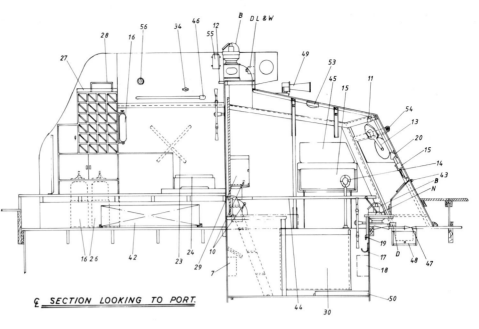

₵ _SECTION LOOKING TO PORT._

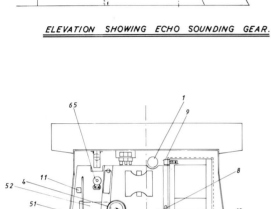

SECTION LOOKING AFT ON AFT BULKHEAD.

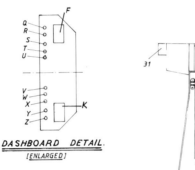

DASHBOARD DETAIL.

[ENLARGED]

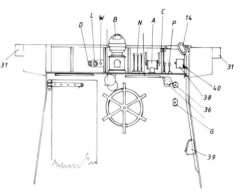

SECTION LOOKING FOR'D. ON AFTER BULKHEAD.

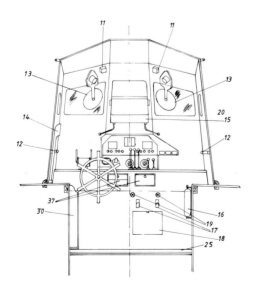

SECTION AT FORE END LOOKING FOR'D.

Dashboard instruments

A Engineroom telegraph (not fitted in this position on MTB 74 onwards)
B Magnetic compass
C Telegraph illumination socket
D Compass illumination socket
E Dimmer navigation lights
F Trip clock
G Socket for telephone handset
H Revolution counters
J Boost gauges
K Helm indicator
L Dimmer compass illumination
M Dimmer instrument panel lights
N Throttles (not fitted in this position on MTB 74 onwards)

P Torpedo firing levers (not fitted in this position on MTB 74 onwards)
Q Alarm push
R Switch – port wiper
S Switch – anchor light
T Switch – shaded stern light
U Switch – navigation lights
V Switch – instrument panel lights
W Switch – compass illumination
X Switch – helm indicator
Y Switch – starboard wiper
Z Siren push

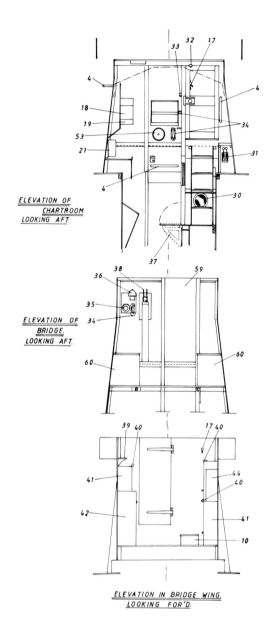

ELEVATION OF
CHARTROOM
LOOKING AFT.

ELEVATION OF
BRIDGE.
LOOKING AFT.

ELEVATION IN BRIDGE WING,
LOOKING FOR'D.

**MTBs 347–362 arrangement of
wheelhouse and bridge**

1   Engineroom orders signal box (V)
2   Boost gauges (V)
3   Compass (magnetic) (A)
4   Handrails (C)
5   Throttles (V)
6   Telegraphs (V)
7   Torpedo firing levers (V)
8   Wood wiring grounds (C)
9   Orders telegraph and casing (V and C)
10 Grenade stowage box (A)
11 Training gear (RDF) (A)
12 Windows permanently blocked out with ply (C)
13 Fixed cover plate (V)
14 Voice pipe (V)
15 Folding seat (V ex MG)
16 Navigation panel switches etc (V)
17 Door latch finger nut and plug for hole (V)
18 Echo-sounding amplifier (A)
19 Echo-sounding recorder (A)
20 Navigation horn (V)
21 Loudaphone (A)
22 Roof light (V)
23 Tachometer box (V)
24 Voice pipe (V)
25 Compass and chart light dimmers (V)
26 Binocular box (V ex MG)
27 Fire extinguisher (A)
28 Pencil rack (V ex MG)
29 Chart table light (V)
30 Loudspeaker with protective shelf over (A and C)
31 Remote control anti-fire levers with flap over (A and C)
32 Roof light door switch (V)
33 Roof light switch (V)
34 Phone band sets (A)
35 Buzzer (A)

36 Electric bell (A)
37 RDF director's folding seat (V ex MG)
38 Depth charge release gear and casing (A and C)
39 Stowage for recognition pistol and ammunition (V ex MG)
40 Canvas cover (V)
41 Flag lockers (V ex MG)
42 Locker and stowage for Aldis lamp (V ex MG)
43 Sponge rubber mat (V)
44 Stowage for semaphore flags (V ex MG)
45 Stowage for books, notepad and writing lamp (V ex MG)
46 Watch holder (Admiralty supply) (A)
47 Mat for DC (V ex MG)
48 Torpedo sight socket (A)
49 Fresh water tank sounding pipe (V)
50 Wood fillet in angle (C)
51 RDF training wire lead bracket (A)
52 Helmsman's stool (V ex MG)
53 Eight day clock (A)
54 6in wide handrail as protection for RDF training wires
55 Seat locker and stowage for six recognition lights
56 Quicktho opening window
57 Chart table
58 Chart stowage
59 Bullet-proof door
60 Seat locker
61 Bookcase
62 Navigation lights

V   = Vosper supply
C   = Contractor supply
A   = Admiralty supply
MG = Morgan Giles

*Close-up view of the bridge of MTB 523 (73ft
Type II). This is more solid, with better
armour protection (see drawings for detail).*
Vosper Thornycroft (UK) Ltd

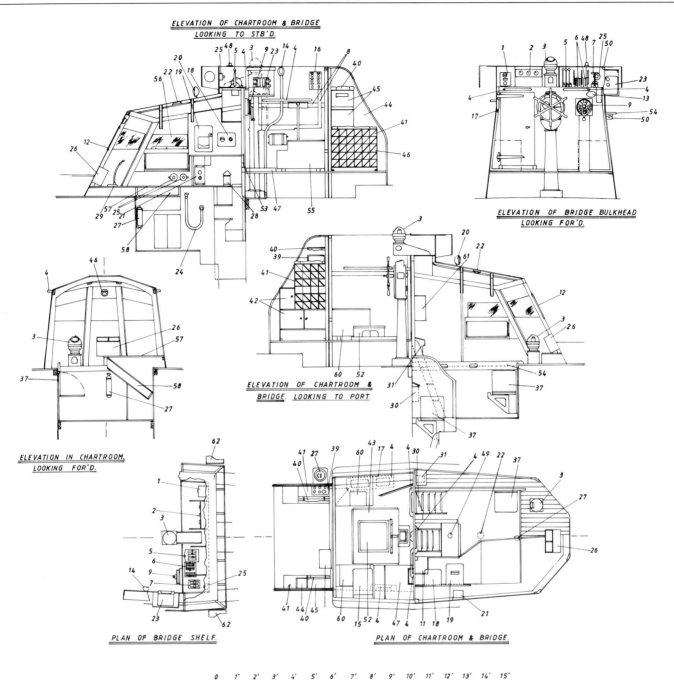

ELEVATION OF CHARTROOM & BRIDGE
LOOKING TO STB'D.

ELEVATION OF BRIDGE BULKHEAD
LOOKING FOR'D.

ELEVATION OF CHARTROOM &
BRIDGE. LOOKING TO PORT.

ELEVATION IN CHARTROOM,
LOOKING FOR'D.

PLAN OF BRIDGE SHELF.

PLAN OF CHARTROOM & BRIDGE.

SCALE   0 1' 2' 3' 4' 5' 6' 7' 8' 9' 10' 11' 12' 13' 14' 15'   FEET

Bridge instruments on MTB 524 (73ft Type II). Many more aids for combat: torpedo sights between the voice pipes, boost gauges, engine throttles, torpedo firing levers, morse key, etc (see drawings for detail).
Vosper Thornycroft (UK) Ltd

237

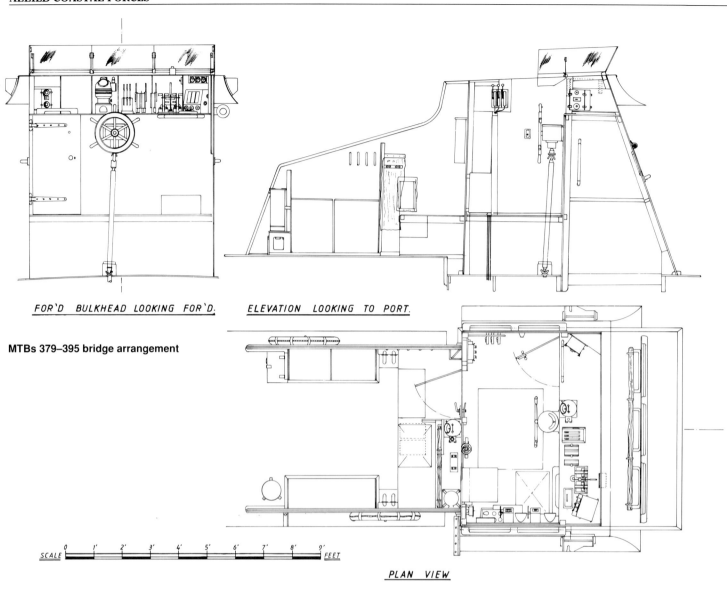

FOR'D BULKHEAD LOOKING FOR'D.   *ELEVATION LOOKING TO PORT.*

MTBs 379–395 bridge arrangement

SCALE |0 1' 2' 3' 4' 5' 6' 7' 8' 9'| FEET

PLAN VIEW

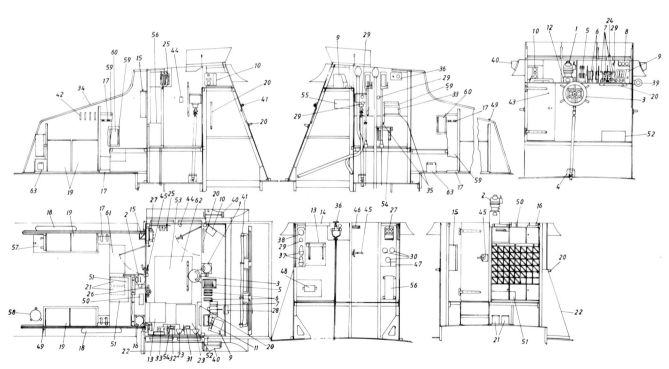

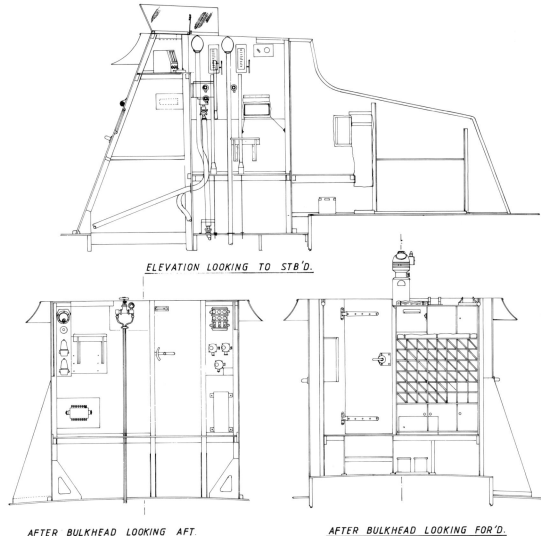

ELEVATION LOOKING TO STB'D.

AFTER BULKHEAD LOOKING AFT.

AFTER BULKHEAD LOOKING FOR'D.

The bridge of MTB 383 in July 1944, showing more electrical aids but still rather basic (see drawings for detail).
Vosper Thornycroft (UK) Ltd

MTBs 379–395 bridge arrangement

1 Steering compass
2 Navigation compass
3 Steering wheel
4 Watertight gland
5 Engine throttles
6 Engine telegraphs
7 Torpedo firing levers
8 Boost gauges
9 Revolution indicator box
10 Engineroom orders box
11 View plot
12 Box seating
13 Skipper's seat
14 Padded back rest
15 Semaphore flag box
16 Aldis ready use seating
17 Carbine stowage
18 Lifebelts
19 Locker seats
20 Handrails
21 Torpedo tool box
22 Stiffening bracket
23 Voice pipes
24 Torpedo sight bracket
25 Fire control levers
26 Chemical smoke-producing apparatus controls
27 Navigation light plugs
28 Torpedo ready lights
29 Press button switches
30 Electric dimmers
31 Engineroom order telegraph
32 Engineroom order revolutions
33 Recognition light box
34 Wood capping
35 Eyes to secure cover
36 Remote control unit
37 Electric bells
38 Buzzer
39 Navigation horn
40 Navigation light brackets
41 Canvas blackout
42 Halliard cleats
43 Oddie fasteners
44 Oddie fastener catch
45 Door catch
46 ½in slip bolt
47 Night signalling lamp
48 Junction box
49 Eye for mast stay
50 Clips for hand lamp
51 Portable stool
52 Skipper's stool
53 Rubatex mat
54 Foot rest
55 Windsail mast chock
56 Intermediate signalling lamp
57 Cartridge box
58 Foam extinguisher holder
59 Canvas cover
60 Magazine boxes
61 Step up to bridge
62 Helmsman's mat
63 Water excluding vent

Modifications

Very light cartridge box added (item 57); holder for foam extinguisher added (item 58); addition of canvas cover over rifles (item 59); second box added for torpedo tools (item 21), 26 May 1944 (dated). Halliard cleats moved aft of bridge wing stiffener (item 42); small arms magazine boxes added (item 60), 6 June 1944 (dated).

**MTBs 523–530 and 532–533
arrangement of bridge instruments**

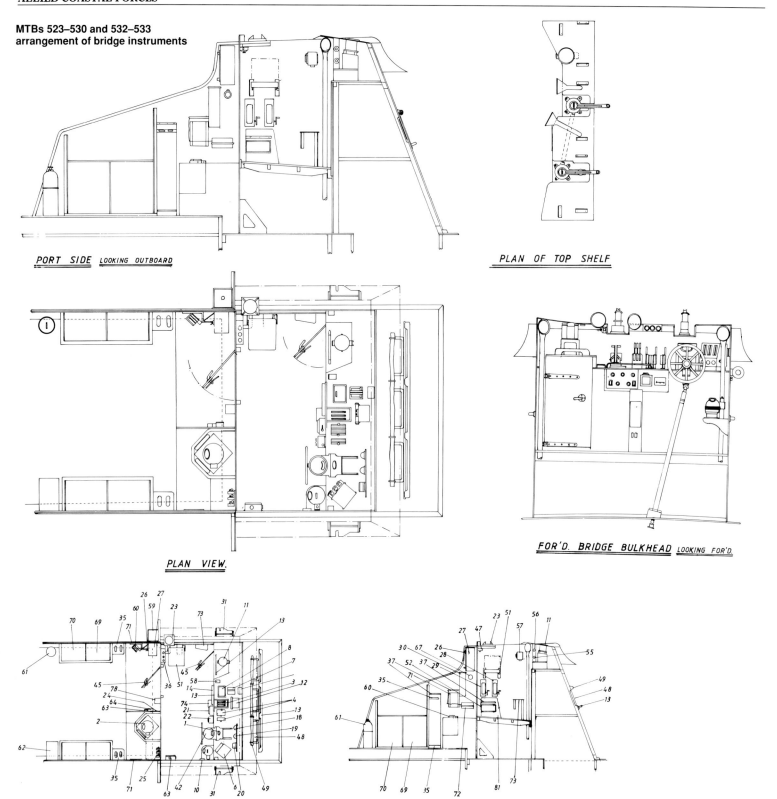

PORT SIDE *LOOKING OUTBOARD*

PLAN OF TOP SHELF

PLAN VIEW.

FOR'D. BRIDGE BULKHEAD *LOOKING FOR'D.*

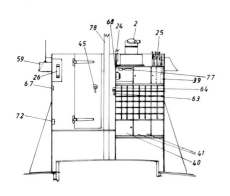
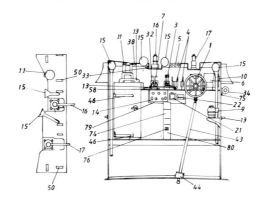
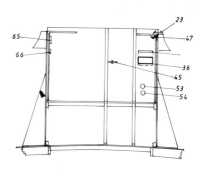

**MTBs 523–530 and 532–533
arrangement of bridge instruments**

1 Steering compass
2 Navigation compass
3 Throttles
4 Telegraphs
5 Boost gauge
6 Revolution counter
7 Torpedo firing levers
8 View plot
9 Standard compass
10 Radar call-up
11 Aerial gyro repeater
12 Engineroom order box
13 Handrail
14 Push bell panel
15 Voice pipes
16 Skipper's torpedo sight
17 Coxwain's torpedo sight
18 W/T reply bell
19 Radar reply bell
20 Gun reply buzzer
21 Recognition light switch
22 Fighting light control
23 Aldis lamp ready use stowage

24 Chemical smoke-producing
   apparatus control
25 Fire control levers
26 Hand lamp clips
27 Intermediate lamp box
28 Engineroom telegraph
29 Engineroom order revolutions
30 Semaphore locker
31 Navigation light brackets
32 Torpedo ready light
33 Torpedo sight lamp switch
34 Navigation horn
35 One rifle and three carbines
36 Recognition pistol rack
37 Canvas cover
38 Loud-hailer microphone
   stowage
39 Very pistol stowage
40 Aldis stowage
41 Flashing lanterns
42 Steering gear
43 Transmission shaft
44 Water excluding box

45 Door handles
46 Door hinge
47 Aldis lamp socket
48 Fixed windows
49 Canvas blackout
50 Windscreen brackets
51 CO's tip-up seat
52 Recognition pistol cartridges
53 Engine orders dimmer
54 Revolution telegraph dimmer
55 Loud-hailer microphone socket
56 Hydrophone plug
57 Armament communication
58 Torpedo stand-by switch
59 Whip aerial
60 Bolt for bullet-proof door
61 Fire extinguisher
62 Ammunition locker
63 Fighting light switch
64 Loud-hailer socket
65 Steering compass dimmer
66 Standard compass dimmer
67 Intermediate lamp dimmer

68 Navigation compass dimmer
69 Recognition lights stowage
70 Steel helmet stowage
71 Lanchester magazine stowage
72 Detonator stowage
73 Foot rest
74 Telephone handset stowage
75 Rocket cease-fire lamp
76 TCS microphone stowage
77 Lamp and switch
78 Mast
79 Ply panel
80 Ply protection round electric
   cables
81 Ply protection round Chadburn
   control rods

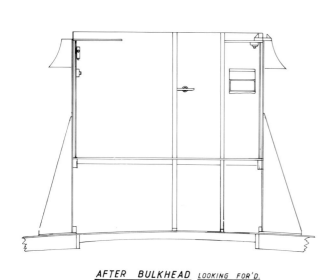

AFTER BULKHEAD LOOKING FOR'D.

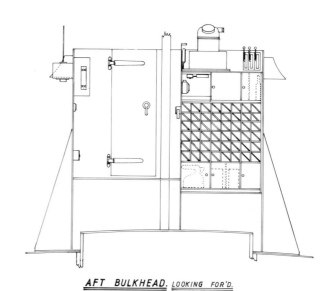

AFT BULKHEAD. LOOKING FOR'D.

SCALE   0   1'   2'   3'   4'   5'   6'   7'   8'   9'   10'   11'   12'   13'   14'   15'   FEET.

Notes on operating Royal Navy Packard engines

This information was kindly provided by a former Petty Officer Motor Mechanic who joined MTB 85 in April 1942, to join the newly-formed 24th MTB Flotilla in June, remaining with her until August 1944, when he returned to England on promotion to Sub Lt (E). After further training he left Coastal Forces to return to general service, where his last appointment was as engineering officer of an *Algerine* class minesweeper. He says:

Most of the modifications I recall were carried out as a result of the seagoing motor mechanics' observations and recommendations to their respective base engineer officers. Some of these officers were enthusiastic, some disinterested, and the worst were the EOs who constantly put down our ideas, then wrote detailed reports claiming that the modifications suggested were their own idea. A water tank modification, mentioned later, is one example.

Most of the so-called engine problems were in fact, on this boat series, the result of poor installation design by the builders and RN Constructors. All of the early 1942 Packard boats had severe problems with engine oil overheating. This was caused by the constant failure of the bellows-type automobile thermostat controlling the water bypass on the oil heat exchanger. At sea the remedy was to force 'cod line' between the bellows of the thermostat, which kept the valve permanently open. Eventually a hand controlled bypass valve was fitted and adjustment could then be set to obtain the required oil temperature as engine loads demanded.

The Vosper Packard boats inherited some design features from the previous Isotta-Fraschini-engined boats. Both designs employed two auxiliary engines which were side valve Ford V8 engines, which could also be used as propulsion units for silent running. The arrangement called for a reduction gearbox incorporated at the side of the main engine gearbox and arranged to drive the main shaft independent of the main engine, the engagement of the reduction gearbox was by a straightforward 'dog-clutch' operated by a short foot operated lever.

The Isotta-engined boats employed a 'crash start' procedure in order to quickly transfer from auxiliary to full power, the method being to engage the main engine ahead mechanism which was by a handwheel (about 10 turns) and when the engine fired the throttle was opened, and the foot-operated clutch kicked out to disengage the reduction gear. During exercises it was mandatory to use this procedure on the Packard boats, which was not needed as the gear box engagement was by a lever which was instantaneous in operation. Also, the Packards had excellent electric starting. There were a number of nasty accidents, especially at Weymouth during the working-up period, caused by the dog-clutch failing to disengage, the main engine coming on to full power, causing the Ford V8 to turn over as far above its designed speed. Imagine the main engine at 2000rpm driving the Ford at 18 times that speed through the still engaged gearbox.

These problems, and the fact that the heavier

A typical engineroom of the 1942 series MTBs, (MTB 351 in April 1943), looking forward. Note the watchkeeper's desk fitted above the starboard engine – space was at a premium.
Vosper Thornycroft (UK) Ltd

beamier Packard boats could just about make 6 knots on the auxiliary engines, meant that we all removed the intermediate drive shaft between the Ford and the Packard. Silent!! running before the advent of the Dumbflow silencers was carried out on the centre engine only, running at about 1000 to 1200rpm with a heavy coir doormat hung over the exhaust outlet to muffle the noise. (First used on MTB 85 on winter operations from Newhaven 1942–43.)

All the original Vosper Packard boats suffered from severe water leaks from the welded seams of the cylinder water jackets. This problem did not seem to exist on the Fairmile D boats or on American-built units. The official remedy was to place a number 10 Jubilee clip around the leaking cylinder, place a ribbed rubber patch over the leak and tighten the clip around the patch. The heat between the cylinders was considerable and normally the engine was shut down during this repair. This problem became so acute, however, that most engineroom crews soon became adept at doing this job under way, in order that patrols could continue.

Although the welding of the cylinders was questionable, pressure tests must have been carried out during the manufacturer's engine tests. The problem on our boats was that excess pressure was being generated internally above the designed maximum. The water system was individual fresh water cooling, the fresh water being cooled through a normal salt water heat exchanger. The header tank on each engine was a small brass affair with an internal sight glass which was most difficult to read. There was also no proper provision to relieve excess pressure. When a leak occurred and it was not noticed in the header tank sight glass, the water level became low enough to cause steam to form and consequently a rise in pressure. Many complaints were made to the flotilla EOs, whose only solution seemed to be to increase the supply of number 10 Jubilee clips. Finally the chief ERA (engine room artificer) of the base solved the problem. He first removed the header tanks and brazed a U-pipe on the bottom with one end connected to a glass water gauge which was clipped on to the front of the tank, and, what was more important, the open top of the gauge glass acted as a pressure relief. This was a most successful modification I wonder who got the credit for it?

Dumbflow silencers were not fitted to boats of the 24th Flotilla until they arrived at Bone, North Africa, in April–May 1943. For some reason the original shafts and bushes fitted to the transfer baffle were made of steel, and although grease points were fitted, the operation from the closed to open position became harder each time it was used. This was obviously caused by salt water corrosion. The silencers on MTB 85 finally seized completely in the open position the day we started night patrols in the Strait of Messina. Needless to say the ubiquitous coir mats were soon hanging over the side again. The fitting of bronze shafts and bushes to the silencers eliminated this problem. One other serious problem occurred later on, however. Where the actual silencer was bolted to the inner exhaust, the flange was split, so that the inner exhaust had a fresh water cooling jacket, while the silencer side was salt water cooled. There must have been some kind of

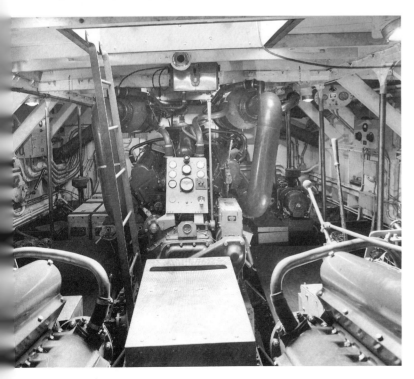

The engineroom on MTB 54 in June 1941, looking aft. Note the huge exhausts, still cluttered in appearance but less sophisticated than later Vosper units.
Vosper Thornycroft (UK) Ltd

chemical reaction taking place because seemingly nearly all the boats at about the same time experienced severe leaks at the fresh water end of the flange connection. Several boats including my own experienced these failures away from base in Komiza. The only solution was to fit a new exhaust system, which was a major base job. A drastic though effective method was evolved, namely the spare set of gun turret hydraulic pipes fitted from the auxiliary engine were taken down and connected to the main engine fresh water system from the salt water circulating pump, thus ensuring that adequate water was available to the main engine system. This was a real emergency solution, as in most cases the engine, once subjected to a diet of salt water, was taken out of service. I believe this emergency system was used by the POMM on MTB 226 during the raid on the cruiser *Dalmatia*.

The 1941–42 Vospers were fitted with large thrust blocks situated between the gearbox output drive and the tail shaft. These thrust bearings were enclosed in a water-cooled jacket fed from the salt water circulating system. In fact they would not have been out of place in a destroyer. The bearings were constantly overheating, mostly caused by air locks in the water circulating system. The usual drill was to cool the bearings externally, usually [with] a bucket of water. One member of the engineroom staff was constantly monitoring the condition of the thrust blocks. This problem was eventually overcome when we discovered in Malta that the US-built Vospers had no thrust blocks fitted; the reason being that a large adequate thrust bearing was fitted at the rear of the main engine gearbox. As these gearboxes were identical to those fitted to the British boats, intermediate shafts were soon made and fitted in place of the very troublesome thrust blocks. One stoker's comment being, 'We modified those . . . thrust blocks by throwing them away'.

The starboard V8 auxiliary engine main function was to generate electrical power for the radar outfit. As this type of radar was not very effective it was hardly used. As the power was 100 volt AC we decided to adapt this engine to provide lighting etc. An outfit of 110-volt bulbs was acquired, suitable connections made and on board 'shore' lighting was obtained. We were once asked by a visiting boat's coxswain at Komiza, 'Where can we connect the shore lighting?'. (At that time there was no power on the Island.) The power obtained could easily supply the needs of two or three other boats.

Another source of information was a flotilla engineer officer with the 5th MGB Flotilla. He made the following comments after reading the previous text:

Cylinder jacket water leaks It is clear that your informant is writing of a slightly later date than most of my experience. Whether I had (in the 5th MGB Flotilla) the first leak, I do not know. What I remember is that in the first year or so we had no leaks. When one of my boats did return from an operation with a single leak I promptly removed the engine and sent it for overhaul. However, within a very short time we were inundated with leaks and there was no question but that we must find a suitable palliative. This turned out – devised by a MM – to be a chain of Vickers clips and a pad of sponge rubber soaked in *Heldite*. Most, but not all, leaks could be remedied in this way and I can remember engines with 15 or 20 patches which continued in use. The 5th MGBs were British Power Boat Co boats and no question of over-pressure in the water system ever arose to my knowledge.

When I had the chance I made enquiries and the explanation was simple. Rate of production of early Packard engines was such that all cylinder jacket welding could be done by one skilled man. When he could no longer cope he was made a supervisor to instruct other welders on how to do the job. (Stainless steel is not the easiest material to weld.)
I cannot be certain but I think my first leak was early in 1942.

Thrust bearings　It may be of passing interest that when the first British Packard-engined boat (MGB 18) was run aground on the Brambles at 36 knots the thrust bearings were nearly pulled out of the gearboxes. The rings retaining them were saucer-shaped instead of flat and all the studs were bent outwards!

Some unusual happenings

Boost coils　Late one evening in Great Yarmouth I was working with my chief ERA in the engineroom of MGB 21, trying to find some obscure fault, and we wanted to switch on the boost coil. There was an air-raid warning in force at the time and we were forbidden to start these big engines because the noise upset the defenders. I said to the chief, 'The engine won't start on coil only so I'll switch it on for you'. I did and the engine burst into life without use of the starter. I never knew this happen on any other occasion.

Scoop cooling　This was fine so long as the boat was running more or less in accordance with the designer's intentions, but if a severe overload occurred it failed. In March 1942 after action off the Belgian coast MGB 91 (CO Pete Thompson) started to tow a disabled E-boat but had to give up because of engine cooling problems (and the unwanted attentions of the enemy).

Bearing failures　I can recall a week early in 1942 at Lowestoft when, out of a total of 12 operational boats of the 5th and 7th MGB flotillas, we had to change 17 engines. Many of these were bearing failures. At about that time the average engine hours achieved by a Packard was 140. I had the first engine to reach 500 and was ordered to see how much more it would do. We finally removed it – still apparently OK – at 600 hours.

The same boat (MGB 21) had a rogue engine (or engines). The first starboard engine had always registered an oil pressure about 5psi low. When it failed the replacement showed a similar low pressure and we failed to discover why. The second engine failed during the action referred to above (Pete Thompson and 91). I had to argue with the Engineer Cdr Barnard to be allowed time to investigate this properly. We were almost at our wits' end and the chief ERA (George Smith) and I were sitting thinking late one evening when George said, 'I once had a Riley 9 which had low oil pressure due to leakage from the camshaft'. I said 'OK, let's take the covers off and start up'. We did. A huge quantity of oil was emitted from the end of the camshaft fitted with the tachometer drive gear. It turned out that this gear did not have a blank fitted and that it had been fitted to

the original engine in this boat and then transferred to the second and third engines. We hurled the offending part into Hamilton Dock.

I personally believed that distortion of the engine due to the way it was mounted in the boat was a cause of bearing problems. I considered trying to measure movements due to hull flexing but never got around to it. An event in a 1942 Vosper MTB – I think it was 348 – had some bearing. We had been working on her at Portland and were delayed in doing trials by a spell of bad weather. Eventually we attempted it on a far from ideal day and had got up to nearly full power with the boat pounding heavily. There was a sudden shrieking noise which caused me to throttle down to investigate and at first we could see nothing amiss until I looked at the air intake screen on top of one of the carburettors. It was smothered in shredded asbestos which we quickly found had come from the expansion joint in the exhaust pipe between the engine and ship side. This gave an indication of just how much movement had occurred.

I think the most important development as regards bearings was the experiment carried out by the AEL, which disclosed how much and where a Packard engine distorted under its own weight when one corner or another was left unsupported. I do not know about other peoples' experience, but mine was that when this information was properly used bearing failures were few.

There is no doubt in my mind that the method of mounting the Merlin engines in boats was superior in that it eliminated distortion of the engine. It did however introduce another problem in the form of the flexible (pendulastic) coupling. Hichens has something to say about these in his book *We Fought Them in Gunboats*.

This reminds me that the rubber couplings used in the Fairmile D were the cause of a lot of vibration trouble because the input and output sides were seldom sufficiently accurately aligned with one another. One of the myths is that because couplings are flexible or self-aligning, accurate alignment does not matter. My experience was that poor alignment led to quite severe vibration if nothing worse. I once sent a D out on a short trip with a brass lining-up jig in one shaft because we were short of a decent coupling. It behaved perfectly well.

I was never directly concerned with the major overhaul of Packards so my knowledge is very incomplete. This does remind me of one further item. We had one engine which would not deliver full power although we could find nothing wrong. Eventually changing the magneto did the trick, so the duff one was returned to an overhaul establishment with a request to let us know what was found to be at fault. The answer lay with the contact-breaker spring. Although it met all the Packard specifications, when fitted to a magneto it caused the spark to retard above a certain speed.

This chapter on the running problems of the Packard under operational conditions has been made possible by the help received from the people mentioned above, one of whom I never met. Without their assistance, with other members of the Coastal Forces Veterans' Association, who provide much of the practical background to these volumes, our efforts would be of much less interest.

Free French Vosper MTBs: Free French naval forces involvement in Coastal Forces craft in home waters

In 1941 the 20th ML Flotilla (Fairmile B MLs) were in two divisions and based at Portland. The 1st Division was British manned, and all its boats were lost during the attack on St Nazaire in March 1942; the 2nd Division was manned by the Free French. Four boats were in service in 1941 – ML 123 (*St Ronan*), ML 245 (*St Guénolé*), ML 246 (*St Yves*), and ML 247 (*St Alain*). Both divisions were employed as convoy escorts in the English Channel during the winter of 1941–42. Following the loss of the 1st Division boats in the St Nazaire operation, four more Fairmile Bs were allocated to the flotilla, the whole of which was then manned by the Free French. The new boats were ML 182 (*Sein*), ML 205 (*Molène*), ML 269 (*Béniguet*) and ML 303 (*Ouessant*). The flotilla, then based at Weymouth, continued its coastal convoy escort duties together with defensive patrols and air-sea-rescue work when required. In August 1942 all eight MLs of the 20th Flotilla were decommissioned and returned to the Royal Navy. The Free French officers and crews then formed the nucleus of a new flotilla of eight 70ft MTBs, which became the 23rd MTB Flotilla.

During the brief interval between the 20th ML Flotilla and the forming of the 23rd Flotilla, the French officers and crews underwent further Coastal Forces training at Royal Navy establishments, including torpedo courses at HMS *Vernon* (Portsmouth) and torpedo firing practice aboard old MTBs at HMS *St Christopher* (Fort William, Loch Eil) together with signal and tactical courses for the officers.

The boat numbers were MTBs 90, 91, 92, 94, 96, 98, 227 and 239; 90 was the first to be commissioned (September 1942) and 92 the last, in January 1943. Following completion they went to HMS *Hornet*, the Coastal Forces base at Gosport, for final handing over to the Free French and for preliminary sea trials of the boats, machinery and equipment.

The officers and crews were entirely French, with the exception of the telegraphists and radar operators, who were Royal Navy ratings in British uniforms and subject to Royal Navy discipline, and on loan to the Free French boats. The British ratings aged over 18, who would have been eligible for rum issue if aboard a Royal Navy ship flying the White Ensign, could not receive such issue (tot) while serving aboard a FNFL ship flying the Tricolour. Instead, they received the same standard issue of red wine as did their French shipmates; that ration was a quarter-litre (0.44 pint) of *vin ordinaire* issued to each rating twice a day with the main meals, midday and evening. At shore establishments both British and French ratings could purchase tobacco and cigarettes from the NAAFI.

As for operational requirements, the British ratings were under the orders of the French officers, but any disciplinary or administration matters affecting them were handled by the British liaison officer with the flotilla. The liaison officer was a lieutenant RNVR familiar with France and French people, and fluent in the language. He had an important role to play, with the supervision of the British ratings only a fraction of his duties; the major part of his work was to smooth the path of communication between the French officers and their British colleagues of the base maintenance departments and stores, and the British authorities under whose operational orders the flotilla had to work.

As each boat completed its initial sea trials at *Hornet*, it went to HMS *Bee* at Weymouth where the personnel underwent a period of intensive training, including exercises at sea during which tough tests of all kinds were set by the senior instructional officer from the base, so that all officers and crew members should become proficient in the use of weapons and equipment as soon as possible. These culminated in exercises in which the boats operated together in close company at high speed, and at night. At the end of four weeks of this exhaustive training, known as 'working-up', the boats and personnel were deemed fit to take on operational duties. Some boats took part in a few operations, and the flotilla left *Bee* to go to *Cicala*, the Coastal Forces base at Dartmouth, from which an Anglo-Dutch flotilla of MTBs had been operating. That flotilla left to go to HMS *Wasp* at Dover once all the French MTBs had completed arrival at Kingswear.

Three other Royal Navy Coastal Forces flotillas also operated from *Cicala* – the 1st MGB Flotilla (short gunboats), and the 52nd and 65th flotillas, which had the large and heavily armed Fairmile Ds – the 65th being manned by Canadians.

The operations office for all Coastal Forces craft based there, regardless of nationality, was at the Station Hotel, Kingswear. Brookhill, a large mansion some distance away near the mouth of the River Dart, was the *casern* (barracks) for the crews of the French MTBs; the officers were lodged and had their wardroom mess in the villa of Longford at Kingswear.

The boats themselves were moored alongside *Belfort*, an old French sloop built in 1919, which had escaped from France and come to Britain at the time of the German invasion in 1940. Bearing in mind that HMS *Cicala* comprised a group of shore establishments in various hotels and villas, a certain amount of amusement was caused when, in a broadcast from 'Gairmany Calling' by 'Lord Haw-Haw', it was announced that, in a *Luftwaffe* air raid on the south coast of England, HMS *Cicala* had been bombed and sunk!

The 23rd Flotilla boats exercised daily between Start Point and Teignmouth, awaiting their first operation orders: those came on 6 March 1943, requiring four boats to patrol in an area off the north coast of Brittany that night, taking care to return to within 20 miles of the English coast by daybreak. By nightfall the four boats were well across the Channel, cruising in calm conditions at 22 knots; unfortunately, at 2130, MTB 227 had a fire in her engineroom and all three engines had to be stopped. Not a happy situation whilst within about 15 miles of the enemy-held coast. However, the fire was mastered, but with only two engines now working, 227 had to return, leaving her three sisters to continue the patrol. This proved uneventful and the boats returned to base at dawn.

The flotilla did not have long to wait before their first brush with the enemy. Four days later, during the evening of 10 March, MTBs 94 and 96 were on patrol approaching Sept Iles, where they were stopped, lying close to shore, to wait in ambush for any enemy shipping that might turn up. As it had been four nights previously, it was calm and quiet, and it seemed that this patrol might also be uneventful. However, shortly before the time fixed for the end of the patrol and the start of the return trip, a ship of about 2000 tons and an escort vessel were spotted, quite close by. The SO detached 96 to create a diversion by approaching the enemy vessels at speed and attacking with gunfire: this was done, and worked perfectly – as soon as 96 opened fire, the enemy reacted at once and all his guns and concentration was focused on the speeding 96. Meanwhile 94 approached slowly and quietly the other side, and fired both torpedoes at the cargo ship, then disengaged at high speed. The enemy vessels immediately took on 94, but reacted too late to avoid the torpedoes. After a heavy explosion the ship was seen to stop, then slowly its bows rose in the air and it slid below the surface. Both units then disengaged and returned to base without suffering damage. (M4620, a converted trawler, was sunk.)

Following that successful action, many other patrols were made in spring 1943, mostly without success, and in weather which varied from calm to awful; nights from bright moonlight to pitch dark; visibility from 10 miles or more to 50 metres or less in thick fog. Still operations went on. One by one various defects appeared, so one by one the boats were dispersed to various south coast ports to refit; meanwhile, the others continued with frequent patrols. One, on a dark night in April, searched for and almost miraculously found an RAF pilot whose aircraft had been shot down; he had come down in the sea a few miles off Ushant, and was discovered in his rubber dinghy, calmly awaiting rescue. One wonders whether he ever realised how lucky he was to be found at night by a French MTB, instead of being discovered in daylight and spending the rest of the war in a POW camp.

On 5 May luck turned against the 23rd Flotilla: one of their patrols ran slap into an ambush by a large enemy force in the region of Sept Iles. Torpedoes were fired but missed their objectives, and the boats were subjected to heavy and accurate gunfire of various calibres. Much damage was caused and the boats returned with several wounded, one very seriously. MTB 96 returned to the Dart in a sinking condition, having 73 holes in its hull and its bows a metre deeper in the water than normal, only kept afloat by keeping way on. As it had to lose way approaching the base, it began to sink, and to prevent that happening it had to be grounded on the slipway at once.

Another patrol on 10 September discovered an enemy convoy with armed trawlers as escort to the south of Guernsey. The MTBs succeeded in torpedoing one of the trawlers, then attacked the convoy with gunfire. Due to the blinding effect of tracer fire, from both sides, it was not possible to state with certainty whether the torpedoed trawler had been sunk.

On 11 October, near Ile Vierge, two of the boats came face to face with two German torpedo boats, fast and well armed, which reacted very quickly. The MTBs had no chance of mounting an attack – indeed they were lucky to escape from their larger adversaries without damage.

A longer patrol than was usual was ordered for the night of 26–27 December, as the previous evening two British cruisers had damaged one or more German torpedo boats in the Gulf of Gascony, and it was thought possible that the damaged vessels might try to limp back to Brest for repairs. The MTBs were therefore sent south of Ushant just in case that happened, and the damaged ships could be intercepted. However, nothing transpired, although the boats waited off the Brittany coast until daylight, a risky thing to do since by 0900 the boats were still not far from Ushant, and one of the boats being low on lube oil could not use full speed. An escort of Spitfires was sent over to guard the boats on their return trip in daylight. Seemingly when these aircraft were first seen from the boats, they were flying towards the MTBs almost at sea level, their RAF roundels not yet visible, and thus causing a certain amount of alarm. As the boats had been continuously at sea for 26 hours on this patrol, the base had begun to fear for their safety, and when they did eventually reappear they received a very warm welcome.

In the meantime the enemy forces had been stung by the growing strength of British and Allied Coastal Forces craft patrols which were disputing the ability of the enemy to run his coastal convoys safely, anywhere off the occupied coasts all the way from the Northern Netherlands coast right down to the Bay of St Malo and Brittany. As a result the Germans worked strenuously to double and sometimes treble the number of escort craft for each convoy, and in addition, to rearm those escorts with more, and where possible, larger-calibre guns. The Allied Coastal Forces craft found that by the close of 1943 it had become increasingly difficult to mount successful attacks, and when made they were increasingly met with fierce resistance. The 23rd Flotilla, like others elsewhere in the Channel and North Sea, noticed this too.

On 31 January 1944 they tried an attack on a convoy off the Channel Islands, but it was very strongly escorted and the three MTBs, coming under a storm of defensive fire, were unable to close the range to make a torpedo attack.

The flotilla went to Plymouth for another retraining and exercise course, in which revised techniques of tactical combat were explored following the experience gained from Coastal Forces operations of all kinds during the preceding months. This kind of revision was to bear much fruit later on, but success did not come at once.

The flotilla's next action, on 20 March 1944, was also frustrating. Three MTBs of the 23rd were operating in conjunction with three Fairmile Ds off the French coast. Both groups were intercepted by a strong enemy patrol which opened a heavy fire. Some heavy guns in coastal batteries ashore also added the weight of their shells, and the battle lasted for half an hour, before the Allied units were able to disengage, fortunately without loss.

Luck favoured the 23rd Flotilla on the night of 7–8 May. Four MTBs were out that night, split in two divisions; two boats 6 miles south of Hanois on course towards the southern end of Sark; the other two cruising at 10 knots towards Corbière lighthouse on the southwest point of Jersey. It was not an ideal night for an MTB attack; visibility was good, the moon bright, and a stiff easterly breeze was kicking up a short steep sea resulting in frequent showers of spray over the decks and bridge. In the direction of Corbière the dark mass of the coast could be seen, and in between frantically cleaning spray off his binoculars every few minutes, the SO suddenly noticed some smaller shadows detaching themselves slowly from the large one of the coast. It was an enemy convoy on a northerly course bound either for St Peter Port or perhaps Cherbourg. It soon became clear that the convoy was an important one; two large ships, one of them deep-laden, with four escort vessels [of the 2nd Patrol Boat Flotilla] ahead of them and three more astern. In the bright moonlight, the SO decided not to attempt a direct attack, but to creep slowly across the stern of the convoy at a safe distance, to avoid being seen, then to come up on the starboard side of the convoy and attack it after the 2nd division, near Sark, had been able to fire torpedoes at it.

The situation changed suddenly; the convoy made a sharp alteration of course, and it became obvious that it intended to enter St Peter Port. The SO at once decided that the only hope of success was to open up to full speed straight for the convoy to make a noisy and very visible diversion, and hope that the 2nd division might profit by it to launch a quiet torpedo attack from under the shadow of Sark. The plan worked perfectly: by the time the 1st division trailing huge white wakes and with open exhausts had closed the range to 3500 metres, the enemy convoy opened a storm of fire on them. Sheets of red and green tracer passed close overhead; meanwhile the other division from the dark background of Sark had crept in slowly to within 800 metres, and fired their torpedoes at the heavily-laden ship of 'about 3000 tons' [the steamer *Bizon* of 750 tons].

An immense column of white and grey water, and smoke, rose from the ship, and, when it dispersed, the ship had gone. At once both divisions came under heavy fire, including large-calibre shells from shore batteries on Guernsey. MTB 227 had its twin 0.5in turret put out of action, the gunner inside it miraculously escaping injury. Soon after, two shells hit the engineroom, one starting a fire, the other putting one engine out of action. Within a few minutes, under the shelter of a smoke screen, the fire was put out and the engine, not seriously damaged restarted. Meanwhile the 1st division had disengaged, and the SO decided to come round in a wide circle and attempt to use his division's torpedoes on one of the other ships of the convoy. By then, the enemy well alerted, the 1st division came under fire again, including some 88mm and heavy shrapnel shell from the shore batteries. Again the SO disengaged, then stopped to take stock once the enemy fire had ceased. It was seen that the second cargo ship had entered St Peter Port by then, and the three armed trawler escorts which had brought up the rear of the convoy were almost stationary outside, probably picking up survivors from the torpedoed ship. The SO then tried to take his division round to the north, to approach the trawlers from inside the shadow of Guernsey. It seemed that the trawlers had completed their task and were about to enter St Peter Port in line ahead – torpedoes were at once fired, although the range was about 2000 metres, but it was then or never, any delay meaning that the escort would be in shelter of the harbour. As luck would have it, two minutes after firing, an explosion was heard; one of the torpedoes had hit the leading trawler [V 211]. The MTBs then went in at 30 knots to 'shoot up' the last trawler before it could enter port. This they did, silencing the trawler's return fire. Circling away from the harbour, the MTBs spotted what appeared at first to be a fishing boat on their port side. A fishing boat, outside St Peter Port, at 0300 in the morning? And with its sail swinging about in such an odd way? The two units slowed down to inspect. It was soon realised that it was no fishing boat, but a balloon – moving around in the breeze, not far above the water, and with its steel cable still attached and leading down into the sea: at the other end of that cable there must have been a ship. Big spouts rose around the boats as the shore batteries once more opened fire on them. The SO ordered the balloon to be burned, then the boats to disengage. With a few bursts of tracer the balloon went up in a great flash.

One result of this successful and well conceived action was the award to the four boats concerned of the Ordre de L'Armée, by Général de Gaulle. (The Ordre de L'Armée was awarded to a ship, not to its CO.)

Another result, not quite so pleasing, was the inevitable reaction of the Germans. Five nights later four MTBs of the 23rd, again in two divisions, were operating again in Channel Islands waters. One of the divisions had come across a small patrol vessel leaving St Peter Port and shot it up, causing considerable damage. Evidently a patrol of enemy torpedo boats or perhaps destroyers was ready to be vectored on to the MTBs, and one after the other each division was intercepted, and a very tough 30 minutes' action followed. During this time the MTBs had to make violent alterations of course at speeds of up to 40 knots. They were indeed lucky to 'get away with it'.

A week later on the night of 19–20 May four boats were out in the same waters. This time they were under specific orders: they were instructed to be at a spot 6 miles west of La Corbière at midnight and to lie there in wait. The Admiralty had information that three German torpedo boats had left Brest a few hours previously and were thought to be on passage to Cherbourg. It was hoped that if their route led through the Channel Islands, a group of MTBs might have the chance of torpedoing them. The MTBs, however, were forbidden to use torpedoes on any lesser target, indeed they were told to do their utmost not to be seen by the enemy, and to avoid all contact between midnight and 0300. If by that time the targets had not appeared, then they would be free to attack anything they could find. That would not give them much opportunity

though, as they would need to start their return trip by 0330 in order to be well clear of the enemy coast by first light.

The four MTBs had to cross the English Channel at 30 knots (faster than usual on passage) in order to reach the rendezvous in time. Once there, they split into two divisions so that any attack could be mounted on opposite sides of the target. Then they waited uneasily, bearing in mind the vigorous response to the previous two actions, and being fully aware of the potential of the torpedo boats if they did arrive.

They had not waited long before interesting 'fireworks' broke out in the air over the south of Guernsey . . . an RAF raid perhaps? At 0130 the boats' radar operators reported echoes from four ships about 4000 metres to the south, two medium-size and two small vessels, and all stationary; evidently not the expected torpedo boats. At about 0215 two E-boats were detected, moving north very fast – and they were sighted soon after, passing only 200 metres or so from the stationary MTBs, and without spotting them. At long last 0300 came, and the division which comprised MTB 90 and 96 felt free to move south to investigate the four radar echoes, moving off at 10 knots or less. Eventually the dim shapes of two trawlers and two small motor craft were seen. When the range had closed to 700 metres, 96 was seen by the enemy and fired upon. She at once crossed ahead of her sister at high speed, making smoke as she did so, thus allowing 90 to prepare her torpedoes for firing and to creep quietly through the smoke screen undetected, to fire as she emerged from the smoke. One of the torpedoes was seen to hit the trawler between its mast and the bridge. MTB 90 then increased to full power, and was shot at by the second trawler, the tracer fortunately going high. As 90 passed, she returned fire and effectively silenced it. She then returned into the smoke screen and rejoined her consort, leaving astern the burning wreck of the first trawler, sinking; the rescue lights on the lifejackets of her crew were seen in the water. For this successful action MTB 90 was awarded the Ordre de l'Armée by Général de Gaulle.

On the night of 10 June in thick fog patches, six MTBs of the 23rd Flotilla intercepted a patrol of armed trawlers to the north of Guernsey and mounted a torpedo attack on one of them. The result was not known, but in the return fire one of the MTBs suffered considerable damage and a number of seriously wounded.

On 23 June six units of the flotilla were in two divisions of three boats each; one of these groups, patrolling at 10 knots between Jersey and the Minquiers, came across a group of small enemy vessels about 4000 metres to the north of them; as it was too small for torpedo attack, the SO decided on a gun attack. The division crept up astern, closing the range to less than 600 metres. The rearmost enemy vessel was then seen to be a small coaster of about 150 tons. It opened fire with a machine gun, whereupon the MTBs increased speed to 30 knots, leaving the enemy to port at about 100 metres and firing with all guns at the coaster's bridge as each boat passed in turn. The MTBs then came under fire, including 40mm, from the R boat escorts ahead of the coaster. Soon the coastal batteries also opened fire, beginning with star shell to illuminate and following up with shrapnel shell. Things became 'hot'; the SO turned all three boats to starboard through 180 degrees, leaving the enemy ship silenced and with its bridge on fire, and now, apparently, being fired on by its own escort craft. Once the MTBs were out of range they stopped to compare notes. There were plenty of holes in their hulls, but no one was wounded, although a telegraphist had been much shaken up when a 20mm round had shaved his head and buried itself in his radio set!

Some of the boats, including 94 with the SO aboard, were ending an uneventful patrol in the neighbourhood of the Minquiers on 4 July; it was almost 0400 and time to consider returning to Dartmouth. Before leaving the SO decided to plant a flag bearing the Cross of Lorraine on the NE Minquiers buoy. This was done, though not without some risk and difficulty for the *Officier en second* designated for the task, due to the pronounced swell at the time. The officer succeeded and jumped back to the boat's foredeck, liberally smeared with red lead paint from the buoy. This was repeated on the NW Minquiers Buoy, this time in broad daylight, before 94 set course for England. Back in Dartmouth the gesture was greatly appreciated, and all British or French Coastal Forces craft operating in that area reported back on how those Free French flags were keeping.

Six boats of the 23rd were returning from a patrol in the Bay of St Malo at 0630 on 19 July. It was daylight with fog patches. MTB 239 had lost one of her screws, so her division of three boats were restricted to her maximum speed of about 15 knots. Suddenly large columns of water were raised about them, as six M class minesweepers emerged from a fog bank and opened fire on the boats. The M types were armed with one or two 105mm guns, two 37mm and six 20mm, and as they could steam at 17 knots things looked bad for the MTBs, particularly the division containing 239. However, the two divisions split up to mount diversionary attacks, while 239 set course at right angles to that of the enemy, making smoke to confuse the issue. These tactics confused the M types, and the MTBs managed to extricate themselves from a highly unpleasant situation. The engagement lasted 45 minutes and was one of the toughest in which the flotilla had been involved. The boats were fortunate to escape with only a few wounded, who were taken aboard MTB 90 which detached at 35 knots in order to get them ashore as soon as possible. The remaining units returned with a considerable list of damage for the base staff to rectify.

On 6 August two MTBs of the 23rd were involved in a combined operation with six US Navy PT boats and two Royal Navy destroyers in an attack on four M class minesweepers off Jersey. The US ships were primarily involved, and caused some damage to two of the enemy, but were unable to mount a successful torpedo attack.

The 23rd flotilla left Kingswear on 25 August to be based temporarily at L'Aber-Wrac'h in Brittany, to join a flotilla of British Fairmile Ds which had gone there a few days before. The intention was to strengthen the blockade of Brest. The boats took some spares, engine oil and some of the base staff engineers. Their refuelling was done from a Royal Fleet Auxiliary tanker sent on ahead from Plymouth with 100 octane petrol, which at that time was not available in France. The Allied blockade of Brest was successful and no German vessels attempted to leave. Brest itself was retaken by the US Army on 21 September, following a series of heavy air raids by the RAF and the USAAF. The 23rd Flotilla returned to Dartmouth on the 25th, exactly one month after leaving it. During that month the personnel of the 23rd, none of whom had been able to set foot in France for up to four years, had received a rapturous reception from the local Bretons – all the more so for those whose own homes, families, relations and friends were in that region.

By the end of September 1944 the western end of the English Channel had been virtually cleared of enemy shipping, apart from four M class minesweepers still based in the Channel Islands. These were four older coal burners which had their supply of fuel cut off when the Allies completed occupation of the Cotentin peninsula and remained virtually isolated. The small reserve of coal left to them was kept unused so that they could go to sea if the Allies attempted an invasion of the islands.

From then the British Admiralty rather lost interest in the 'short' MTBs and decided to close down some of the smaller Coastal Forces bases, including HMS *Cicala*, but kept operating the larger bases further east from which the large Fairmile D MTB/MGBs were still operating.

The 23rd flotilla was anxious to continue operations off the Belgian coast, perhaps later even on the River Rhine. The Commander-in-Chief Plymouth, when consulted, suggested that after two years of very active operations it might be better to pay off the 'short' boats and re-equip the 23rd with D types. However, the Admiralty did not agree to this and sent the boats of the 23rd to HMS *Aggressive* at Newhaven for the time being. The MTBs moored alongside the quay there on 25 October.

With little prospect of further operations in the immediate future, and accommodation ashore inadequate, some crew members moved aboard the boats despite the inconvenience. Others were housed in the Free French Bir-Hackheim barracks near Portsmouth. Steps were taken to send as many men as possible on leave to France, in batches. Two officers and about twenty men remained with the boats as a care and maintenance party.

While this was taking place, the Free French admiralty requested the continued use of the boats off the Atlantic coast of France, and pointed out that if such use of the boats were approved, a base in France would be essential because of the operational distances involved. The request was eventually approved. From 15 December the boats were put on the slips in batches of three for equipment overhaul. This work, and the acquisition of the necessary machine tools and spares required to establish a base in France (for British-built boats with British armament and equipment), took time, argument and bargaining.

Eventually the boats completed their refits and sea trials, and put to sea again on 31 January 1945, en route for Brest, calling at Portland and Plymouth. They found Brest in a terrible state, and were not cheered by the discovery that the local headquarters had not prepared to receive them – they did not seem to be aware that they were coming, despite the flotilla having previously received a signal from the French admiralty that Brest would be ready to receive them.

The boats were sent to the former German U-boat base, where they were allocated the only basin which had been cleared of wreckage. The men were assigned to the neighbouring quarters. These had suffered heavily both from the recent Allied air raids and from destruction by the Germans as they evacuated. They were not yet fit to live in, so the men lived aboard the boats, whilst working to clean up some of the quarters in the naval school to provide a barracks for their base staff colleagues who were due to arrive shortly. This also included the rebuilding of doors and windows (replacing the shattered glass in the latter with sheets of plywood), repairing electrical services, and clearing rubble.

In the meantime the SO, the British liaison officer, and the base staff personnel had been working frantically to get over 300 tons of tools, spares and equipment of all kinds transported from Newhaven to Plymouth, where it was to be sorted and loaded aboard *Barfleur*, together with all kinds of consumable provisions sufficient to keep the base running for at least six months. This was to be done in just over seven days. Somehow it was done, though time did not allow for everything to be cased up before loading. By the time *Barfleur* arrived in the roadstead on the 13th, repairs to the naval school were sufficiently advanced to allow quarters for the base staff to be made use of. Unloading was started, first into lighters, thence to the basin in which the boats were moored, to be finally unloaded on to the quayside by a travelling crane, the only one left working in Brest.

It was all very different from the comfort and ordered routine of the 23rd Flotilla's former base on the River Dart, which was greatly missed by many. As one of the officers wrote at the time, 'In the life of the flotilla, this period of setting-up the new base must be counted as one of the most distressing'.

Despite the difficulties and frustrations, the new base and barracks were cleaned up and in full working order before the end of

March, and it became possible to resume operations. Four of the MTBs left Brest on 3 April on a reconnaissance patrol off the Biscay coast as far south as Quiberon, with orders to return to Benodet, which was to be used as the advanced operational base. During that patrol no enemy ships were seen, but the MTBs were detected and fired on by coastal batteries during the night; fortunately no casualties or damage were suffered. From Benodet operations were resumed on all nights when the weather allowed and any boats with major defects were sent back to Brest for repairs. Despite frequent patrols, no German vessels were to be found off the Biscay coast, but dark nights, strong currents and the occasional spell of bad weather combined to provide their own form of excitement.

At the end of April, orders were received to send four of the boats to Rochefort to act in concert with the attack by Général de Larminat and his troops on Ile d'Oléron, to prohibit the use of Pertuis d'Antioche to the Germans, and to prevent their escape from La Rochelle. For a day or two the sea was too rough for operations to be undertaken, but conditions had eased somewhat by 30 April, so at nightfall three of the boats left for the south. (The fourth boat had an engine breakdown.) At 0400 they were detected by two British destroyers who, thinking they must be E-boats, opened fire on them; however the MTBs escaped damage and entered the port of Sables d'Olonne at dawn. There they took on board some local fishermen to assist in the pilotage on the River Charente, and to inform the COs where the Germans had laid nets or moved channel buoys. The next night they got under way to pass through the Pertuis d'Antioche. That channel is only 6 miles wide at most, so there was a real risk of trouble from the coastal batteries. Fortunately due to a thick mist the boats made it unmolested, and once inside, found themselves coming up astern of a trawler proceeding at about 6 knots; the ship was alert, and challenged them. This gave the units no time to position themselves for a torpedo attack, and the SO decided on a gun action. Passing the trawler at 30 knots the boats fired broadsides at point blank range, silencing return fire from the trawler and setting its bridge alight. The coastal batteries then opened up with starshell and 130mm, forcing the MTBs to disengage to the south. When clear, they discovered a small motor launch which they circled whilst firing at it. This brought the coastal batteries back to life, and the boats started to take hits. The leading MTB had one engine hit and put out of action, followed by an engineroom fire. The boats disengaged again, but at reduced speed. In doing so they came across another trawler which did not seem to notice them, and the boats returned the indifference. The SO took his crippled boat close to Ile d'Aix for shelter, transferred himself to one of the remaining boats, then led them back at speed to find and engage the remaining trawler. By the time the two boats had returned to their former position their quarry had gone.

Two nights later, with the two boats which remained in full operational order, the SO made a reconnaissance patrol as far as La Pallice. There was still a hint of daylight left when they reached Ile d'Aix. The boats then slowed, awaiting darkness before closing La Rochelle. When there, they detected six dim shadows moving slowly and occasionally using signal lamps. As the MTBs crept closer, the leading ship was recognised as an M class minesweeper, one of their old and formidable enemies. Visibility being good, the SO decided to fire torpedoes at a range of 1000 metres, rather than risk detection by going closer. No sooner had the torpedoes been fired than the target altered course, causing the torpedoes to miss astern. The minesweeper completed her turn and trundled slowly back to La Rochelle, her engineroom ventilator fans clearly audible to the MTBs and apparently unaware of the MTBs' presence.

The next evening a fierce storm blew up, preventing any further patrol. Three of the officers decided to have a run ashore, during which they had a car accident, resulting in two being killed and the third badly injured. These two deaths were the only fatalities sustained by the 23rd flotilla throughout the war!

The end of the European war came officially at midnight on 8 May 1945. The boats were then dispersed to 'show the flag' among the islands. Three of them finally wore the Cross of Lorraine in the heart of Paris on 15 June 1945.

The boats were all Vosper 70ft MTBs of the 1940–41 Programme. The first six were ordered on 14 May 1940 and the last two on 22 February 1941.

Free French MTBs

No	Builder	Comp.	Comm.	Withd'n
90	Harland & Wolff	21. 9.42	11.11.42	24.5.46
91	Harland & Wolff	28.10.42	17.11.42	25.4.46
92	Harland & Wolff	1. 1.43	29. 1.43	25.4.46
94	Berthon Boat Co	24.12.42	24.12.42	25.4.46
96	Morgan Giles	17.11.42	24.11.42	25.4.46
98	Vosper	17.10.42	24.10.42	25.4.46
227	Hugh McLean	31.10.42	2.12.42	20.6.46
239	Camper & Nicholson	5.12.42	5.12.42	20.6.46

Commanding Officers of Free French MTBs

MTB 90   Enseigne de Vaisseau R Courtois
MTB 91   Enseigne de Vaisseau Douet
MTB 92   Officier des Equipages Laurent
MTB 94   Capitaine de Corvette Meurville; later Lieut de Vaisseau Iéhlé*
MTB 96   Lieut de Vaisseau Bourcey**
MTB 98   Lieut de Vaisseau Lagersie
MTB 227 Enseigne de Vaisseau de Bigault de Cazanove***
MTB 239 Officier des Equipages Abraham

Note *These were the SOs (senior officers) of the flotilla. Capitaine Meurville from the commencement of commissioning and the CO of MTB 94 until 12 April 1944. Lieut Iéhlé was the flotilla SO from 13 April 1944 for the remainder of the commission while under the French ensign, but elected not to command one of the boats; he went on operations aboard various boats of the flotilla. The new CO of 94 was Ens de Vaisseau Baudère.
**The CO of MTB 96 was also the deputy to the flotilla SO; that is if the latter was killed or seriously wounded, Bourcey would have taken over as SO. Bourcey's *Officier en Second* was the son of General de Gaulle, then Enseigne de Vaisseau 2 cl (Sub-Lt) Philippe de Gaulle. He eventually became an *Inspecteur-General* before his retirement. It was a military post, not naval.
***This officer remained in the French Navy postwar, and rose to Admiral, becoming NOIC (Brest) before his death in 1990.

Free French MTBs awards and decorations

Motor torpedo boats of the 23rd Flotilla carried out 451 patrols, of which 128 were 'operations of war' and during which 15 combats with enemy ships were involved.

Enemy ships confirmed sunk were 5, totalling 7200 tons. Other ships were damaged and some possibly sunk, the details are not confirmed. Both Wehrmacht and Kriegsmarine prisoners were taken from time to time and landed at HMS *Cicala*.

British decorations to officers and men

1 Distinguished Service Order
5 Distinguished Service Cross
2 Distinguished Service Medal

6 Mentions in Despatches

French decorations to officers and men

1 *Croix d'Officier de la Légion d'Honneur*
3 *Croix de Chevalier de la Légion d'Honneur*
3 *Médailles Militaires*
85 *Croix de Guerre*

French citations to the MTBs of the Flotilla

7 *L'Ordre de l'Armée de Mer*

Boat technical data

Tonnage 47 (60 tonnes)

Dimensions See drawings of that group

Engines 3 Packard V12 supercharged main engines, max 1250bhp each; 2 Ford V8 auxiliary engines, each 75bhp; one of these drove the electric power supply dynamo.

Initially these auxiliary engines could be clutched in to the two outer propeller shafts to allow main engines to be stopped and the boat to run silently at about 6½kts. Later in 1943 most Vosper boats of the class were modified by having 'Dumbflow' silencers fitted to the main engine exhaust pipes. One of the Ford V8 engines was then removed. This allowed main engines to be used for quiet running at low speeds without the clutching and declutching delays previously necessary. (See remarks in engineering section). The use of the auxiliary engines for quiet running was universally disliked, and on operations was fraught with danger.

Fuel 2500 gallons (11,400 litres of 100 octane petrol (essence)

Maximum speed 40 knots (sea state permitting)

Range about 300 miles (cruising speed 25kts); about 400 miles (cruising speed 20 kts)

Armament Two 21in (533mm) torpedoes, initially Mark V (500lb warhead, 35kts); later Mark VIII** (750lb warhead, 45kts). Fired from the deck tubes by small explosive charge at the rear of the tube.

Twin 0.5in (12.7mm) Vickers machine guns. HA/LA. 700rpm. Belt feed with mixed rounds of armour-piercing/incendiary/tracer; mounted in an hydraulically power-operated turret (Mark V) on centreline abaft the bridge, pressure-fed from a pump on the centre main engine. Later, some boats had this turret replaced by a pair of hand-operated twin 20mm Oerlikons. (Mark IX mounting). Most boats also mounted, when they became available, a single manual 20mm Oerlikon forward of the bridge.

Two twin Vickers 0.303in (7.69mm) gas operated machine guns on stands each side of the bridge*

Two illumination-rocket launchers, one on each torpedo tube*

Two Mark VII, 410lb (186kg) depth charges, one on each quarter*

One CSA smoke laying apparatus fitted right astern*

Note *These weapons systems are fully described in Volume 1

This chapter has been kindly provided by M René Courtois, (onetime CO of MTB 90). It was translated from the French by a mutual friend and the facts checked where possible with two British former liaison officers of the 23rd MTB Flotilla. It gives some indication of the trials and isolation undertaken by people whose country and home was under enemy occupation. They served in exile, in the *Forces Navales Française Libres* or FNFL.

A heavily censored photograph of the Free French 23rd MTB Flotilla at Folkestone in 1943 (MTBs 90–92, 96, 98, 227, 239 and 94). The French pom-pom cap can be seen on the crewmens' heads. Note only two depth charges and two rudders.
Courtesy D J Marshall

The Vosper survivors

Considerable interest was shown in our chapter about surviving Fairmile types and 72ft HDMLs described in Volume I. Here, from the same source, are described some of the surviving Vosper designs around the British coastline.

It is plain that the faster Vosper craft, with stresses imposed by the greater speeds required, had by necessity to be more strongly constructed, and this can be seen by study of the detailed construction drawings. In general similar material was used for their construction – quality seasoned wood, and care went into their in design and construction. This has produced a number of survivors, very few in use as boats, albeit re-engined but most ending their days as houseboats.

Whenever I am in the area I visit the Chichester Yacht Basin, where on the adjacent Birdham fresh water canal lies ex-MTB 71,

View of the East Bank, River Itchen, Southampton, in July 1985. Left: houseboat Meridian *(ex-MTB 245), moored at 73, Whitworth Crescent, Bittern. Right: houseboat at No 75, Whitworth Crescent. This was later renamed* Ancasta III *and towed to West Bank. It was one of the MTB 412–497 series.* Courtesy David Fricker

now named *Wild Chorus* after Sir Peter Scott's book. She is in first-class condition, and a credit to her owner the late Cyril Pudney, who purchased her in 1949.

I first visited her in May 1988, when Cyril Pudney allowed me to take photographs of her upper deck and bridge. She is largely still in her original condition, the bridge is of alloy and shrapnal damage can still be seen. Cyril told me that MTB 71 still had her tube beds and gun turret mountings when he purchased her. However, her maintenance in later years is causing problems, as are the mooring fees. I understand that the Norwegian authorities were making encouraging noises to acquire what was one of their original orders requisitioned by the Royal Navy. Unfortunately Cyril died in the summer of 1992, but efforts are under way to save MTB 71 for the nation and restore her to her wartime appearance.

Her sister, another 60ft Vosper – the houseboat *Chrysalis*, ex-T4, ex-CT 19, ex-MTB 70, ex-T4, was another requisitioned unit. Up for disposal in September 1945, she was formerly a houseboat at Hayling Island, and was towed to her Bursledon mooring on the River Hamble in 1972. When acquired by Jonathan Eastland she was due to be dismantled before being burnt to make way for a new marina. However, after a great deal of effort, and the removal of an accumulation of debris from her engineroom, she was towed to her present berth, and restoration work commenced. She is seen here in

March 1986, and was the subject of a series of articles in *Motor Boat and Yachting* in 1972. I have no information on her since then.

The only working exhibit is the original Vosper Job 1763, the original private venture design, later to be purchased to become MTB 102. She is in first-class condition, but bears little resemblance to her original lines. She had a busy operational life, and was transferred to the War Office in 1943, being returned to the Admiralty in 1945 and sold to J Van der Ould in 1948. In 1973 ex-MTB 102 was found by a Norfolk Sea Scout group at Brundall, converted into a houseboat and in need of attention, and was acquired as a base with the intention to reactivate her. In 1976 Kelso Films wanted an MTB for the film *The Eagle Has Landed*, and to the joy of the Scout group used the refurbished 102 as a Second World War MTB (albeit German), handing her back to the Scouts as a fully-operational sea-going training ship.

Maintenance and upkeep is largely carried out on a voluntary basis, but in 1983 it became necessary for major work to be carried out on her hull and decks and the sum of £20,000 was spent to ensure a sound and seaworthy boat, but it was then apparent that her old engines were the next problem. Perkins Engines Ltd came to the rescue with the generous provision of two diesel turbocharged V8s and 102 came back to life in much of her original glory.

As a Sea Scouts training ship she has taken part in the Queen's Silver Jubilee Pageant, attended gatherings of the Dunkirk Little Ships Association, represented 'Yesterday's Navy' at Portsmouth Navy Days, returned to Dunkirk for the 45th Anniversary in 1985, and was inspected by HRH the Duke of Edinburgh in 1986, as well as providing a full programme of weekend training for an average 200 boys a year. These activities continue up to the present, but maintenance, upkeep and preservation of this unique vessel remain costly and time-consuming for the very willing volunteers, and funding is always required. She is shown here on 6 September 1984 alongside at the Vosper Camber Yard, Portsmouth, her home early in the war. The yard has since been demolished.

Another surviving Vosper is the houseboat *Gemini XXII* (ex-MTB 22) on the mud flats at The Saltings, Tollesbury, near Maldon, Essex. Another of the early units, completed in June 1939, she is basically intact, and her original bridge has been lifted and moved right forward.

The houseboat *Freedom* (ex-MTB 224) was broken up and burnt *in situ* at Temple Boatyard at Strood on the River Medway in September 1991.

A scene of tranquillity below the Cobden Bridge on the River Itchen, Southampton, in July 1985 shows two old warriors. The houseboat *Meridian* (ex-MTB 245) is moored at Whitworth Crescent, Bitterne, with a 71ft 6in British Power Boat MTB at the adjacent berth.

A former Free French Navy boat, previously based at Dartmouth, the houseboat *Sarie Marais* is ex-MTB 239, and was at the Medway Bridge Marina, Rochester, on the River Medway in September 1989.

The houseboat *Nonsuch II* appears to be in superb condition at Ash Island Hampton on the River Thames. Her exact origin remains to be established but she is probably in the 200 series.

A later 73ft Vosper, the houseboat *Brincadeira*, is shown at Portchester Creek, Portsmouth Harbour, in May 1985. Formerly MTB 1001, ex-MTB 386, she is a veteran of the 31st MTB Flotilla operating out of Lowestoft. She was a Type I unit. She was finally used for 'timber and plywood tests' both afloat and on mud banks. She has been at this location at least since 1955 and lost her original bridge after 1959.

A source of a number of 73ft Vosper survivors is (or was) the river bank at Shoreham, East Sussex. In Berth No 3 was the houseboat *Heron*, purchased from the Admiralty Marshal in 1962. She reputed saw no active war service, and has been identified as a Type II.

A sister 73ft Type I, the houseboat *Moidore* (named after the former Portuguese gold coin), is shown in September 1984, during her reconstruction at No 27 berth, Riverbank, Shoreham (a source of much of my original interest in 'the survivors'). She is shown again post-rebuild in July 1986. Further along, at berth 36, is the houseboat *Enstone*, another 73ft boat shown at the same date. I suspect that none of the wartime boats of all types, including Fairmile Ds, are still at this location, having been moved on by the local council or destroyed.

Another 73ft Type I is the houseboat *Fourwinds*, shown here in July 1985 at Pettinger Gardens, St Denys, Southampton. I have been informed that she was sold shortly after the photograph was taken, believed scrapped and replaced by *Fourwinds II*, a former Royal Norwegian Navy 'Nasty' class FPB.

Another 73ft boat is an 'unnamed' houseboat moored at Cobden Bridge on the River Itchen, shown in July 1985. By 1989 she had been towed away and replaced by another houseboat, and is believed to have been discarded and scrapped.

Detail of bridge and bipod mast of the 60ft ex-MTB 71 in January 1987.
Courtesy David Fricker

Others still survived. On the West Bank, Pettinger Gardens, River Itchen, in July 1985, there were the houseboat *Sungo* (ex-MTB 486, ex-MGB 167 (British Power Boat); alongside her sister the houseboat *Shearwater* and houseboat *Latona* (ex-MTB 533) a Type II Vosper. This was a rare example of postwar civilian use of a Type II, which alas was towed across the River Itchen, broken up and burnt in December 1989.

The boats illustrated here are not a full list of all the surviving Vospers. Others are still in use as houseboats – *Grayling* (ex-MTB 98) at Conyer Creek, Kent; MTB 219 on the Chelsea Embankment, London; *Silverstream* (a 73ft MTB) at Laleham, and another unidentified short boat, *Pendlewitch,* at Wootton Creek, Isle of Wight.

The Ex-MTB 71 (the former houseboat Wild Chorus). *It is hoped that she will be restored to her original glory and re-engined by 1995, in the Chichester Fresh Water Canal in April 1993.*
Author's collection

Ex-MTB 102 departs Portsmouth harbour on 8 September 1984.
Courtesy David Fricker

Restored Elco PT 617

In 1968, James 'Boats' Newberry, founder of the PT Boat Museum, acquired the former PT 619 from the South Korean Navy with the idea of restoring her as a permanent exhibit. One of four boats transferred to South Korea in January 1952, 619 served under the name *Koroki*. Sixteen years later, the boat was lying derelict at the Chin Hae Naval Base, completely stripped and abandoned. Following discussions, Rear Admiral Kim Chun Tai presented the boat to Newberry. Transport arrangements were made with the US Navy through Rear Admiral John Bulkeley and the boat was eventually shipped back to Memphis, Tennessee, in 1970. Unfortunately, 619 was beyond economical restoration. The boat was completely gutted, the starboard side of the hull from the day cabin aft was non-existent, and portions of the port side were missing. In 1985–86 she was cannibalised for the restoration of 617 and the remains burned.

In 1979, the PT organisation purchased the former PT 617 from a Miami-based company which was using her as a salvage support boat. She too was in sorry shape: waterlogged, worm-eaten, and rotten; still, she was in far better shape than 619. After purchasing the boat, the PT group had the makeshift superstructure removed and the boat made ready for the long tow to Melville, Rhode Island. In June 1980 PT 617 arrived at the Bend Boat Basin and the long task of restoration began.

Fran Baratta, the yard manager at the basin, had her surveyed and discovered extensive rot. The exterior planking was removed and the condition of the inner planking indicated that the entire boat would have to be replanked. Removing a steel reinforcement from the keel revealed further serious problems. About 30 feet of the keel was badly rotted and nearly 70 per cent of the ribs and frames in the keel area were completely rotted away. The hull was nearly 1ft 6in longer on one side than the other, due to wracking. Seven of the eight watertight bulkheads required repair. Quite simply, she was a wreck! I saw her after the planking had been removed from the starboard side and can attest to her terrible condition. The hull planking was so rotten that I was able to push my hand through both layers with little effort.

What followed was five years of masterly restoration, all the more remarkable in that the boat yard had to work from incomplete blueprints. The keel was repaired, frames sistered, new decking and superstructure fabricated, and the interior completely reconditioned. Fittings were scrounged or fabricated, armament acquired from the Navy, and a large amount of volunteer effort expended. Finally, on 25 June 1985, the completed boat was barged to Battleship Cove, Fall River, Massachusetts, joining PT 796 on display. Two years later she was housed in specially-built Newberry Hall, protecting her from the elements.

I had the opportunity to go aboard PT 617 while she was on outside display in 1986. As a member of PT Boats, I was allowed below and was thoroughly impressed with the results of the restoration. Baratta and crew had done a magnificent job restoring the interior to as near as possible the original configuration. It was quite a thrill to walk through the compartments and imagine what life aboard must have been like. The compartments were generally quite spacious, although I was surprised at the limited clearance between the bulkhead and ladder leading from the cockpit to the charthouse and the galley.

Above decks, things are much the same as the original, although there have been some concessions. A decision was made to install both torpedo tubes and roll-off racks to illustrate the different types of weapons used on the PTs. The tubes and roll-off racks had to be fabricated, as originals were not available. Apparently, neither were the Mark 17 machine gun mounts; in their place are two Vietnam era Mark 56 mounts. The 37mm forward and 40mm aft are originals.

This is a 'must see' exhibit for anyone interested in Coastal Forces craft.

A view of the restored PT 617 at Battleship Cove before Newberry Hall was built over it.
Tom DelRossi

Bibliography

Articles

Hersey, John 'PT Squadron in the South Pacific', *Life*, 10 May 1943, pp74–86.

Holt, W J, RCNC 'Coastal Force Design', *TINA*, Vol. 89, No. 3, 1947. Institution of Naval Architects.

Palmieri, Del 'USN Camouflage of WW 2', *Scale Models*, April 1979–June 1982.

Peters, S A 'The Motor Torpedo Boat', *Ordnance*, Vol. XXXVIII, No. 204, May–June 1954, pp943–6. American Ordnance Association (1954).

Peters, S A 'The PT Boat', *Bureau of Ships Journal*, Vol. 2, No. 4, August 1953, pp2–8. Bureau of Ships (1953).

Ross, Al 'RN 77' Elco PT Boats', *Warship*, Vol. VIII, pp33–7. Conway Maritime Press (1984).

Stebbins, John 'Fast Fighting Patrol Boats: A "Nasty" Perspective'. *Transactions, Patrol Boats 86 Technical Symposium*, pp1–76 to 1–100. American Society of Naval Engineers (1986).

Sumrall, Robert 'Ship Camouflage (WWII): Deceptive Att'. *US Naval Institute Proceedings*, Vol. 99, No. 2, February 1973, pp67–81. US Naval Institute (1973).

Various *Yachting*, Vol. LXXIV, No. 5, November 1943. Yachting Publishing Corporation.

Published books

Bagnasco, Erminio *I Mas e Le Motosiluranti Italiane* Ufficio Storico Marina Militare (1969).

Bagnasco, Erminio *Le Motosiluranti Della Seconda Guerra Mondiale* Ermanno Albertelli Editore (1977).

Brown, Leo *Motor Torpedo Boat Squadron 37* published by the author (1981).

Buckley, Robert J *At Close Quarters* Naval History Division, Washington (1962).

Campbell, John *Naval Weapons of World War II* Conway Maritime Press (1985).

Chun, Victor *American PT Boats in World War II – A Pictorial History* published by the author (1976).

Dickens, Peter *Night Action* US Naval Institute Press (1974).

Donovan, Robert J *PT 109* McGraw-Hill Book Company (1961).

Du Cane, Peter *High-Speed Small Craft* Temple Press Ltd (1951).

Ferrell, Bob, and Al Ross *Early Elco PT Boats* PT Boat Museum (1980).

Ferrell, Robert *US Mosquito Fleet* PT Boat Museum (1977).

Fock, Harald *Fast Fighting Boats 1870–1945* Nautical Publishing Company (1978).

Friedman, Norman *Naval Radar* US Naval Institute Press (1981).

Friedman, Norman *US Naval Weapons* US Naval Institute Press (1982).

Friedman, Norman *US Small Combatants* US Naval Institute Press (1988).

Geburzi, Hans-Ulrich *Torpedo-Schnellboote* Militarverlag der Deutschen Deomkratischen Republik (1985).

Gröner, Erich, Dieter Jung, and Martin Maass *Die Deutschen Kriegsschiffe 1815–1945, Band 2: Torpedoboote, Zerstorer, Schnellboote, Minensuchboote, Minenraumboote* Bernard & Graefe Verlag (1983).

Hichens, Robert *We Fought Them in Gunboats* Michael Joseph Ltd (1944).

Hodges, Peter *Royal Navy Warship Camouflage 1939–1945* Almark Publishing (1973).

Holman, Gordon *The Little Ships* Hodder & Stoughton Ltd (1943).

Lambert, John *Anatomy of the Ship – The Fairmile D* Conway Maritime Press (1985).

Lambert, John, and Al Ross *Allied Coastal Forces of WWII*, Volume I Conway Maritime Press (1990).

Lenton, H T and J J Colledge *Warships of World War II* Ian Allan (1980).

Lord, Lindsay *Naval Architecture of Planing Hulls* Cornell Maritime Press (1954).

Marczak, Jan *Kutry Torpedowe* Wydawnictwo Morskie (1968).

Meister, Jurg *Soviet Warships of World War II* Doubleday (1977).

North, A J D *Royal Naval Coastal Forces, 1939–1945* Almark Publishing (1972).

Pope, Dudley *Flag 4* William Kimber (1954).

Rance, Adrian *Fast Boats and Flying Boats* Ensign Publications (1989).

Reynolds, L C *Gunboat 658* William Kimber (1955).

Schiffner, Manfred *et al Torpedobewaffnung* Militarverlag der Deutschen Demokratischen Republik (1990).

Scott, Peter *The Battle of the Narrow Seas* Country Life (1945).

White, W L *They Were Expendable* Harcourt, Brace, & Co (1942).

—— *Knights of the Sea* Taylor Publishing Co (1982).

Government/Company documents

Bagnasco, Erminio 'The Development of the Motor Torpedo Boat in the Italian Navy, 1915–1945'; paper presented at the 4th Naval History Symposium, Annapolis, MD (October 1979).

Jolie, E W *A Brief History of US Navy Torpedo Development* Naval Underwater Systems Center (1978).

Swasey, David L *Camouflage and the PTs* Elco (1945).

Tredinnick, Frank and H Bennett *An Administrative History of PTs in World War II*, unpublished manuscript Naval Historical Center (1945).

OP 951: *.05 Inch Machine Gun Mounts MK17 Mods 1 and 2* Bureau of Ordnance (1943).

FM23–55 *Browning Machineguns Caliber .30 M1917A1, M1919A4, M1919A4E1, M1919A6, and M37* Department of the Army (1955).

TM 9–252 *40mm Automatic Gun M1 (AA)* War Department (1944).

TM 9–225 *Browning Machine Gun, Cal. .50, M2, Aircraft, Basic* War Department (1943).

Letter from Office of Captain, Coastal Forces Mediterranean to Preston Sutphen (Elco) 18 October 1945.

Handbook on Ship Camouflage C and R – 4 Navy Department, Bureau of Construction and Repair (1937).

The Camouflage of Ships at Sea – CB 3098R (45) Tactical and Staff Duties Division, Naval Staff, Admiralty (October 1945).

Light Coastal Craft Operating in the North Sea and the English Channel (BR 834) The Admiralty (September 1943).

OP 911 *20mm AA Fun MK2 and MK4* Bureau of Ordnance (1943).

Ship Camouflage Instructions – March 1943 Navy Department (1943).

Ship Camouflage Instructions – Ships 2 (Second Revision) Navy Department, Bureau of Ships (June 1942).

General Board Studies 420–14 (1923–1940) – Small Craft General Board.

Ship's Data US Naval Vessels. Navships 250–011, Vol. 2 Government Printing Office (1945).

Motor Torpedo Boats – Tactical Orders and Doctrine. Government Printing Office (1942).

Detail and Special Specifications for Building Motor Torpedo Boats PT 565–624 Government Printing Office (1944).

BuShips Allowance List, PT 565–622 Bureau of Ships (1945).

Detail and Special Specifications for Building Motor Torpedo Boats PT 761–790 (NAVSHIPS 451) Government Printing Office (1945).

Detail Specifications for Building 80-ft Motor Torpedo Boats PTs 103–138 Bureau of Ships (1942).

Operating Instructions, the Dewandre-Elco Power-Operated Machine Gun Turret MK II Electric Boat Company 1940(?).

Manual for the Installation, Running, & Maintenance of the 'Scott-Paine' 70ft. Motor Torpedo Boat Canadian Power Boat Company (1941).

OP 950 Torpedo MK 13 Type Bureau of Ordnance (30 November 1944).

Operator's Manual, Gun Sight MK 14 Mod 2, 3, and 4. Sperry Gyroscope (1942).

Parts Catalog – Motor Torpedo Boat, Elco Type (NAVSHIPS 312–0003) Elco (undated).

Sources

Douglas, Dr W A B letter on RCAF and RCN use of experimental USN PTs (29 January 1990).

Henzell, Lt Cdr Max RNVR Notes written on the operation and performance of 70ft Elco motor torpedo boats in the Mediterranean (July 1945).

Schade, Gene, Momm, RON 9. Diary entries from 12 December 1942 to 13 February 1944.

Factory, C and R, and BuShips drawings for the various boats.

'Potted history' of *MTB 261* (ex-*PT 12*).